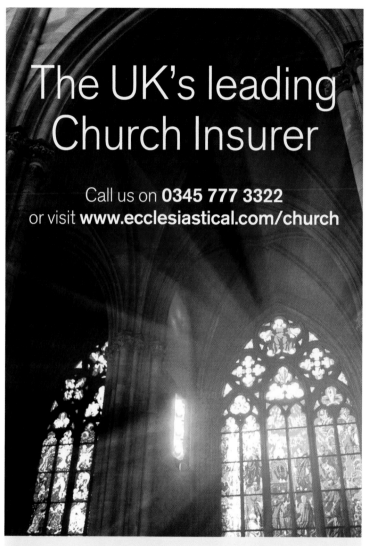

The UK's leading Church Insurer

Call us on **0345 777 3322**
or visit **www.ecclesiastical.com/church**

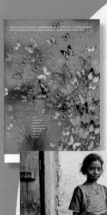

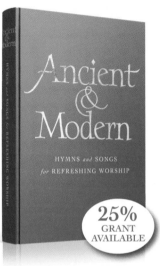

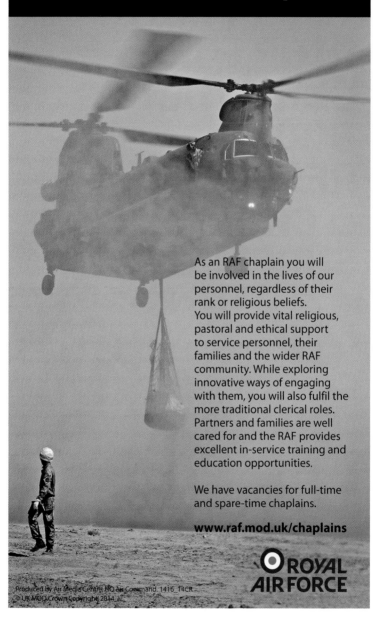

"In this easy-to-read book, pastor Jack Haberer helps you seek God's will for your life. You'll move from deep theological considerations to street-level, daily-life practicalities—and you'll learn to chart a course through life's complexities, guided by the Scriptures, in the company of the church. My only complaint is that it wasn't available thirty years ago!"

—BRIAN D. McLAREN,
author, speaker, and activist

9780664261245
Paperback • £10.00

Jack Haberer's *It's Complicated* helps Christians figure out what to do when life gets complicated and the distinctions between good and bad are not so clear. Using Bible passages as a guide, Haberer affirms and then challenges many closely held beliefs, making traditional distinctions between "conservative" and "liberal" Christians obsolete.

WESTMINSTER
JOHN KNOX PRESS

Order from Norwich Books and Music + 44 (0)1603 785925
or email: orders@norwichbooksandmusic.co.uk

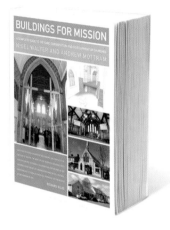

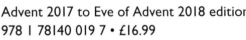

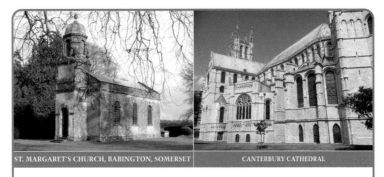
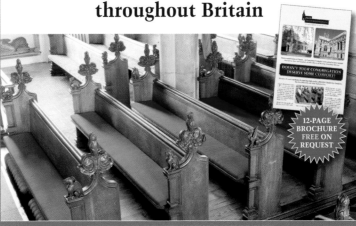

The Canterbury Preacher's Companion 2018

This book is also available on Kindle

Some other books by Michael Counsell:

A Basic Bible Dictionary (Canterbury Press)

A Basic Christian Dictionary (Canterbury Press)

2000 Years of Prayer (Canterbury Press)

Every Pilgrim's Guide to the Journeys of the Apostles
   (Canterbury Press)

Every Pilgrim's Guide to England's Holy Places
   (Canterbury Press and on Kindle)

Every Pilgrim's Guide to Oberammergau and its Passion Play
   (Canterbury Press) New edition 2008

The Little Book of Heavenly Humour by Syd Little with
   Chris Gidney and Michael Counsell (Canterbury Press)

Kieu by *Nguyen Du*, translated into English verse
   (amazon Createspace and Kindle)

She was the First Apostle (amazon Createspace and Kindle)

The
Canterbury Preacher's
Companion 2018

Sermons for Sundays, Holy Days,
Festivals and Special Occasions
Year B, the Year of Mark

Michael Counsell

CANTERBURY
PRESS

Norwich

First published in 2017 by the Canterbury Press Norwich
Editorial office, 3rd Floor, Invicta House
108–114 Golden Lane, London ECIY OTG, UK

Canterbury Press is an imprint of Hymns Ancient & Modern Ltd
(a registered charity)

H
Y
M **Ancient**
N **&Modern**
S

Hymns Ancient & Modern® is a registered trademark of
Hymns Ancient & Modern Ltd
13A Hellesdon Park Road, Norwich,
Norfolk NR6 5DR, UK

www.canterburypress.co.uk
www.norwichbooksandmusic.co.uk

British Library Cataloguing in Publication data

A catalogue record for this book is available from the British Library

Scripture quotations are mainly drawn from the New Revised
Standard Version Bible © 1989 by the Division of Christian
Education of the National Council of Churches of Christ in the USA

Readings are from *Common Worship: Services and Prayers
for the Church of England* (with later amendments), which is
copyright © The Archbishops' Council 2000:
extracts and edited extracts are used by permission. Readings for days
not covered by that book are from *Exciting Holiness*, second edition
2003, edited by Brother Tristram, copyright © European Province of the
Society of Saint Francis, 1997, 1999, 2003, published by Canterbury
Press, Norwich; see www.excitingholiness.org

ISBN 978 1 84825 941 6

Typeset by Manila Typesetting Company
Printed and bound by CPI Group (UK) Ltd, Croydon, CRO 4YY

Contents

vi

vii

In Memory of Michael Counsell

It is with great sadness that we announce the death of Michael Counsell, who passed away following a short illness in 2016.

Michael was a very popular Canterbury Press author, whose books include the *Canterbury Preacher's Companion* series, along with *A Basic Bible Dictionary, A Basic Christian Dictionary* and *Every Pilgrim's Guide to Oberammergau*.

Michael was unable to complete this 2018 edition of the *Canterbury Preacher's Companion*, and we are grateful for the generosity of Bridget Nichols, who allowed us to use some of her *Church Times* Sunday readings. And Rosalind Brown also kindly supplied a sermon.

We are also grateful to Hannah Ward for her invaluable advice in completing the 2018 edition.

Preface

I enjoy preparing sermons, and when I lack ideas for a fresh approach to a subject, I have learnt where to look. I have also been keeping a note in my diary of phrases I hear in conversation or read in books and magazines, or events in my experience, which I think would make a stimulating approach to a sermon.

Like other preachers, however, I sometimes look at a sermon I have written and think, that is not good enough. If I cannot think of a way of improving it, I sometimes go ahead and preach it anyway, trying to put enough into my delivery to keep the interest of the hearers. I do not go to the extremes of the preacher who was found to have put in the margin of his sermon notes, 'Argument weak here – shout!' But if I deliver the sermon imaginatively and keep eye contact with the congregation, sometimes someone will come up to me after I have preached a sermon which I felt myself was a dud, and say to me, 'Thank you. That was the best sermon I've heard for a long time. I felt you were speaking directly to me, and it was just what I needed to hear!' And that restores my faith in the Holy Spirit's power to use even the most ordinary servant of God.

So whether you read one of my sermons directly from the book, or paraphrase it into your own words, preach confidently, without apologizing. Since these volumes first appeared I have spoken to several preachers who said they had copied out the main points of one of my sermons to make them the basis of what they were going to say, and then torn them up, crying, 'That's not what I want to say to these people. But now I've done that, I've realized what I do really want to get across!' And then they've gone on to write a better sermon than they would have done without the help of my book. So there are as many ways of using it as there are preachers. God bless you in your ministry.

Michael Counsell

How to Preach

Why do we preach?

Life's greatest privilege is:
    to share what God is saying with his people.
    to proclaim God's love for them.
    to help them to serve God in the power of the Spirit.
    to change their lives for the better.
So we must communicate,
    our thoughts about God,
    our experience of God.
This means exposing who you are, and becoming vulnerable.

Forming the structure

Methodist ministers on ordination are issued with a magic hammer:
    strike any verse from the Bible with this,
        and it will immediately fall into three points, with introduction
        and conclusion.
This is not the only possible structure,
    but it's a good one to begin with.
People can't absorb more than three points in one sermon.
Resist the temptation to put the whole of your training into the first
sermon.
    An author's best friend is his wastepaper basket.
    An author must be willing to murder his children.
Let the skeleton show: for example, 'I've finished discussing the
background, now let's look at what it means for us today.'
Afterwards they should remember what your three points were,
and how one led into the next.

Sum up the whole of what you want to say in the final sentence.
(If you can't, there's too much material and you've wandered.)
Then plan everything to lead up to this.
Write layout notes,
with numbered paragraphs, sub-paragraphs, and paragraph headings.
(When you've been preaching for 40 years you can begin to do this in your head without writing it down.)

Notes or full text? Style?

Compiling clear notes first is essential,
to make the structure plain.
Most beginning preachers need next to write out in full what they're going to say.
It mustn't sound like a read essay,
or the listeners will fall asleep.
So the style must be simple, colloquial, conversational.
No long subordinate clauses.
Always use contractions: don't, won't, haven't and so on;
(but never use etc. or e.g.).
No more than one long or new word per sermon, and explain it.
Commas no more than ten words apart, to show where you breathe.
Full stops no more than 20 words apart.
Deliberate use of repetition, but not careless repetition.
There must be plenty of eye contact: at least once per sentence.
Therefore, the preacher needs to read the text through several times beforehand,
until it's almost memorized.
Then glancing at the first few words
will be enough to remind you what you want to say,
so that you can say it, while looking the listeners in the eye.
After a couple of years preaching, aim to make the notes longer
(always write out quotations in full)
until you can tear up the text and preach from the notes.
Then you'll really begin to communicate.
A few years after that you may be able to do without writing a full text,
making up the sentences in your head based on the notes.
But you can never do without making clear notes first.

Length

'I don't know what to preach about.'
> Preach about God, and preach about ten minutes.

If you're really interesting,
> you may be able to hold the listeners' attention for 15 minutes;
> more than that, and they'll fall asleep.

Audibility

It is a waste of time to preach a sermon that nobody can hear.
Many people are more deaf than they realize:
> 'I don't need a hearing aid – what did you just say?'

Why can't people speak up these days?
Such people always sit at the back of the church!
To be able to speak louder, practise singing:
> Stand up straight but relaxed.
>
> Begin to hum with your lips closed: 'Mmmmmmm'.
>
> Feel the top of your mouth vibrating:
>> this brings your voice up into your mouth;
>> if you sing or speak from your throat it will turn into a shout
>> and if someone shouts you can't hear the words.
>
> Then open your mouth while singing 'Mmmmmmm-eeeeeeee-aaaaaaaah' on any note you like.
>
> Feel the top of your mouth still vibrating.
>
> Feel your 'diaphragm' pushing up a firm column of air, from the
>> bottom of your ribs to the top of your mouth.

Then stop singing and talk using the same part of the mouth to produce the sound.
Think of someone at the back of the church and talk directly to them in such a way as to attract their attention.
However, it is often not the volume but the melody that makes people inaudible.
If you speak always on the same note (musical pitch, high or low),
> it'll be terribly boring.

If you always speak with the same melody, which falls at the end of the sentence,
> nobody will be able to hear the last few words, and the sentence
>> won't make sense.

If you vary the melody from sentence to sentence, without being sing-song,
> you'll be interesting to listen to.

Elocution is a form of verbal gymnastics between the tip of the tongue and the teeth:
  always exaggerate the final consonant.
A preacher needs to be a good actor,
  remembering humbly that they are acting the part of Christ.

Communication

'Who has believed what we have heard?' (Isaiah 53.1).
Even if the congregation hear every word,
  it'll do them no good unless you communicate.
You must be quite clear what ideas you want to get across:
  the words are only aeroplanes for the ideas to ride in.
Try to think up striking phrases, graphic images and metaphors;
  remember the *Readers' Digest* column, 'Towards more picturesque language'.
Above all you must communicate yourself, your own personality:
  Eye-contact is essential.
  Never preach anything you don't personally believe – and you don't really believe anything until you've struggled through doubt to reason it out for yourself.
  Make it heartfelt, the fruit of your own experience.
If the listeners say,
  'I can't remember a word they said, but what a nice/interesting/challenging person they are', then you've succeeded in communicating.
If the listeners say,
  'I can't remember a word they said, but my faith is much stronger', then you've succeeded even better.
If you've just preached a brilliant sermon on 'justification by faith', and a listener says,
  'Your sermon on "the way to ask for God's guidance" was just what I needed to hear', then you've allowed the Holy Spirit to succeed!

Personal experience

Preach as well as you can,
  but don't try to imitate somebody else.
Even if it is in stumbling, ungrammatical English,
  a sermon tells the listeners what your faith has meant in your own life and
  it will have ten times the effect of an abstract theological discourse.

Try to describe in each sermon at least one event in your life,
 which has taught you something about God.
But avoid embarrassing stories about the charming things your children have said!

Stories

I listened to the people in the supermarket checkout line.
Most of them were discussing last night's soap opera on the TV.
They were making moral judgements:
 'Wasn't it terrible when he did this?'
 'What she should have said was that!'
So they were making use of stories to train themselves in moral theology!
Next time they're faced with a similar situation,
 they'll have already made up their minds, subconsciously, how they should behave,
 and they'll behave a bit better because of the story they've heard.
So it is in sermons.
A sermon is dull as ditchwater if it doesn't include at least one story, true or fictional:
 from your own experience;
 from a book you've read, but put into your own words briefly;
 from the Bible;
 a joke, so long as it isn't a 'shaggy dog'!

Exegesis

Jesus is the Word of God.
The Bible contains the word of God.
The prophets proclaimed, 'Thus saith the LORD.'
'But how shall they hear unless they have a preacher?' (Romans 10.14).
Our task is to allow God to speak through Jesus,
 then through the Bible,
 then through us.
Almost every sermon should be an exposition of the Bible readings set for the day; (here liturgical churches have an advantage over Free Churches, because we're forced to preach on all the important passages in the Bible every three years).
It's good to find a single verse out of the readings,
 which summarizes what you want to say,
 then repeat this 'text' enough times,

at the beginning, in the middle and the end of the sermon,
so that the hearers will learn it by heart, without trying.
If they forget the sermon and remember the text, they will have
heard God.
Always look for the original context:
what the text means when surrounded by the verses that come
before and after it;
what the text meant to the original Bible writers;
what the text meant to the first people to hear it read out;
and explain this context to the congregation.
But it's very easy to decide on what you want to say,
then hunt for a text to hang it on;
in this way you're communicating your own prejudices,
and not what the Bible says.
Exegesis is the art of
drawing out what the Bible originally meant *in its own time*; then
applying that inner meaning to the changed circumstances of *our*
time.
This is the task of the preacher,
and we dare not miss out either step.

Check

When you have prepared your sermon, ask yourself (or have your
spouse ask you):

1 Where is the gospel? (Kerygma)
   I have heard Billy Graham and Desmond Tutu preach,
   and both kept coming back to one simple phrase: 'God loves
   you.'

'A text without a context is a pretext'

   If you haven't communicated this good news, you ought not to
   be in the pulpit.
2 What should they do about it? (Didache)
   Unless a sermon results in some practical action or change of
   behaviour,
   the listeners will go away frustrated.
   Don't be 'so heavenly minded that you're no earthly use'.

Practical considerations

Never use paper any bigger than A5, or you'll lose your place.
Write or type large, with frequent new lines and much indenting,
    (like this paper), or you'll lose your place.
Number the pages clearly, in case you drop them on your way to
the pulpit.
When you find that you've left your sermon notes at home two
miles away,
    and have to preach entirely off the cuff,
    as I did when I had been ordained only seven years,
    then you'll discover whether you've learnt anything about
    preaching!

Leading intercessions

The Anglican minister was asked to preach in the Methodist church,
    and found he was expected to lead the prayers as well.
Fortunately he had brought a spare set of sermon notes,
    and he found it quite easy to turn these into a prayer . . .
    until he heard himself saying,
    'And now, Lord, I'd like to illustrate this with a funny story,
    I hope you haven't heard it before.'
Many of the points in this paper about preaching
    can be applied to leading intercessions,
especially careful preparation;
    writing it out in your own words;
    clear diction;
    being always short and concise;
    and absolute sincerity.

Common Worship suggests five headings:
1 The Church of Christ (worldwide, all denominations, and this
   congregation).
2 Creation (thanksgiving, ecology) human society, the nations of
   the world and their leaders.
3 The local community (families, the caring professions).
4 Those who suffer (the sick, at home or in hospital –
   mention names if you have permission – the sad and the hungry).
5 The communion of saints (remember those who have recently
   died –
   mention names if you have permission – and those who mourn;

any saints whose saint's day occurs at this time;
the patron saints to whom this church is dedicated).

(*Common Worship*, page 174)

And it gives the responses that should be used after each section:

Lord, in your mercy

All   hear our prayer.

And after the fifth section:

Merciful Father,

**All   accept these prayers
for the sake of your Son
our Saviour Jesus Christ.
Amen.**

Prayer

St Paul told the Christians in Thessalonica to 'Pray without ceasing'
(1 Thess. 5.17).
Our preaching and intercessions will fail
unless they are undergirded by constant prayer:
    daily at set times;
    as we work;
    the evening before we preach;
    before the service;
    on the way to the pulpit.
Memorized words can help,
but if you trust the Lord like a child trusts his father
    you can use your own words, or even no words at all,
to draw on the grace he has promised
    to enable you to carry out the work to which he has called you.

YEAR B, the Year of Mark

*(Year B begins on Advent Sunday
in 2017, 2020, 2023 etc.)*

ADVENT

Advent consists of the four Sundays leading up to Christmas. It is a penitential season, so altar frontals and vestments are purple (except that the Third Sunday in Advent may be rose), and there needs to be an air of solemnity in the services. 'Glory to God in the highest' is often omitted. 'Advent' means 'coming'; there is a sense of eager expectancy looking forward to the coming of Christ into the world at Christmas, but, except in carol services, it is a shame to introduce many Christmas carols during Advent as this robs us of the chance to enjoy some splendid Advent music, and leads to a sense of anticlimax when Christmas comes. We also celebrate the coming of Jesus into our lives daily, at our death and at the end of the world. Traditional themes for sermons on the four Sundays are Death, Judgement, Heaven and Hell. Candles can be lit, mounted on an Advent wreath, one on the first Sunday, two on the second, and so on, leading up to five on Christmas Eve.

First Sunday of Advent, 3 December 2017
Principal Service **Mark Thirteen**

Isa. 64.1–9 Rend the heavens; Ps. 80.1–8, 18–20 Repentance;
1 Cor. 1.3–9 Blameless on the Day of the Lord; Mark 13.24–37
Ready for the coming of the Son of Man

> *'[Jesus said to his disciples,] "What I say to you I say to all: Keep awake."' Mark 13.37*

Apocalypse

The thirteenth chapter of St Mark's Gospel is sometimes called 'The Little Apocalypse', in contrast to the last book of the Bible, The Revelation to John, which is just called 'The Apocalypse'. The word means something that *was* hidden, and has now been made public. Like the book of Daniel and other in the Old Testament, they are a style of writing that appears, at first glance, to be a prediction of the end of the world. But is that really what they are? There are several problems with that approach. For instance, according to St Mark, Jesus said, 'Truly I tell you, this generation will not pass away until all these things have taken place.' If Jesus meant that some of those listening to him would be still alive when life on earth came to an end, then he was mistaken. Or worse still, he was lying. And that doesn't seem in character for the sort of person described in the Gospels.

Non-existence

If you search on the internet, you will find lots of idiots spouting their opinion that the whole New Testament is a lie, and that Jesus never in fact existed. I call them idiots because most of them have no qualifications to speak on these matters, and have never submitted their views to a university degree course, or even to peer review by fellow students. Jesus is mentioned in several documents, written by people who were not Christians, which can be dated with certainty to within 40 years of his death. Fragments of manuscripts of one or other of the four Gospels have been found which can be proved to have been written down within the first century; and you can't get away with publishing lies when there are still people alive who witnessed what really happened.

AD **70**

Therefore many Christian scholars have said that Jesus was predicting what happened in AD 70, when the Romans destroyed Jerusalem by fire, as described by the Jewish historian Josephus. Now Mark 13 does not mention fire; it predicts that 'not one stone will be left here upon another', which anyone who has seen the Wailing Wall knows is not literally true. But that is the sort of small mistake you would expect in somebody predicting where history was heading, judging by present trends. Terrorism was first invented 2,000 years ago, when Jewish Zealots, or 'dagger-men', used to stab Roman soldiers in the back. Jesus wanted to warn his fellow countrymen that if they carried on like that, the Romans would retaliate and destroy them. Which actually happened during the lifetime of some of those who heard Jesus preach. So Jesus said, 'I'm warning you.'

AD **40**

More recently, some have suggested that Jesus was not referring to the events of AD 70 but of AD 40, when the Emperor Gaius threatened to erect a statue of himself in the Jerusalem Temple. Jesus could have predicted this when he spoke of 'when you see the desolating sacrilege set up where it ought not to be'. When it happened, Jews called it an idol, and uproar broke out. Whichever date it refers to, however, Jesus is warning his followers to be ready for the worst.

Death

If Jesus *had* been talking about the end of the world, most people would shrug it off, saying, 'It hasn't happened yet and probably won't take place in my lifetime if at all. Nothing to do with me, mate!' But supposing Jesus was saying, in a poetic way, 'Death comes to us all.' 'What I say to you I say to all: Keep awake!' Then that would be relevant to each one of us. We don't have to wait for Judgement Day; any of us could fall under a bus today. But that is not as gloomy as it sounds, because we Christians believe that death is the gateway to a better life. We need to prepare for it, simply by loving God as our friend and loving our neighbours to the best of our ability, telling our family that we love them, being reconciled to anyone we have quarrelled with, and making a will. That is not the whole of the Advent message, but it is the part that is most relevant to all of us. '*What I say to you I say to all: Keep awake.*'

3

All-age worship

Make a list of things you want to do before you die. How soon can you start?

Suggested hymns

Abide with me; Come, thou long-expected Jesus; Sleepers, wake! the watch-cry pealeth; Soon and very soon.

First Sunday of Advent   3 December 2017
Second Service   **Teilhard de Chardin**
Ps. 25 Forgive me; Isa. 1.1–20 Social Justice; Matt. 21.1–13
Triumphal Entry

> *'Hear, O heavens, and listen, O earth; for the LORD has spoken: I reared children and brought them up, but they have rebelled against me.' Isaiah 1.2*

Purpose

Advent is a time for looking forward, asking what the purpose is of our life on earth. The story of the Garden of Eden answers this question; it's a story about the future, not about the past. Genesis says that God created human beings so that we might become his friends; but we spoil this plan by disobeying him. Yet because this is taught through the form of a myth, modern people, unfamiliar with that teaching method, get confused about whether it's historically true. We need a new way of proclaiming this timeless truth in modern terms.

Teilhard de Chardin

One of the first to do this was a Jesuit priest called Pierre Teilhard de Chardin. Born in France, he studied theology and philosophy in Hastings in Sussex, and then went on to study human evolution. He spent much of his life in China, and was one of the team who discovered and studied the fossil remains of 'Peking Man'. He wrote many books, most of which were banned by the officials of the Roman Catholic Church. That was because, by rejecting the historical interpretation of Genesis, they thought he was denying St Augustine's

4

doctrine of Original Sin, which alleges that we are all born sinful because we are descendants of sinful Adam and Eve. Yet after his death in 1955, Teilhard's ideas influenced several of the reforms introduced by the Second Vatican Council. Pope John Paul II showed a positive attitude towards some of Teilhard's opinions, and in 2009 Pope Benedict praised Teilhard's ideas. Teilhard wrote a moving paper entitled *A Mass on the World*, describing how, on a train journey without any bread and wine, he said Mass in his heart, offering up the world as a sacrifice to God. His book *Le Milieu Divin* was a mystical meditation on God's work in the world. But his most influential work was a book, not published until after his death, entitled *The Phenomenon of Man*.

The Phenomenon of Man

In this book Teilhard de Chardin pictures the whole history of the universe, down through many millennia, as a drama in which God gradually unfolds his purpose of creating human beings who are capable of dwelling in love with him in eternity. This climax he describes as the Omega Point, when we shall all be one in God, and he describes this triumphal conclusion to the history of evolution as 'pulling all Nature towards it'. The story begins with God creating 'primordial particles'; the Big Bang theory hadn't been invented then, but it is basically this that he is talking about. Then, under God's guidance, these particles condense into galaxies and stars, and on this particular planet earth, an environment develops, planned by God, with water and carbon and the right atmosphere and range of temperatures so that life can evolve and survive. Under God's guidance, these life forms evolve into more and more complex creatures, but are controlled by a central nervous system. The climax of this development is *Homo sapiens*, which develops the power of rational thought, able to ask questions, make choices and form relationships. The story of evolution doesn't end there, however, writes de Chardin, but sets off in another direction, that of co-operating with others in increasingly complex societies, with a deeper and deeper cultural life. De Chardin writes that this gradual unification of the human race under God mirrors the unification of the human body under the control of the brain. Eventually he foresees the human race becoming one in Christ, as the Bible says, either in this world or in the dimension of eternity, at the Omega Point. That is the purpose towards which the whole cosmic history has been heading, and was the purpose of creation.

Advent

That is a gross oversimplification of Teilhard de Chardin's very profound philosophy. But I think we can see it as a retelling for the people of today of the Advent message. We are not here as the products of random chance, as the atheists would have you believe. We are here for a purpose, planned by God with the intention that, by learning to love each other and to love him, we should progress towards a blissful fellowship where all are one in love, with each other and with God. But, because love requires free choice, God leaves us able to choose whether to accept or reject this glorious future he has planned for us. I think that's a much more helpful and inspiring way of painting the choices that lie before us than talk of haloes and wings, demons and eternal flames.

Suggested hymns

Immortal, invisible, God only wise; Lord of the boundless curves of space; Morning glory, starlit sky; O Lord of every shining constellation.

Second Sunday of Advent   10 December
Principal Service   Salvation
Isa. 40.1–11 Comfort my people; Ps. 85.1–2, 8–13 Salvation is at hand; 2 Peter 3.8–15a The Day of the Lord like a thief; Mark 1.1–8 John the Baptist, the voice in the wilderness

> *'Truly, [God's] salvation is near to those who fear him, that his glory may dwell in our land.'*
>
> *Psalm 85.9 (Common Worship)*

Isaiah

The middle section of the book of Isaiah was written by an anonymous prophet, about 200 years after the man called Isaiah who wrote the first part. This was because it was a piece of undercover subversive literature, promising that the Jews who were trapped as exiles in Babylon would soon be set free. The nameless prophet was passionate about this. It was as though the Lord God would build a motorway across the hostile desert, keeping his promise to lead his people all the way from Babylon to Jerusalem. Jerusalem was to proclaim that God will save his people, crying out, 'Don't be afraid, here comes your God!'

Post-exilic

After the exile, the Jewish people saw their God as a God who saves. God had made a covenant to save them, provided they obeyed his laws. In which case the exile must have been his punishment for their disobedience. The emphasis moved from salvation from their enemies to redemption from the slavery of sin. They carried a heavy burden of guilt.

Sinners

These days, if you tell people they are sinners, they feel resentful and insulted. Everybody commits sexual sins, they think, and they laugh at it. But *real* sin means murder, and they are not guilty of that. So God sends you and me to be voices crying in the wilderness with a different message of salvation. Many of them realize they are entrapped by bad habits: mainly overeating, or addiction to shopping or a bad temper. So we must promise them that God will set them free. How is he going to do that? By healing them.

Healing

You see, the word used in the New Testament for 'salvation' also means 'healing'. In those days, there were a few doctors like St Luke who healed people with herbs and massage, but otherwise their only hope was prayer. Now, with the advances in medical science, we expect the doctors to be able to heal us without any spiritual assistance. But the doctors would be the first to admit that they are not infallible, and that the mental attitude of the patient counts for a lot in the speed of their recovery, and sometimes can frustrate everything the doctor does for them. So now most churches and many doctors have realized there must be a partnership in the process of healing.

Respect

This requires mutual respect. Christians must not undo the doctors' work by telling patients to refuse the treatment they offer. Our part in the healing process is mainly to assure people that God really loves them. Sometimes he works a miracle, but you can't count on it every time you fall sick. But the peace and calm that comes from knowing that they are loved, and that there is a congregation of Christians surrounding them with loving prayer, usually has a calming effect that allows the self-healing powers that God has put in our bodies to do their work, unhindered by tension and worry. In this and other ways God gives us salvation from sickness without apparently breaking any laws of nature.

Death

The problem for a Christian comes when it seems that a patient's death is probably quite close. Even the most skilful doctor cannot usually tell you with certainty whether the patient is going to die soon, or how long they have to live. Many families don't wish to frighten their sick relative and so never mention death; but although that seems kind, it robs them of the chance to prepare for their death, by establishing good relations with those around them and with God. So a Christian may have to say something realistic like, 'I pray you will have a speedy recovery with God's help; but we all have to die sometime, and I pray that you will have a deep trust in God's promises of a better life to come when he calls us.'

Exorcism

Finally and briefly, if someone tells you they are frightened of haunting by ghosts or curses and evil spirits, try to get them to see an experienced minister for a blessing. But assure them with all the faith you can summon that the love of Jesus is stronger than any other force in the world, and that he will bring them salvation. God says, 'Bring comfort, bring comfort to my people', and each of us has a part to play in that.

All-age worship

Make a card with a verse from the Bible to give to somebody who is ill.

Suggested hymns

Hark the glad sound, the Saviour comes; I cannot tell why he whom angels worship; Long ago, prophets knew; On Jordan's bank the Baptist's cry.

8

Second Sunday of Advent   10 December
Second Service   **Secularization**

Ps. 40 I waited for the Lord; 1 Kings 22.1–28 Conflict between
prophets; Rom. 15.4–13 Hope for Jews and Gentiles; *Gospel at
Holy Communion*: Matt. 11.2–11 Jesus praises John

> *'Whatever was written in former days was written for our instruc-
> tion, so that by steadfastness and by the encouragement of the
> scriptures we might have hope.' Romans 15.4*

Scripture

St Paul wrote that whatever was written in the Bible, even though
it was written centuries ago, is still necessary to instruct us today.
Today's Old Testament reading speaks of kings and prophets who
were not willing to listen to the word of the Lord, with disastrous
consequences. Yet a vocal minority today claim that the Christian
religion is not only outdated, but is a dangerous delusion. They call
themselves 'secularists'. The word 'secular' literally means 'a generation'; then it came to mean the parish clergy not under control of
the monasteries; and then 'not controlled by the Church at all'. But
militant atheists have used it as a slogan for denying religious folk
any influence at all over the way people live.

Secularism

The apostle of secularism is Richard Dawkins, who argues that
religion is dangerous nonsense. He suggests that there should be no
connection between Church and State, no bishops in the House of
Lords, no prayers at great state occasions, and no church schools.
Certain Christians would agree with some of those points. But
when he says that all wars are started by religion, he needs to be
reminded that three famous atheists, Mao Tse-tung, Pol Pot and
Stalin, each individually caused more deaths than all the religious
wars put together. He is on record as suggesting that although
over half the population of the country claim to be Christians, they
can be ignored because very few of those go regularly to church
on Sundays. In fact the UK average Sunday church attendance is
about 6 per cent of the total population. But most of those calling
themselves Christians come occasionally to special services, and
agree that Jesus was 'the Son of God, the Saviour of mankind'. The

trouble is that we have not educated people in what the Christian message is, and in our busy lives many do not want to be tied down to doing something at the same time every week.

Muslim

But Baroness Warsi [pronounced 'Varsi'] – a British-born Pakistani Muslim, who became co-chair of the Conservative Party and was the Senior Minister of State for the Foreign and Commonwealth Office, before resigning in 2014 because of a disagreement over the Gaza conflict – took the opposite view to that of Dawkins over secularism. She claimed that Europe needs to become more confident in the face of 'militant secularism'. She warned of the increasing marginalization of religion, fuelled by a misguided belief that the country's majority religious heritage must be erased, in order to create equality for minority faiths. 'This militant secularism . . .', she said, 'at its core and in its instincts . . . is deeply intolerant. It demonstrates similar traits to totalitarian regimes: denying people the right to a religious identity.' 'The societies we are, the cultures we've created, the values we hold and the things we fight for, stem from . . . centuries of Christianity. You cannot and should not erase these Christian foundations from the evolution of our nation.' She said it was what she called 'the strong Christianity' of the UK that had given her confidence in her own Muslim faith!

Humanism

The other name that some atheists use to describe themselves is 'humanists'. This we can agree with, while denying them a monopoly on the word – all Christians ought to be humanists; which means that we should be keen observers of human nature, and set the effect one's actions have on other humans above any abstract philosophy. We should seek to influence events, not by use of power or compulsion, but by persuading others of the rightness of our views, and setting them an example by the kindness of our character.

Love

People with any experience of bringing up children know that you cannot change their human nature by fear and threats of punishment, only by loving them. So anyone who believes that God loves them, will become loving to other people. We shall treat them as

God treats us. Anyone who doesn't know that God loves them has no motive for behaving unselfishly. So we need reminding of that fact by meeting regularly with a caring community; and, with all our faults, a church is the best place to look for that sort of fellowship. It is religion that raises us above our natural selfishness and builds up a loving society. The secularists don't know what they are missing! We feel sorry for them, but it is in everyone's interest that we should resist their attempts to destroy religion as outdated superstition.

Suggested hymns

Faith of our fathers, taught of old; Firmly I believe and truly; If you believe and I believe; Jesus, where'er thy people meet.

Third Sunday of Advent   17 December
Principal Service   **John and the Jews**

Isa. 61.1–4, 8–11 The year of the Lord's favour; Ps. 126 Salvation, *or Canticle*: Luke 1.46–55 Magnificat, Justice; 1 Thess. 5.16–24 Pray without ceasing; John 1.6–8, 19–28 Words of John the Baptist

> *'This is the testimony given by John [the Baptist] when the Jews sent priests and Levites from Jerusalem to ask him, "Who are you?" . . . Now they had been sent from the Pharisees.' John 1.19, 24*

Messiah?

A deputation of Jewish priests and Levites were sent to cross-question John the Baptist. John's father was a priest, so he had the right to call himself a priest, too. The priests were worried that some eccentric priest might cause an uproar. They were sent by some Pharisees, members of a strict moralistic movement, who may have been members of the council that governed the religious life of every Jew. It was the job of the council to investigate rogue prophets, who regularly popped up and started a riot against their Roman rulers. Many of these errant priests and wayward prophets claimed to be the Messiah, the new King of the Jews. So the deputation asked John whether *he* was the Messiah. 'No,' he answered, 'but he's coming soon, so you'd better watch out.' The next day, John recognized that Jesus was the perfect King that he had been preparing them for. Yet many were not ready for his arrival.

Preparedness

We read the story of John the Baptist at this time of year because we are busy preparing for Christmas, when Jesus came into the world. We believe he was the Messiah, but not the military conqueror that the Jews had been waiting for. He was the Prince of Peace, and the prophet of God's universal love. Yet sometimes we are too busy buying presents to remember that Jesus comes into our lives daily, but we often don't recognize him. John the Baptist's message to the Jews applies to us, too: 'He's coming soon, so you'd better watch out.' It is not that Jesus is going to convict us of murder; he simply asks us, 'Do you make loving God and loving other people the very centre of your lives? Because,' Jesus continues, 'if you don't, there's not much I can do to help you.'

Jews

You see, we are not much different from the Jews. We are so busy with what *we* think is important, that we forget to do what is most important to God: that is, to make love our absolute priority. The Jews kept the petty regulations of the food laws and the ritual ceremonies, but it took Jesus to show them that the Law of Love is what all the other laws and the preaching of the prophets 'hang on'. St John's Gospel mentions 'the Jews' about 70 times, usually to condemn them. That seems to us to be very anti-Semitic; but we should remember that Jesus was himself a Jew, and so was John the author of the Fourth Gospel. He appears to have been writing to convince other Jews that Jesus is the God whom the Jews worship, incarnate in a human body.

Enigma

There are two possible answers to the enigma of why the Fourth Gospel appears anti-Semitic. It may be that John came from the region around Lake Galilee, but it was the people from Judaea, the area around Jerusalem, who caused all the problems for Jesus and John the Baptist and their disciples, and also for John the Gospel-writer and the small congregations of new Christians that he was writing for. Or it may be that, outside Jerusalem, 'the Jews' simply meant the people in authority: the priests, Levites and Pharisees, who had sent the deputation to enquire about John the Baptist, and were opposed to all forms of change in their society and their religion.

Ready?

So John the Baptist's message applies to us, too, as I already said: 'He's coming soon, so you'd better watch out.' He came to earth at Christmas; but he comes to us every day. He said, 'When you help the sick, poor, prisoners and homeless, you are doing it to me.' We must recognize Jesus in the faces of the needy. 'Because,' Jesus said, 'if you don't, there's not much I can do to help you. Be prepared! Watch out! Be ready when I come, asking you to show my love to somebody who is starved of love.' That is what Jesus is saying to you. If you are ready, then you will have a very happy Christmas. But if you are too busy to recognize Jesus in the poor and needy, there is not much he can do for you.

All-age worship

Find out about Crisis at Christmas and similar charities.

Suggested hymns

Christ is surely coming; 'The Kingdom of God is justice and joy';
Thou didst leave thy throne; To Mercy, Pity, Peace and Love.

Third Sunday of Advent   17 December
Second Service   **Rejoice**
Ps. 68.1–19 A God of salvation; Mal. 3.1–4; 4 My messenger; Phil.
4.4–7 Rejoice in the Lord always; *Gospel at Holy Communion*:
Matt. 14.1–12 Death of the Baptist

> *'Rejoice in the Lord always; again I will say, Rejoice.'*
> *Philippians 4.4*

Have a nice day

'Rejoice in the Lord always.' Choristers know those words as the *Bell Anthem* by Henry Purcell. They come in the closing chapter of St Paul's letter to the Philippians. Letters written in Greek still end with the word 'Rejoice!' Yet some readers might feel like answering,

'But I don't feel like rejoicing.' When you're having a tough time, being told to rejoice may sound as unsympathetic as 'Have a nice day!' To which grumpy people sometimes answer, 'Who are you to tell me what sort of day to have?' Many of our days are 'bad hair days'. If things go badly, we don't have much to rejoice about, either.

Philippians

Yet Paul's letter to the Christians in Philippi is full of joy. It was the first church that he founded in Greece, and was led by a business-woman called Lydia, who had been converted when she welcomed him into her household. There were no major splits in the congregation, like in Corinth. Yet little squabbles were hindering the spread of the gospel. Paul wrote, mentioning two women by name, 'I beg of you, Euodia and Syntyche, [you-OWE-dear, SIN-ticky] that you would agree with each other . . .', and you can almost hear him adding underneath his breath, 'just for once!' Visitors to that congregation would probably say, 'I'll not join a fellowship where those two are always arguing.' In the film *Secrets and Lies*, a character cries in frustration, 'Why is it that the people I love should hate each other?' Paul loved the Philippians, and instead of rebuking them, he told them to rejoice.

Reasons to rejoice

Despite their squabbling, Paul wrote: 'I thank my God every time I remember you.' They'd prayed for him while he was in prison. An Australian member of the Anglican congregation in Saigon was captured by the Vietcong in 1968; he was marched every night to a fresh camp in the jungle, starved and taunted for almost a year. When at last he was released, he told the church members that he used to say to himself the words of the communion service, which he knew by heart, every Sunday at the time when he knew his friends would be saying them and praying for him, and that kept him going. Paul rejoiced because the Philippians prayed for him, and believed the gospel, and so hoped for God's help in this life and a joyful eternity in the world to come. So he quotes to them a hymn about Jesus who 'emptied himself . . . and became obedient to the point of death – even death on a cross . . . therefore God also highly exalted him'. Maybe this was the hymn that Paul and Silas sang at midnight in the prison at Philippi. Even in prison they found something to rejoice about.

Happiness

Joy is much greater than mere happiness. Happiness depends on chance: if there are no mishaps, and good hap comes your way by happenstance, then you may be happy. So happiness depends on what's happening to you – joy doesn't. You can be joyful even in the most awful circumstances, knowing that the good things God has promised us far outweigh any suffering in this life. To know that you are loved by another human being helps you through the bad days; to know you're loved by God turns even the worst days into days of joy.

Positive thinking

So Paul recommends the power of positive thinking:

> Finally, beloved, whatever is true, whatever is honourable, whatever is just, whatever is pure, whatever is pleasing, whatever is commendable, if there is any excellence and if there is anything worthy of praise, think about these things. (Philippians 4.8)

For as Maria sang, in *The Sound of Music*, if you're thinking about your favourite things, there's no room for gloom.

Advent hope

Advent is a season of hope. We look forward to Christmas – not only the family gathering and the presents, but the remembrance that God loves us enough to come to earth for us and be born as a baby in a stable. In Advent, we also look forward in hope to the joys of heaven, when we shall live for ever in one great Christmas party with Jesus, and with those we love who've died. So we can sing with St Paul:

> Rejoice in the Lord always; again I will say, Rejoice. Let your gentleness be known to everyone. The Lord is near. Do not

worry about anything, but in everything by prayer and sup-
plication with thanksgiving let your requests be made known
to God. And the peace of God, which surpasses all understanding, will guard your hearts and your minds in Christ Jesus.
(Pilippians 4.4–7)

Suggested hymns

*Come, thou long-expected Jesus; Hark, a herald voice is sounding;
O come, O come Emmanuel; Rejoice! the Lord is king.*

Fourth Sunday of Advent   Christmas Eve,
24 December
*(For an evening service that is not a Eucharist, see
'Christmas Eve' below)*   **The Virgin Birth**
2 Sam. 7.1–11, 16 God promises King David peace; *Canticle*:
Magnificat, *or* Ps. 89.1–4, 19–26 Covenant; Rom. 16.25–27
The mystery promised long ago; Luke 1.26–38 The Annunciation
to Mary

> *'Mary said to the angel, "How can this be, since I am a virgin?"'
> Luke 1.34*

Truth?

The Gospels tell us that Mary the Mother of Jesus was still a virgin when her son was born. And that is the gospel truth. But what
sort of truth is that? There are two types: scientific truths are those
investigated by the logical left side of the brain; they are analytical,
of the type: 'If A, therefore B.' The scientific approach to the question 'Why are we here?' is to discuss, 'How did this come about?'
But the narrative approach to the same question uses the right side
of the brain. It is intuitive, rather than analytical, and searches for
meaning, rather than logic. It approaches the question 'Why are we
here?' by discussing the purpose of our existence. And many people
think that to treat the virgin birth as a scientific question misses the
whole point of what the Gospel-writers were saying, and demeans
the value of the Scriptures.

Myth?

Yet if you call it a myth, people assume that means that it is an ancient fairy story, of no importance for today. On the contrary, the dictionary definition of a myth is 'a story offering an explanation of some fact or phenomenon; a story with a veiled meaning'. Very often it explains something of vital importance, which could never be explained by the scientific method. Many ancient kings asserted their authority by suggesting that some god had raped a human female, and they are the fruit of that liaison. Against that background, the virgin birth myth is a story explaining the one true God's spiritual involvement in the birth of Jesus, with the full consent of Mary who said, 'Let it be with me according to your word.'

Interpreting

The words we know as 'a virgin shall conceive' are quoted by Matthew from Isaiah 7.14, which is accurately translated as 'The Lord himself will give you a sign. Look, the young woman is with child and shall bear a son, and shall name him Immanuel.' Isaiah tried to persuade King Ahaz that God favoured the Israelites, and would give them a new king. The word 'Immanuel' means 'God is with you'. Maybe the wife of Ahaz was already pregnant, and would call her son 'God is on our side'. Matthew wanted to show that the birth of Jesus fulfilled this prophecy; his version was left brain, to persuade us that Jesus is our king, promised by God, God incarnate in a human body. That is a very profound teaching; but to be distracted by arguments as to whether the story was literally true is to destroy the whole point that Matthew was making.

Remote

When people spoke about God, they used to think of an old man on a cloud. But who wants to be friends with an old man on a cloud? Nowadays, we tell ourselves that God is the creator of the trillions of light-years-wide universe, and perhaps other universes, too. How can you possibly conceive of such an infinite being, let alone relate to him or her? But God neither wants us to be patronizing nor terrified towards her or him. God is not a person, in any normal sense of the word; God is far greater than that; but God wants, believe it or not, a relationship with us rather like that between two loving

17

human beings. The only way God could achieve that was to become a human person. So God crammed as much of himself or herself as was possible into a human body; then showed how much God loves us when that incarnation sacrificed his life to save us from our selfish and inconsiderate habits. That was the only way God could get through to us.

Birth

To show that Jesus was not just a human being like the rest of us, but rather the distillation of the nature of godhead, his birth had to be unique, unlike any other human birth. So it is quite possible that God performed a miracle that first Christmas. But God does not want us to concentrate on what literally happened, but on what it means. This Christmas, try to believe that God has come to earth for *your* sake, to persuade you that God is with you every minute of the day, and loves you more than anyone else could love. Then you really will have a happy Christmas!

All-age worship

Try to squeeze yourself into a small cupboard or box (careful!). Draw it. Imagine what it would be like for God to squeeze into a human body.

Suggested hymns

Creator of the starry height; O come, O come, Emmanuel; O Lord my God, when I in awesome wonder; Of the Father's love begotten.

CHRISTMAS, EPIPHANY AND CANDLEMAS

Despite our weariness from all the preparations, Christmas retains its magic as a season of joy. The churches are brightly decorated, vestments and hangings are gold, if possible, on Christmas Day and white on the Sundays following. On 6 January we celebrate the Epiphany, which means the revelation or revealing of who Jesus really is. On that day we read about the visit of the Wise Men, who were the first non-Jews to recognize Jesus as 'King, and

God, and Sacrifice'. The following Sundays have readings about other occasions when Jesus was 'manifest': when the Father spoke at his baptism, when he 'revealed his glory' at the wedding in Cana, when he proclaimed his programme in Nazareth, when Nathanael (and the demons!) recognized him as Son of God, and when he called the first disciples and sent them out as 'fishers' to reveal him to all races. The Epiphany season is a time therefore to remember our own missionary task of evangelism. Then on 2 February comes 'The Presentation of Christ in the Temple', when old Simeon recognized Jesus as the Messiah, and sang of him as 'a Light to lighten the Gentiles'. This is therefore also called 'Candlemas', and candle ceremonies are held in some churches. Simeon also predicted that a sword would pierce Mary's heart, looking onward to the crucifixion; so Candlemas is a watershed between the Sundays following Christmas and those leading up to Holy Week, and is often celebrated on the Sunday falling between 28 January and 3 February. From then until Ash Wednesday there are a number of 'Sundays before Lent', using, if necessary, readings for Propers 1–3 in Ordinary Time.

Christmas Eve   Sunday 24 December
Evening service when not a Eucharist
Revelation at Christmastime
Psalm 85 His salvation is near; Zechariah 2 I will dwell in your midst; Rev. 1.1–8 Who is and was and is to come

> *'The revelation of Jesus Christ, which God gave him to show his servants what must soon take place; he made it known by sending his angel to his servant John . . . Blessed are those who hear and who keep what is written in it; for the time is near.'*
> *Revelation 1.1, 3*

Christmas Eve

Once in about seven years, Christmas Eve falls on a Sunday. Many churches use the readings for the Fourth Sunday in Advent for their principal service in the morning. If there is a Holy Communion in the evening, then we should call it 'the first Mass of Christmas' and use one of the sets of readings for Christmas Day. But for any non-eucharistic evening service special Christmas Eve readings are suggested, and it on these that I shall be preaching. The New Testament reading is the first eight verses of the book of Revelation; and the first three occur nowhere else in the three-year cycle.

Revelation

The first words of what is properly called 'The Book of the Revelation to St John the Divine' are, 'The revelation of Jesus Christ . . . to his servant John'. It doesn't say 'John the apostle', and John was a very common name; the John who was one of 'the Twelve', and the author of the Gospel and Letters of John, and the author of the Revelation may or may not have been the same person. 'Revelation' is an English translation of the Greek word 'apocalypse', which means 'no longer veiled'. Think of a new painting or a sculpture, hidden behind a veil of opaque material until the opening ceremony, when the veil is pulled back and everybody gasps at the beauty and the truthfulness of what has been revealed.

Truth

Truth is not often obvious. We usually have to work hard to discover the truth; and Christians believe that God gives us the grace and perseverance to do so. Or sometimes God may reveal a new truth to one of his servants in a flash of inspiration, and then instructs them to pass it on to others until everybody learns the truth. That is what happened in this case; but either way, all truth comes from God.

Near future

The truth unveiled in the last book of the Bible is there described as 'what must soon take place . . . for the time is near'. Many books were written between the Old Testament and New Testament periods describing the distant future, when God would come to earth to put the Jewish race in control of everything, destroying their enemies before them. They use symbolic language, and some are called apocalypses; John used the same style, but it is a serious mistake to think that he is describing something that will happen in the distant future; people have been waiting for that for 2,000 years, but it still has not come. It is a complete misunderstanding of the Bible writings to take their symbols literally. No, as John says, he is talking about how Jesus comes to us in our own lifetime. This makes it very suitable for the day that links the season of Advent, which means 'coming', with Christmas, when we commemorate God coming to earth as a little baby.

Recognize

So the question this reading raises is, shall we recognize God when he comes? In the unlikely event that we are alive when human life ends on this planet, we must understand that this is not only the effect of global warming, but is also because God has completed his plans for us here, and is continuing them in another, better world. But we must learn to expect the unexpected at any time. As a modern carol puts it, 'Who would think that what was needed to transform and save the earth . . .' is the birth of a powerless baby in a dirty stable in an obscure village in a remote corner of the Roman Empire? If you had dropped into that stable by accident that night, would you have realized what was happening?

Apply to yourself

So we must apply the Bible prophecies to ourselves, in our everyday lives. Christmas didn't just happen 2,000 years ago: the coming of God to earth happens daily when some human being does an act of kindness, or stands up for the truth, or gasps at the beauty of creation, or performs some beautiful music, or obeys their conscience against their human desires. Only, we have to be on the lookout for the God of Surprises, to recognize him when he comes. God never forces himself on us; he waits for us to be open to his unexpected unveilings of himself, his daily apocalypses.

Suggested carols

Hark, what a sound, and too divine for hearing; People, look east; Tell out, my soul; Who would think that what was needed?

Christmas Day   25 December

Any of the following sets of readings may be used on the evening of Christmas Eve and on Christmas Day: Set III should be used at some service during the celebration.

Set I   A Messy Christmas

Isa. 9.2–7 A child is born; Ps. 96 Tell of his salvation; Titus 2.11–14 Salvation has come; Luke 2.1–14 [15–20] The birth of Jesus

> '[Mary] gave birth to her firstborn son and wrapped him in bands of cloth, and laid him in a manger, because there was no place for them in the inn.' Luke 2.7

Childbirth

Three women, all of them mothers, were praying together at Christmas time. They had just been singing the carol, 'O little town of Bethlehem', with the memorable lines:

O holy child of Bethlehem,
descend to us, we pray;
cast out our sin, and enter in:
be born in us today.

One of the women tried to imagine what this meant for her, and prayed earnestly, 'Let the Christ child be born in us this year.' The others thought about this for a while, and then the second thought back to her own experience of childbearing, and blurted out, 'But without any labour pains.' And the third added, 'Or at least with an epidural.' Then they all burst out laughing. 'Of course,' they thought, 'for Jesus to be born in our hearts is a spiritual experience, nothing like the agony of human labour pains.' But in that they were wrong.

Messy

Neither was the physical birth of Jesus 2,000 years ago free from the searing agony that most women experience in the labour ward. It was, in fact, a very messy business, like every other human birth. If you have never been in a 'birthing suite', think back to the TV series, *Call the Midwife*. Some Christian heretics shied away from this idea. One said that Jesus passed through Mary's body like

22

light passes through glass. Even today, we sing 'How silently, how silently the wondrous gift is given'. A rich woman commissioned the colourful windows in Birmingham Cathedral from the artist Edward Burne-Jones, and protested that he had put the ox and ass in the stable with the newborn baby. She insisted that he move them outside, saying, 'They are dirty! You can't put them near a newborn baby!' But such squeamishness robs the nativity story of its most important lesson: that Jesus became completely human, *just like us*!

Census

St Luke emphasizes this when he begins his account by dating the birth as 'when Augustus was emperor in Rome, and Quirinius was governor of Syria'. It was also while Herod the Great was King of Judaea. That was a most terrifying period in politics – all three ordered pogroms of suspected enemies. To secure his power, Augustus instituted regular censuses, to calculate what taxes he could levy on his subjects to pay his army.

Peasants

And then Luke's gaze switches from the wider world scene to a family of peasants in an obscure village in an obscure corner of the Empire, and a very messy birth in a dirty stable, with nowhere to put the baby down but in the animals' feeding trough. We can be sure that Mary had labour pains, and howled like every other mother, then promptly forgot them for joy that a new human being was born. She was not the plump blonde Italianate Madonna of the Renaissance paintings, but a dark-skinned, black-haired, undernourished, adolescent Jewish peasant. But that is just the point. The Prince of Peace was not born in the wealthy but cruel courts of the Emperor, but among ordinary down-to-earth people like you and me; because he came to save ordinary messy people like me and you.

In us

If we understand that, it may be easier to say to Jesus, 'Be born in us today.' For God did not shun us, but embraced us, with all our messy bits. He came among us to bring love and glory in a way that humanity had never known before. But receiving him into our hearts, to love us but also to rule us, may be quite painful, and certainly very messy. He may expect us to do unpleasant things if we serve him by serving others. There will definitely be no epidural. But there will certainly be rejoicing in heaven when each of us, in our own good time and our own personal way, opens our eyes to this wonderful truth: that we can carry around in our own heart of hearts the eternal love of the Saviour. The God who was even willing to be born as a blood-smeared squalling baby, just as we were once, to become one of us and show how much he loves us.

All-age worship

Examine the instruments and drugs, or pictures of them, which a modern midwife uses to diminish the pain of childbirth. Say thank you to Mary for willingly having a baby without any of these aids.

Suggested carols

Away in a manger; Behold, the great Creator makes; Once in royal David's city; O little town of Bethlehem.

Christmas Day   25 December
Set II   Shepherds are Human Too
Isa. 62.6–12 Prepare a way; Ps. 97 God comes to rescue his people; Titus 3.4–7 Salvation by grace; Luke 2.[1–7] 8–20 Shepherds go to Bethlehem

> *'All who heard it were amazed at what the shepherds told them.'*
> *Luke 2.18*

Shepherds

Shepherds in the time of Jesus were usually employed at shoestring wages by a farmer. They owned no land, and spent much of their time in the open air, defending their flocks against wild animals or sheep-stealers, and at lambing time helping the ewes to give birth to their lambs. For this reason, shepherds were regarded by the rest of society as the lowest of the low. It is all the more surprising, therefore, that a group of shepherds are praised in the Christmas story.

Imagine

Can you imagine it? Suppose you are one of those shepherds in the fields near Bethlehem. It is a cold winter's night, but your flock needs you to be near them in the fields. You can't go to sleep, for a wolf might appear at any moment and run off with one of the lambs. If your boss finds out, the value of that lamb might be deducted from your wages. If a sheep gets lost, all the shepherds would have to fan out and search for it, leaving the other sheep at the mercy of thieves and predators.

Grumbling

So you have nothing to do to pass the time, but grumble to your fellow shepherds about how unfair your life is. You are stuck in this job, paid a pittance, you say, and there is no getting out of it. You can never leave your sheep to attend the synagogues, so the rabbis show no interest in you. You have heard that they sing a song there which compares God to a shepherd, but you tell your mates that the all-powerful God would have no time for the likes of us. So you stare at the stars.

Angels

One of the stars looks a bit odd, you say. It seems to be moving. And it's no longer star-shaped, but more like a human being. The other shepherds are getting excited, because more and more of the stars are looking like tiny human beings, far off, high up in the sky. Then one of them starts talking! He – or is it she? – comes close to you, and starts talking to you – you, whom people cross the street to avoid. Mostly it's about God; synagogue-talk that you have never learnt to understand. But the bit that sticks in your memory is when the thing in the sky says to you, 'Tonight, God is going to save you shepherds from the hopeless mess you are in. A baby will be born in that tiny village on the hillside opposite. The baby will save you, because he is actually the Lord God himself, come down to earth for ordinary people like you. So tell everyone you meet.' Then the sky is filled with light, and the things start singing, much more wonderful than the folk songs the shepherds sing when they're bored.

25

Response

So what are you to do? Obviously you and your mates drop everything, leave the sheep with only the things-in-the-sky to look after
them, and rush off to the tiny village of Bethlehem, which claims to
be where the shepherd-king David was born. But tonight it's full of
strangers, something to do with a 'census', they tell you. You soon
find the baby, though, because the sky-creature had told you that he
would be 'wrapped in bands of cloth and lying in a feeding trough'.
His young mum looked delighted; and so did the much older man
who, you guess, was the baby's dad. So you congratulate them, and
say welcome to the wee one, and rush out to tell everybody, like the
thing had told you to.

Disbelief

But nobody believes you. Nobody! You tell all the people in the
village, visitors included, that God himself has come down to save
ordinary people like us from the mess we've got ourselves into. And
they all waggle their finger against their foreheads to show they think
we are completely mad. 'They're only shepherds,' they say. 'God
wouldn't have time for common people like that.' But you mark my
words, you tell them. One day, people will believe us. Not everybody; not those who are too snobbish. But some will recognize that
what happened to us tonight means that God has time for everybody.
Even the lowest of the low. So just you mind your 'know-it-all' attitude doesn't make you too proud to recognize the truth: God can tell
us he loves us all, even through the child of penniless parents, like the
one who was born tonight. Remember, even shepherds are human.

All-age worship

*Make a shepherd's crook and use it to 'rescue' a toy lamb that is
straying, Learn to sing 'The Lord's my shepherd'.*

Suggested carols

*Hark! The herald angels sing; It came upon the midnight clear; The
first Nowell; While shepherds watched.*

Christmas Day 25 December
Set III What is 'the Word'?

Isa. 52.7–10 The messenger of peace; Ps. 98 God's victory;
Heb. 1.1–4 [5–12] God speaks through a Son; John 1.1–14
The Word became flesh

> *'The Word became flesh and lived among us, and we have seen his glory, the glory as of a father's only son, full of grace and truth.' John 1.14*

Meaning

The first chapter of St John's Gospel is all about 'the Word'. It uses simple words, yet we are aware of depths in this passage, and it is worth spending some time to study the different meanings of the word, 'Word'.

Communication

First, words are used to communicate. So this passage tells us that God wants to communicate with us. Religion is not the story of our search for God, but of God's search for us. He tells us of his love for us, first through the words of the Bible, but more importantly, through the words and life of Jesus.

Create

But the desire to communicate is creative. An author pours words into his books, or the politician into her speeches, in the hope of creating new ideas in people's minds, and new relationships in society. A democratic nation cannot be formed unless the people talk to each other. So, at the beginning of the story of our universe, 'God spake and it was done.' St John says that:

> In the beginning was the Word, and the Word was with God, and the Word was God. He was in the beginning with God. All things came into being through him, and without him not one thing came into being.

27

Logic

The Greek word for 'word' is *logos*, which gives us our word 'logic'. So God used reason to create the world, and uses his words to reason with us until we see the truth.

Explain

For words are also used to explain ideas that we cannot yet grasp. God speaks to us, to explain that all we see and are is actually here because God intended it to be so.

Promise

When you find it hard to believe what somebody says, they may protest, 'I give you my word; my word is my bond.' The word of God is his guarantee that we can depend on him; above all that we can trust his promise to give us eternal life.

Bible

The promise is found in the Bible, which we call 'the word of God'. We have to take into account the context in which those words were first spoken, and ask ourselves whether they were meant to be understood literally or symbolically. As George Gershwin joked, 'The t'ings dat yo' li'ble To read in de Bible, It ain't necessarily so.' But that is probably because you are misinterpreting the words as literal history; the overall message of the Bible is that God loves us, and that is certainly so.

Aspect

Parts of the Old Testament and Apocrypha talk about God's *wisdom* as being almost a separate person. Of course there is only one God, so it might be better to speak of Divine Wisdom as being an aspect of God's personality. St John appears to have taken up this idea to suggest that Jesus and the one he called 'Father' are so close that you could call Jesus 'the Word of God', an aspect of God's multi-sided divine nature.

Revelation

By our words we gradually reveal aspects of our character to other people. So we learn of the character of God through the life of Jesus, his passion for truth, his healings, his compassion for the needy, his willingness to forgive those who repent, his encouragement of those who were lonely or depressed. God is not a remote stern tyrant; God is like Jesus. So, at last, we grasp that Jesus is the Word of God. Jesus is God's means of communication, his means of creation – of the universe and of a society of loving people. Jesus is God's logic, the reasoning through which he explains his promises. The Bible contains the word of God; Jesus *is* the Word of God. Jesus is an aspect of the One God, through which God reveals his character.

Home

So, writes St John, 'The Word became flesh and dwelt among us.' We could not form a close relationship with God while he remained remote in another world, so one aspect of God's personality became incarnate as a human being at Christmas time. Not only that, but, when many of those he loved rejected him, he made his home among and in us who love him. He also gave us the power to become children of God, and to live with him in eternity. And that is the meaning of Christmas – God gives you his word.

All-age worship

How many English words do you know which are borrowed from another language? How could you communicate with somebody who speaks that language using only those words?

Suggested hymns

Christians, awake; Love came down at Christmas; O come, all ye faithful; Of the Father's love begotten.

Christmas Day 25 December
Second Service Baby of Bethlehem

Morning Ps. 110 This day of your birth, 117 Steadfast love; Evening
Ps. 8 Out of the mouths of babes; Isa. 65.17–25 A new creation;
Phil. 2.5–11 Jesus emptied himself, *or* Luke 2.1–20 Shepherds go to
Bethlehem (*if it has not been used at the Principal Service of the day*)

> *'Jesus . . . though he was in the form of God, did not regard
> equality with God as something to be exploited, but emptied him-
> self, taking the form of a slave, being born in human likeness.'
> Philippians 2.6–7*

Emptying

One of the possible readings for this service is taken from St Paul's
letter to the Christians in Philippi [though sometimes, if the story
of the shepherds has not been used at any of the earlier services,
that is used at this service and Philippians is omitted]. It describes
Jesus 'emptying himself of his glory' when he left heaven to become a
human being. It is a lovely phrase for describing his utter humility.
He becomes like us; not like one of the great people on the earth, but
humbly like you and me. One of the difficulties about Christmas is
that people are so familiar with the story that they treat it as utterly
unreal, a fairy story, which has no message for ordinary people. So
here is a poem I read, in which each verse emphasizes that Jesus came
here for everyone – 'even for me!' The first verse is like a Christmas
carol, telling how Jesus was 'born among humble men, cared for and
shared with them'. The villagers of Bethlehem were a peasant society,
as were the fishermen of Galilee; and the all-powerful God chose to
become incarnate among ordinary poor people like that. But that is
only the introduction to the whole story of his life, which was lived
in the same spirit of self-sacrifice for other people – 'even for me!'
The poem could be sung to the tune of the folk song, 'Blow the wind
southerly', though it has to be said that the even-numbered verses go
rather high for a congregation, and if it is sung by a choir, only the
higher voices should attempt those verses.

Christmas

So here is the first verse, all about Christmas:

Baby of Bethlehem,
born among humble men,
cared for and shared with them;
you help me see
this is God's sympathy,
shown unreservedly
for all in poverty – even for me.

Childhood

The second verse is about the childhood of Christ. It makes the
same point as Mrs Alexander makes in the carol 'Once in royal
David's city', that 'he is our childhood's pattern, day by day like us
he grew; he was little, weak and helpless, tears and smiles like us he
knew; and he feeleth for our sadness, and he shareth in our gladness'. So here is the modern poem:

Jesus of Nazareth,
lowly you came to birth,
lived as a child on earth
by Mary's knee.
This you have done for us,
lovingly come to us,
just like each one of us, and just like me.

Temptation

Each verse begins with one of the names of Jesus, and one of the
places where he displayed his humanity and his divinity. Next we
come to the struggle Jesus fought in the garden against the temptation to renege on his vocation. We tend to think it was easier for
Jesus to live a good life than it is for us; but the story of his temptation, which he received in the Garden of Gethsemane, to avoid suffering and death, shows that it was as hard for him as for us, and he
sympathizes with how we have to struggle to be kind:

Christ in Gethsemane,
dreading your destiny,
wishing from agony
you could be free;

tempted to run away
and fight another day;
but all the world can say, 'tempted like me'.

Crucifixion

Verse four is about his crucifixion. We are accustomed to hearing people say that he died to save sinners, or even that he was born to die, to save all mankind. But have you made it personal: imagine you are about to be hit by a train and someone leaps on to the tracks and dies saving your life. That gratitude is what we should feel when we say, 'Jesus died for me':

Jesus on Calvary,
divine vitality
killed by brutality,
hanged on a tree.
God's love that never ends
down to death's depths descends,
dying for all your friends – dying for me!

Resurrection

But the poem ends with the triumph of the resurrection. We have done nothing to deserve eternal life, yet he promises it, even to you:

Risen by Galilee,
Jesus in majesty,
living eternally
for all to see!
Bring us before God's face,
in heaven prepare a place
for all the human race – even for me!

© 1992 Michael Counsell

Suggested carols

I cannot tell why he whom angels worshipped; I danced in the morning; What child is this?; Who is he in yonder stall?

First Sunday of Christmas   31 December
Principal Service   Titles of Jesus

Isa. 61.10—62.3 Garments of salvation; Ps. 148 Young and
old together; Gal. 4.4–7 God sent his Son, born of a woman;
Luke 2.15–21 The shepherds visit Bethlehem

> *'When the fullness of time had come, God sent his Son, born of a
> woman, born under the law, in order to redeem those who were
> under the law, so that we might receive adoption as children.'*
> *Galatians 4.4–5*

Naming

Tomorrow, New Year's Day, commemorates the Naming of Jesus.
Just as we give our babies their official names when they are christened, so Jesus was named at his circumcision. His name, Jesus,
a dialect form of Joshua, means 'God saves'. But Jews were also
named after their parents. If they had named him 'son of Mary',
that would have revealed to everyone the shameful fact that his
parents were not married when he was born; so presumably they
swiftly tied the knot, and he was named 'son of Joseph'. St Paul
calls Jesus 'Son of God', and also 'the Christ', which is Greek for
'the anointed [King]'.

Titles

But many other titles are given to Jesus, indicating his nature, his
character and his achievements. He was called the Second Adam,
Son of David, King of the Jews, Lamb of God, Son of Man, Word
of God, and Emmanuel. There are other names, too numerous to
mention, but let us concentrate on a few of the names that were
given to Jesus at the time of his birth.

Jesus

The name given to him by the angel before he was born was 'Jesus'.
As we have seen, this means 'God saves', and shows us that Jesus
was born to save us, from sin and death. He reveals a loving God,
who creates a universe with the intention of populating it with

creatures that God can love, and in the case of humans, beings who can love God in return. To do this, God has to give us free will, which means we are sure to behave selfishly, hurt others and disobey God. There are only two ways God could prevent that: take away our free will, which he will never do; or reveal how much he loves us by coming to earth himself and dying in our place. Then, when we love him in return, he can take us to heaven to love and be loved eternally by God and our neighbours. Jesus is our Saviour because he takes away the guilt of sin and the fear of death.

Christ

'Christ' means the 'Messiah', the anointed King of all the nations on earth. The Jews, God's Chosen People, were disappointed by a series of selfish, tyrannical kings. So God promised them a new type of king, a servant king, who would come soon to form a new type of kingdom, a society based on mutual love. To become the Prince of Peace, God had to become incarnate as a babe in a manger, humble and powerless, brought up among poor people and proclaimed by simple shepherds.

God's Son

Jesus is called 'the Son of God', a phrase that is easily misunderstood. Notoriously, our Muslim friends declare confidently that 'God has no sons'. That is because they are thinking of God coming down to earth and begetting children in the normal human way. 'Son of God' must be treated as a metaphor, attempting to convey the indescribable relationship between the man called Jesus and the ineffable Creator of the world. Like a human son, Jesus is the 'image' of the Father, meaning that he resembles him in his loving character; he is his Father's representative, speaking for God and acting on his behalf. So Jesus needed to have a fully human birth, but with unique features to show that his relationship with God was a special one. So Jesus had to be born of a virgin, announced by angels, and welcomed by wise men from the East, who had followed a travelling star.

Conclusion

I have spoken about just a few of the titles of Jesus. But you will see from that how all the others have to be studied in depth, to help us to an understanding of why the divine Christ had to come to earth as a human being, just like us, but to live a life of loving service to others, to inspire us to understand what we could become. All those details in the Christmas story, which charm us so, have something to say about how we should behave. All the titles given to Jesus should remind us what an astonishing privilege this is: the Creator of the stars and planets cares so much about you and me that he has come to earth to be our Saviour, our Master and our Friend.

All-age worship

Make a sign to attach to the Christmas crib: 'The Son of God: isn't he like his dad?'

Suggested hymns

Angels from the realms of glory; Come and join the celebration; Meekness and majesty; Thou didst leave thy throne.

First Sunday of Christmas 31 December
Second Service **A Twelve-Year-Old**
(*Suitable for New Year's Eve, but see also the Naming and Circumcision of Jesus, page 280.*)
Ps. 132 God's dwelling in Zion; Isa. 35.1–10 The redeemed return to Zion; Col. 1.9–20 The firstborn of creation, *or* Luke 2.41–52 Jesus aged twelve

> 'When the festival was ended and they started to return, the boy Jesus stayed behind in Jerusalem, but his parents did not know it . . . Then they started to look for him among their relatives and friends. When they did not find him, they returned to Jerusalem to search for him.' Luke 2.43–45

Same

Now we've got to plod all the way back to Jerusalem, Mary, where we came from yesterday. It's all his fault. Well, you know what children are like, don't you?

Yes, Joseph, I know what children are like. And our baby Jesus has grown up to be a 12-year-old, just like they all do. Smiles and tears like us he knew.

Well, Mary, young Jesus is just like all the rest – rebellious and argumentative. He's having a teenage rebellion a year before he's a teenager. As his mother, you should have brought your son up differently.

Well, he's your son too, Joseph. Remember . . . you adopted him soon after he was born? Yesterday he had his bar mitzvah ceremony, that means he's officially a grown-up now. He's learning all the time, how to be loving and kind to his family and even to strangers; he's learning from you what fatherhood means. But he only argues with you when he's right and you're wrong, my darling!

According to you, Mary, that's most of the time. You always take his side. This time he's behaving like a typical 12-year-old, and vanished without trace. I tell you, I've had enough of him. Where can your son – sorry, *our* son – have got to?

Yes, I'm just as worried about him as you are, husband of mine. But he can't have gone far. I feel sure he stayed behind in Jerusalem, darling; you know he was enjoying himself. And you and I were so busy looking after the other pilgrims in our group that we didn't notice he wasn't among us.

Yes, well, this lot are so daft they couldn't have found their way back home to Nazareth without me and my wife – that's you, my darling – to show them which way to go. I dread to think where they've got to now we've left them. And it's only the same road we came up to Jerusalem on, to bring our sons for their bar mitzvah ceremony in the Temple courtyard. Ooh, just thinking about that place gives me the shivers. It was awful! Full of rabbis arguing with each other.

I'll bet Jesus was having such a good time he's still there in the Temple, discussing with the legal experts what the Lord really meant when the Scriptures were written down. You know, before Jesus could become bar mitzvah he had to . . .

Yes, Mary, I know, I did it myself when I was 12, all those years ago. I had to learn huge chunks of the Scriptures by heart, so that I could trick the rabbis into thinking I could read when I was tested for shouting them out from the scrolls. But if you ask me, I think young Jesus really *can* read.

Yes, of course he can, Joseph. I think he's probably read nearly all the Scriptures to himself by now. That's why he was having such a furious row with the rabbis. They think it's all about what you can't eat and mustn't do; Jesus told them it's all about love.

Well that won't make him popular with the authorities, Mary; if people start believing that, the rulers will lose all their power. I think we'd better hurry up and find him; I'm afraid the rabbis may have arrested him by now, and thrown him into jail.

No, not yet, Joseph.

What do you mean, Mary, by 'not yet'?

I don't quite know, my darling husband. I just have this dreadful premonition that the happiness that surrounded his birth won't last for ever.

Oh no, Mary, you're just being pessimistic. I hope the last few days have taught him to obey those who are in authority, and not to get at cross purposes with those who have the power in the land – under the Romans, of course. Maybe he'll decide to be more obedient to his parents in the coming years. But if he does get into trouble, I pray to God that I shan't be there.

Mmm. We shall see, Joseph. I just hope, if I am there, God will give me strength and courage to stand by my son in all his difficulties.

Suggested hymns

A stable lamp is lighted; For Mary, Mother of our Lord; Lord of the home, your only Son; The maker of the sun and moon.

Baptism of Christ (First Sunday of Epiphany)
7 January 2018

*(If the Epiphany is celebrated today, the Baptism of Christ
is transferred to Monday 8 January.)*

Principal Service   **The Spirit over the Waters**

Gen. 1.1–5 The Spirit over the waters; Ps. 29 The voice of the Lord
over the waters; Acts 19.1–7 Baptism and the Spirit; Mark 1.4–11
The Baptism of Jesus

> *'The earth was a formless void and darkness covered the face
> of the deep, while a wind from God swept over the face of the
> waters.' Genesis 1.2*

Waterworks

The readings at this service could be connected by the word 'water-
works': they all refer to works of God performed over some water!
The book of Genesis tells how, when God created the heavens and the
earth, God's Holy Spirit was brooding, like a dove, over the waters.
[The NRSV translation referred to 'a wind from God'; the same word
is used in Hebrew for both 'wind' and 'spirit'.] Psalm 29 speaks of a
storm at sea: 'The voice of the LORD is upon the waters; the God of
glory thunders.' The Acts of the Apostles refers to the water of baptism:
the believers in Ephesus 'were baptized . . . [and] the Holy Spirit came
upon them . . .'. In all these quotations, God is behaving creatively.

Creation

For instance, in the first reading, God creates the universe through
his Spirit. If you take science seriously, you are driven to this conclusion. Science says that everything must have a cause. You can
picture all those pairs of cause and effect as links in a chain, each
link hanging from the link above. But there must be a top link
somewhere, hanging from a nail or something like that, otherwise
the whole chain would fall down. The Big Bang was the topmost
link in the creation of the universe, when space and time began. But
a cause must always come before its effect. So the Big Bang *must*
have been caused, whether you like it or not, by a timeless, spatially
unlimited spiritual intelligence; which is poetically represented as

the Spirit of God brooding over the waters of chaos, or the mighty voice of God shouting creatively above the storm.

Baptism

The same imagery describes the baptism of Jesus. 'Just as he was coming up out of the water, he saw the heavens torn apart and the Spirit descending like a dove on him. And a voice came from heaven, "You are my Son, the Beloved; with you I am well pleased."' Human sin was turning the first creation back into chaos; so God began a new creation, beginning with Jesus, who is often called 'the Second Adam'. Jesus was the origin of the spiritual body of believers who build the new kingdom of love. The baptism of Christ was the beginning of a new creation.

Christening

What about your own christening, then? Was that a new beginning? Well, it was the outward and visible sign of the start of a new Christian life. But you knew little of what was happening to you then; so christening needs following up by the discovery that God loves little you with all his heart. This realization can have a shattering effect on anyone; call it conversion if you like; but it needs a visible, outward, sacramental form, which in many denominations takes the form of a confirmation service. The bishop speaks God's words over you, welcoming you into God's family, and promising the Holy Spirit. Every time someone decides to take God seriously, that is a new creation.

New creation

Many people apparently imagine that they know better than God. 'If *we* had been in charge of creation,' they seem to think, 'we would have eliminated pain and suffering, and done everything at once, instead of dragging it out like this.' But that is to misunderstand love. You cannot attract another human being to love you without a prolonged period of courtship. It is even harder for God, whom we cannot see, to win our love. God cannot force us to love him; so God must give us free will to refuse him, and cause immeasurable hurt to other humans when we do so. Creatures that can be given freedom may take millennia to evolve. There was a watershed at the baptism of Christ, when the first stage of kingdom-building was complete; now it is up to each of us to build the kingdom of love. But worry not: we have plenty of opportunities to enjoy the love of God in the meanwhile; and we shall be part of God's kingdom when we die.

All-age worship

Put blue paper 'water' in empty bottles and 'pour' it over each other. Then put paper crowns on each other's head, labelled 'a new creation'.

Suggested hymns

Lord Jesus Christ, you have come to us; Love divine, all loves excelling; O Jesus, I have promised; When Jesus came to Jordan.

Baptism of Christ (First Sunday of Epiphany)
7 January 2018
Second Service **Baptism, Sign of Grace**
Ps. 46 Our refuge [47 King of the nations]; Isa. 42.1–9 The servant a light to the nations; Eph. 2.1–10 From death to life; *Gospel at Holy Communion*: Matt. 3.13–17 Calling disciples

> *'For by grace you have been saved through faith, and this is not your own doing; it is the gift of God – not the result of works, so that no one may boast.' Ephesians 2.8–9*

Forgiving myself

Even a person who is thought by their neighbours to be a model of uprightness and virtue often has a secret. It may be something that you and I would regard as quite trivial; a little sin that is called a peccadillo. The person who has done this naughty deed worries about it, telling themselves, 'That wasn't like me; I really let my usual standards drop then.' And then they say, 'How can I ever forgive myself?' And there they give themselves away. It isn't God's forgiveness they want, or even their neighbour's. They want to regain their self-respect.

Atheists

Atheists are particularly vulnerable to these strange attitudes, which is quite illogical, actually. It is very fashionable to call yourself an atheist these days. Maybe you just want to be like your friends, or other people whom you admire; or maybe because some religious person has done or said something that upset you. But logically, if you are an atheist, you can do what you like. If there is no God, there is nobody to tell you what is right and wrong, and nobody to apologize to. Yet it is very difficult to be an atheist, particularly at this time when everybody is singing Christmas carols, and you are overcome with nostalgia and envy of those who have a religion. A television presenter a while ago went to a Buddhist festival, and said, 'What I remember of religion is a man in a black cassock telling me I was a sinner; yet these people are enjoying their religion so much!' I have never met a Christian, cassock or no cassock, who told me I was a sinner, though I expect there are some; what I have heard is preachers telling me I was a forgiven sinner, if only I would accept God's forgiveness.

Paul

That is what St Paul was writing about in his Epistles. He gets a bad press because he talks so much about sin, but it is only because Paul wants us to know that we are forgiven, even though we can never deserve it. The phrase that sums up Paul's teaching is: 'For by grace you have been saved through faith, and this is not your own doing; it is the gift of God – not the result of works, so that no one may boast.' The opposite extreme to the type of person I mentioned at the beginning is the one who says, 'The church walls would fall down if I went in there; that's no place for a sinner like me.' To which I want to reply, 'If God won't accept you, he won't admit me either. We're all sinners, and you can't judge between us. Two men were jumping a river; one got three-quarters of the way across and the other only reached the half-way point; yet they both got equally wet. If only those got to heaven who deserved it, there would be no hope for any of us.' That is the message of St Paul: we are saved from the punishment we deserve because we trust God to forgive us by his kindness, not because of anything we have done. Or in Paul's words, 'By grace you have been saved, through faith . . . not the result of works.'

Baptism

This Sunday we remember the baptism of Christ, when he went down into the River Jordan with his cousin John the Baptist, who symbolically washed him as a sign of God's forgiveness. Not that Jesus had done anything he needed to be ashamed of; but he wanted to identify himself with all of us who have. Washing is a good symbol, because it leaves no trace of the filth that was on us. Whether you were christened as a baby, or came forward as an adult, you only need to be washed once.

Response

But when you realize how generous and gracious God has been in forgiving you, you will want to do something to say thank you. That is where the good works come in. William Barclay, in his commentary on this passage, wrote, 'If some fine person loves us, we know that we do not and cannot deserve that love. At the same time, we know with utter conviction that we must spend our lives *trying* to be worthy of it. That is our relationship to God.'

Suggested hymns

All for Jesus; Amazing grace! How sweet the sound; Guide me, O thou great Redeemer; I heard the voice of Jesus say.

Second Sunday of Epiphany   14 January
Principal Service   **The New Moses**
1 Sam. 3.1–10 [11–20] The child Samuel in the Temple; Ps. 139.1–5, 12–18 God knows us; Rev. 5.1–10 Worthy is the Lamb; John 1.43–51 'You are the Son of God'

> *'Philip found Nathanael and said to him, "We have found him about whom Moses in the law and also the prophets wrote, Jesus son of Joseph from Nazareth."' John 1.45*

Jews

In the time of Jesus, his fellow Jews were certain that every commandment in the Hebrew Scriptures is absolutely true for all people

42

for all time. One commandment forbids working on the Sabbath day. The Scripture also tells us to love others as we love ourselves, and do for them what we would like them to do for us. Suppose someone falls sick on a Saturday, to heal them on the Saturday would be a sin, according to Moses. What are you to do: obey the Law of Moses or the Law of Love? Jesus said the latter; so the law experts spread a rumour that he was telling people to disobey Moses. His disciples answered by saying that Jesus was the New Moses, who made the old one out of date. Shock, horror among the Jews!

Philip

So the apostle Philip 'found Nathanael and said to him, "We have found him about whom Moses in the law and also the prophets wrote, Jesus son of Joseph from Nazareth."' To begin with, Nathanael dismissed out of hand the idea that anyone could replace the great Moses. But when Jesus said he had seen Nathanael beneath the fig tree, the traditional place for Jews to say their private prayers, he suddenly realized they were not dealing with a human messenger like Moses, but one who was completely human, but also divine!

The New Moses

This idea was taken up several times in the New Testament. This was to attract liberal-minded Jews, who wanted a moral code that was adaptable to modern circumstances, yet without losing the idea that God cares how we treat each other. It was also to attract non-Jews, who were seeking a religion that would have a higher standard of morality than the libidinous gods their ancestors had worshipped, yet without having to adopt the whole Jewish law, including submitting to circumcision. Jesus, as the New Moses, was the answer to all these problems.

John

Already, in the prologue to his Gospel, St John had recognized the superiority of Jesus over Moses, when he wrote: 'The law indeed was given through Moses; grace and truth came through Jesus Christ.' This was because the law tells you what you must not do, in certain narrowly defined circumstances; but the truth brought by Jesus tells you to behave lovingly in all circumstances, and offers you God's

43

strength, his 'grace' to enable you to do it. John actually represents Jesus as giving us commandments, as Moses did; but in the teaching of Jesus it was the commandment to love that was central, and overrides all the others: Jesus said, 'If you love me, you will keep my commandments.' Jesus did not regard the Ten Commandments as of no value; we should read them carefully, because they are like witnesses in a law court, confirming the truth of what Jesus said: 'You search the scriptures because you think that in them you have eternal life; and it is they that testify on my behalf.'

Hebrews

The anonymous 'Letter to Jewish Christians', in the New Testament, which we call 'The Epistle to the Hebrews', takes this idea even further. We must remember that Jewish scholars taught that Moses did not see God, and the commandments were carried to him by the angels. But 'Hebrews' says:

> If the message declared through angels was valid, and every transgression or disobedience received a just penalty, how can *we* escape if we neglect [the message of Jesus]? . . . Jesus is worthy of more glory than Moses . . . Now Moses was faithful in all God's house as a servant, to testify to the things that would be spoken later. Christ, however, was faithful over God's house as a son.

Matthew

But the New Testament doesn't tell you that the Old Testament Law can be totally ignored.

That would only lead to a sort of 'do-what-you-like' immorality. So Jesus said, 'Do not think that I have come to abolish the law or the prophets; I have come not to abolish but to fulfil.' So he confirms that the Law of Love does not cancel the Law of obedience to God, but brings out its inner meaning. It is also much harder than obeying a set of rules.

All-age worship

Role-play a parent telling their child not to cross the road, expecting instant obedience. At what age is the child able to understand the reasons why this command is given?

Suggested hymns

A New Commandment I give unto you; I want to walk with Jesus Christ; Love divine, all loves excelling; When we walk with the Lord.

Second Sunday of Epiphany   14 January
Second Service   **Mission**

Ps. 96 God will judge the peoples; Isa. 60.9–22 Nations shall bring their wealth; Heb. 6.17—7.10 Melchizedek; *Gospel at Holy Communion*: Matt. 8.5–13 Foreigners in the kingdom

> Sing to the Lord and bless his name;
> tell out his salvation from day to day.
> Declare his glory among the nations
> and his wonders among all peoples.
>   Psalm 96.2–3 (Common Worship)

Magi

The wise men, who brought to Jesus their gifts of gold, frankincense and myrrh, came from the land of Persia, which is today known as Iran. Many Jews in those days hated and despised foreigners as much as any right-wing politician does today. They were followers of another religion, which is called 'Zoroastrianism'. This embodied the teachings of its founder, called Zoroaster or Zarathustra. Centuries before the Jews under Abraham began to believe in monotheism, he taught that there is only one God, called Ahura Mazda. Under him there were two opposing forces, those of good and evil. Its followers were taught to join in this struggle firmly on the side of good against the forces of darkness. So far so good. But Zoroastrians tried to predict the future by studying the stars; what we call 'astrology'; and by working magic, which is why they were called 'magi'. Yet despite these dangerous delusions, their studies led them to believe that they would find the fulfilment of their hope in Jesus.

Epiphany

So the message of the Epiphany is that God is not only interested in one race and one religion. God can use even the wrong beliefs of other religions to bring people of all nations to worship God as he is found in Jesus. The first followers of Jesus were called 'apostles', which means 'missionaries'. The early disciples were the first Jews to accept that they had a duty to share what they had learnt of God with other races. The Epiphany season is a time for thinking about evangelism: sharing the good news, first with your near neighbours, and then to the ends of the earth. But we can't do that by denying that there was any truth at all in what they previously believed. We must assure the followers of other religions that, like the Magi in the time of Jesus, the best things in their religion can lead them to the feet of Christ.

How?

How do we set about this? Not by wading in with criticism, but by getting to know them as friends. We must first learn their language and their culture, and help them to see Jesus not as some foreign interloper but as one of them. Find out what we have in common. Treat them with respect. Remember, when Jesus was approached by one of the pagan officers of the hated foreign army of occupation with a story about obedience to one's superiors, he said to his Jewish followers, 'Truly I tell you, in no one in Israel have I found such faith. I tell you, many will come from east and west and will eat with Abraham and Isaac and Jacob in the kingdom of heaven, while the heirs of the kingdom will be thrown into the outer darkness.' So effective mission must offer an inclusive, non-judgemental, passionate and heartfelt welcome.

Conversion

Then, as a great missionary once said, we must encourage them to 'take Christ into their own religion'. Not press for conversion, but let them decide for themselves. For people in some countries, to convert to Christianity would cost them their lives, or at least they would be cut off by their families. So we must allow them to be secret Christians, honouring God and loving Jesus in their hearts, if seldom with their mouths. Effective evangelism will be done by the second generation. Another missionary, David Bosch, in his book *Transforming Mission*, wrote: 'God's mission is something in which we join, not something we create.'

Hymn

There is a hymn that has recently been made popular by the Salvation Army which illustrates this theme. The opening and closing of each verse are:

> They shall come from the east,
> they shall come from the west,
> And sit down in the Kingdom of God.

Then the verses run:

> Both the rich and the poor,
> the despised, the distressed,
> They'll sit down in the Kingdom of God.
> And none will ask what they have been
> Provided that their robes are clean.
>
> To be met by their Father
> and welcomed and blessed,
> And sit down in the Kingdom of God.
> The black, the white, the dark, the fair,
> Your colour will not matter there;
>
> Out of great tribulation to triumph and rest
> They'll sit down in the Kingdom of God.
> From every tribe and every race,
> All men as brothers shall embrace;
> They shall come from the east,
> they shall come from the west.
> And sit down in the Kingdom of God.

Suggested hymns

Hills of the north, rejoice; In Christ there is no east or west; They shall come from the east; We three kings of orient are.

Third Sunday of Epiphany   21 January

See also 'Week of Prayer for Christian Unity', p. 289.

Principal Service   **Marriage**

Gen. 14.17–20 Melchizedek brought bread and wine; Ps. 128 God will bless your family; Rev. 19.6–10 The wedding feast of the Lamb; John 2.1–11 A wedding at Cana

> *'There was a wedding in Cana of Galilee, and the mother of Jesus was there. Jesus and his disciples had also been invited to the wedding.' John 2.1–2*

Pro-marriage

Politicians argue about how to encourage couples to become legally married. Obviously not everyone agrees, for an increasing number of couples continue to live together without tying the knot. But even those who are pro-marriage fear that neither tax breaks nor any other governmental action could succeed in stemming the flow away from legal marriage. Jesus was obviously in favour of marriage; he accepted an invitation to a marriage reception at Cana of Galilee, and when asked his opinion on divorce, he said that it was God's intention from the beginning that 'the two should become one'. Yet it is complicated, because many of the words in the Bible have changed their meaning, and the whole structure of society has changed.

Polygamy

Throughout the Old Testament, polygamy was the norm, at least for those who could afford it. That was because of two things: the appalling rate of infant mortality, and the number of mothers who died in childbirth. It has been estimated that the norm for a girl in the time of Jesus was to be married at 13, then bear a baby every year until she died at 30. In old parish registers in this country, many families had ten or more children, only a minority of whom lived to adulthood; two or more wives in succession; and more mothers mentioned at the christening of their babies than ever appeared in the marriage registers. Without any social security, if a man died without leaving any property to his heirs, his widow had to find another partner quickly or become a prostitute. If a woman died, her husband had to find another partner to bear enough surviving children to support him and their siblings when he was too old to work. Many could not afford a church wedding, so they were united by 'jumping over the broomstick' or, as at Cana of Galilee, by throwing a party.

Purpose

All of which stops us talking sentimentally about 'traditional marriage'. Nowadays we have working mothers, from choice or necessity, and some couples who choose not to have children. So let's ask realistically, what is the purpose of 'getting hitched'? Obviously, it is to stop our species from becoming extinct, and to care for the children. Most importantly, it is to teach every couple what a demanding task it is to love somebody else sacrificially and caringly, despite difficulties and the inevitable ups and downs in your feelings. If enough people learn to do that in their nuclear family, we may develop a whole society of people who have learnt to love others in that way, nationwide or even worldwide. That truly would be the kingdom of God. But you can never teach people to love by telling them to: they must have the experience of being loved; ideally, in the family in which they were brought up.

Divorce

So we can see why Jesus was anti-divorce. If your partner is violent towards you and your children, you have a duty to divorce them. In all other cases you should, ideally, love them in such a way that they will want to love you in return 'till death us do part'. Not easy, but true love is an act of the will, regardless of your feelings.

Legalities

The Church got involved in marriages when it was decided that all unions should be recorded in writing, and the parish clerk was the only person within less than a day's walk who could read and write. But that has got caught up into many complicated and expensive legalities. So perhaps in present circumstances we should return to the way most other countries do it, and have the legalities fulfilled by a simple promise and some signatures in the registrar's office. Then those who wish could come to church for a service of prayer. Here they should make more profound promises in the eyes of God, asking for God's help in keeping them. This would be a blessing in the sense that everyone present would join in that prayer, and a sacrament because it makes the couple's invisible love visible, and God's love also. But it is not magic: praying in church does not ensure that you have no difficulties in your marriage – only that God will give you strength to overcome them. Then, if you wish, have an expensive reception; but that is not an essential part of getting married: the white wedding dress was invented by Queen Victoria!

All-age worship

Play at weddings. Write some realistic modern vows.

Suggested hymns

Come down, O love divine; Father, hear the prayer we offer; Gracious Spirit, Holy Ghost; Love divine, all loves excelling.

Third Sunday of Epiphany   21 January
Second Service   **Christianity in Germany**
Ps. 33 All the inhabitants of the earth; Jer. 3.21—4.2 Nations blessed by him; Titus 2.1–8, 11–14 Pastoral care; *Gospel at Holy Communion*: Matt. 4.12–23 Ministry in Galilee

> *'At that time Jerusalem shall be called the throne of the* Lord, *and all nations shall gather to it, to the presence of the* Lord *in Jerusalem, and they shall no longer stubbornly follow their own evil will.' Jeremiah 3.17*

Mission

Jesus was a Jew, and his Jewish apostles spread his message of inclusive love into Europe. Greek Christians influenced the Celts; our Anglo-Saxon ancestors will have required German Christians to translate the words of the Italian missionaries. As we think at Epiphany-tide of how the gospel is spread to all nations, we must also reflect on how various people's national pride can sometimes be a hindrance to worldwide evangelism. Particularly this year, as we celebrate the centenary of the end of the First World War, we should reflect on Christianity in Germany, and how the struggle between that nation and ours has hindered the growth of the Christian faith.

Origins

Roman Catholicism was strong in the German-speaking nations in the monastic period, and contributed many great thinkers and teachers to our understanding of God. Martin Luther was a German and a loyal Catholic but he protested against what he saw as corruption and false teaching in the hierarchy, and was excommunicated with all his followers. So the Reformation began in Germany, and greatly influenced Protestantism in this country, including many of our hymns. The German princedoms were not united into a single country until 1871; until then, the people's religion was decided by their rulers, so there were separate Protestant churches in each of the 28 Protestant states.

War

The reasons for the outbreak of the First World War were complicated, but one of the causes was certainly because of territorial ambitions by the new German Empire, opposed by the British Empire. Yet fresh understanding of the widespread Christmas Day truce in 1914 shows that the war was opposed by many people on both sides. The poet Wilfred Owen dreamt of meeting, after he died, a dead German soldier who said, 'I am the enemy you killed, my friend . . .'

Hitler

But the Treaty of Versailles, which ended the war, imposed a heavy burden of debt on the Germans, which was one of the causes of the collapse of their economy and the colossal unemployment in the following years. Hitler, however, blamed the recession on communists and Jews, and persuaded many of the ordinary Germans that he was the only person who could save them. That, and the four-hundredth anniversary of Luther's Reformation in 1917, persuaded the majority of German Protestants to form a federation called the German Evangelical Church, and within it a movement called 'the German Christians' for whom the German nation was almost more important than God. Hitler delighted in this, and sought to control the Church more firmly.

Opponents

Fortunately not all were hoodwinked, and an opposition movement started called the 'Confessing Church'. Karl Barth was one of those who drew up their declaration rejecting the 'Führer Principle'. Dietrich Bonhoeffer was jailed for joining a plot to assassinate Hitler, and executed. Martin Niemoeller was also placed in a concentration camp, but he survived, and became a leading, if controversial, Christian, opposing the post-war rearming of Western Germany. He wrote: 'They came for the Jews, and I did not speak out because I was not a Jew; they came for the socialists and communists, and I did not speak out because I was not one of them; when they came for me, there was nobody left to speak out for me.'

Decline

While Christianity has been growing like wildfire almost everywhere else in the world, it has been declining in Western Europe. One reason may be because people here saw terrible things done in the name of religion during the two world wars, which gave them the idea that we are all warmongers. But let us not forget that on our side, too, there was bombing of innocent civilian populations, and we left much of Germany a wasteland of ruined buildings. There was right and wrong on both sides, and good and bad people also. If we want to resume spreading the gospel of love in heathen Europe, we must, to begin with, recognize that Jeremiah was right when he said that all nations draw their knowledge of God from the Jews, and stop persecuting them. Then, at the very least, we must stop blaming each other for the things our ancestors did, and learn to make friends with our fellow Christians in Germany.

Suggested hymns

A safe stronghold our God is still; Now thank we all our God; Silent night, holy night; Sleepers wake, a voice is calling.

Fourth Sunday of Epiphany   28 January

(or Candlemas; see p. 293)

Principal Service   **The Muslim View**

Deut. 18.15–20 God will raise up a prophet; Ps. 111 Salvation; Rev. 12.1–5a A woman in heaven; Mark 1.21–28 Demons recognize Christ

'I will raise up for them a prophet like you from among their own people; I will put my words in the mouth of the prophet, who shall speak to them everything that I command.' Deuteronomy 18.18

Prophets

Today's Old Testament reading predicts the coming of a prophet like Moses. John the Baptist said he was not the one, but pointed to Jesus, and Christians regard this as foretelling the birth of Christ. But some 600 years later, Muhammad was born in Arabia; he claimed to be the great prophet, predicted by Moses and Jesus. Muslims accept that Jesus, whose name they pronounce 'EE-sa', was the second greatest prophet, but that Jews and Christians have altered their Scriptures to suggest that he was crucified, and was the one-and-only Saviour. Our first reaction, as Christians, is to be furious, dismissing Muhammad as a false prophet, and his followers as a bunch of terrorists. But before jumping to that conclusion we must look more deeply. I am not arguing that you should all become Muslims, or that the differences between religions do not matter; that would be quite wrong in a Christian pulpit. But if you look carefully at the Bible there is evidence that our God wants us to be tolerant of other religions, and even to learn from them.

Unique

The first thing to look at is the claim of Jesus to be unique, when he said, 'I am the way, and the truth, and the life. No one comes to the Father except through me.' This is absolutely true. No religion other than Christianity dares to address the infinite God by the intimate term, 'My Father'. Jews call him the father of the nation; but otherwise it is considered blasphemy to address the Almighty as Jesus suggested. But does not the Bible condemn all other gods as idols? Not quite; we are forbidden to *worship* an image, in wood, stone or metal; but there is nothing wrong with using it as a visual aid, otherwise, like the Muslims, we could have no religious pictures.

But Jews, Muslims and Christians believe there is only one God. St Paul said to the philosophers in Athens, 'What you worship without knowing him intimately is the same God we are revealing to you.'

The Qur'an

Muhammad believed that Moses was the prophet for the Jews, and Jesus for the Christians; a lot of Muslim doctrine is based on the Bible, and the Qur'an warns Muslims to respect 'the people of the Book'. But where could the Arabs find a prophet 'from among their own people', as Deuteronomy prophesied? Muhammad went into the desert to meditate, and there the Archangel Gabriel dictated to him the word of God, which formed the Qur'an. It is a confusing but deeply spiritual book – you should read it sometime. But many fellow Arabs and idolatrous tribes fought against him, so it justifies the use of force in self-defence, and makes no protest against polygamy. Then Muslims wanted to spread their faith to other nations, regrettably by defeating them in battle. Christians retaliated, and so the Crusades started. But it was only in the twentieth century, when European nations started dividing up the Arab lands among themselves, that some Arabs decided the only way to defend themselves was terrorism.

Learning

That is an over-simplification of a complicated period of history; but it shows we should not jump to conclusions. We have learnt much from Islam. In the Middle Ages much of Greek culture would have been lost had it not been preserved in Arabic. Al Ghazali was one of the world's greatest philosophers. Their beautiful architecture showed what could be done with the arch and the dome, and they have left us many masterpieces of poetry. They made a comprehensive study of botany, revealing the distinctions of gender in plants; they built the world's first observatory, and taught us much about astronomy. Words like 'algebra' reveal how much the Arabs have taught us about mathematics; though an old joke asks, 'What has western mathematics learnt from the Arabs?' Answer: 'Zero'! Think how complicated Roman numerals were because there was no figure nought. For many centuries Muslim and western scientists worked in happy harmony, especially in Spain, until the Christian kings forbad it.

54

Respect

This has been a brief survey, with no time to mention the tragic division that led to Sunni and Shia Muslims fighting each other, nor the beautiful mysticism of the Sufis. In many places Christians and Muslims are meeting together and seeking to resolve their differences. There may not be much agreement yet, but there is no need to kill each other in the meanwhile.

All-age worship

Read stories from 'The 1,001 Nights'.

Suggested hymns

As with gladness men of old; From the eastern mountains; God is working his purpose out; God's Spirit is in my heart.

Fourth Sunday of Epiphany   28 January

(or Candlemas; see p. 293)

Second Service   **Samuel's Story**

Ps. 34 Taste and see; 1 Sam. 3.1–20 The boy Samuel in the Temple; 1 Cor. 14.12–20 Pray with the mind also; *Gospel at Holy Communion*: Matt. 13.10–17 The purpose of parables

> 'The LORD came and stood there, calling as before, "Samuel! Samuel!" And Samuel said, "Speak, for your servant is listening."' 1 Samuel 3.10

Samuel

The prophet Samuel's mother was a poor woman, mocked by her husband's other wife because she was old and had not borne any children. She prayed, and then Samuel was born, to everyone's surprise. In gratitude to God, when her baby was weaned, she gave the child to God as a Temple slave. He slept in the Temple. One night, when he was still young, he heard a voice calling him by name: 'Samuel! Samuel!' He thought it was his boss, Eli the priest, but Eli was annoyed at being woken and told Samuel to go back to sleep. This happened several times, till Eli realized it must have been

God speaking. 'The next time it happens,' he told Samuel, 'you must reply, "Speak, Lord, for your servant is listening."' The Lord told Samuel he wanted him to speak on God's behalf, as a prophet calling for justice. The first task was to speak up against the corruption among the priests, who were mostly Eli's sons. It was risky, as the slave might have been sold off to some other owner; but the people respected God's prophet, even if he was only a slip of a lad. Samuel went on speaking for God for the rest of his life, and it was he who rebuked the bad King Saul, and appointed David to be the king of Judah in Saul's place.

Vocation

A small number of people today claim to have heard the voice of God, like Samuel did; most of them say it was in a dream. More often, people who are praying, or thinking about a decision they must make, suddenly have a strong inner conviction that God wants them to make a particular decision. Commonest of all is the experience when the answer to your prayers starts as a suspicion, grows into a hunch, and finishes as a conviction that this is what God wants you to do. Maybe an unlikely sequence of events makes you exclaim, 'I think God is trying to tell me something by this!' Your friends may say the concatenation of circumstances was only a coincidence; but there is a popular saying that 'coincidences are when God wishes to remain anonymous'. In all these ways, God is trying to persuade you to do something for him. When we believe that God is calling you to a particular job of paid or unpaid work, we name it a 'vocation'; but the same thinking applies to quite trivial decisions. Some people wear a bracelet that reads, 'What Would Jesus Do?', or simply the initials WWJD? Then whenever they have to decide between two options, they glance at the bracelet, and try to imagine what Jesus would have done if he had been confronted by the same dilemma that they are facing.

Response

If you suspect that God is calling you, then say, as Samuel said, 'Speak, Lord, for your servant is listening.' If you realize that God wants you to do something for him, because of a heavenly voice, a dream, an inner conviction, a process of reasoning or an unlikely coincidence, what should be your response? The correct answer is to say, 'Oh no, I could never do that; I haven't the skills, the strength, the brainpower.' That is to keep you humble. When you have said that, follow it with, 'But of course God has promised me the grace to achieve great things for him by *his* power, not my own.' Next pray for grace and for guidance. Then just get on with it, persevering until the job is finished, or until somebody more qualified than you offers to take your place.

Future

When we see the future spreading out before us, the pessimist will slump down and moan: 'Oh, how terrible, but there is nothing we can do.' The casual-minded will relax on the sofa, sighing, '*Che sera sera*, we must learn to put up with it.' But the Christian leaps up and says, 'Oh good, I think God is calling me to put this situation right.' God's Jobcentre is there to provide opportunities for the underprivileged: a chance for people who have never done anything memorable in their lives to say, 'With God's help, I can make a difference.' If you do that, God will be proud of you, and the prophet Samuel will give you a cheer.

Suggested hymns

Forth in thy name, O Lord, I go; God forgave my sin; Jesus calls us o'er the tumult; Will you come and follow me?

The Second Sunday before Lent   4 February
Principal Service   **Portraits of Jesus**
Prov. 8.1, 22–31 Wisdom in creation; Ps. 104.26–37 Creation; Col. 1.15–20 The head of the Church; John 1.1–14 The Word in creation

> '[Jesus] is the image of the invisible God, the firstborn of all creation.' Colossians 1.15

Head

The first words of the Bible are 'In the beginning, God . . .'. Only, in Hebrew, the word for beginning is the same word they used for 'head'. St Paul, writing to the Christians in Colossae, played a word game, listing all the possible meanings of 'head', and applying them to Jesus. A head is a portrait, painted on canvas or carved in marble; so Jesus is the image of the invisible God. A head is the origin, so Jesus is the origin of creation. A head comes first, so Jesus is the first cause of all that followed after. A head is a leader, so Jesus is the leader of the Church, which is his body. The head of a family is the firstborn child of the father, so Jesus was the first to be reborn from the tomb at his resurrection. The trouble is that humour is untranslatable, and it is doubtful if anyone but a Jew like Paul could fully enjoy the joke.

Portraits

So let us concentrate on the first pun: a head is a carved or painted portrait; so Jesus is the image of the invisible God. God was the creator of the visible universe, so he must have existed before it came into being. Therefore God is not located in the universe, so he must be invisible. Yet mere humans find it almost impossible to think of an invisible being larger than the universe, let alone speak to him. But God wants to hold a conversation with us, so that he can tell us he loves us. So he hit on the brainwave of entering the visible world in the form of a human being, Jesus Christ, who would fully reveal God's character, albeit in a miniature form. So Jesus is like a portrait of God, to help us to imagine the God we have never seen.

Portraits of Jesus

There have been many portraits of Jesus, in paint or in print; in stone, bronze and wood; and on the screen, played by actors or in CGI. But as none of the artists saw the living Jesus, these are artistic images of a mental image, formed by the artist's imagination. They are a good starting point, but if you are to hold a conversation with the living Christ, you need to use your own imagination, and think of Jesus as a warm, living human being standing just a few feet from you. Have you tried to do that?

Nationality

The first problem is what nationality or ethnicity will you choose? Jesus was a first-century Jew, but can you imagine what that means?

Many paintings of Jesus represent him as a man from the same area as the artist. So Italians painted him as a black-haired, olive-skinned Italian; British children's books show him as a fair-haired, blue-eyed Englishman. This is good if it helps you to become his friend; but you must never let a trace of racial prejudice creep into your mind by thinking that 'Jesus was not like *them*', meaning the people you hate. An English minister visited a theological college in China, and asked why all the pictures of Jesus on the walls showed him as a blond man with fair skin. The Principal replied that these were the only type in print. The Englishman pointed out that in the 1930s many pictures had been painted of Jesus with slanted eyes, in classical Chinese clothes; in fact they are still being produced in Hong Kong. 'You mean,' asked the surprised Principal, 'that Jesus was not white-man like you nor yellow-man like me, but brown-man from the countries in-between?' 'Yes,' was the reply, 'but it will be most helpful if you think of him as yellow-man in modern dress.'

Method acting

The same Englishman was speaking to an up-and-coming sculptor in London, who had been helping to make a bust of the Queen. The secret, she said, is to imagine you *are* the person whose image you are making. 'Like a method actor imagining he is the character he acts?' he asked, and she nodded agreement. So when I pray to Jesus, the image of the invisible God, he thought, I should imagine Jesus as being just like me. Only without all my faults, and with many virtues that I haven't yet acquired. Me as I could become if I gave Jesus a free hand. I could talk, in my imagination, to a person like that – then I should be talking to the image of the invisible God!

All-age worship

Paint what you think of when you pray to Jesus.

Suggested hymns

Immortal, invisible, God only wise; Jesus, these eyes have never seen; Love came down at Christmas; Of the Father's love begotten.

The Second Sunday before Lent   4 February
Second Service   **The Selfless Gene**

Ps. 65 Fecundity of nature; Gen. 2.4b–25 The Garden of Eden;
Luke 8.22–35 Demons into pigs

> *'The Lord God formed man from the dust of the ground, and
> breathed into his nostrils the breath of life; and the man became
> a living being . . . And the Lord God commanded the man, "You
> may freely eat of every tree of the garden; but of the tree of the
> knowledge of good and evil you shall not eat, for in the day that
> you eat of it you shall die."' Genesis 2.7, 16–17*

Important?

What is the point of the story of the creation in the Bible? What
message was it trying to get across? Well, it was trying to get across
a number of things that were of vital importance to the people
when it was first written, and still are to us today. Among them are:

1   We are dependent upon God for our existence, for the food we
    eat and the beauty we see.
2   We must care for the environment.
3   All nations are descended from common ancestors, so all are
    sisters and brothers.
4   We were meant to love God and our neighbours, but instead we
    all choose to be selfish.

These messages are a matter of life and death. So if anyone says
that the message of the story is that the world was created in seven
days a mere six thousand years ago, they are turning away from
the crux to concentrate on trivialities, and distracting their hearers
from what God is trying to tell us.

Language

But God had to put this message in words that people could
understand. The first hearers knew all about how to grow things,
and how a potter creates things out of clay; but they knew nothing
about what we call science. Was God to wait until the twenty-first
century before revealing these things? Surely not, that would have

been cruel; so he used the language they were most familiar with: the language of story and legend. But for us today that is not helpful, because we have fallen into the delusion that legends are unimportant, and can safely be ignored. We have forgotten that legends often have vital lessons to teach us about how we lead our lives.

Darwin

The geologists of the nineteenth century proved conclusively, from the layers in the rocks and the different species of life found in the fossils, that life had originated much earlier than previous generations had assumed, and had progressed to new and more elaborate life forms as the millennia passed. Charles Darwin suggested that new species had originated by random changes in their ancestors' bodies, and the survival of those that were fittest to adapt to their environment. Many Christians welcomed this new insight into how God brought his creation to progress to more and more complex life forms, until *Homo sapiens* emerged which was capable of responding to his love. But some Christians reacted violently against Darwinism, because it disagreed with the timetable given in the Bible, bringing many to believe that there is a conflict between science and religion. Thus the literalists and creationists focused on the superficial surface meaning of the legend, and distracted readers from delving into the deeper, spiritual meaning of the text. Thereby they prevent God's vital message from being heard: dependence on God, care for the environment, the oneness of humanity and mutual love.

Dawkins

Nevertheless, science does not answer all our questions. Richard Dawkins tried to suggest that human behaviour also evolves by the survival of the fittest. He argues that we have 'memes' of behaviour (which nobody has ever observed), so that those who behave in the most selfish way, by having sex with the maximum possible number of partners, will ensure the survival of their particular genetic make-up. Yet when you think of it, praising the 'selfish gene' is fatally harmful to society as a whole. Those who contribute most to the quality of human life are those who love unselfishly, and if need be sacrificially. The opposite of selfishness is altruism, putting the needs of other people before your own. Some animals will sacrifice themselves to ensure the survival of their family, swarm or tribe; but putting the needs of total strangers before your own is only found in humans. Where does altruism come from? Certainly not by the survival of the fittest. So we have to conclude that God caused evolution to progress to this point, where we can understand that our creator loves us, and respond by loving him in return, and by loving our neighbours as much as we love ourselves, for God's sake. There is nothing unscientific about that; but it takes you much deeper in your understanding of life than any scientist ever could.

Suggested hymns

For the beauty of the earth; Jesus is Lord! Creation's voice proclaims it; O Lord my God! When I in awesome wonder; The spacious firmament on high.

Sunday next before Lent   11 February
Principal Service   **Resisting Change**
2 Kings 2.1–12 Elisha sees Elijah's ascension in glory; Ps. 50.1–6 God speaks from heaven; 2 Cor. 4.3–6 The glory of God in the face of Jesus; Mark 9.2–9 The transfiguration

> *'Peter spoke up and said to Jesus, "Teacher, how good it is that we are here; we will make three tents, one for you, one for Moses, and one for Elijah." He and the others were so frightened that he did not know what to say.' Mark 9.5–6 (Good News Bible)*

Tradition

We should all be proud of our traditions. We like to do things like we have done them all our lives, and like our ancestors used to do them before us. Tradition guides us down a comfortably familiar path, helping us to do the right thing without having to agonize over it, because those are the things we have always done. There is a lot to learn from tradition, and it is the foundation of society. People from another nation may have a quite different way of behaving, and we say, 'Ah, well that is the way they do things over there; we respect that, but we shall stick to our own traditions.' On the whole, this works quite well.

Peter

St Peter was brought up in the Jewish traditions, which stretched back a very long way. One of their customs was to celebrate every year the Feast of Tabernacles – 'tabernacles' is an old word for 'tents'. On that night they would celebrate and then sleep in a tent, in the open air or on the flat roof of their house. This was partly a harvest festival, for when you are bringing in the crops you have no time to go home, but must make your living arrangements in the fields. But even earlier, the Jews were originally nomads, wandering from place to place as they followed their flocks. When Moses led the Israelites out of Egypt at the Exodus, God led them in the form of a pillar of cloud to guide them by day, and a pillar of fire to give them light in the night-time. But they couldn't keep up this 24-hour travelling for long, so Moses made a tent called 'the tent of meeting', outside the camp, so that people could go there to say their prayers; it was a visible sign that the invisible God is always with us. But when it was time to move, they packed up the tent of meeting and carried it before them to the next campsite. So it became a sign that God is always with us, but always on the move. When Jesus took Peter and his friends up a high mountain and was transfigured, shining brightly with Moses and Elijah, Peter wanted to keep them there. You don't find houses on mountaintops, so he offered to erect three tents so that they could stay there for a good long time. Perhaps it was the Feast of Tabernacles, and that gave him the idea. Then he would know where Jesus and the authors of the Scriptures were when he needed them. But as the Gospel says, he was talking nonsense – in a short while Moses and Elijah were gone, Jesus had returned to his normal human appearance, and he led them off down the mountain towards a very challenging future in Jerusalem. Peter wanted to trap religion in a tent, but you can't do that, because it is always changing.

Resisting change

The Romans had a saying, 'Times change, and we change with them.' Our traditions provide us with a stable foundation, but we must not cling to them. The foundations of the gospel never vary, but the words we express them in must change as the people around us change their attitudes, their metaphors and their vocabulary. Traditional worship is very beautiful, but we must be constantly alert to the views of the people around us, or they will reject us, saying, 'I'll have no truck with all that old-fashioned nonsense.' I am not saying we must reject the past completely all at once; but we must be flexible, always ready to explore new ideas and new ways of doing things, because God is constantly on the move. God leads us to new experiences, new challenges, and new opportunities to love our neighbours and spread the good news of God's love. He promised us the Holy Spirit to lead us 'into all truth', and that process never stops; if *we* stop, we shall be left behind. That sounds a bit frightening, but once you take your courage in both hands and make the leap of faith, following Jesus is exhilarating and fun.

All-age worship

While some members sing the hymn 'I danced in the morning', the rest can improvise a miming dance, expressing the words of the hymn in their actions.

Suggested hymns

Faith of our fathers, taught of old; I danced in the morning; One more step along the world I go; 'Tis good Lord to be here.

The Sunday next before Lent   11 February
Second Service   Silence
Ps. 2 He who sits in heaven [99 He spoke in the cloud]; 1 Kings 19.1–16 God speaks through silence; 2 Peter 1.16–21 We heard this voice; *Gospel at Holy Communion*: Mark 9.[2–8] 9–13 John the Baptist and Elijah

> *'He said, "Go out and stand on the mountain before the LORD, for the LORD is about to pass by." Now there was a great wind, so strong that it was splitting mountains and breaking rocks in pieces before the LORD, but the LORD was not in the wind; and after the wind an earthquake, but the LORD was not in the earthquake; and after the earthquake a fire, but the LORD was not in the fire; and after the fire a sound of sheer silence.' 1 Kings 19.11–12*

Elijah

Elijah spent the night in a cave, and then came out hoping to hear the voice of God. But God was not in the wind, nor the earthquake, nor the fire. In the old translations of the Bible it says that God spoke to him in a 'still, small voice'. Many people took that as referring to the voice of conscience, whispering into your ear, 'Stop, you're going the wrong way, you've made the wrong choice, go back before it's too late.' Thank God that we do have these inner voices. But the Hebrew words actually mean that God spoke to Elijah in 'a sound of utter silence'. If we are to hear God speaking with us, we need to quieten not only the voice of the busy world around us, but also the voice of our inner attempts to wrestle with the truth.

Seeking silence

There are all too few opportunities for silence in the world today. If you get a brief chance to be silent, seize it gladly. The first thing to do is to remember that you are in the presence of God. You don't have to say anything to him. Just enjoy reflecting that Jesus is very near, and he loves you. But it is also a blessing if you can make some longer periods of silence, maybe five minutes when you wake up, or after lunch, or before you go to bed, or in church. Yes, I know that after a few seconds your brain will start running off on to some other subject than God. If you are thinking about something important, stick with it, and just ask God to help you make the right decision. Just lead your thoughts back gently to the subject of Jesus and his love for you.

Using silence

Then try to relax. Take a few words from the Bible, and repeat them slowly over and over, in rhythm with your breathing. While you are doing that, the name of somebody who needs your prayers may flash into your mind, so commend them into the gentle arms of Jesus; maybe relating to them the words of the Bible verse you have been repeating. If you find it hard to relax, read a passage from the Bible, or some poetry, prayers or hymns, and reflect at your leisure on what they mean for you. Visual people can meditate over a picture; tactile folk can hold a stone or a crucifix. You can choose a passage from the Gospels and imagine that you are present at the scene. What can you see? Hear? Feel? When you have had enough of that, say the Lord's Prayer slowly, pondering on what each line meant to Jesus, and what it means to you.

God uses silence

God uses silence. The three greatest events in the life of Jesus took place during moments of silence: he was born on a cold winter's evening in the silence of a stable; he died in the silence of the crucifixion; and he came back to life in the silence of early dawn. So God will speak to you in the silence, if you will only give him a chance, and listen out for what God is saying to you, today. Try repeating the words, 'Be still and know that I am God.' After a few repetitions, shorten it to 'Be still and know that I am'; then 'Be still and know'; then 'Be still'; then simply 'Be'.

Relax

I am aware that in telling you to do this or do that in the search for silence I may have sounded like a disciplinarian. On the contrary, my aim has been to help you relax. If anything I have said makes you tense, ignore it. One little trick is to use a string of beads, then repeat a prayer or a Bible verse as you count off the beads in your hand. If you fall asleep while you are doing that, it has certainly helped you relax, and it may be that you will feel God close to you in your dreams.

Suggested hymns

Be still and know; Come, living God, when least expected; Dear Lord and Father of mankind; There's a quiet understanding.

LENT

Lent is observed in the 40 days leading up to Holy Week. The figure 40 is based on the 40 days that Jesus fasted in the wilderness after his baptism, before he began his ministry. It is calculated either by omitting the Sundays, when the Lenten discipline is relaxed, or by finishing on Palm Sunday. In the early Church, candidates for baptism at Easter prepared for it by 40 days of learning and fasting, and soon the rest of the congregation wanted to join with them. Instead of doing without food, today Christians 'give up something for Lent'. This is a good lesson in self-control, but mustn't lead to self-righteousness. More important is to train oneself to do something good in Lent: to read the Bible, spend more time in prayer, attend extra services or a study group, or do something to help others. Like Advent, Lent is a penitential season, so altar frontals and vestments are purple, or unbleached linen representing sackcloth (except that the Fourth Sunday in Lent may be rose), and 'Glory to God in the highest' is often omitted. It is good to examine our lives, accept responsibility for our sins, and confess them to God. Sermons in Lent are often linked together on a common theme; a series on the Sermon on the Mount or the Ten Commandments can help with self-examination, or sermons on aspects of Christian living can lead to practical action. There are some fine Lenten hymns, but they can be too gloomy unless mixed with others on lighter but relevant themes.

Ash Wednesday   14 February
Valentine

Joel 2.1–2, 12–17 Rend your hearts, *or* Isa. 58.1–12 Care for the needy; Ps. 51.1–18 Cleanse me from my sin; 2 Cor. 5.20b—6.10 Suffering of an apostle; Matt. 6.1–6, 16–21 Secret fasting, *or* John 8.1–11 Adultery and forgiveness

[This sermon is based on the second Gospel reading]

'The scribes and the Pharisees . . . said to [Jesus], "Teacher, this woman was caught in the very act of committing adultery . . . Now what do you say?" . . . When they kept on questioning him, [Jesus] . . . said to them, "Let anyone among you who is without sin be the first to throw a stone at her."' John 8.3–5, 7

Valentine

I wish you a blessèd Ash Wednesday . . . and a very happy Valentine's Day! It is not often that the two occur on the same day, but it is appropriate, because they both celebrate love: God's love for us, and romantic love, respectively. There were two saints called Valentine. In the second century AD Bishop Valentine of Terni, in Italy, was martyred for his faith. And in the third century, a priest in Rome called Valentine was arrested for trying to help other Christians. While in prison he tried unsuccessfully to convert the Emperor Claudius II to Christianity, and healed his jailer's daughter of her blindness. Then he was beheaded outside Rome's Flaminian Gate. Nobody is quite clear how Valentine became the patron saint of lovers. Some say it was because there was a pagan festival at this time of year called Lupercalia. Young men and women used to draw names out of a hat and pair up for the period of the festival. Another suggestion is that it is due to the English poet Geoffrey Chaucer, who wrote:

This was on St Valentine's Day, when every bird cometh there to choose his mate.

Romantic love is one of God's greatest gifts to the human race. I think it is no accident that the Romantic Movement, with its emphasis on romantic poetry, art and music, arose in a Christian continent at a time when Christian influence was strong. However, like any good thing, romantic love can be misused, such as when someone uses romantic means to lure away somebody else's partner. Jesus, in the Gospel reading chosen for today, warns us against judging and condemning other people for their sins, because all of us have done selfish things at some time or other.

God's love

It is moving, then, to compare God's passionate love for you and me with the devoted love between two human lovers. God will not force us, but he woos us to respond to his love. If we fail to do so, and ignore him, God is wounded just as much as a human lover who finds their overtures are not returned. Jesus on the cross shows us that God's love for us is marked by willing self-sacrifice, just as human love should be. But the agony of the cross also reveals

68

how deeply God suffers when we ignore him, and fail to return his generous love. When we realize that, we suffer from guilt, thinking how deeply our selfish love has wounded the most passionate of all lovers. But God does not want our lives to be wrecked by an endless burden of guilt, so he sent his Son to assure us that as soon as we say sorry we are forgiven. Jesus says to us, as he said to the woman in the Gospel story, 'Neither do I condemn you; go and sin no more.' Of course God forgives us, for he wants to be reconciled to those who have rejected him. But God's love, too, can be misused. If we say that we are sorry, without really meaning it, and then go out and do the same wrong things again because it is so easy to be forgiven, we are taking advantage of God's indulgence. So we need Ash Wednesday, when we can make a fuss of our penitence, to convince God and convince ourselves that it is sincere, and we really mean it. Then we can forget our wrongdoing, certain that God has forgotten it too.

Personal

We can learn a lot about God's love by studying the ways of human lovers; and about how generous human love should be by looking at how God loves you and me. So I wish you, once again, a blessèd Ash Wednesday . . . and a very happy Valentine's Day!

All-age worship

Divide into couples, emphasizing that this is play-acting, not the truth about how we feel. Then one says, 'I really love you.' The other replies, 'I couldn't care less, go away.' The first speaker says, 'This play-acting shows me how it hurts God when we ignore him.' Then repeat it the opposite way round. Make Valentine cards for everyone in the congregation, marking them, 'To you from God'.

Suggested hymns

Drop, drop, slow tears; Forty days and forty nights; Jesu, lover of my soul; O for a closer walk with God.

First Sunday of Lent   18 February
Principal Service   Noah's Baptism
Gen. 9.8–17 Noah's covenant; Ps. 25.1–9 God's grace and
forgiveness; 1 Peter 3.18–22 Jesus speaks to Noah's generation;
Mark 1.9–15 The baptism and temptation of Jesus

> '[God said to Noah:] "When the bow is in the clouds, I will see it
> and remember the everlasting covenant between God and every
> living creature of all flesh that is on the earth . . . This is the sign
> of the covenant that I have established between me and all flesh
> that is on the earth."' Genesis 9.16–17

Environment

The story of Noah in the Bible makes some profound spiritual
points. It suggests that human beings have disobeyed God's instructions about caring for the environment, to such an extent that God
would be quite justified in destroying his whole creation and starting over again with a less stubborn set of creatures. This gives an
ominous slant to what environmentalists have recently realized,
about the way in which humans have contributed to global warming. Is it possible that we may be rapidly making the earth uninhab-
itable, and preventing God's plans of building the kingdom of God
'on earth, as it is in heaven', from being fulfilled?

Remnant

But rather than destroying everyone and everything, God chooses
a single family to rescue a breeding pair of every species to build a
new future. It is often through a wise minority that the disruptive
policies of the majority may be frustrated. The Bible often refers
to such a group as 'a remnant': St Paul writes to the Romans that
the Christian Church is such a minority: 'So too at the present time
there is a remnant, chosen by grace.' Whether it is small or large,
the Church is vital to human survival – which side are you on?

Rainbow

Next we come to the symbol of the rainbow. Knowing nothing of
diffraction and wavelengths, people for thousands of years have
wondered what this beautiful arch in the clouds, after a rainstorm,

could possibly be. Genesis picturesquely suggests that God is a warrior, armed with a bow and arrows, seeking to destroy the evil in the world. But rather than destroy the whole human species in the process, God signs a contract or 'covenant' with Noah, that if the remaining human beings, all now descendants of Noah, agree to care for the planet, God will hang up his bow and arrows in the clouds and promise never to use them again. Hence it is called a 'rain-*bow*'. Think of that, every time you see one.

Unity

Finally, the story of Noah replaces that of Adam, in teaching that all races are descended from a common ancestor. That means that we must all treat each other as brothers and sisters: Jews and Arabs, Africans and Asians, black, white, brown or yellow, if we attack each other we are killing members of our own family. No room for racism there.

Truth

Did you realize there was so much teaching in one story? There are stories of a man surviving a flood in many of the cultures of the ancient Middle East, but none with such a depth of spiritual wisdom. So whether it is historically true, or whether God inspired the author of Genesis to take an old legend and rewrite it to become a work of genius, does not really matter. It is the moral wisdom that counts.

Baptism

Then Christians took this Jewish story and made a Christian parable out of it. Sometimes we refer to the effects of surviving great danger as 'a baptism of fire'. But in Noah's case it was a baptism of water. He came through the waters, and emerged into a paradise of multicoloured light. When a new convert to Christianity is baptized, especially if it is by immersion in a baptismal pool as in the early Church, then the candidate comes out of the moral darkness of atheism – no reason for behaving kindly, and no grace to help them to do so – through the waters of baptism, into the glorious multicoloured light of Christ's love. Nowadays most people are baptized as babies, and it would be a little dangerous to immerse little babies in a pool. But many churches have the Easter candle standing beside the baptismal font, and the symbolism is still there: out of the godless darkness, through the water, washed clean from sin, and welcomed into the light of Christ. That is what your christening meant.

All-age worship

Make paper cut-out figures of Noah's ark, the people, the animals and the rainbow. Stand them on or by the font, and explain why.

Suggested hymns

Just as I am, without one plea; Lead us, heavenly Father, lead us; Lord Jesus, think on me; O love, that wilt not let me go.

First Sunday of Lent   18 February
Second Service   Original Sin
Ps. 119.17–32 The wonders of God's law; Gen. 2.15–17; 3.1–7 Adam's sin; Rom. 5.12–19 Adam and Christ, *or* Luke 13.31–35 Jesus grieves for Jerusalem

> 'The LORD God commanded the man, "You may freely eat of every tree of the garden; but of the tree of the knowledge of good and evil you shall not eat, for in the day that you eat of it you shall die."' Genesis 2.16–17

Blame

If you ask people what they would say to God if they met him, many will answer that they would give him a good telling-off for making a world so full of pain, suffering and death. Maybe you feel like that yourself, sometimes. But in effect, that is placing the blame for all these terrible things in the wrong place. God wanted this world to be a paradise, where men and women could live contented and happy, as the lovely story of the Garden of Eden assures us. But the only way that would work would be if these privileged human creatures would live in the way that God advised them to. Yet we are a stubborn lot, and as soon as someone gives us a piece of advice, even if it is obviously going to be good for us, we obstinately do the opposite, and then howl if we hurt ourselves in the process. As soon as human beings evolved the power of choice, we started making the wrong choices. So God had to change to Plan B. That is not God's fault, it is ours.

Plan B

We now know what the first readers of Genesis could not possibly have known, that evolution is the way that God has chosen to create more and more complex creatures. But pain, and even death, are essential parts in this process. Individual animals develop new features that help them adapt to their environment. To pass them on, they must give birth to another generation, and soon there will be no room for everyone to live, so the older ones must die. Then, if they are to adapt to a new environment, there must be pain to warn them that they are behaving in an unsuitable way – you would never learn to take your feet out of the fire unless it hurts you to leave them there. We howl about pain and death, but they are an essential part of the process. We all have to die sometime, and we all long for a few more years. But God has given us the hope of a life after death; and we learn important lessons about our total dependence on God from our suffering.

Copying

But we are such copycats. As soon as we see somebody doing something wrong, we always want to do the same ourselves. We inflict pain and death on each other, because we imitate the villains and not the good people. Let's call selfish and disobedient behaviour by its Bible name of 'sin'. Then most of the pain and early death we suffer from is caused by our own sins and the sins of others.

Slaves

We are all, even the good people, slaves of sin, living in a world of universal sin. This goes back to the origins of the human race, so we sometimes call it 'original sin'. We need somebody to set us free. The word for setting a slave free is 'redemption', and that is what Jesus came to bring us. But I have to warn you that a lot of nonsense is talked about original sin, not least by Christian preachers. Yes, our sinful environment goes back to the origins of the human race, or to

Adam, in St Paul's terminology; but no, we have not inherited Adam's guilt, because guilt cannot be passed on. The prophet Ezekiel wrote:

> The person who sins shall die. A child shall not suffer for the iniquity of a parent, nor a parent suffer for the iniquity of a child; the righteousness of the righteous shall be his own, and the wickedness of the wicked shall be his own. But if the wicked turn away from all their sins that they have committed and keep all my statutes and do what is lawful and right, they shall surely live; they shall not die.

Jesus set us free from guilt, not by paying a fine to the devil or to God, but by revealing how our sins hurt God, and setting us an example of unselfish love. He delivers us from original sin, by offering us the chance to make a fresh start in life.

Joke

To finish on a lighter note: somebody once said that there is no such thing as an original sin: they've all been tried before!

Suggested hymns

Be thou my guardian and my guide; O for a heart to praise my God; Oft in danger, oft in woe; Walking in a garden.

Second Sunday of Lent   25 February
Principal Service   Self-denial
Gen. 17.1–7, 15–16 The covenant with Abraham; Ps. 22.23–31 Witnessing grace to all; Rom. 4.13–25 The covenant with Abraham was through faith; Mark 8.31–38 Take up your cross

> '[Jesus] called the crowd with his disciples, and said to them, "If any want to become my followers, let them deny themselves and take up their cross and follow me."' Mark 8.34

Self-centred

Some people are completely self-centred. They are in love with themselves – full of themselves and their big ideas; and need somebody to praise them all the time. When they were two years old, if they needed something, they would yell until they got it; if they didn't get what they wanted they would throw their rattle out of the pushchair. This is quite natural, and has been programmed into our brains since caveman days. If they carry on such behaviour into adulthood, the psychological name for them is 'narcissist'. It may be because they did not receive enough love from their parents, that they try to draw attention to themselves. This may make them successful in some fields of endeavour, but it has disastrous effects on the harmony of society.

Me

Of course, there is nobody like that in this congregation. But the tendency to think and talk all the time only of 'Me, me, me' is one we have to be careful to avoid. I think this is what Jesus was thinking of when he said, 'If any want to become my followers, let them deny themselves and take up their cross and follow me.' Self-denial is not a matter of just giving up chocolates for Lent. Jesus calls us to deny, and say no to, all these self-centred attitudes that make us not very nice people to know. Of course we don't *think* we are not nice to know; we imagine that everybody adores us.

Genetics

Self-centredness is really what the Bible calls sin. But it is perfectly natural. Charles Darwin's theory of 'natural selection' implies that only very selfish people are able to survive in the struggle for existence. Therefore only those men who ruthlessly spread their sperm into as many wombs as they can will contribute to the next generation many copies of themselves with the necessary self-centredness to dominate and push their rivals out of the way. Darwin himself was aware that this was a problem with his theory if it is ruthlessly applied: for in fact most human beings are not like that. Most of us will, sometimes at least, sacrifice our own wishes for the benefit of those among whom we live. This is called 'altruism'. Darwin wrote, in *The Descent of Man*, that, according to his theory, the bravest, most self-sacrificial people 'would on average perish in larger numbers than other men'. An unselfish person, he wrote, 'would often leave no offspring to inherit his noble nature'. It seems scarcely possible, he admitted, that virtue 'could be increased through natural selection, that is, by survival of the fittest'.

Communities

Darwin recognized that 'survival of the selfish' is true when we talk of individuals, but not when we are discussing the behaviour of groups, tribes or societies. Darwin wrote:

> A tribe including many members who, from possessing in a high degree the spirit of obedience, courage and sympathy were always ready to give aid to each other and to sacrifice themselves for the common good, would be victorious over most other tribes; and this would be natural selection.

Yet how to get people to progress from the level of the individual to the group was at present much too difficult to be solved. But Jonathan Sacks, who was then the Chief Rabbi, suggested some nine years ago that this was the function of religion.

Self-denial

So it is in religion that we find the key to the evolution of human society. In both the Old and the New Testament we are recommended to love our neighbours as ourselves, to welcome the stranger, care for the poor, feed the hungry, shelter the homeless and temper justice with compassion. Jesus commended self-sacrifice when he said, 'take up your cross and follow me'. It is only in a community or a church, in which you discover that the other members care for you for Christ's sake, that you can learn that caring for others is worth all the effort and inconvenience it causes you – because ultimately it leads to more happiness than always being self-centred and greedy.

All-age worship

Share a piece of cake among a group giving one member, chosen randomly, twice as much as the others, and another gets none – but don't eat it. What do you all feel about living in such an unjust society? Now divide the cake in equal amounts between all in the group. Are you happier?

Suggested hymns

Follow me, follow me; God's Spirit is in my heart; Take up thy cross, the Saviour said; Will you come and follow me?

Second Sunday of Lent   25 February
Second Service   **Impossible Callings**

Ps. 135 Their land a heritage for Israel; Gen. 12.1–9 Abram's call;
Heb. 11.1–3, 8–16 Abraham's faith; *Gospel at Holy Communion*:
John 8.51–59 Abraham rejoiced

> *'By faith Abraham obeyed when he was called to set out for a place that he was to receive as an inheritance; and he set out, not knowing where he was going.' Hebrews 11.8*

Readings

The Old Testament reading set for this service is from Genesis, and describes how God called Abraham, the ancestor of the Jewish and nearby races, to leave his home in Iraq, travel across the hostile desert, and build a new homeland in the land of Canaan. But then, he protested, where was he to get the strength to obey God and do what God had told him to do? The answer comes in the New Testament reading, which describes Abraham's faith.

Journeys

Abraham was the son of Terah, who came from Ur of the Chaldees, and we first read of Abraham when he was living in the Mesopotamian town of Haran, with his wife Sarah, His two sons were called Ishmael and Isaac. Then God appeared to him, and:

> the LORD said to Abram, 'Go from your country and your kindred and your father's house to the land that I will show you . . . and in you all the families of the earth shall be blessed.'

So Abraham travelled as a wandering nomad to the area we now know as Israel. His son Isaac was the father of Jacob, who was renamed Israel, and whose 12 children were the ancestors of the 12 tribes of Israel. But the Bible is clear that many of the neighbouring tribes were also descended from Abraham and his relatives. Abraham bought a plot of land and a cave in which to bury his wife Sarah, but otherwise he did not own any land. Like the twentieth-century Jews who were promised a 'homeland' in Palestine, this did not mean that Abraham was to have exclusive possession of the land and to drive out the original inhabitants. The task that God had set Abraham, of finding a place to dwell in where he would live in harmony with all the neighbouring tribes, may have seemed well-nigh impossible. There were times when he wished he could return to Mesopotamia; where was he to get the strength to be obedient to God's call?

Monotheism

There was a spiritual dimension to this challenge, also. The name 'Abraham', or in its earlier spelling 'Abram', actually means 'the Father is exalted'. The surrounding tribes had many gods, which encouraged them to go to war with the neighbouring tribes who followed different gods. Abraham was the first to introduce the idea that there is only one God, for all the tribes, who regards himself as the father of them all. So the Lord was calling Abraham to introduce monotheism to the neighbouring tribes, at no matter how high a cost to himself. In fact, the worshippers of different idols co-existed with the monotheists among the many descendants of Abraham. The task to which Abraham was called seemed to be getting harder and harder. But the Lord called him to trust our heavenly Father, who was the only one who could give Abraham that power, which Christians call 'grace'.

Faith

God offers us the ability to bring unbelievers to trust in the one true God, not in our own strength but by drawing on God's power. But we cannot claim that we deserve it. We must have faith and trust in God before we can be make use of the strength that the Lord offers to us for free. The Letter to the Hebrews says:

> By faith Abraham obeyed when he was called to set out for a place that he was to receive as an inheritance; and he set out, not knowing where he was going . . . By faith he received power of procreation, even though he was too old – and Sarah herself was barren – because [Abraham] considered [God] faithful, who had promised. Therefore from one person, and this one as good as dead, descendants were born, 'as many as the stars of heaven and as the innumerable grains of sand by the seashore'.

So Abraham, says the Bible, is our spiritual ancestor, too. I wonder what apparently impossible task God is calling *you* to? Yes, of course you cannot do it on your own. But you can if you have faith. Jesus said, 'For mortals it is impossible, but not for God; for God all things are possible.' If you trust God, he can use you as his tool for getting impossible things done.

Suggested hymns

Amazing grace; The God of Abraham praise; Through the night of doubt and sorrow; Will you come and follow me?

Third Sunday of Lent 4 March
Principal Service Cleverness or Wisdom?

Ex. 20.1–17 The first four commandments; Ps. 19 The heavens declare God's greatness; 1 Cor. 1.18–25 The cross is greater than human wisdom; John 2.13–22 Cleansing the Temple

> *'God's foolishness is wiser than human wisdom, and God's weakness is stronger than human strength.' 1 Corinthians 1.25*

Cleverness

I hope you never say of those who preach to you, 'Oh, they are very clever people.' Because cleverness is very dangerous. A 'clever-clogs' can easily turn into a 'know-all', imagining that every useful fact or idea is already in their brains, and there is no need for them to learn any more. They think that they know more than anybody else, and everybody should come to them for knowledge. Yet, in fact, a person who has formed their own ideas and never listened to anyone else may believe that their ideas are wholly true, when in fact they are full of logical holes that they have never noticed. I hope none of the people whom you hear preaching are proud of their cleverness. Knowledge is no use without wisdom.

Jews

St Paul knew this when he said that what the Christians were preaching – the message that the one who is King of all the earth was hanged on a cross – is a stumbling block to Jews and foolishness to the Greeks. The Jewish people thought that God had promised them a conquering Messiah who would defeat their enemies and help Jews to rule the world. The idea of such a king being executed as a criminal was one obstacle too many for them to climb over, and they tripped over it: it was 'a stumbling block'. The more pious they were, the harder it was for them to become Christians.

Greeks

The Greeks, on the other hand, were clever philosophers. We owe a lot to their habit of logical thinking. But once they had a good idea, they took it to extremes. For instance, they believed the Greek gods are spiritual beings; they are far above this material world, the world that makes you and me happy or sad. They can ignore the earthly provocations that give you and me emotions. So the gods, they reasoned, lived in a perfect world and had no feelings at all. Why should any god who lived in heaven put all that aside and come down to this messy old world? The idea of incarnation was to the Greeks, and therefore to most people in the Roman Empire, utter foolishness. But, Paul wrote:

> God's foolishness is wiser than human wisdom, and God's weakness is stronger than human strength.

Today

But those mistakes are still made today, by clever atheists and pious followers of other religions. Courteously we need to explain to our friends that cleverness and piety are neither of them any use without wisdom. Science is very clever at explaining how things happen, but cannot begin to ask why they happen. Other faiths, though they convey to us some wonderful truths, do not help us to live in a world where good people suffer, and where the only thing that can turn us into better people is knowing that God loves us. But Jesus on the cross can supply us with both those things.

Learning

So we all need to set about learning wisdom, because it is the only thing that matters. The best place to learn it is from the Bible. But that's no good if you try to read it on your own, because you may make all sorts of clever mistakes. The Bible will make you wise if you read it with a set of wise notes, or in a group. You can learn wisdom from other people: ask them how they cope with the unfairness of pain, and the loneliness when we feel that God is no longer nearby. What lessons have they learnt from their own experience, about how we should behave, how we should treat other people. Often the best people to learn wisdom from are those who are humble enough to imagine they are not wise at all, for it is wise to be humble. And ignore your preacher when he or she tries to show off how clever they are; but listen with rapt attention when they unconsciously reveal some wise idea that will help you to live your life better.

All-age worship

Draw two columns. Mark one 'Knowledge, Knowing facts', and the other 'Wisdom, Knowing what to do for the best'. Discuss which is the right column in which to write these phrases: 'Knowing a tomato is a fruit'; 'Knowing not to put a tomato in a fruit salad'; 'Kindness'; 'Mathematics'; 'Saving for a rainy day'; 'How to play cricket'; 'Learning to drive a car'; 'Helping those who are arguing to calm down'. If you disagree, discuss. Add more words.

Suggested hymns

All my hope on God is founded; Dear Lord and Father of mankind; 'The kingdom is upon you!'; We sing the praise of him who died.

Third Sunday of Lent 4 March
Second Service The Lord My Refuge
Ps. 11 In the Lord I take refuge, 12 Help, Lord; Ex. 5.1—6.1 Bricks without straw; Phil. 3.4b–14 Pressing on for the prize, *or* Matt. 10.16–22 Coming persecutions

> *'In the Lord have I taken refuge;*
> *how then can you say to me,*
> > *"Flee like a bird to the hills"?'*
> > *Psalm 11.1 (Common Worship)*

Despair

Have you ever felt overwhelmed by troubles? Your life goes pear-shaped; and you despair of the human race? Yes, haven't we all, at one time or another? So you want to hide in a corner, crawl into a hole or by some means or another escape from the fray and enjoy a bit of peace and quiet. Only, when you curl up by yourself, you discover that your brain is still churning round and round, and there is no peace anywhere. The psalms, in the Old Testament, have many passages describing an agony like that. 'Where shall I find a hiding place?' is the burden of their complaint.

Refuge

The writers of the psalms are surprisingly open and honest, and they often describe this agonizing dilemma. And over and over again they offer the solution: *God* is my refuge. It is as if God is the air-raid shelter in which we can escape the bombing. Don't rely on yourself, they say, imagining that, if only you can be alone by yourself, you will calm down. Often the opposite can happen. But if you learn to be alone with God, he will fling his arms invisibly around you, saying to you, 'Come here, my child, and cry on my shoulder for a while. Remember, I love you, and always will. If you remain in my arms, the evil forces can never conquer you.'

Psalm

Psalm 11, which is set for this service, begins with the words:

> In the Lord have I taken refuge;
> how then can you say to me,
>   'Flee like a bird to the hills'?

In the ghastly situation in which he had found himself, the psalmist's friends could offer no better advice than to throw in the towel. 'Run away from your problems,' they said, 'like a small bird which is being attacked by an eagle, and flies off towards the hills in the hope of finding a safe and secure nest.' But this is bad advice; if you find one apparently safe nesting place, the raptor will search it out, and destroy you, leaving your mate as a widow or widower, and your chicks as orphans. Much better to fly into the arms of God, remember his loving presence with you, and he will strengthen you. If you must be a refugee, seek asylum with God.

Reconciliation

For God's purpose is not for you to escape from the struggle, but to return to it refreshed and renewed. If everybody is criticizing you from different directions, listen carefully to what they say, think about it, then return to God, your refuge, and ask him for his advice. It may not come in words, but if you have flung yourself upon his mercy, a conviction may grow in your mind: the direction that God wants you to follow. You can't please all the people all the time, but if you let them all know that they have been listened to, and that some sort of compromise is essential, they will admire you for your firm leadership. God has called you to the ministry of reconciliation, and called you to be a leader; his grace is the only thing which can enable you to follow that call. In God is your refuge.

Strength

Or think of the times when you have just run out of steam. So many tasks are laid upon you by your family and your employer, and from the various voluntary tasks you have taken on, that you feel that you haven't yet grown strong enough to shoulder them all; or that you are growing older and no longer have the energy to cope with so many challenges all at once. Well, how about giving yourself a breathing-space, and relaxing in the consciousness of the presence of God? Then sally forth again in the strength of God, and you may find a surge of strength that enables you to do what hitherto you had thought was beyond you. Or if not, maybe God wasn't actually calling you to do that job, but to find somebody else to whom you can hand over one of your responsibilities. Who knows, they might be able to do it better than you would have yourself.

Escape

So we none of us need to run away from challenges and puzzlements, like a bird flying off to the hills. Instead we should turn to the only place where we shall find peace and renewal. In God is your refuge.

Suggested hymns

A safe stronghold my God is still; Jesu, grant me this, I pray; My spirit longs for thee; Say not the struggle nought availeth.

Fourth Sunday of Lent   11 March
Principal Service   **This is the Judgement**
(For Mothering Sunday, see the Second Service.)
Num. 21.4–9 The bronze serpent; Ps. 107.1–3, 17–22 Thanks for healing; Eph. 2.1–10 Salvation by grace through faith, not by works; John 3.14–21 As Moses lifted the serpent, so must I be lifted

> *'This is the judgement, that the light has come into the world, and people loved darkness rather than light.' John 3.19*

Discipline

Parents would like to give their children total freedom to do as they wish; but it wouldn't work. The children will hurt their brothers and sisters, because they don't realize what the results of their actions may be. So the parent says, 'Don't do that. If you do that again, I won't give you that treat you were expecting.' Then the child repeats the dangerous action, is denied the treat, and there are tears. 'One more time,' says the parent, 'and I will slap the back of your hand.' So there is disobedience, pain and tears. But the parents suffer more than the child, because they want the loving relationship with their child to be restored. But they know there must be no cuddles just yet, or the lesson will never be learnt.

Tribe

If the family joins a tribe, the tribal leader cannot discipline every member, so he delegates it to wise people, called 'judges'. But if the judges are left to make their own judgements, one will be lenient and another strict. The result will be chaos. So kings have to issue laws for all the judges to adhere to. The Jews were chosen to spread the idea of obedience to God's laws to other nations.

Legalism

But by the time of Jesus, the danger of passing more and more laws was apparent: the nation had become too legalistic, ensnared in the detail of the written laws, ignoring the principles of mutual care and co-operation that lie behind them. This problem is still with us today: Parliament passes far too many laws, some of which have never been tested in court. People fear the day when their case comes up to be heard by the judge. How far we have come from the aim of creating customs of tolerance and care within the family! Even God came to feared as a fierce judge.

Judgement

'You've got the wrong end of the stick,' snorted Jesus. 'God our loving parent doesn't judge you: you declare yourselves guilty by your refusal to recognize goodness when you see it.' Or more precisely, according to John's Gospel, Jesus said:

> This is the judgement, that the light has come into the world, and people loved darkness rather than light because their deeds were evil. For all who do evil hate the light and do not come to the light, so that their deeds may not be exposed.

Warnings

God our Father, like any wise parent, gives us warnings for our own benefit. He tries to persuade us that our self-centred behaviour is destroying us. Society will fall apart if we do not tolerate and love even people who think differently from us. So the law of love overrides all other laws. Law is essential as a starting point, but we must progress beyond it to basing our lives on love, not law.

Example

Not only that, but God showed us what self-sacrificing love means. He turned himself into a human being, and the cross was the example of how far we should go on the path of sacrificing ourselves for others, but it also showed how our disobedience hurts our loving heavenly Father. This came as a flash of light, a revelation, to many of his contemporaries. But there were still some who saw the light of love in the eyes of Jesus, but rejected him. If we sin, and then feel regret for what we did, God is just waiting for us to say, 'I'm sorry, Dad', and he will tear up the charge sheet, and take us to heaven when we die. But if we see the light of love, and reject it, there is nothing God can do for us. If we lose our opportunity to go to heaven because we refuse to repent, it will be our fault, and not that of God. We shall have judged ourselves, and declared ourselves guilty.

All-age worship

Role-play a law court, with a judge in a wig, the accused, and counsel for the defence and the prosecution. The judge declares the prisoner guilty and sends them for punishment. Then replace the judge with God, who says, 'not guilty', and welcomes the guilty party to go with him to heaven.

Suggested hymns

In a world where people walk in darkness; Judge eternal, throned in splendour; Lead, kindly light; To God be the glory, great things he hath done.

Mothering Sunday   11 March
Postnatal

(This is the first set of readings for Mothering Sunday in *Common Worship*.)
Ex. 2.1–10 His mother hides Moses; Ps. 34.11–20 Advice to the young to be righteous; 2 Cor. 1.3–7 Helping others because God helps us; Luke 2.33–35 Simeon predicts Mary's suffering

> '[God] helps us in all our troubles, so that we are able to help others who have all kinds of troubles, using the same help that we ourselves have received from God.' 2 Corinthians 1.4 (Good News Bible)

Postnatal

Happy Mothering Sunday! I hope to bring some very encouraging points out of discussing briefly a medical condition that you have probably heard of, called postnatal depression. After giving birth to a baby, about one mother in ten feels low, lacking energy, and can no long take pleasure in things they used to enjoy. Some mothers hide it because they feel ashamed, but like any other medical condition it is not the patient's fault. We call it 'postnatal depression'; 'post' means 'after', 'natal' is connected with the word 'nativity' and means 'giving birth'; it is spelt the same as, but has nothing to do with, the South African area called 'Natal' (natt-TARL). It can develop within the first six weeks of giving birth, but is often not apparent until around six months. With proper treatment, it usually goes after a few months. I only mention it as yet another example of what many mothers go through in bringing us their children into the world.

Mothering Sunday

So Mothering Sunday is very important, because it reminds us to say thank you to our own mothers, and mothers all over the world. There is no true love without sacrifice. It is important to realize that, because at some point of your life you, too, may have to make sacrifices, of your time and money, your personal preferences and your pleasures, to look after someone you love. So we should look at our mothers and learn a lesson from them, so that we can follow their example.

Equality

An old proverb says, 'The hand that rocks the cradle rules the world.' In these days of feminism, many people would object to that, saying that women are frequently discriminated against, and have far less power than most men. That is true, of course, because in many fields of life there is a 'glass ceiling' that seems to prevent women from rising to senior positions. Women who choose to have a baby usually need to take time off work while they care for the new child. Well, thank God they do, or all of us would feel neglected. But nowadays, some fathers are also taking a break to share in the parenting, so that is no excuse for inequality. Thank God, also, that we now have women bishops in the Church of England, showing that we are in line with modern understanding of a woman's place in the world; they seem to have brought the virtue of motherliness to a place where it was sorely lacking! But mothers do rule the world in another sense, too. They set an example to their children of what love truly means. Jesus told us, and showed us, that true love must involve self-sacrifice; so in any family, mothers, fathers, children and grandparents all need to be willing to yield their own preferences and time for the benefit of the whole family. St Paul wrote:

Let us give thanks to the God and Father of our Lord Jesus Christ, the merciful Father, the God from whom all help comes! He helps us in all our troubles, so that we are able to help others who have all kinds of troubles, using the same help that we ourselves have received from God.

Influence

But no matter how many times preachers tell us that this was the love that Jesus showed, we need an example to look at now. So our mothers show us how to take time and trouble in caring for those you love, even when you would rather be doing something else. In this way they have an influence on the next generation that is beyond measure. Jesus taught us that God wants everybody to show this form of altruistic love, so that we can form a society where all live together in harmony, tolerance and mutual self-sacrifice. What a wonderful world that would be! So Jesus taught us to pray, 'Thy kingdom come, thy will be done, on earth, as it is in heaven.' And that will only happen if we all follow the example of self-sacrifice set us by our mothers, from bearing the depression that sometimes follows after giving birth, to the daily treats they think up for us as we grow older. Thank God for mothers, on this their special day.

All-age worship

Make Mothering Sunday cards listing some of the sacrifices our mothers make.

Suggested hymns

All things bright and beautiful; For the beauty of the earth; Teach me, my God and King; Tell out, my soul, the greatness of the Lord.

Fifth Sunday of Lent   18 March
Principal Service   **The Death of the Seed**
Jer. 31.31–34 A new covenant; Ps. 51.1–13 Forgiveness, *or*
Ps. 119.9–16 Law; Heb. 5.5–10 Jesus the priest; John 12.20–33
The death of the seed

> *'[Jesus said] "The hour has come for the Son of Man to be glorified. Very truly, I tell you, unless a grain of wheat falls into the earth and dies, it remains just a single grain; but if it dies, it bears much fruit."' John 12.23–24*

Glory

The apostles Andrew and Philip were Jews, but they had Greek names. They reported that some Greek-speaking people wanted to learn the teaching of Jesus. Most people in the Roman Empire could speak Greek, and that represented most of the then-known world. The Jews had learnt some precious truths: that there is only one God for every single nation on earth, who cares how we treat each other, and wants to give eternal life to everyone. But they kept this to themselves, the chosen few. When Jesus heard that other nations were enquiring about the outward-looking version of Judaism he taught, he rejoiced. This was the moment God was waiting for, when Jesus would be glorified. Only, paradoxically, by 'glory' Jesus meant death and burial.

Death

Why? Because nobody listens to a live prophet; they suspect their motives. But if a preacher is willing to die rather than recant their teachings, everyone knows they really mean it. If a holy man has been telling us to love others in a self-sacrificing way, we can follow his example; his actions bear out his words.

Burial

Then Jesus turned our idea of death and burial on its head. Death is not defeat, it is victory; a burial is not a cause for sadness but for overwhelming joy. He compares it to planting a seed: 'Unless a grain of wheat falls into the earth and dies, it remains just a single grain; but if it dies, it bears much fruit.' That's true, provided you remember that the cells of the seed don't die, they are transformed into a much more glorious creature. When Jesus was alive, he was an obscure prophet; after he was buried he grew into the Saviour of the world. Perhaps something similar is true of you and me, also. So the burial of Jesus is a key moment in the story. All his disciples were sad; most just hid themselves away; Joseph of Arimathea and Nicodemus, Mary Magdalene and the other Mary, followed the body to the cave, but they were broken-hearted and sobbed, because they thought this was the end of everything. But if they had known what would happen on the third day, they wouldn't have wept – they would have been jumping up and down for joy, laughing and embracing. '[After I am crucified,]' said Jesus, 'you will weep and mourn, but the world will rejoice; you will have pain, but your pain will turn into joy.'

Funerals

If Jesus was right when he said that, surely it means that most of us take entirely the wrong attitude to funerals. Don't mistake my meaning: I am not saying that you shouldn't be tearful at a funeral; it is dangerous to repress your emotions. But if you call yourself a Christian, and believe what Jesus taught, it is not for the person who has died that you should be sad; only for yourself.

Heaven

The teaching of Jesus concentrates, first, on building a more just and loving society here on earth, without prejudice, divisions or fighting. The second emphasis is on the promise that after we die, we shall go to a new and happy life. We call it 'heaven', because we have no words to describe a life free from the restrictions of time and space, where we live eternally with those we love, and with Jesus. So if somebody has died, you should be delighted for their sakes. For yourself, you can weep and mourn, because for a good few years you are going to miss them terribly; you will miss their words of advice and the warmth of their embrace. But if you ask God to give you strength, he will bring you through this deep feeling of loss. After you have had a sufficient time of mourning, you will think of the deceased as still invisibly present with you, wanting you to be brave and dry your tears, and rejoice for their sake.

Just as the sobbing friends of Jesus would have done at his burial if they had known what would happen later.

All-age worship

List some people you know who have died. Would they want you to be sad or rejoice for their sake?

Suggested hymns

Awake, our souls – away, our fears; Be still, my soul; Come, let us to the Lord our God; Give rest, O Christ.

Fifth Sunday of Lent   18 March
Second Service   **Grace Abounding**
Ps. 34 God rescues the righteous; Ex. 7.8–24 Water turned to blood; Rom. 5.12–21 Adam and Christ; *Gospel at Holy Communion*: Luke 22.1–13 Preparing for Passover

> 'Law came in, with the result that the trespass multiplied; but where sin increased, grace abounded all the more,' Romans 5.20

Ad hominem

St Paul was writing to a group of Jewish rabbis in Rome, and those who had been influenced by them. So he wrote in ways that rabbis would understand. They were accustomed to heated arguments on how the Jewish Scriptures were to be interpreted, going into great detail, using metaphor and allegory, and emphasizing the importance of the Old Testament Law. So Paul did the same; this is what is called an *ad hominem* argument, from the Latin for 'to the man'. This was the best way of arguing with first-century rabbis; but for twenty-first-century non-Jews it is hard to understand. Yet the letter contains some important ideas, which we ignore at our peril – such as the concept of grace, which is God's help, which we can never deserve or earn, but which is given to us by God as a free gift of his love. Modern translations show us that the heart of Paul's argument is that it is no use hoping to earn a place in heaven as a reward for obeying the Jewish Law; heaven must be freely and gratefully accepted as an undeserved gift of God's love.

Grace

To understand what the Bible means by 'grace', think of the 'grace and favour' houses that the Queen gives rent-free to those who acknowledge her. The Greek word also refers to a 'present' that you give to someone you love, whether or not they deserve it; and the forgiveness you offer to a guilty person in the hope that they will reform. This is the way God treats you and me. His forgiveness is abundant to pardon us, however great our sin; as St Paul wrote: 'Law came in, with the result that the trespass multiplied; but where sin increased, grace abounded all the more.'

Abounding

For this reason, the word 'grace' occurs in the title of many works of Christian literature. Not only 'Amazing grace', 'which saved a wretch like me', but also the wonderful book, *Grace Abounding to the Chief of Sinners*, by John Bunyan. Bunyan, of course, was the author of *Pilgrim's Progress*, an allegory telling how a Christian pilgrim travels through the Slough of Despond, Vanity Fair, and many other obstacles, to arrive at the ford that leads to heaven, 'and the trumpets sounded for him on the other side'. *Grace Abounding to the Chief of Sinners, or The Brief Relation of the Exceeding Mercy of God in Christ to his Poor Servant John Bunyan*, to give it its full title, is his spiritual autobiography. Bunyan was a Puritan, and the book was written while he was serving a 12-year prison sentence in Bedford jail, for preaching without a licence, and was first published in 1666. 'Grace abounding' is a quotation from the verse in St Paul's Letter to the Romans which I have quoted; in his first letter to Timothy Paul describes himself as 'the chief of sinners'.

Quotations

I confess that I have not read the whole book myself, but here are two quotations to give you the flavour of it:

I thank God for each of you as I am imprisoned here in the wilderness. I enclose just a bit of the honey with which God has refreshed me, with the hope that your soul will be refreshed by reading of His work upon me. My intent is to be plain and simple in expressing to you what God has done for me. May you receive this discourse in the humbleness that I intended. First, let me explain my beginning so that you may truly comprehend the goodness of God toward me. My descent is from the meanest and most despised family in all the land. I cannot boast of noble blood or a high-born state; still, I thank God for this beginning, for it was through this door that He brought me into this world. As for my own nature, I was without God. I was filled, at a very tender age, with unrighteousness to a degree of which I had few equals for *'cursing, swearing, lying, and blaspheming the holy name of God'* . . .

Of all the temptations that ever I met with in my life, to question the being of God, and the truth of His gospel, is the worst . . . Sometimes, when, after sin committed, I have looked for sore chastisement from the hand of God, the very next that I have had from Him hath been the discovery of His grace.

Suggested hymns

Amazing grace; And can it be?; God moves in a mysterious way; Rock of ages, cleft for me; Who would true valour see.

HOLY WEEK

The final week of Jesus' life on earth is celebrated from Palm Sunday to Easter Eve. Long readings of the Passion Narrative are set at all the services. Palm Sunday is often marked with a procession of palms, Maundy Thursday by the washing of feet, Good Friday by the veneration of the cross, and Easter Eve by a vigil with the lighting of the new fire. An informal Passover supper to commemorate the Last Supper can be held on any day but is especially suitable for Maundy Thursday. A series of sermons on the Passion, or on the seven words of Christ from the cross, can be preached throughout Holy Week, or to mark the Three Hours on Good Friday. Most of the sermons provided in this book for specific days in Holy Week could be used on other days instead.

Palm Sunday   25 March
Principal Service   Anger against God

Liturgy of the Palms: Mark 11.1–11 *or* John 12.12–16 Triumphal
entry; Ps. 118.1–2, 19–24 Blessed is he who comes. *Liturgy of the
Passion*: Isa. 50.4–9a I gave my back to the smiters; Ps. 31.9–16
Assurance in suffering; Phil. 2.5–11 Jesus' obedience unto death;
Mark 14.1—15.47 The Last Supper to the burial, *or* Mark 15.1–39
[40–47] The trial to the death on the cross

'*They brought Jesus to the place called Golgotha . . . And they
crucified him.*' Mark 15.22, 24

Outburst

How dare he? He's behaving like the worst sort of criminal! He beats
me up and makes me suffer; he deprives me of the resources I need. He
takes away the people I love, and employs me to work among a load
of people I can't stand. And all this is after he promised me . . . *promised me*, I tell you . . . that he would look after me, rescue me when I
was in trouble, and be my friend. Well, if that's friendship, I'll be a . .
. I don't know what. I hate him! I think he's the worst . . . well, words
fail me. No, it's not one of you sitting there that I'm talking about. In
case you haven't guessed, it's God who is the cause of this outburst.

Anger

Of course, none of us would dare to say those words out loud. Even
if I wasn't scared that a thunderbolt would strike me dead, I know
we are *supposed* to be respectful towards the Almighty. But even
if we don't say it, many of us think this from time to time. Life *is*
unfair; innocent people *do* suffer; we get painful diseases, and family members die younger than they ought. How can Jesus say his
Father is a God of love, if God allows these things to happen? It's
the old dilemma of innocent suffering and the problem of evil.

Closure

Most people agree that if you feel strong emotion, it is better to
let it out than to bottle it up. Say what you feel, to a third party if
necessary, and that may well bring you what people call 'closure'.

But what if you still feel you were right to be angry? And what if the one who provoked you was God?

The Shack

In the novel entitled *The Shack*, by William Paul Young, the story is supposed to be told by a man who is very angry with God, because his young daughter disappeared, and was then found murdered near a shack in the mountains. Later, the bereaved father received a message inviting him to meet God at the shack. I won't spoil the story for those who have not yet read it, by revealing what form God took. Suffice it to say that God embraced the angry man and let him cry on God's shoulder, telling him that it is OK to get mad with God. And that is true: God is strong enough to take it, and God is the only person who, you can be sure, will not get angry with you in return, because God is love through and through.

Jesus

So let us forget ourselves and our problems for a moment, and think, on this Palm Sunday, of Jesus. 'They brought Jesus to the place called Golgotha . . . And they crucified him.' Jesus was the best man that ever lived, and God could have saved him from the cross, so why didn't he? If that isn't unfair I don't know what is. Jesus cried out, 'My God, my God, why have you forsaken me.' We assume he said it in despair, but what if he said it in anger: '*My GOD! MY . . . GOD! Why, oh WHY . . . have you left me to SUFFER like this?*' Jesus had so successfully become fully human that he had put aside . . . not his faith, but his omniscience. For one short moment, Jesus felt anger against his Father, and grief just as we do. But at the end he said triumphantly, 'My task is finished.'

Justified

The world does seem unfair, and nobody has successfully managed 'to justify the ways of God to men'. All we can say is that, if you think you can design a world in which human beings can evolve with free will, but without pain and death, you had better apply for God's job. No atheist, no believer, has done that yet. So if you get angry with God, shout at him, then say sorry, and ask God's forgiveness. Finally, ask for God's grace, to uphold you through the pain. Then Jesus, who has known pain and anger like ours, will hold your hand, now and in eternity.

All-age worship

Learn the words of one verse of 'Christ triumphant, ever reigning' and sing it during the procession of palms.

Suggested hymns

All glory, laud and honour; Christ triumphant, ever reigning; Ride on, ride on in majesty; There is a green hill far away.

Palm Sunday   25 March
Second Service   **Salvation for All**
Ps. 69.1–20 Save me, O God; Isa. 5.1–7 The Song of the Vineyard; Mark 12.1–12 The parable of the wicked tenants

> *'[Jesus asked the priests,] "What . . . will the owner of the vineyard do? He will come and destroy the tenants and give the vineyard to others."' Mark 12.9*

Vineyard

A vineyard is a place that produces fruit. Today's reading from Isaiah describes the people of Israel as God's vineyard, which he cares for tenderly. They have been chosen to produce fruit for God – but what sort of fruit? Two phrases are used in Scripture to describe this: the fruit of the Spirit, and the harvest of souls. St Paul says the fruit of the Spirit is love, joy, peace, patience, goodness, kindness, faithfulness, gentleness and self-control. So the reason God has chosen certain people is so that they should grow that sort of a character – a demonstration of love in action. And the parable of the sower suggests that 'bearing fruit a hundredfold' means that each believer is intended to bring in many new believers – people who have been converted by their words and example to believe, as they do, in a God of love. But both Old and New Testament readings today warn that if the nation, or the Church, fail to do this, God will choose another group to do the work for him.

Salvation

Today's psalm is a cry for salvation: 'Save me, O God.' It is the same for everyone: we all need saving from those who disagree with us, and from the temptation to behave in an unloving way. The message that every Christian is called to spread is of a God who saves us from these things. But, says the Bible, if we fail to spread this message, the job will be taken away from us and given to others who will 'bear fruit' for God.

Ethnicity

So who will receive God's gift of salvation? We must not be anti-Semitic. Jesus in the parable, himself a Jew, suggested that the task of evangelism will be given to other, non-Jewish people; but the Jews, who were the first to believe in only one God for every nation in the world, are still invited to share this message with those around them. Yet Jesus was startlingly anti-racist in his lifetime.

Samaritans

He several times mentions Samaritans. After the time of David and Solomon, their descendants split into two nations: Israel in the north, and Judah in the south. The people of Judah were exiled to Babylon around 587 BC, though they later returned to their capital in Jerusalem. Many people from the *northern* kingdom were exiled to Assyria in 722, but never returned; their place was taken by immigrants from Assyria and several of its colonies. Some of this mixed-race community settled at the former capital city of Samaria, and were called Samaritans. They only recognized the first five books of the Old Testament, and were despised as heretics. Yet when Jesus healed ten lepers, a Samaritan was the only one to thank him. Jesus said, 'Was none of them found to return and give praise to God except this foreigner? . . . Get up and go on your way; your faith has made you well.' Jesus spoke to the Samaritan woman at the well about life-giving water, saying 'Salvation is from the Jews. But the hour . . . is now here, when the true worshippers will worship the Father in spirit and truth, for the Father seeks such as these to worship him.' And, most famously, he told his story about the good Samaritan to show that even heretical foreigners can be an example to us of godly compassion and love.

Syrian

Jesus teased a woman from Syria to test her faith, saying he had no time left to preach to foreigners, and she responded, 'Yes, Lord, yet even the dogs eat the crumbs that fall from their master's table.' Jesus answered, 'Woman, great is your faith!'

Centurion

A centurion, a sort of sergeant-major in the Roman army, asked Jesus to heal his 'boy', saying, 'When I tell my servants to do something, they obey immediately'. [Surely that's also true of the One God you speak about?]' Jesus replied, 'Truly I tell you, in no one in Israel have I found such faith . . . many will come from east and west and will eat with Abraham and Isaac and Jacob in the kingdom of heaven.'

Universalism

So God's kingdom has no boundaries. Salvation, from guilt and temptation, is available to all, even sinners, of whatever race, provided they say they are sorry and trust in Jesus. We call this belief, 'universalism'. But if we fail to share the good news with all our neighbours, then God may turn away from us, and choose foreigners to spread the good news to the unbelieving people of this country.

Suggested hymns

Give me oil in my lamp; Make way, make way, for Christ the King; They shall come from the east; You are the King of glory.

First Three Days in Holy Week   26–28 March
Covenants

(Following are the Monday readings, but this sermon may be used on any day this week.)

Isa. 42.1–9 The servant brings salvation; Ps. 36.5–11 Defend me against the wicked; Heb. 9.11–15 The sacrifice of the new covenant; John 12.1–11 Mary anoints Jesus for his death

> *'For this reason Christ is the one who arranges a new covenant, so that those who have been called by God may receive the eternal blessings that God has promised.' Hebrews 9.15, Good News Bible*

Hebrew

The Letter to the Hebrews, in our New Testament, was written to explain Christianity to Jews. So it was written to appeal to people who think in a Hebrew way. This means that every sentence in the letter uses Jewish metaphors, similes, ideas and phrases; which was fine when most people who read were immersed in the Old Testament, but it is very difficult for the rest of us to read. That is why I read my text from a modern translation, almost a paraphrase.

Covenants

One of the most important words in the Old Testament is usually translated 'covenant'. It actually means a legally binding contract, and is one of the words the Bible uses to explain what Jesus was doing during Holy Week. Probably the earliest forms of written contract were those that dealt with the ownership of land, buying and selling it. It was important that everybody should know which land belonged to whom, and where the boundaries lay. If the contract was between individuals, they might cut themselves and mingle their blood; then sign the document in the presence of witnesses – except that most of them could not write, so they would make the sign of a cross. If the contract was between a people and their god, they sacrificed one of their most precious belongings, usually the best sheep in their flock; poured its blood on the altar, together with a small burnt offering for God to enjoy the smell; then cooked and ate the rest themselves as a shared meal with God. In the book of Genesis, God makes a covenant with Noah, promising never again to flood the earth; with Abraham, promising to give him land and protect his descendants; also with Isaac; and Abraham made a covenant with Abimelech, a foreign king, both of them promising not to attack the other. In Exodus, the Lord God promises to Moses that God will protect the Israelites provided that they obey the Ten Commandments. In the book of Joshua, the tribes make a covenant with each other, allocating land to each and promising to work together as one nation, and calling God as a witness to their contract.

Jesus

So we can understand when Jesus said at the Last Supper that the wine was his blood of the new covenant. Another word for a contract was a testament. The Old Testament, which depended on the observance of more and more complicated codes of law, was now outdated and void. The New Testament was a contract of love: if we love God, and love other people for God's sake, the Lord will love and care for us, forgiving us all our sins as soon as we repent of them. So the author of the Letter to the Hebrews writes:

> For this reason Christ is the one who arranges a new covenant, so that those who have been called by God may receive the eternal blessings that God has promised. This can be done because there has been a death, which sets people free from the wrongs that they did while the first covenant was in force.

Sacrifice

Yet, today, this reference to the need for a death puts some people off. It sounds as though Jesus had to pay a bribe, by sacrificing his own life, either to God or the devil, before we can be forgiven. We think that, because we live in a century when animal sacrifices are rare. The first readers of the Bible could see them taking place daily in every temple. They were not bribes, but a present, made to the god, of something that is worth a lot to you, to show how much you love him. So the bread at the Last Supper symbolizes Jesus offering his life to God, and the cup of wine is God's signature, in his own blood, of his promise to forgive, protect and care for us. Remember that it is all about love: God did not make a covenant that if we are pure he will destroy our enemies, but that if we are considerate to all he will help us not to make enemies.

Suggested hymns

All ye who seek for sure relief; And now, O Father, mindful of the love; Glory be to Jesus; Wherefore, O Father, we thy humble servants.

Maundy Thursday   29 March
Eye-gate and Ear-gate

Ex. 12.1–4 [5–10] 11–14 The Passover; Ps. 116.1, 10–17 The cup of salvation; 1 Cor. 11.23–26 The Last Supper; John 13.1–17, 31b–35 Foot-washing

> *'[Jesus said to his disciples,] "You call me Teacher and Lord – and you are right, for that is what I am. So if I, your Lord and Teacher, have washed your feet, you also ought to wash one another's feet."' John 13.13–14*

Eye-gate

People sometimes refer to the five senses as the eye-gate, the ear-gate, the mouth-gate and so on. Educationists remind us that information that enters the brain through the eye-gate will be remembered far longer that what comes in through the ear-gate. Visual aids are vital in teaching. If you see a picture, a diagram or words on the blackboard, you will absorb their message far more efficiently than by listening to the spoken word, which may go straight over your head. Best of all, however, is a visual aid that is then explained in words.

Jesus

Jesus had been telling his disciples for three years that God loves us, and wants us to love each other; that we must be humble and willing to serve. To judge by the way they kept on squabbling, none of this had gone home at all. So he decided to mount a life-sized visual aid. To explain the meaning of his death on the cross, Jesus arranged a Passover meal, which we know as the Last Supper. This was full of unforgettable visual images; in particular when he washed his disciples' feet, and when he broke the bread, poured out the wine, and shared them around. None of them would ever forget those moments. Then he said, 'Do this to remember me.' Surely he intended us all, every human being, to repeat these actions, whenever possible. In this way his teaching would sink into our heart of hearts. And we should never forget it, because it entered our souls through the eye-gate, and was then explained by the words Jesus said.

Foot-washing

The disciples had been arguing about which of them was the most important. 'You call me Teacher and Lord,' said Jesus, quietly: 'and you are right, for that is what I am. So if I, your Lord and Teacher, have washed your feet, you also ought to wash one another's feet. For I have set you an example, which you also should do as I have done to you.' Bang! That went straight to the heart of the matter, and for ever after they would judge their own actions against the humility of Jesus.

Sacrament

Jesus had told them he was not going to use force to bring in the kingdom of God, no matter what his enemies did to him. His disciples tried to persuade him to take a safer course, but he replied that there is no love without sacrifice. Then Jesus broke bread and poured out wine, before their very eyes, saying that the bread was a symbol of his body; the wine an image of his blood. He may have spoken about our willingness to make unlimited sacrifices for each other, but they forgot those words. What stuck in their brains was the visual image of the meaning of the cross. If even God's Son was willing to sacrifice his body and blood for us, then there is no limit to the acts of kindness we must be willing to do for others, even when we don't feel the least bit like it. You cannot *see* love, but you *can* see bread and wine, and you can see acts of self-sacrifice. So it is no use telling other people about love unless we show it in our own lives by the sacrifices we are willing to make for others. The traditional definition of a sacrament is 'an outward and visible sign of an inward and spiritual grace' – and through the sacraments the idea of what love means enters our brain through the eye-gate.

Noisy

So, after all that noisy arguing between the disciples at the Last Supper, Jesus quietened them down with his visual aids: the washing of their feet, the breaking of the bread, and the pouring out of the wine. Afterwards he did one more thing; he invited them to eat the bread and drink the wine, showing that God's love is best experienced in community. Then he explained all these visual aids in a teaching session. But it was not a one-man show – he encouraged them to ask questions. You can find the whole dialogue in St John's Gospel, chapters 13 – 17. What a brilliant teacher Jesus was, speaking about love through the ear-gate; making it memorable by visual aids through the eye-gate; demonstrating it in his own life; and then leading us to think deeper by the profound discussions he encourages between Christians.

Suggested hymns

I hunger and I thirst; Let all mortal flesh keep silence; Now my tongue, the mystery telling; Strengthen for service, Lord, the hands.

Good Friday   30 March
Jesus the Priest

Isa. 52.13—53.12 The suffering servant; Ps. 22 Why have you forsaken me?; Heb. 10.16–25, *or* Heb. 4.14–16; 5.7–9 Jesus the priest; John 18.1—19.42 The blood of the covenant

'We have a great priest.' Hebrews 10.21

Daring

How can we possibly dare to speak to God? He is infinitely great, why should God be concerned about our little problems? He is infinitely good, how can we approach him when we have done things that we are ashamed of? These are questions that people often ask; and the answer is to be found in the cross of Jesus. But tons of paper and gallons of ink have been used in trying to explain how this can be.

Hebrews

The problem is that you must speak in a language your readers can understand. By that I don't just mean where they come from; but also the metaphors, comparisons, stories and images they use when speaking of the deep things of the heart. The first converts to Christianity were Jewish by race and language. Most Jews spoke a late dialect of Hebrew called Aramaic, but no documents about Jesus in Aramaic have survived. But a large number of Jews, living outside the Holy Land, spoke Greek, the common language of the Roman

Empire. Many of the disciples of Jesus had Greek names, and the Greek translation of the Old Testament was widely distributed. But it was Greek adapted to a Jewish way of thinking. The Letter to the Hebrews, in the New Testament, was addressed to Jews like that.

Temple

Jewish religion, in the time of Jesus, was mostly focused on the Temple in Jerusalem. Those who lived a long distance from there would aim to visit Jerusalem at least once a year if they could, but otherwise only once in their lifetime. Because of the Old Testament emphasis upon the Law of God, most Jews were horribly guilt-ridden. It was so easy to break one of the minor regulations unintentionally, and that made you ritually unclean. Then you were like a leper, unable to mix with good people, to go out in public or to enter any holy place. There were elaborate regulations about washing before meals, which were supposed to wash you clean of sin; but how could you be sure that you had washed sufficiently? Washing became an obsessive behaviour, in the desperate attempt to become worthy to enter God's presence.

Priests

The only answer to this dilemma was the Day of Atonement. Once a year, the High Priest of the Jerusalem Temple would go through an elaborate cleansing ritual, and then pass through the 'veil of the Temple' into the 'Holy of Holies'. Only this one man, on one day of the year, was allowed to do this. There he would sacrifice an animal, pour its blood over the altar and burn its flesh, in the belief that this would make 'atonement' for all the sins of the Jewish people in the world, making them acceptable to God and allowing them to enter the Temple once more. But the fact that this ritual had to be repeated every year still left them feeling dirty most of the time, and conveyed an image of a fierce unforgiving God. Jesus had taught of a loving heavenly Father, more ready to forgive than we are to repent. Finally, the letter was probably written after the Temple had been destroyed in AD 70, so there was no hope for those who depended on its ministrations.

Christian

So the author of 'Hebrews' gave the perfect Christian answer, to appeal to Jews. We have a new, effective and permanent atonement process. Jesus is the new High Priest; he ascended into where God lives in heaven, the new 'Holy of Holies'; his death on the cross was the perfect sacrifice, made once and for all; and so, those who believe in Jesus are cleansed from guilt in the waters of baptism, and remain cleansed for ever because of the eternal sacrifice of Jesus in the spiritual world. So the author wrote:

> Since we have confidence to enter the sanctuary by the blood of Jesus, by the new and living way that he opened for us through the curtain (that is, through his flesh), and since we have a great priest over the house of God, let us approach with a true heart in full assurance of faith, with our hearts sprinkled clean from an evil conscience and our bodies washed with pure water.

Cultures

It is a brilliant argument. It may not mean as much to us as it did to the original readers. But it is a good example of how the eternal truths of the Bible may be re-expressed in each generation to adapt them to the ways of thinking in a fresh culture. Good Friday is the answer, however you formulate the question.

Suggested hymns

Morning glory, starlit sky; There is a green hill far away; There's a wideness in God's mercy; When I survey the wondrous Cross.

EASTER

The 40 days of Easter, up to Ascension Day, are a season of joyful celebration. We celebrate the resurrection of Jesus from the dead, and are filled with hope as inheritors of eternal life. The altar frontals and vestments are white, or gold on Easter Day, and the wonderful Easter hymns resound with alleluias. If the 'Gloria in excelsis' has been omitted in Lent, it is sung again for the first time at the Easter Vigil. At the Vigil, the Easter candle may be lit; it then burns at all services during the season, and at baptisms in the rest of the year. At the Vigil, or some other service, there may be a renewal of baptism promises. There may be an Easter garden with a model of the empty tomb. Eastertide sermons expound our reasons for believing that Jesus is alive, and for hoping for an eternal future for ourselves.

EASTER
Easter Vigil   31 March–1 April
Coming through the Water

(*A minimum of three Old Testament readings should be chosen. The reading from Exodus 14 should always be used.*)

Gen. 1.1—2.4a Creation, Ps. 136.1–9, 23–26; Gen. 7.1–5, 11–18; 8.6–18; 9.8–13 Noah, Ps. 46 Our refuge and strength; Gen. 22.1–18 Sacrifice of Isaac, Ps. 16 The path of life; Ex. 14.10–31, 15.20–21 The Exodus, *Canticle*: Ex. 15.1b–13, 17–18 The song of Moses; Isa. 55.1–11 Come to the waters, *Canticle*: Isa. 12.2–6 Great in your midst; Bar. 3.9–15, 32—4.4 God gives the light of wisdom, or Prov. 8.1–8, 19–21; 9.4b–6 Wisdom, Ps. 19 The heavens declare God's glory; Ezek. 36.24–28 I will sprinkle clean water on you, Ps. 42 and 43 Faith and hope; Ezek. 37.1–14 The valley of dry bones, Ps. 143 A prayer for deliverance; Zeph. 3.14–20 I will bring you home, Ps. 98 Salvation and Justice; Rom. 6.3–11 Baptism, death and resurrection, Ps. 114 The Exodus; Mark 16.1–8 The empty tomb

> '*Do you not know that all of us who have been baptized into Christ Jesus were baptized into his death? Therefore we have been buried with him by baptism into death, so that, just as Christ was raised from the dead by the glory of the Father, so we too might walk in newness of life.*' Romans 6.3–4

Water

Have you ever wondered why there is so much about water in the readings at Easter time? At this service, for instance, we can choose any readings from a list of over 20, including:

The Holy Spirit moving over the waters at the creation; Noah's flood; crossing the Red Sea at the exodus; Isaiah's song: 'Come to the waters'; Ezekiel reports that God says 'I will sprinkle clean water on you'; the waterless valley of dry bones; and St Paul writing to the Romans about baptism, death and resurrection.

The probable reason was that Easter was the time of year when the Church focused on God's offer of resurrection and new life to all those who repent, believe and are baptized. So Easter was a good time to baptize by immersion adult converts to Christianity 'and their whole households', though the infants would be baptized by sprinkling for safety reasons. Lent was the time for candidates to prepare for baptism, by fasting and confessing their sins, until it became popular as a time of self-discipline for all Christians.

Night-time

Baptism was probably performed at night-time, because slaves and labourers worked a seven-day week, and could not get any time off during the day. Also, in those days, a day ran from sunset to sunset; Easter Sunday began at sunset on the Saturday; soon after that there would be the baptism, followed by a shared eucharistic meal, either on a river bank or by the ornamental pool in the courtyard of a rich man's villa. Nowadays most baptisms are infant christenings, and most people have a work-free day on Sundays. So there is no need for a night-time service; yet many churches like to keep up the ancient tradition, by holding an evening vigil service, or an early communion service on Easter Day morning.

Baptism

In this context, the meaning of the readings becomes as clear as a mountain pool. Whether we were baptized as babies or as adults, or are preparing to be baptized, these words apply to us. Baptism is a time when we receive God's Holy Spirit, as Jesus did at his own baptism. The Church, like Noah's ark, welcomes people out of the evil world and keeps them safe through the storms of wickedness to deposit them where life begins again. Baptism is our exodus, when we leave the land of our slavery – to bad habits and temptations – pass through the waters, and then enter the Promised Land of heaven. And we can each of us apply to ourselves the words of St Paul:

> Do you not know that all of us who have been baptized into Christ Jesus were baptized into his death? Therefore we have been buried with him by baptism into death, so that, just as Christ was raised from the dead by the glory of the Father, so we too might walk in newness of life.

The message of baptism, whether at the christening of a small child who will not understand it for several years to come, or of an adult who was baptized years ago, is very simple. It is also the message to you of the Easter festival. It can be conveyed in nine words, which anyone can commit to their memory:

God loves you and has a purpose for you.

Suggested hymns

As the deer pants for the water; Alleluia, alleluia, give thanks to the risen Lord; At the Lamb's high feast we sing; Come, ye faithful, raise the strain.

Easter Day   1 April
Principal Service   All Fools' Day

Acts 10.34–43 Peter and other witnesses to the resurrection, *or* Isa. 25.6–9 Swallow up death; Ps. 118.1–2, 14–24 I shall not die but live; 1 Cor. 15.1–11 Resurrection appearances, *or* Acts 10.34–43 Peter and other witnesses to the resurrection; John 20.1–18 Magdalene at the tomb, *or* Mark 16.1–8 Women see the empty tomb

> *'[The women] went out and fled from the tomb, for terror and amazement had seized them; and they said nothing to anyone, for they were afraid.' Mark 16.8*

Mark

According to St Mark's Gospel, a group of women disciples saw that the tomb where the body of Jesus had been laid was empty. Then a 'young man', probably an angel, assured them that Jesus was not dead but had risen to new life. He told the women to go and tell everyone this wonderful news. But, if what we read there is true, they disobeyed their orders, but ran away quickly and told nobody, because they were afraid. In that case, they were very foolish women. God called them to spread a crucial piece of information, and they messed it up. Fortunately for gender relationships, many people believe that is not the whole story. In the very oldest manuscripts of St Mark's Gospel, it ends quite suddenly there, apparently in the middle of a sentence. But many scholars of the Bible text believe that Mark wrote another few sentences, and maybe another chapter, to explain how the women soon plucked up courage to tell the other disciples. In fact many Bibles add a longer or shorter ending to Mark, quoting from the other Gospels, describing the resurrection appearances and his ascension into heaven. So we talk about 'the lost ending of Mark'. There is no agreement on this, so you must decide for yourself. But Mark would clearly never have even started his Gospel unless he was quite sure that Jesus was alive.

Fools

But that debate about a possibly foolish action means that, on this day of all days, I cannot resist the temptation to tell this joke:

> An atheist Member of Parliament complained to the House of Commons that there are many religious festivals, but no day dedicated to atheism. Another MP promptly replied that Psalm 53 begins with the words: 'The fool has said in his heart, "There is no God."' So the atheists already have a day; it is 1 April, called 'All Fools' Day'.

Pullman

But we must not be discourteous to atheists, among whom there is as great a variety of opinions as you find among Christians. A few years ago a newspaper carried an interview with Philip Pullman, author of the series of children's books entitled *His Dark Materials*. These strongly attack religion, though this was not obvious from the only one that was filmed, *The Golden Compass*. Yet he said he disliked the harsh, mocking atheism of Richard Dawkins – let alone Dawkins' argument that children shouldn't be taught fairy tales full of magic. 'We don't teach children that frogs turn into princes, we tell them a story in which a frog turns into a prince . . . [Dawkins] is on shaky ground when he attacks religion because it isn't true. My attack on religion is not that it isn't true, it's that it does bad things when it gets its hands on power.' That is what Pullman said, and I think many Christians would agree with him.

Resurrection

But the difficulty comes when you try to define what 'true' means in talking about the resurrection of Jesus. The women were certain that the tomb was empty, but disagreed at first as to what the young man meant when he said that Jesus was alive. But the risen Christ was seen by a few individuals, then by two or three together, by eleven disciples all at once, and by more than five hundred people at one time. A vision by one person *could* be a hallucination, but when seen by so many it has to be true. Though, since the risen Christ could pass through locked doors there is still room for discussion on what sort of body he had. Some of the stories in the Bible are fiction, though they still have important truths to convey. But the resurrection is historically true, and many people have been willing to risk their lives to defend that truth, and spread it to others. You would be a fool to reject that truth, for that would be turning your back on the opportunity to have love for living with, and heaven to hope for. So to all atheists, and all believers, and all who are still unsure, I wish a very happy Easter!

All-age worship

Which of the stories in children's books are historically true? What truths can we learn from fiction? Why is the resurrection of Jesus important to us? Make Easter cards.

Suggested hymns

Jesus Christ is risen today; Light's glittering morn; The day of resurrection; This is the day, this is the day.

Easter Day   1 April
Second Service   Abide with Me

Morning Ps. 114 The Exodus, 117 God's faithfulness endures forever; Evening Ps. 105 The Exodus, *or* 66.1–11 God holds our souls in life; Ezek. 37.1–14 The valley of dry bones; Luke 24.13–35 The road to Emmaus

> '[The disciples on the road to Emmaus] urged [Jesus] strongly, saying, "Stay with us, because it is almost evening and the day is now nearly over." So he went in to stay with them.' Luke 24.29

Hymn

Many people, whether or not they were regular church-goers, used to be able to join in the hymn 'Abide with me', because they knew the words by heart. It was popular at football matches, at Remembrance Sunday ceremonies, funerals and solemn evening gatherings. Alas, it is not so familiar these days, mainly because fewer and fewer schools hold religious assemblies. Some of those who know the words are aware that they were written in 1820 by Henry Francis Lyte, the incumbent of the fishing village of Lower Brixham in South Devon. Fewer still realize that it is based upon the story of how two followers of Jesus met him on the road from Jerusalem to Emmaus on the evening of the first Easter Day.

Disciples

The people concerned are simply referred to as 'two of them', but earlier in the same chapter St Luke described how the women who had seen the empty tomb returned and told 'the eleven and all of the rest' about it. 'The rest' must refer to the friends and followers of Jesus, shattered at the fact of his death, who nonetheless had clung together in the 'upper room' for mutual support and comfort in the face of disaster. But in spite of what the women told them, Luke says, 'these words seemed to them an idle tale, and they did not believe them.' The eleven, who were also called apostles, stayed in the Upper Room, and Jesus appeared to them there later that evening. But the rest must have given up hope and returned to their homes in despair, including these two, who were heading to their family home in the village of Emmaus. The exact site of Emmaus is uncertain; there are several possibilities, all to the west of Jerusalem, but nobody can be sure which is the village referred to in the Bible. One of the two is called Cleophas, but the other is not named; it is possible that the other was his wife.

Unrecognized

Jesus walked beside them along the road, though they did not recognize him. I wonder how often Jesus walks beside you and me, and we don't realize he is there, anxious to help us understand the things that are puzzling us, if only we would ask? Whether it was because these two were walking towards the sunset that they did not see who was beside them, or because they were convinced he was permanently dead that their minds refused to believe their eyes. Anyway, Jesus began to explain how the Old Testament had predicted that the Saviour, when he came, would be rejected and killed, but would rise again to new life. One of the proofs that the Bible is telling the truth is the number of times that events in the New Testament fulfil prophesies made in the Old.

Hospitality

So intrigued were the two by what Jesus said they invited him, a complete stranger as they thought, to come into their home and spend the night with them. It was probably only a tiny dwelling; but the Bible commends the virtue of hospitality; and anyway they wanted to hear what he had to say. So they uttered the memorable words, 'Abide with us', which gave rise to the hymn. A modern translation would be, 'Come on in and spend the night with us.' But the resonance of the old words stays in our minds. But that is good, because it reminds us to ask ourselves, 'When was the last time I invited Jesus into my home?' Yes, we know in the abstract that he is there always. But it is often not until you deliberately invite him in that you are consciously aware of his presence.

Prayer

Here is a lovely prayer by the seventeenth-century Welsh poet and physician, Henry Vaughan:

Abide with us, O most blessed and merciful Saviour, for it is toward evening and the day is far spent. As long as thou art present with us, we are in the light. When thou art present all is brightness, all is sweetness. We discourse with thee, watch with thee, live with thee and lie down with thee. Abide then with us, O thou whom our soul loveth, thou Sun of righteousness with healing under thy wings arise in our hearts; make thy light then to shine in darkness as a perfect day in the dead of night. **Amen.**

Suggested hymns

Abide with me; Good Christians all, rejoice and sing; This is the day the Lord has made; Through the night of doubt and sorrow.

Second Sunday of Easter   8 April
Principal Service   **But is it Gospel Truth?**

Ex. 14.10–31; 15.20–21 The Exodus (*if used, the reading from Acts must be used as the second reading*), *or* Acts 4.32–35 Witnessing to the resurrection; Ps. 133 Unity, life; 1 John 1.1—2.2 The word of life; John 20.19–31 Thomas' doubt and faith

> *'Jesus said [to Thomas], "Have you believed because you have seen me? Blessed are those who have not seen and yet have come to believe."' John 20.29*

Gospel

The word 'gospel' means 'good news'. Christians are convinced that the good news that God loves each one of us, and that Jesus died on the cross to convince us that our sins have been forgiven, is absolutely true. So when somebody wants to convince us that what they are saying is true, they sometimes say, 'And that's the gospel truth!' There is disagreement between Christians as to whether the whole Bible is literally true; some say 'yes', because it was all dictated by God, and the scribes simply wrote down what he told them to. Others say that there are accurate historical sections, but there are also many prophetic or poetic and fictional parts, which convey important truths, but should not be seen as accurate history.

Resurrection

So, you may ask, what about the resurrection; is that gospel truth? Again, almost all agree that the heart of the Easter message is undoubtedly truthful: we believe that Jesus died on the cross, and afterwards many people have seen him, and he is alive and close to us now. Also that he has promised that all who trust in him, after they die, will live again a life of joy and love with him. But just as there are different types of truth, there are different meanings of the word 'resurrection'. The first reference in the Bible is in the prophet Ezekiel, who had a vision of a valley of dry bones being brought back to life. But that was a metaphor for the revival of the nation of Israel, who were so shattered by their defeat and exile to Babylon that they felt as dead as a dodo; but God would give them fresh hope to revitalize the nation when they returned to Jerusalem.

Resuscitation

Secondly the prophets Elijah and Elisha, and Jesus himself, brought back to physical life people who had been dead. But this resuscitation was only temporary; when they reached old age, they also died the same as everyone else. But by the time of Jesus, it seems that most Jews believed that physical resuscitation of the dead would happen to all dead fellow countrymen and -women, when the Messiah had defeated their enemies.

Spiritual

A group called the Sadducees denied this. They tried to trick Jesus with the story of the woman who had seven husbands – whose wife would she be? His reply showed that he believed not in a physical resuscitation but a spiritual resurrection, untrammelled by time and free from the hindrances of the flesh; he said:

'In the resurrection they neither marry nor are given in marriage, but are like angels in heaven.'

So with those words from Jesus we can be certain that we enter a spiritual eternity immediately when we die. He said to the thief on the cross: 'Today you will be with me in paradise.'

Problems

Two problems remain: what happened when Jesus rose again; and why is there so much talk about the last judgement? We may have to keep an open mind on these. The risen Christ appeared and disappeared at will, even behind locked doors; so his was what St Paul called 'not flesh and blood but a spiritual body'. Yet the tomb was empty, and Jesus invited Thomas to touch him. He was determined that his disciples should not mistake him for a ghost. And there was a type of poetic symbolism in the centuries just before Christ, which we call 'apocalyptic imagery'. This was designed to shock people into realizing that quite soon, in their own lifetime, the struggle between the forces of good and the forces of evil would come to a head, and they must decide now which side they are on. You have only to read today's newspaper to realize that this is true now; perhaps it always was and always will be. So this sort of language could be imagery or metaphor; not literally true, but proclaiming a true spiritual message nonetheless. Jesus said to Thomas:

'Have you believed because you have seen me? Blessed are those who have not seen and yet have come to believe.'

So the spiritual resurrection of Jesus is gospel truth; the rest of the Bible is true also, provided that you interpret it in the right way.

All-age worship

Make paper puppets of the risen Christ appearing to the eleven disciples in the upper room.

Suggested hymns

Alleluia! O sons and daughters; Christ is alive! Let Christians sing; Jesus is Lord; Thine be the glory.

Second Sunday of Easter   8 April
Second Service   Why do You Seek for the Living?
Ps. 143.1–11 Remember the days of old; Isa. 26.1–9, 19 Your dead shall live; Luke 24.1–12 The resurrection

> *'The women were terrified and bowed their faces to the ground, but the men said to them, "Why do you look for the living among the dead? He is not here, but has risen. Remember how he told you, while he was still in Galilee, that the Son of Man must be handed over to sinners, and be crucified, and on the third day rise again."' Luke 24.5–7*

Cummings

e e cummings was a controversial American poet of the first half of the twentieth century. Many of his poems contained no capital letters at all, so his name is often written similarly: entirely in lower case, or small, letters. Sometimes it is hard to discover whether his poems express his own feelings or are a satire on the views of others. One poem, entitled 'More of the Day', begins by describing the reaction of the women at the empty tomb of Christ, as described in St Mark's Gospel.

[Preachers may quote the poem in full by searching the internet for e e cummings, 'They came as dawn was breaking' or 'More of the Day', but the copyright situation is complicated so it is unwise to print it out in full.]

Poem

The first verse describes the women coming to the tomb, intending to grieve over their loss, and the painful death of Christ on the cross. Then it quotes the words the angels said, 'Why do you look for the living among the dead?' But in the second verse it is the grieving women who object to people who believe in the resurrection disturbing them as they mourn. In the third it sounds like many modern people, who want to wallow in their grief, and resent Christians telling them we shall rise again after we die, as Jesus did. It is almost as if they feel at home with hopeless grief, whereas those who believe in resurrection interrupt the unbeliever's search for meaning in the grave. They had been nursing their wounds, but their feelings of loss have been made public, and their attempt to follow the path less trodden spoilt because Christians have paved it.

Attitudes

I believe the poet has put his finger here on a common modern attitude. Sometimes mourners even say to the funeral director, 'We would like a minister to take the funeral, because they dress and speak solemnly, but we don't want any of this religion nonsense.' They want pop music, not hymns, at the funeral, partly because they don't know any hymns, but also because they take a perverse pride in rejecting talk of the afterlife as old-fashioned nonsense. Which is sad, because nobody tries to 'ram religion down their throats', but we do offer a message, coming from Jesus himself, that death is not the end, but the gateway into a better life. Sharing that good news is a far better use of time than reciting endless tributes to the departed.

Heaven

Of course, the sceptic is right in saying that much of the language we use in talking about heaven is very outdated and unscientific. Enough people have been up in an aeroplane to convince us that the New Jerusalem is not somewhere above the clouds. But many people like using words that have been in use for a couple of thousand years to describe an afterlife that we have to admit is indescribable. Yet we need to say openly that these are metaphors for something that goes beyond language.

Resurrection

But hundreds of people saw Jesus, when he returned to life after his crucifixion, and the fact that these events happened 2,000 years ago does not make their evidence inadmissible. Many people today become strongly aware of the presence of their departed loved ones after they die; too many for us to dismiss their experience as superstition or wishful thinking. So there is nothing to be ashamed of in saying, 'I believe there is a spiritual dimension to the material world.' Like the angels, we can say to those who mourn, with sympathy and understanding, 'Why do you look for the living among the dead? He [or she] is not here, but has risen.'

Suggested hymns

Give us the wings of faith to rise; I serve a risen Saviour (He lives); Jesus lives! Thy terrors now; Now is eternal life.

Third Sunday of Easter   15 April
Principal Service   **Witnessing by Caring**
Zeph. 3.14–20 The Lord is in your midst (*if used, the reading from Acts must be used as the second reading*), *or* Acts 3.12–19 Witnessing by caring; Ps. 4 Sleep in peace; 1 John 3.1–7 Adoption; Luke 24.36b–48 The upper room

> 'When Peter saw [the lame man walking], he addressed the people, "You Israelites, why do you wonder at this, or why do you stare at us, as though by our own power or piety we had made him walk?"' Acts 3.12

Sermons

Have you ever wondered what the first Christian sermons were like? Well, we have in the Acts of the Apostles one sermon by St Stephen, several by St Peter, and a lot by St Paul. Some are addressed to a Jewish audience, others are adapted to be understood by non-Jewish listeners also, and it is interesting to see how the same message can be rephrased using the words of a different language, and addressing the concerns at the forefront of the minds of different groups.

Lame

In today's reading, we heard what St Peter said to a crowd that assembled spontaneously when they heard that he had healed a man who had been lame since he was born. They were astonished, and ready for the first time to respect the words of this new 'heretical' group. As they were entirely Jewish, he began by reminding them that Jews of their generation were responsible for the death of Jesus. One idea that gripped Jewish thought at that time was the expectation of a Messiah, a new anointed King of the Jews, who would defeat the Romans and usher in the kingdom of God when Jews would rule the world. It was because Jesus refused to accept that role that they had him killed. But now that miracles were being performed in the name of the risen Christ, they began to wonder whether they had been disastrously mistaken.

Sin

St Peter didn't pull his punches. He told them they were all sinners, because they had blocked God's plan for a kingdom of peace. He didn't try to shift the blame onto the high priests, or Pontius Pilate. They were not so individualistic in those days. If a nation had sinned, or a society, then every member of that society was responsible for the harm they had done. That knocked his Jewish audience back on their heels; but some of them, at least, recognized the truth in what Peter was saying. Yet he did not grind their faces in the mud – as soon as they began to feel sorry for what their nation had done, he proclaimed God's promise of immediate forgiveness to those who repent, and are willing to accept it.

Compassion

Once again they were knocked back on their heels. Nobody had spoken of a compassionate God like this before. They had been brought up to think of God as a judge, who would punish sinners, unless they paid him off with a sacrificial offering. But St Peter described a God who looked at a handicapped person and did not blame him – 'probably a punishment for some sin of his parents,' they muttered – but cared for him as a person and cured him. Then they were told that God is anxious to forgive us our sins as soon as we confess them, without any punishment. And they were flabbergasted. So St Peter bore witness to Jesus by proclaiming, and demonstrating, the caring personality that was also the character of the God that Jesus proclaimed.

Healing

But how can we witness to God's care if we have never seen a healing miracle? I wouldn't be so sure that you haven't. A Christian watched a lad come into a coach station where he was to change coaches. The lad sat down with his head in his hands, shivering violently. The Christian could not hear what was said, but he prayed for that lad as he had never prayed before. Soon the shivering subsided, and the lad seemed asleep. When his coach was called his family woke him, and the lad walked calmly away before the Christian could say anything. Of course, it could have been quite natural; but the Christian felt sure it was not, and he thanked God for all the unobserved miracles that he performs every day, but people are too sceptical to notice.

Witness

So we too must witness, as Peter did, by our confidence in a compassionate God, who cares for the marginalized and forgives as soon as he is asked. And then show that in our own lives, as we seek to serve the handicapped, the sick and the poor, and to reconcile those who feel that people who have sinned against them can never be forgiven.

All-age worship

Have a first-aid class, learning how to help people who have been injured until trained help arrives.

Suggested hymns

Christ is alive! Let Christians sing; Christ triumphant, ever reigning; Come, my soul, thy suit prepare; Peter and John went to pray.

Third Sunday of Easter   15 April
Second Service   The Seven Sleepers of Ephesus

Ps. 142 Bring me out of prison; Deut. 7.7–13 Redeemed from slavery; Rev. 2.1–11 Letters to Ephesus and Smyrna; *Gospel at Holy Communion*: Luke 16.19–31 The rich man and Lazarus

> *'To the angel of the church in Ephesus write: These are the words of him who holds the seven stars in his right hand, who walks among the seven golden lampstands . . . Do not fear what you are about to suffer . . . Be faithful until death, and I will give you the crown of life.' Revelation 2.1, 10*

Ephesus

When St Paul visited Ephesus, in about AD 52, it was a huge city – population estimated at a quarter of a million – the capital of the Province of Asia in what is now called Turkey. It is one of the great archaeological sites of the Mediterranean, and tourists love to visit the vast Roman theatre, where the crowd baying for Paul's death assembled. He left behind a small Christian community, which was one of the seven churches to which letters are addressed by the risen Christ in the book of Revelation. Persecution and imprisonment was foretold for them, and they were encouraged to 'be faithful until death'.

Legend

This is also the location for a wonderful legend, the tale of the Seven Sleepers of Ephesus. It is not in the Bible, so we have no need to treat it as fact. But it is one of the great stories of world literature, and we can enjoy it as such. It was first found in the writings of a Syrian bishop who lived from 450 to 521, based on an earlier Greek original. It is quoted by many writers, notably in the late medieval book called *The Golden Legend*.

Sleepers

The story goes that seven youths who lived in Ephesus during the reign of the pagan Emperor Decius, in about 250, were tortured until they admitted to being Christians. They were offered their freedom if they would renounce their faith and become pagans. Here the story resonates with the suffering of many Christians in the Middle East and Africa today. When they refused to do so, they fled the prison and hid in a cave outside the city, where they fell asleep. The Emperor gave the order for the cave opening to be walled up, as their punishment for being Christians. There they slept for 180 years. Then the farmer who owned the land broke open the entrance, intending to make it a cattle pen. But the Seven Sleepers woke up, thinking they had been asleep for a day or a day-and-a-half. It was now the rule of the Christian Emperor Theodosius II, and Christianity had become the established religion of the Roman Empire. The seven sent one of their number with some money that they had brought into the cave, to buy food. He was amazed to see buildings with crosses on them, when he assumed that Christianity was a forbidden faith. The shopkeepers were astonished to be paid in ancient coins from the reign of the Emperor Decius. The local bishop interviewed all seven, and then, the story says, they died praising God. They were buried in the cave, and a chapel was built over it; Roman Catholics and Eastern Orthodox honour them as hundreds of saints and pilgrims go to visit the chapel and the Christian catacombs beside it, which were used for hundreds of burials in the following centuries. The site was discovered and re-stored in 1927. What a story!

Qur'an

One of the fascinating aspects of this tale is that it also appears in the Muslim holy book, the Holy Qur'an, Surah 18. There the young men are called the Companions of the Cave, and their number is not specified. Nor is the location and date. Several places in the Muslim world claim to be the cave in the story, and the time the young men slept is described as 300 or 309 years. All we can say is that the story of people waking after a long sleep is a widespread legend. It has been told of Joseph of Arimathea in the cave at Glastonbury, and most recently emerging in the story of Rip van Winkel.

Moral

But all good stories have a moral; what can we learn from this one? The first is that any Christian may suffer persecution, if not life-threatening, at least by mockery. In those circumstances we must hold fast, and refuse to deny our faith. Second, the story is a parable of the resurrection, appropriately for the Easter season. Remember that when we 'fall asleep' in death, that is not the end, and we shall wake up again in heaven. And finally, never tell God what you are going to do tomorrow, as he is quite likely to do something that will force you to change your plans completely!

Suggested hymns

Alleluia, sing to Jesus; For all the saints; Give us the wings of faith to rise; Wake, O wake! With tidings thrilling.

Fourth Sunday of Easter 22 April
Principal Service **The Good Shepherd**
Gen. 7.1–5, 11–18; 8.6–18; 9.8–13 Noah's flood (*if used, the reading from Acts must be used as the second reading*), *or* Acts 4.5–12 Peter's witness to resurrection; Ps. 23 The Lord is my shepherd; 1 John 3.16–24 Law, faith and love; John 10.11–18 The good shepherd

'[Jesus said,] "There will be one flock, one shepherd."' John 10.16

Lambs

Have you seen any lambs yet? When you see them gambolling in the fields, it is a sure sign that spring has come. Nowadays we keep them in fields, with a hedge round, so they can't wander off, and they stay there all day and all night. In the days of Jesus, the dry climate meant that grass could be scarce, so the shepherd led the sheep from one place to another, in search of pasture. No fences means no protection. When the wolf comes, the sheep panic, and run in all directions. Then the lamb who gets stuck in a corner by itself can easily be caught. The safety of the sheep was the concern of the shepherd. He lived with them, spent his days and nights with them, fought off wild animals with either a sling shot or his bare hands. If the wolf mortally wounded him, he could probably die for them, being far from help. This helps us understand what Jesus meant when he said, 'I am the Good Shepherd.'

Persecution

In the Acts of the Apostles, Peter and John are under attack, if not from wolves, from people even more dangerous. The very same people who had Jesus killed. Today's reading is part of a long story, where a lame man was healed right in the Temple gateway. A spectacular healing, as the man was well known, and there were many witnesses. The man himself was leaping and jumping about, so there was no hushing this up. The priests discussed what to do, and came up with a possible compromise. They told the disciples to give God the credit, and not to mention Jesus. But Peter and John are living in the power of the resurrected Jesus. Jesus is the link between heaven and earth. The name of Jesus is the key. Jesus had commissioned Peter with the feeding and care of his sheep, and Peter had seized this opportunity to demonstrate the power of the name of Jesus. Peter had a new purpose in life, and he was not to be deflected. I am sure that Peter's prayer each morning would be: 'Show me who needs help this day, and give me strength to help them.' If that is our prayer, then we go out and *look* at people – see them through God's eyes. In today's reading from his first letter, St John writes:

> We know love by this, that he laid down his life for us – and we ought to lay down our lives for one another. How does God's love abide in anyone who has the world's goods, and sees a brother or sister in need and yet refuses help?

Under-shepherds

So the loving character that Jesus showed should be reflected in the lives of those who follow Jesus. You cannot sit by and say, 'What a wonderful life Jesus lived, I could never live like that. If you try, Jesus will give you his Holy Spirit to help you. You cannot leave it to your minister and the other church members. Remember the Lord's Prayer: the kingdom of God will not come until everyone is doing God's will – which is for us to love each other. In Bible times shepherds didn't work alone: there might be a shepherd and a group of under-shepherds, or a group of independent shepherds who joined together for company, protection and flexibility. Jesus calls you to be his under-shepherd, loving other people in practical ways, and especially the poor and needy. He said:

I have other sheep that do not belong to this fold. I must bring them also, and they will listen to my voice. So there will be one flock, one shepherd.

The Jews who heard this will have been shocked: 'You mean, the Chosen People is not limited to Jewish people?' But we can be equally prejudiced in this country. We have little interest in the growth of Christianity in the developing world; we want to reduce the number of poor foreigners entering this rich country; we give small sums to overseas aid charities, and resent government support for other countries when our own standard of living is going down a little. Remember, you are an under-shepherd, and should be willing to make big sacrifices to build one flock, under one shepherd.

All-age worship

Make paper and cotton-wool models of sheep and shepherds. Put them on a board with a model Jesus in the centre, and flocks approaching him from all four corners.

Suggested hymns

Faithful Shepherd, lead me; Great Shepherd of thy people, hear; Loving Shepherd of thy sheep; Shepherd divine, our wants relieve.

Fourth Sunday of Easter   22 April
Second Service   Son of God
Ps. 81.8–16 I would feed you; Ex. 16.4–15 Manna; Rev. 2.12–17 Letters to Pergamum and Thyatira; *Gospel at Holy Communion*: John 6.30–40 I am the bread

> *'To the angel of the church in Thyatira write: These are the words of the Son of God, who has eyes like a flame of fire, and whose feet are like burnished bronze . . .' Revelation 2.18*

Son of God

Jesus is called 'Son of God' in the four Gospels more than 30 times. There are numerous uses of the term in the other New

Testament books. But what exactly do we mean by those words? In today's reading from the book of Revelation they are used to describe an unearthly, heavenly being: 'the Son of God, who has eyes like a flame of fire, and whose feet are like burnished bronze.' Similar words are used to describe God the Father in the Old Testament. So in Revelation you can say that they assert that Jesus is equal with the Creator. But that is not what the words originally meant.

Qur'an

The Muslim sacred book, the Holy Qur'an, has many respectful references to Jesus, and to his mother Mary, but to Muslims, Jesus is a great prophet, no more than that. There are quotations, familiar even to the least educated Muslim, which are claimed to deny the basic truth of Christianity. I quote:

- Allah forbid that he should have a son.
- It is not fitting for God to have children.
- He begets not, nor is he begotten, and there is none like unto him.
- No son did Allah beget, nor is there any god along with him.
- It is not consonant with the majesty of the Most Gracious that he should beget a son.
- How can [Allah] have a child when there is no consort for him?

The problem here is that Muhammad assumed that Christians meant a physical son, engendered by sexual intercourse. Which of course we don't, and never have.

Bible

Psalm 2 shows the King of Israel referred to as God's son, but there is no suggestion here of a physical relationship: God says, 'Yet have I set my king upon my holy hill of Zion . . . You are my Son; this day have I begotten you.' Everybody knew who the monarch's physical parents were, so this must be a way of expressing the close loving relationship between God and the king. Next it came to be used of any Jewish king, and especially of the Messiah, the long-hoped-for ideal ruler who would bring about the kingdom of God. The Old Testament was written in Hebrew, a language lacking in adjectives. If you wanted to say that a woman was born in Jerusalem, you said that she was 'a daughter of Jerusalem'. When two disciples had violent tempers they were called 'Sons of Thunder'. When Daniel wanted to describe a figure in his dream as looking almost human, he had to write 'one resembling a son of man'. There is no word in Hebrew that translates our word 'divine', so you have to talk about 'the Son of God'. But that doesn't mean a physical, biological descent – heaven forbid!

Meaning

So what *does* it mean? We say, 'like father, like son'. So the loving, forgiving character of Jesus of Nazareth reveals the nature of God. The close relationship between a child and its parents resembles the intimacy between Jesus and the Creator, whom he called 'Abba', which is what we roughly translate as 'Daddy'. That is what the disciples meant at first. Yet it goes beyond that. By the time they had lived with Jesus for three years, watched him die and rise again, they felt that God was revealing himself to them through their friend Jesus. As St Paul put it, 'God was in Christ, reconciling the world to himself.' And they felt that the Holy Spirit was God working through them. Yet we agree with the Muslims, and the Jews, that there is only one God. So we have to say that the eternal God reveals himself to us in three ways: as God the Father and Creator; as God the Son, revealing God's love through the life of Jesus; and God the Holy Spirit, revealing God's power to work through you and me. Those words, 'Son of God', have travelled a long way: now they express an indescribably close spiritual relationship between the Persons of the Trinity, the three ways in which we experience the one God. But it is still definitely not a physical relationship. I wonder whether the Christians in Thyatira understood all that? Of course, it is not what we understand with our minds which counts, but what Revelation calls our 'love, faith, service, and patient endurance'.

Suggested hymns

Love of the Father, love of Christ the Son; Son of God, eternal Saviour; The Son of God his glory hides; The Son of God his glory hides.

Fifth Sunday of Easter 29 April
Principal Service **The True Vine**

Bar. 3.9–15, 32—4.4 Wisdom, *or* Gen. 22.1–18 Abraham willing to sacrifice Isaac (*if used, the reading from Acts must be used as the second reading*), *or* Acts 8.26–40 Baptism of an Ethiopian; Ps. 22.25–31 The poor shall eat; 1 John 4.7–21 Our love for one another, God's love for us; John 15.1–8 The true vine

> '[Jesus said to his disciples,] "I am the vine, you are the branches. Those who abide in me and I in them bear much fruit, because apart from me you can do nothing."' John 15.5

The future

Jesus had gathered his disciples together for the Last Supper, and told them he was going to die – 'I am the Good Shepherd,' he said, 'the good shepherd lays down his life for the sheep.' This made them sad, and each worried about their own future – would the priests come after them, as they had after their leader? Would they be able to survive in hiding? How could they continue to spread the kingdom of love as he had called them to? So Jesus reassured them by saying, 'I am the True Vine.'

I am

This is no accident. In the Old Testament, Moses asked God how he should answer if people asked him who had sent him. God replied, 'My name is "I am". Tell them that "I am" has sent you.' The Hebrew word for 'I am' sounds a bit like 'Yahweh', the Jewish name for God. So whenever Jesus said, 'I am', he was claiming to be one with God, our Saviour. Followers of Jesus need have no worries.

Bad vines

The image of a vine is often used in the Bible to describe the nation of Israel. But usually it describes a bad vine that bears no fruit. Psalm 80 describes 'a vine being brought out of Egypt'. Hosea refers to Israel as 'a spreading vine'. Isaiah contains a 'Song of the Vineyard', in which God speaks of his care for the vine, that is, Israel, but in return he received only bad grapes. Therefore the vine was destroyed. In Ezekiel, Jerusalem was described as a 'useless vine'. Jesus is the true vine because he, unlike Israel, produces good fruit; and you and I and all his other disciples are branches of the true vine, provided that we stay connected to the trunk and bear fruit also.

Fruit

What does Jesus mean by fruit? St Paul answers that question when he describes the 'fruit of the spirit' as the qualities of a good character: love, joy, peace, patience, kindness, goodness, faithfulness, gentleness and self-control. Anyone who shows those characteristics is bearing good fruit for God. Anyone who attracts others to that way of life is grafting new branches into God's vine.

Connected

Many Jews would agree with that. God will not destroy the whole nation of Israel, just those who are only interested in exclusive nationalism. Those who bear the fruit of love remain part of his Chosen People. It was Paul, the Jew, who said that non-Jews had been 'grafted into' Christ. Jesus was also born a Jew; the true vine started in Israel, but God's plan is for it to grow to embrace every nation of the world. The way towards this goal is for more and more individuals to grow the fruit of love in their lives. But now Jesus moves on to another important point: branches can only bear fruit if they are firmly attached to the trunk; individuals can only grow love if you are intimately connected to Jesus. Not just a nodding acquaintance; you need a daily conversation with Jesus in the life of prayer.

The Church

That is hard to achieve on your own. So Jesus gives us the Church, to teach us to pray and to encourage us to go on with it even when we don't feel like it. Your relationship with Jesus goes on growing all through your life. You can't persuade people to be loving by telling them to; only by showing them that they are loved; and the community of the Church is the best place to do this.

Rambling free

One final point: the branches of a vine ramble all over the place. They try one direction, and if that doesn't work, they go off in another. That's how we Christians are. We are all different, and free to discover the version of Christianity which is most helpful to us. Ritual, happy-clappy, social service, silence – we can try all of them from time to time. It doesn't matter, so long as we remain united to Jesus in prayer. So we must not judge each other, saying, 'You're not a Christian, because you don't do as I do.' The Christian Church should be the most open, accepting, tolerant institution in the world.

All-age worship

Train up a pot-plant.

Suggested hymns

Bread of heaven, on thee we feed; Gracious Spirit, Holy Ghost; I hunger and I thirst; You are the vine, we are the branches.

Fifth Sunday of Easter   29 April
Second Service   Change
Ps. 96 A new song; Isa. 60.1–14 Arise, shine; Rev. 3.1–13 Letters to Sardis and Philadelphia; *Gospel at Holy Communion*: Mark 16.9–16 Mary Magdalene

> *'These are the words of him who has the seven spirits of God and the seven stars: "I know your works; you have a name of being alive, but you are dead. Wake up, and strengthen what remains and is at the point of death."' Revelation 3.1–2*

Change

The only things that never change are those things that are already dead. So I think the risen Christ was talking to a congregation that was resistant to any form of change, when he said to the church at Sardis, in the book of Revelation, 'I know your works; you have a name of being alive, but you are dead. Wake up, and strengthen what remains and is at the point of death.' I don't know of any churches that are completely dead today; and if I did suspect one of being so, it is not my place to judge. But I know many in which large sections of the congregation are reluctant to make any changes in their hallowed traditions. Now, I am very reluctant to preach on this, because I am very fond of the old ways myself. But I recognize we shall never attract people who are not brought up in our traditions if we do not make at least a few small changes. If not, they will write us off as already dead. Certainly change must be gradual, and start from where we are now. If we change too suddenly, we shall lose some ardent traditionalists. But it was God who said. 'See, I am making all things new.' It was Jesus who encouraged Peter to step boldly out of the boat in the storm. The gospel is described as 'new wine', which will burst the old wineskins. The Psalms tell us to 'Sing to the Lord a new song.' In a very balanced way, Jesus said: 'Every scribe who has been trained for the kingdom of heaven is like the master of a household who brings out of his treasure what is new and what is old.' So I shall look briefly at what changes are possible, and which are desirable, in worship, doctrine and society.

Worship

The Church has been changing ever since it was founded, and still is changing in our lifetime. The Roman Catholic Church has changed from a rigid, and not always logical, Latin rite to the present vernacular liturgies, and small changes are continually being made to those. The Church of England has changed, for most purposes, from the 1662 Book of Common Prayer services to the present *Common Worship*, with several stages on the way, and there is plenty of flexibility in the way that is used. Some Protestant Churches have changed from a fixed service to one made entirely of extempore prayers, but the language in which that is expressed has changed. Many congregations in all denominations, without wishing to become completely Pentecostal, have shown new awareness of the Holy Spirit in their services. A minister saw that at a funeral he was to sing, 'Always look on the bright side of life', from *The Life of Brian*; he was horrified, but soon found himself joining in with enthusiasm.

Doctrine

We talk of the 'unchanging doctrine of the Church', but that too has been in constant change since the beginning. In the Bible you can see ideas being formulated, reconsidered, and written down in one language, then translated into another. St Paul's ideas on 'the spiritual body', which we have after death, only emerged gradually. The doctrine of the Trinity is based on biblical experiences, but not finally formulated until AD 325, using Greek terminology based on the writings of Greek philosophers. This strikes many modern people as mere nit-picking over words. The doctrine of the atonement has used many metaphors that were helpful to one generation but a hindrance to the next. Every generation must express the unchanging doctrines in the language of the present.

Society

The most serious challenge, however, is the change in society. Society is constantly changing; as Tennyson wrote, 'The old order changeth, yielding place to new.' If the Church is flexible, it can give useful guidance on new problems. It was Christians who saw the immorality in slavery, who brought about the Abolition movement. But on so many issues today, society has moved more quickly than Christian morality – gender, sexuality, divorce, abortion, race and so on. Therefore many people understandably see us as obsolete and irrelevant. Bishop David Jenkins once said: 'The Church of England is in favour of change so long as it makes no difference.' That was unkind, but there is a grain of truth in it, and not only in the Church of England.

Suggested hymns

New every morning is the love; One more step along the road I go; One shall tell another; Sing to God new songs of worship.

Sixth Sunday of Easter (Rogation Sunday) 6 May
Principal Service **Baptism of Gentiles**

Isa. 55.1–11 Come to the waters (*if used, the reading from Acts must be used as the second reading*), or Acts 10.44–48 Baptism of Gentiles; Ps. 98 In righteousness God shall judge; 1 John 5.1–6 Love and the commandments; John 15.9–17 The commandment to love

> *'The circumcised believers who had come with Peter were astounded that the gift of the Holy Spirit had been poured out even on the Gentiles.' Acts 10.45*

Jewish

If you have any Jewish friends, you will note that they are mostly kind, loving and charming. There are a few exceptions, just as there are among Christians, but on the whole they are just like us. An amateur chorus was singing a piece of Christian music, and a Jew turned to his Christian neighbour, saying, 'These words sound more Jewish than Christian'; to which the other replied, rather rashly, 'Everything in Christianity we have borrowed from you Jews.' 'Well said,' laughed the Jew; 'tell that to everyone!' It was a bit of an exaggeration, but remember that Jesus was a Jew. When he was on earth, his thoughts, words, metaphors and doctrine were based on those of the Jews; if they had not been, he could not have communicated with his Jewish hearers. He saw himself as a reformer of the Jewish faith, not as starting a totally new religion. We have a tremendous lot in common with our Jewish friends.

Pharisees

Jesus did, however, come into bitter conflict with one particular sect of Judaism: the Pharisees. They taught that it was essential for every single Jew to obey all the fiddling commandments in what we call the Old Testament; Jesus said it is all summed up in the commandments to love God and love our neighbours as much as we love ourselves. The priests said that sins could only be forgiven when we offer an animal to be sacrificed in the Temple; Jesus said our sins are forgiven the moment we repent of them. The Pharisees said that only those who had been circumcised and followed all the other customs and rituals of Judaism counted as Jews. They did try to convert members of other races, but circumcision is very painful for an adult; Jesus said, 'Woe to you, scribes and Pharisees, hypocrites, for you cross sea and land to make a single convert, and you make the new convert twice as much a child of hell as yourselves.' The Pharisees were basically racist in their attitude to foreigners; whereas Jesus welcomed the Canaanite woman with a sick daughter, the Greeks who came to Philip, and the Roman centurion, saying, 'Truly I tell you, in no one in Israel have I found such faith. I tell you, many will come from east and west and will eat with Abraham and Isaac and Jacob in the kingdom of heaven.'

Pentecost

So as we prepare to celebrate the coming of the Holy Spirit at Pentecost, it is important to notice that all who were present that day were Jews – many of whom had lived away from Palestine and Hebrew was not their first language – with a few converts who had been circumcised. The real challenge did not occur until, as we heard in today's reading from Acts, St Peter visited the home of another Roman centurion in Caesarea, and found himself proclaiming the good news to a group of Roman soldiers and their families, who also received the Holy Spirit. Then, we read:

> The circumcised believers who had come with Peter were astounded that the gift of the Holy Spirit had been poured out even on the Gentiles . . . Then Peter said, 'Can anyone withhold the water for baptizing these people who have received the Holy Spirit just as we have?'

So these foreigners were baptized and welcomed into the family of God, *without needing to be circumcised*! Shock, horror, for the racist Jews!

Racism

So is there any racism in your heart? I am sure you think there is not. But when you meet somebody of a different race, do you assume that we have a lot to teach them, without asking what they have to teach us? They may not have received the same education as you have, but they may have learnt a wisdom in some areas which is nowhere to be found in western culture. Never slip into the patronizing attitudes of the Pharisees. The Church in the developing world is flourishing and growing at a rate quite unknown in the West. Peter and his friends were forced to admit that the Romans were equal to the Jews in all respects, when they saw what gifts they had received. As Jesus said when showing what lessons could be learnt from a non-Jewish Samaritan, 'Go, and do thou likewise.'

All-age worship

Read about Christians in the developing world.

133

From all that dwell below the skies; He is Lord, he is Lord; In Christ there is no east or west; Ye choirs of new Jerusalem.

Sixth Sunday of Easter (Rogation Sunday) 6 May
Second Service   Royal Wedding

Ps. 45 Royal wedding; S. of Sol. 4.16—5.2; 8.6–7 Many waters cannot quench love; Rev. 3.14–22 Letter to Laodicea; *Gospel at Holy Communion*: Luke 22.24–30 Greatness and service

> 'Kings' daughters are among your honourable women;
> at your right hand stands the queen in gold of Ophir.'
> Psalm 45.9 (Common Worship)

Royal wedding

Psalm 45 is full of memorable phrases, many of which have been set to music for royal occasions in this country, and it is titled 'A song for the king'. The first half is full of flattering phrases about the monarch, who has been anointed by God because he loves righteousness and hates iniquity – the pursuit of justice is a good quality in any government. The second half is sung to his bride, who is 'all glorious within', which probably means she is still inside the palace, preparing to make her grand appearance for her wedding. She is to leave her parents' home and produce sons who will be princes in the country of the king, who will be their father.

David?

The question then arises, which king is getting married? Many people mistakenly thought that, just because 'the Lord is my shepherd' sounds as though it could have been written by the shepherd boy who killed Goliath, then the psalms were all written by King David. It is hard to see how he could have written this psalm, which is addressed to him; and the question is settled by the psalm beginning, 'By the waters of Babylon we sat down and wept', which must have been written at the time of the exile, which occurred around 400 years after the death of King David. They are more likely a collection of songs used in the Temple at Jerusalem, composed in the style that had been originated by King David, 'the sweet psalmist of Israel'.

Solomon?

We also have a reading today from the Old Testament book known as 'The Song of Songs, which is Solomon's'. This a wonderful love poem, which turns into a dialogue between the woman, who is trying to locate her beloved, named as King Solomon, and a chorus of the women of Jerusalem:

> Set me as a seal upon your heart,
>   as a seal upon your arm;
> for love is strong as death,
>   passion fierce as the grave.
> Its flashes are flashes of fire,
>   a raging flame.
> Many waters cannot quench love,
>   neither can floods drown it.
> If one offered for love
>   all the wealth of one's house,
>   it would be utterly scorned.

Solomon had many wives. The poem is a beautiful hymn to the value of love; but whether it was actually used at one of Solomon's weddings must be left an open question.

Marriage

These poems are from a bygone age. Nowadays marriage is not as universal as it used to be. Maybe it is because of the cost, both of marriage and divorce; or a reluctance to enter into a lifelong commitment when we live so much longer than our ancestors did. But a relationship will be much stronger if it is based on mutual commitment, and the power of sexual love has a lot to teach us about the other types of love that are mentioned in the Bible. As the mystics have shown us, there is a lot in common between the love of the Christian for Jesus, and the passionate attraction of two people in a romantic love affair. Moreover, the self-sacrificing love that Jesus tells us we should show to our neighbours and all those we meet is paralleled by the unselfish love in a married couple, both giving priority to the needs of the other and putting their own needs second, which is the only way to a happy relationship.

Love

I have met a few people who had an absolute passion for helping the poor and needy. I know of some who would not feel their life was worthwhile if they were not helping to build community in their neighbourhood. Then there are parents who sacrifice their whole lives to caring for their kids. I am not suggesting that any of us should aim to demonstrate our love in all of these ways. And we do need some leisure time. But I believe that the parallel between erotic love and Christian love makes us think again about the devotion that Jesus calls us to put into loving our neighbour, compared to the casual way we practise Christian love in our lives most of the time. Our lives would be more deeply enjoyable, and the world would be a better place, if we would only put a tenth of the energy and effort into loving our neighbours that the romantics put into their devotion to the beloved. And if we loved God like that, then every day would be a royal wedding.

Suggested hymns

A new commandment I give unto you; Hark, my soul, it is the Lord; Most glorious Lord of life; O love, that wilt not let me go.

ASCENSION, PENTECOST AND TRINITY

At this season of the year, 40, 50 and 57 days after Easter – counting inclusively, as everybody did in ancient times – we celebrate the ascension of Jesus into heaven, the descent of the Holy Spirit, and the threefold nature of God, Father, Son and Holy Spirit. These are vital doctrines, for even when we believe that Jesus rose from the dead at Easter – that is, Passover – it does not affect us until we believe that he has passed 'out of the here into the everywhere', and so is available to hear our prayers. And we are not able to pray, until we allow God the Holy Spirit to pray within us. And we cannot believe that when Jesus died and rose, it was God himself who suffers when we sin, and that it is God himself who lives in our hearts and inspires us, and that it is the same God who made us and is our Father in heaven, unless we believe that God is three and God is one. So on these days we are celebrating God's availability, God dwelling in us, and God who shows love in his very nature. Yet the language used to describe these things in days gone by is obscure to modern people. We do not talk about God being above the clouds, nor of tongues of fire on our heads, nor of separate persons having the same substance these days. So our celebration of these life-changing ideas must be combined with a search for new words in which to share them with scientifically educated folk.

Ascension Day   10 May
Up

Acts 1.1–11 The ascension (*must be used as either the first or second reading*), *or* Dan. 7.9–14 The Son of Man; Ps. 47 God has gone up, *or* Ps. 93 The Lord is king; Eph. 1.15–23 Christ is seated beside God; Luke 24.44–53 The ascension

'As [the disciples] were watching, [Jesus] was lifted up, and a cloud took him out of their sight.' Acts 1.9

Movie

'Up' is the title of an animated cartoon, centring on a grumpy old man called Carl. When he was young he had idolized an explorer who travelled in search of a place called Paradise Falls, and was never seen again. Carl's wife made him promise her that one day he himself would travel in search of the missing explorer. He is very down in the dumps, when he is ordered to go into a retirement home. He has the idea of buying thousands of inflated toy balloons, and tying them to his house, turning it into a sort of airship. Just as it is about to rise, young Russell arrives, who is a sort of Boy Scout, seeking to gain points for a badge by doing good deeds for the elderly. Carl resents Russell's interference, but somehow they are both in the house when it floats into the air and sails off towards Paradise Falls. After many adventures they eventually become friends. The story is a sort of metaphor about how, when people are feeling down, they can rise above their troubles and think on higher things.

Metaphors

Our talking is full of metaphors. In fact we can hardly speak without using metaphors in almost every sentence. Metaphors are not optional extras; they go to the very heart of our communication. One of the commonest groups is the many phrases that refer to 'up' as better, and 'down' as worse; for instance:

- 'Down in the dumps' as opposed to 'having your spirits uplifted' when you feel happier;
- 'Wake up!' and 'early to rise', both meaning that, in the daytime, wakefulness is better than sleep;
- 'He has people working under him', and 'getting on top of the situation' suggesting that being in control is better;
- 'Going up in the world' and 'at the peak of your career' indicating that promotion is good;
- 'A low trick', 'beneath me', and 'underhand', contrast with 'upstanding', 'high standards' and 'high minded' to suggest that virtue is better.

Bible

The Bible, and especially the book of Psalms, has a high-old time with metaphors suggesting that up is better:

- 'God is gone up with a merry noise';
- 'Let God arise, and let his enemies be scattered';
- 'The floods have lifted up their voice';
- 'Mine horn shall be exalted like the horn of the unicorn'.

Ascension

So, as you will already have guessed, I am going to argue that the high point of the life of Jesus is called his ascension, which we celebrate today. This does not mean that heaven is situated so many thousand feet above the surface of the earth; it is a metaphor, implying that Jesus has gone to a higher form of existence. It is right that we should identify with him in his suffering and death, but we must also be one with him in his exultation. Christianity is a religion of joy.

138

Feelings

This has a lot to teach us about how we deal with pain. We are not like the Christian Scientists who say that pain does not exist. Yes, it does, and it is very serious. You cannot just laugh it away. But if we remember that Jesus shared our pain so that we can be raised with him to happiness, we shall endure pain with a positive attitude and trust in God's loving presence with us, to support us through the pain, and either heal us or take us to a life of eternal happiness. It can easily be seen how a positive attitude in the brain can speed up the processes of healing in the other organs.

Identify

However low we may feel from time to time, if we 'put our hands in the hands of the man who stilled the water', he will raise us to a better life of love in this world, and happiness above anything we can imagine in the world to come. Christ came down to earth when he became human, and has been through hell and back for our sakes; but because he identified with us, we must identify with him in his triumph and exaltation. Remember that Jesus has raised us up with him to the very presence of God, who is above all things. You do not need to tie balloons to your house to rise 'up' in the metaphorical sense.

Suggested hymns

Christ triumphant, ever reigning; Hail the day that sees him rise; I danced in the morning; See, the conqueror mounts in triumph.

Seventh Sunday of Easter   13 May
(Sunday after Ascension Day)
Principal Service   Optimism
Acts 1.15–17, 21–26 Choosing Matthias (*must be used as either the first or second reading*), *or* Ezek. 36.24–28 I will put my Spirit in you; Ps. 1 Righteousness; 1 John 5.9–13 Faith and life; John 17.6–19 Sanctified in truth

> *'Those who believe in the Son of God have the testimony in their hearts . . . And this is the testimony: God gave us eternal life, and this life is in his Son.' 1 John 5.10–11*

Optimism

Are you an optimist or a pessimist? Optimism, according to my dictionary, is 'a disposition to take a bright, hopeful view of things'. It is the opposite of pessimism, which is 'a tendency to look on the dark side of things'. Of course, there is the old joke about the two people looking at a glass of a desirable drink that only rises half way up the sides: the optimist describes it as half-full, and the pessimist says it is half-empty! Many people have a tendency to be one or the other. Others will say, 'I am neither; I am a realist, simply accepting things as they are.' But just consider for a moment, which position is most advantageous to you and the people round you?

- **Pessimists** make themselves and everyone round them feel gloomy. They lack the will to change things for the better, which may be quite easy to improve. So things in their life may indeed continue to get worse, and it will be largely their own fault.
- **Realists** accept things as they are, but have no strong motive for changing them, and so make no impact on the world round about, which they could have done if they had taken a more positive view.
- On the other hand, **optimists** are full of hope, and want to prove themselves right by doing everything in their power to make their positive vision come true. Their hope is infectious, and others co-operate in trying to make the world, or their bit of it anyway, a better place. Of course, their vision may never come to pass; some things are on a downward slide, and there is nothing we can do about it. But having tried will make us feel better, and ready to grasp similar opportunities whenever they turn up.

Hope

So let us agree that a hopeful attitude is most likely to change our circumstances for the better, even if it is a false hope that never comes completely true. But where is this hope to come from? St Paul says that hope is one of the fruits of the Spirit; in other words we cannot become optimistic by our own efforts; we have to allow God to dwell in our hearts and inspire us. It may grow gradually, like fruit on a tree. But grow it will if we allow God to have a look-in when we are making up our minds.

Healing

I think this can mostly clearly be seen when somebody is ill. If they allow themselves to sink into gloom and despondency, they may never get better. Whereas most doctors will agree that a positive, hopeful attitude in the patient's mind will trigger and speed up the natural processes of healing which are there in everyone's bodies. The fact that they know that they are surrounded by the love and prayers of their family and friends will assist in this process, too. But the growth of hope requires faith.

Faith

God cannot help you unless you believe in him. You cannot prove that God exists, but no more can you prove that he doesn't. But if you weigh up the probabilities it is more likely that there is a God out there. Don't wait for absolute proof, but put your trust in the most likely alternative. Jesus doesn't seem like someone who would deliberately mislead us. Jesus said that he has blessed us with truth; and that God's word is truth. He said that he does not pray that God our Father would take us out of the world, but that God would protect us from harm. St Paul prayed to be healed, but he writes that God gave him an even greater blessing: the grace to bear his troubles bravely. So whereas we should pray with faith for healing, if God decides that you should go to heaven – where there is no more pain, and all is joy and happiness with those we have loved – then that is an even greater blessing. St John wrote in his first letter: 'Those who believe in the Son of God have the testimony in their hearts . . . And this is the testimony: God gave us eternal life, and this life is in his Son.' Whatever happens, it is always best to be optimistic.

All-age worship

Make up prayers for ill people to pray.

Suggested hymns

Crown him with many crowns; Hail, thou once despised Jesus; Lord, enthroned in heavenly splendour; The head that once was crowned.

Seventh Sunday of Easter   13 May

(Sunday after Ascension Day)

Second Service   **Liberation Theology**

Ps. 147.1–12 God's care; Isa. 61.1–11 The Spirit is upon me;
Luke 4.14–21 Rejected at Nazareth

> '[Jesus said,] "The Spirit of the Lord is upon me,
>   because he has anointed me
>   to bring good news to the poor.
> He has sent me to proclaim release to the captives
>   and recovery of sight to the blind,
>   to let the oppressed go free,
>   to proclaim the year of the Lord's favour . . .
> Today this scripture has been fulfilled in your hearing."' Luke 4.18–
> 19, 21

Needy

At the very beginning of his ministry, Jesus proclaimed that it was to be focused on liberating the poor and needy from their awful conditions. He quoted from the prophet Isaiah about good news for the poor, release to those in prison, and freedom for the oppressed. That implies that the followers of Jesus should be concentrating on the relief of poverty, even the elimination of poverty, in what we do as Christians. But for most of us poverty relief is an optional extra, only talked about once or twice a year. Most of us know little about the grinding poverty under which the majority of the people in the world live. We see film on television of the aftermath of natural disasters, and we hear of those who suffer as a result of war. But we are totally unaware of the lives of those in the urban slums of the developing world, or the rural population who work dawn to dusk in the fields, walk huge distances to find drinking water, and are entirely dependent on the climate giving them a good harvest if they are to have anything at all to eat next year. Many British families have overseas holidays, but never see the areas of grinding poverty. I read of one minister who was in Saigon during the Vietnam War, and visited the slums where people lived in tiny shacks pushed tightly together. There was no drainage, so the only way for adults or children to get from place to place was to teeter along the narrow planks suspended above the sewage that slurped down the tiny alleys between the shacks. It changed his whole attitude to global poverty. But most cities in the developing world have something similar.

Unchangeable?

Some people object to Christians wasting their time on this, when they should be thinking of more spiritual matters. Yet Jesus commanded us to love one another, and you cannot talk about love without putting it into practice. Once a woman anointed Jesus with precious oil, and people objected that it should have been sold and the money given to the poor. But Jesus said she had done it to anoint his body for burial, 'but the poor are always with you'. Some Christians say that means that the fight against poverty is a waste of time, because there will always be poor people around. But put it in context, and you see that Jesus said his disciples must concentrate on his coming death and resurrection first; *then* they can get on with continuing his ministry of universal love.

Liberation theology

But a few people were aware of some serious questions we need to ask: How can we talk of God as love when people are suffering daily from poverty and oppression? How can we talk of a just God when people are dying unjustly? And what does the Bible have to say to such poor and marginalized people? The care of the needy was largely ignored in the Christian Church until the mid-twentieth century, when a new way of looking at things emerged among people working on relief efforts in the favellas, or slums, of South America. They insisted that anyone who wishes to think about God must begin with practical action, ministering to the needy by bringing them food, and then encouraging them to look at the gospel from their own perspective. Mary was not a distant figure; she was a poor woman suffering as they did. This was called 'liberation theology'. Action first, then reflection. Liberation theology soon spread across the Christian world.

Britain

In this country we do valuable work through food banks to limit the effects of local poverty; and in Christian Aid week we raise funds to attack the global crisis, and also educate the general public at the same time. But the gap between comfortably rich and grindingly poor is widening in this country, and is even worse when you consider it on a world scale. The only way we can halt the spread of emigration and wars is if we seriously seek to raise the living standards in other countries until they approach our own. God loves our poor neighbours. We cannot truly say we love God if we do not actively love those whom God loves.

Suggested hymns

For the healing of the nations; In a world where people walk in darkness; Inspired by love and anger; Jesus Christ is waiting, waiting in the streets.

Day of Pentecost (Whit Sunday) 20 May
Principal Service Coming of Age

Acts 2.1–21 The day of Pentecost (*must be used as either the first or second reading*), *or* Ezek. 37.1–14 The valley of dry bones; Ps. 104.26–36, 37b The Spirit in creation; Rom. 8.22–27 The Spirit's prayer; John 15.26–27; 16.4b–15 The Advocate will lead you to truth

> *'We ourselves, who have the first fruits of the Spirit, groan inwardly, while we wait for the adoption, the redemption of our bodies.' Romans 8.23*

Legal

Suppose a child has a rich uncle who dies and leaves all his money to them. That sounds like good news, but it could be disastrous. If somebody didn't stop them, the child could spend it all at once on something they didn't really want, get into bad habits, then finish up deeply in debt, complaining, 'Why didn't you stop me?' To prevent this happening, laws were passed that when a 'minor' inherits, the money must be put into the hands of trustees, until they are old enough, and, we hope, responsible enough, to look after their own affairs. This usually happens when they reach the age of 21, and we call it 'coming of age'. Of course, that phrase is used in other circumstances too; anybody who is considered mature enough to make their own decisions is said to have 'come of age'.

Rome

When St Paul wrote to the Romans, the law there was slightly different. Land and property were so important to them, that if a property-owner was near death and had no adult heirs, he might adopt someone who was responsible but poor, but no relation to them, a slave, even, and appoint him his son, with full power over his property. Distant relatives had no rights at all. This was quite common among rich people, even emperors. So when God is spoken of as adopting us as his children, what a tremendous honour that is! It means God is redeeming us out of slavery to bad habits, and entrusting us with all his riches, to which we have no rights, treating us from now on as his favourite children!

First fruits

Only, in the passage I read to you, it hasn't quite happened yet. The immature Christians in Rome have what Paul calls the first fruits, the early stages, of our inheritance. The metaphors are getting a bit confused now, but in another passage Paul says they have the fruits of the Spirit: love, joy, peace, patience, kindness, goodness, faithfulness, gentleness and self-control. So when they come of age, obviously, they will inherit the fullness of the Holy Spirit, with the right to take full control of their bodies and their lives.

We ourselves, who have the first fruits of the Spirit, groan inwardly, while we wait for the adoption, the redemption of our bodies.

Mature

Do you think you are mature yet? God does, if you have been confirmed. Confirmation is the Christian 'coming of age ceremony'. We confirm children at a surprisingly low age. But that is a very good thing, because it makes them feel the weight of responsibility. We give them a course in the basic principle of your faith. Then the bishop says, 'You're on your own now, Bud.' Or something like that. Up until now your parents and godparents have told you what is right and what is wrong. Now you have to make your own decisions, through the power of the Holy Spirit. The neurologists produce evidence from brain scans that there is a complete change in the brain's architecture between childhood, adolescence and adulthood. What we have to do, with the Holy Spirit's aid, is to adjust responsibly to those changes, and not try like Peter Pan to remain a child for ever.

Adults

So all you mature, adult Christians in this congregation, have you realized what happened to you all those years ago, at the rite of passage that we call confirmation? God pulled the carpet from under your feet. No more laws telling you, 'Do this, don't do that.' Instead, God has given you the Holy Spirit to enable you to make up your own mind. When you have a choice to make between two courses of action, ask God's Holy Spirit, who lives in your heart, to help you decide which is the more loving way to behave. 'What would Jesus do?' You can look at the Bible for precedents, but the final choice is yours, inspired by the Spirit. That's a bit scary, but it's also incredible liberating. Try putting it into practice over some choices that confront you, today.

All-age worship

Make yourself a paper bracelet reading, 'WWJD: What would Jesus do?' Discuss some decisions you may have to take; how would you apply that principle?

Suggested hymns

Gracious Spirit, Holy Ghost; Holy Spirit, come confirm us; O thou who camest from above; Spirit divine, attend our prayers.

Day of Pentecost   (Whit Sunday)   20 May
Second Service   **You Have a Body, You Are a Soul**
Morning Ps. 145 One shall tell another; Evening Ps. 139.1–11 [13–18, 23–24] God is present in death; Ezek. 36.22–28 I will put my spirit within you; Acts 2.22–38 You will receive the Spirit; *Gospel at Holy Communion*: John 20.19–23 He breathed on them

> '[Jesus] breathed on [the disciples], and said, "Receive the Holy Spirit."' John 20.22

Agnostics

Strictly speaking, the definition of an 'agnostic' is somebody who has studied all the evidence and come to the conclusion that it will never be possible to prove that there is a God or there is not. In which case the logical thing to do would be to say, 'Now I shall live as if there is a God, for the effects of living as though there isn't, if there is, are far more serious than those of living as if there is, if there isn't!' Only, few people follow their logic to its conclusion like that. In fact, most people who call themselves agnostics are just too lazy to think things through. There is an old joke about an agnostic of the second, lazy, type, who realized that he was on his deathbed, and uttered an agonized prayer: 'Oh God – if there is a God – have mercy on my soul – if I have a soul!'

Soul

In fact the Bible never answers the question, 'Do we have a soul?' In the Hebrew language there is a word pronounced '*nefesh*', which is sometimes translated soul, sometimes spirit, sometimes being, sometimes breath. In Genesis 2, the second account of creation, but not in Genesis 1, we read: 'The Lord God formed man from the dust of the ground, and breathed into his nostrils the breath of life, and the man became a living being.' But in chapter 1, it says that the earth is full of living creatures that have the breath of life. So it would best be translated as the 'life-force'; there is nothing distinctively human about it. But the Greek philosophers regarded humans as a soul, there pronounced '*psyche*', imprisoned in a body, and only released after death. The early Christians refused to accept this idea. In the New Testament, however, there is some evidence of the human soul surviving death: 'By your endurance you will gain your souls.' Some scientists tried to weigh a human body before and after it died, and decided what the soul's weight is, but their results were not borne out by subsequent experiments. So it is best for practical purposes and clearness of understanding to regard the soul as not a material thing, like the body, but that aspect of our being that can form a relationship with God, and can therefore receive God's gift of life after death. The soul is the whole of our living being, except the material, bodily part.

Soul–body

So the agnostic who wondered whether he had a soul was barking up the wrong tree. It would be better to say that each of us *has* a body, and each of us *is* a soul. It is best to recognize that many other people

147

use those words in different ways, however, but if we ourselves keep to that rule, at least *we* shall know what we are talking about.

Holy Spirit

The minds of the disciples when Jesus gave them the Holy Spirit in the upper room must have flown back to Genesis 2. *Then*, God breathed into Adam and he became a living soul; *now* '[Jesus] breathed on [the disciples], and said, "Receive the Holy Spirit."' So there is a connection between the gift of life and the gift of the Spirit. It is confusing to say, as some do, that human beings are living spirits; better say we are living souls who receive the gift of the Spirit. While we are here on earth, the gift of the Holy Spirit gives us an entirely new dimension to our lives, bringing us new levels of closeness to God, new joy, inspiration and insight. When we die, we shall be one with the God who created us. Jesus breathed into us, and we speak with God's breath. Others ask us to help them, and we share with them the life of God that we have received. We feel incapable, and then find that we can do anything through the life of God that Jesus has breathed into us. Remember, each of us *is* a soul; each of us *has* a body; and each of us *has received* the gift of the Spirit.

Suggested hymns

Breathe on me, breath of God; Our blest Redeemer, ere he breathed; Tell out, my soul, the greatness of the Lord; Wind, wind, blow on me.

Trinity Sunday   27 May
Principal Service   Lord of the Dance

Isa. 6.1–8 Holy, holy, holy; Ps. 29 God's greatness; Rom. 8.12–17 The Spirit makes us heirs of God, with Christ; John 3.1–17 Born of the Spirit

> *'Seraphs were in attendance above him; each had six wings: with two they covered their faces, and with two they covered their feet, and with two they flew. And one called to another and said: Holy, holy, holy is the* Lord *of hosts; the whole earth is full of his glory.' Isaiah 6.2–3*

Noise

We usually think of holy places as being deathly quiet and still. But in the famous description in the book of the prophet Isaiah of the Temple in Jerusalem, there is a lot going on. The Bible just says that 'Seraphs were in attendance', but it doesn't say how many. Artists usually reduce it to three, but it could have been a whole throng. They were flying about, and singing. Sounds pretty noisy to me. Of course, this is a vision that the prophet saw, of legendary creatures, but there is no reason why we shouldn't conceive of the invisible God as a scene with plenty of movement.

Trinity

Christians have always regarded this vision of the prophet as an image of God the Holy Trinity, because the heavenly creatures cried out 'Holy' three times, reminding us of God the Father, God the Son, and God the Holy Spirit, three Persons but one God. I want to suggest that there is a very good reason for this.

Unity

Have you ever had an experience in which you have felt an absolutely free individual, yet completely at one with the people around you? It could be when people are cheering at a sporting occasion. Once, before the Beatles made him famous, Ravi Shankar gave a sitar concert in Singapore. The half of the audience who were of Indian origin knew exactly what to expect; but the Europeans and Chinese had never heard anything like it before. Yet they were all caught up in a wave of emotion in which they felt a tremendous unity with each other. This feeling is even stronger if you are taking part in the music yourself, in a choir or an orchestra. You still have your individual voice, but it is swept up into a corporate experience in which you feel that you are all performing as one unit. Does that help you to understand that in the Godhead there are three distinct Persons, but only one God?

Dance

So I want to take one final illustration, and that is from the world of dance. Many of you may have no talents at all as dancers. But with a bit of imagination, you can conceive how a roomful of people could be so emotionally united in the movements of a dance, whether strictly ballroom or any other sort, that you feel that all those people have combined into one soul, while each keeps their individual personality. There have been numerous attempts to explain the doctrine of the Trinity in terms of dance. First let us remind ourselves what that doctrine is. We experience God in three ways:

- We experience God in the creation around us, and call him God the Father, the Creator of all that exists.
- We experience God in the life and teaching of Jesus, calling him God the Son.
- We experience God active in our hearts, inspiring us to say and do things we could not have done on our own. We call this God the Holy Spirit.
- Yet although we experience God in these three ways, there are not three separate Gods, but three Persons in one God.

There have been many attempts to describe God as dancing. The most famous is the hymn, 'Lord of the Dance'. *Perichoresis* is a theological term meaning 'the dance of God', all three persons of the Trinity interrelating in a totally harmonious fluid way. C. S. Lewis, in his book *Mere Christianity*, described the Trinity as a 'dance', saying, 'God is not a static thing . . . but a dynamic, pulsating activity, a life, almost . . . a kind of dance.'

Illustration

This illustration may help you to understand how God can be three and at the same time one. If not, don't worry. God is infinite, so beyond our capability to describe in mere human words. We can never understand him, only adore him and praise him. And that also is the meaning of Isaiah's vision of the mythical creatures singing 'Holy, Holy, Holy is the Lord God of hosts. The whole earth is full of his glory.'

All-age worship

Create a series of dance movements in threes, each holding the other two's hands in theirs. What does this say of God's three ways of helping us, while remaining one God?

Suggested hymns

Bright the vision which delighted; Father, we adore you; Holy holy, holy holy; I danced in the morning.

See notes at: http://www.prismleadership.org/trinitarian-dance/

Trinity Sunday   27 May
Second Service   **Twins in the Womb**
(For Corpus Christi, the Thursday after Trinity Sunday, see page 314.)
Morning Ps. 33.1–12 All earth's inhabitants; Evening Ps. 104.1–10
God's greatness; Ezek. 1.4–10, 22–28a A vision of God; Rev. 4.1–11
Holy, holy, holy; *Gospel at Holy Communion*: Mark 1.1–13 The
Father sends the Spirit on the Son

> *'Like the bow in a cloud on a rainy day, such was the appearance of the splendour all around. This was the appearance of the likeness of the glory of the* LORD.*' Ezekiel 1.28a*

Vision

The prophet Ezekiel had a vision of God. He tried to describe what he had seen, and failed. He wrote phrases like 'the appearance of the likeness of . . .' to show that he was lost for words: God looks something like a rainbow, but not exactly. Many people have the same problem: they believe there is a God, but he is so much greater than we are, that mere human words are quite inadequate to describe the indescribable, infinite God. On Trinity Sunday we use all sorts of difficult words to describe 'Father, Son and Holy Spirit, three Persons in one God'. So more sceptical people protest, 'How can you expect me to believe in God if you cannot see him or describe him? It's like asking me to believe in fairies!'

Facebook

There is a very funny piece on Facebook which illustrates this dilemma. It was written in Hungarian and translated into English, and has given many people a good laugh. It describes two twins talking to each other before they have been born; they are still in their mother's womb. They are discussing not what grown people would talk about, the question as to whether there is life after death. No, these two foetuses are discussing whether or not there is life after *birth*.

Discussion

One of the twins is adamant. He is quite sure that this foetal life, where they can see and touch the walls of the womb, is all there is. 'When birth takes us,' he insists, 'we just cease to exist. When this life comes to an end,' he says to his twin, 'there is nothing more, nothing beyond it.' The other answers, 'No, you're wrong, of course there is life after birth. I really think we are here to prepare us for the next life. Otherwise, why do we have these arms and legs? I believe they are there so that in the next world, we can walk on the legs, eat with our mouths, and reach out to other people with our arms.' 'Nonsense,' snapped the other, 'walking is impossible, and how could we eat with that ridiculous mouth?' 'Well,' replied the other, 'I'm not sure what happens in the next life, but I expect the mother will help us.'

Sceptic

I think you can guess what is coming next. The more sceptical twin raises his voice: 'Believe in Mother! Of course I don't. You'd be a fool to believe in Mother. You'll be asking me whether I believe in Santa Claus, next. I can't see Mother, what reason would I have to believe in her?' The other says, wistfully, 'I may not be able to see Mother, but I can feel her all around me.'

Unbeliever

The unbeliever laughs at his twin. 'Now, if you're asking me to make life-changing decisions on the basis of subjective feelings, you're going too far! If there was life after birth, you would expect there to be some positive evidence. Nobody has come back to this world from the next life to tell us about it. Anyway, we are totally dependent on our umbilical cords for our nourishment, and look at them: the umbilical cords are far too short to bring us food after we have left this place. We would starve before the day was out.' 'Well,' said the other twin, 'I'm sorry, I can't help it, I really do believe in Mother. I believe that we live within Mother. If you are quiet, you can feel her love, feel her caress, and hear her song as she sings to us.'

Conclusion

The story ends there. It is quaint, isn't it? But if you think about it, the arguments that the sceptical twin in the womb gives for not believing in Mother are almost exactly the ones that many adult humans, called 'atheists', give for not believing in God – and they are rubbish. Whereas the believers, although we may not be able to prove the existence of God, can produce evidence that weighs down the scales of probability firmly on the side of belief. And all this we can learn from two unborn twins in the womb! God bless you all.

Suggested hymns

Firmly I believe and truly; Holy, holy, holy! Lord God Almighty!; Immortal, invisible, God only wise; There is a Redeemer.

See mylifeyoga.com/2013/04/13/two-twins-talking-in-the-womb/

ORDINARY TIME:

There is no such thing as 'Ordinary Time'! Every day is special in some way, and every Sunday in the year is a celebration. In Bible times, days ran from sunset to sunset, and the first generation of Jewish Christians probably worshipped in the synagogues together with their non-Christian Jewish friends in the morning of the Sabbath, which was Saturday. Then they had a special time of worship of their own on the same evening, which was technically Sunday, the 'first day of the week', to celebrate the Resurrection of Jesus on that day. Later, when the majority of Christians were Gentiles, they had no day off, so they could only meet together for worship in the evenings.

But there are no major festivals between Trinity Sunday and the beginning of Advent, so the custom grew up in the Roman Catholic Church of calling these Sundays, 'Sundays in Ordinary Time.' In Britain, White or Gold vestments and hangings were kept for Festivals, Red for Saints and Pentecost, and Violet for Advent and Lent. So in Ordinary Time, they were in Green, the colour of steady growth. This, then, is a time for educating congregations in the basics of the Christian Faith. But in the Church of England, when *Common Worship* was published in 2000, the Sundays in this season continued to be named Sundays after Trinity, as they had

---

been in the *Book of Common Prayer.* As if this were not confusing enough, the readings were drawn from the Common Lectionary of the Roman Catholic Church, though this was edited and renamed the Revised Common Lectionary, and the readings 'Proper' (i.e. appropriate) to the various Sundays in Ordinary Time were called Proper 4, Proper 5, etc. (Propers 1, 2 and 3 are occasionally used between Epiphany and Lent if Ash Wednesday is late.) Then at the Principal Service, churches can choose between readings in the Continuous or the Related sequences. The first Old Testament reading and Psalm given from Proper 4 to Proper 25 is the Continuous Sequence, working steadily through the same book over several Sundays; the second one is 'Related' to the theme of the Gospel Reading. Since I don't know which sequence you are using in your church I have tried to avoid basing the sermons in this book on the Old Testament readings in Ordinary Time. It is a good idea to use The Continuous sequence for three years, and then switch to the Related sequence for the next three years.

Confused? All you have to do is turn to the calendar inside the front and back covers of this book, to see what Sunday it is, what the Proper readings are, and what colour the hangings should be. Then turn to the sermon suggested here to see at a glance what the readings are at each service on that day, with a two or three word summary of what the theme of each reading is. There is always something to celebrate, even in Ordinary Time.

The first Old Testament reading given from Proper 4 to Proper 25 is the (Continuous) Sequence; the second one is (Related) to the Gospel Reading.

First Sunday after Trinity (Proper 4)   3 June
Principal Service   **Sabbath**
(*Continuous*): 1 Sam. 3.1–10 [11–20] Samuel hears God's call, Ps. 139.1–5, 12–18 Known in the womb; or (*Related*): Deut. 5.12–15 Commandments five to ten; Ps. 81.1–10 Salvation and law; 2 Cor. 4.5–12 Clay pots; Mark 2.23—3.6 Healing on the Sabbath, hardness of heart

'[Jesus said,] "The sabbath was made for humankind, and not humankind for the sabbath; so the Son of Man is lord even of the sabbath."' Mark 2.27–28

Internet

The internet is a wonderful thing. It enables us to access information in an instant, which would otherwise take us hours consulting reference books in a library. It gives us answers to questions from the simple to the profound. The web attracts us to take an interest in subjects we might otherwise have ignored. We can compare and buy online necessary things that would have taken us hours before in searching from shop to shop to find. But like all good things the internet can be misused. It can prevent us from thinking for ourselves. It can spread misinformation. It can oversimplify complicated problems. It can turn us into shopaholics, buying things we don't really need simply because we saw them advertised on the web.

Social media

The same applies to an even greater extent to emails and the social media. Emails enable us to send a message to our friends in seconds, which would previously have taken several days through the Royal Mail. We can keep in touch with people we would otherwise have had no time to write to. Social media enable us to carry on a continuous conversation with people who live miles away. But the result sometimes is that people can keep their noses glued to their mobile devices all day, and fail to interact with the world and the people around them. What I call the anti-social media can promote shallow online relationships, with the result that some people forget how to achieve strong face-to-face and serious friendships with people who really matter to us. Facebook and Twitter have been used to organize revolutions, some necessary, some that brought unending misery.

Sabbath

There is another example of good things that can be misused, in the teaching of Jesus. The commandment to keep the Sabbath day holy was intended so as to allow every labourer at least one day off work out of every seven, and provide everyone with some family time, and a chance to think about God and pray to him. But some of the Pharisees had turned it into a minefield of prohibitions, so that Jesus was criticized for doing good things on the Sabbath such as plucking food from the wayside, or even healing the sick, because they were counted as work. Jesus replied:

The sabbath was made for humankind, and not humankind for the sabbath; so the Son of Man is lord even of the sabbath.

Apart from the rather clumsy attempt at inclusive language in this translation, this verse offers us an important principle: things that were intended to be of benefit to people should not be misused to be harmful. We can apply this to the internet and social media. Jesus, however, applies it to the provision of a weekly day off.

Distractions

More and more we need a break from the endless distractions of modern life. We may envy modern Jews, who use the Sabbath to have a complete break from modern technology. They switch off their computers or tablets; televisions and smartphones are not turned on; and time is released for conversations with their family around the meal table, and, at the synagogue, with their co-religionists and with God. Even if you find it impracticable to be quite so self-denying, you could resolve to resist the invasion of modern technology on Sundays, and use the time saved to have some prayer to God, whether silently or aloud. Best of all is if you can make a solemn resolution to be in church for an hour *every* Sunday, except when you are ill, or going to another church on holiday. In church, you will find short periods of silence in which to meditate, and readings from the Scriptures from which to get messages from God to meditate on. But in church, the world of mobile phones and computers is far away, and you will find the whole quality of your life is changing.

All-age worship

Have some quiet time, then pray aloud to God in your own words.

Suggested hymns

On this day, the first of days; There's a quiet understanding; This is the day the Lord has made; This is the day, this is the day.

First Sunday after Trinity (Proper 4)   3 June
Second Service   **Authority**
Ps. 35 You deliver the weak; Jer. 5.1–19 God looks for justice;
Rom. 7.7–25 Law and sin; *Gospel at Holy Communion*: Luke 7.1–10
The centurion's boy (*If this sermon is preached, this Gospel must be one of the readings.*)

> '[The centurion said to Jesus,] "Only speak the word, and let my servant be healed. For I also am a man set under authority, with soldiers under me; and I say to one, 'Go', and he goes, and to another, 'Come', and he comes, and to my slave, 'Do this', and the slave does it."' Luke 7.7–8

Growing up

The problem of authority first arises when a child is told by his or her parents, 'Don't do that!' Yet the process of growing up is meant to be one of learning to be independent; how is this to be reconciled with obedience? In adult life, if you are too obedient to your employer you may be taken for granted as the 'willing horse'; yet as soon as you are given authority, you realize that it is impossible to get anything done unless your orders are obeyed. There are related problems; must one obey the state if it orders you to fight in a war you do not believe in?

Authority

To analyse all these situations we must see that they all have in common the question: what is proper authority? Next we must be able to see both sides. An army unit used deliberately to promote in rank all the trouble-makers, so that they could appreciate what disobedience means when you are one of those who give the orders! It has been said that leadership is the art of sitting on the fence with one ear to the ground – a very uncomfortable position! We can see what would be the results if everybody disobeyed. A naval officer once saw a wire rope about to snap, and shouted 'Lie flat!' His crew obeyed at once; if they had stopped to question they would all have been killed. The novel *Lord of the Flies* by William Golding tells of a group of castaway schoolboys, and how, when authority breaks down, they revert to savages. So perhaps we should obey even a bad authority just to avoid anarchy.

Excessive

Yet what would happen if there were excessive obedience? If employees obeyed their employers when they ordered them to cheat? Would working conditions have improved if there had been no strikes? Is there not a duty to revolt against tyranny? There is a similar problem for the leaders: if you are excessively firm with those under you, they become either resentful or lacking in initiative. Yet if you are excessively lax, those under you will feel insecure. Or laxity also may lead to anarchy; the trouble with feet of clay in a leader is that you can turn them to face any way you like.

Bible

What has Christianity to say to this dilemma? Jesus quoted 'Honour your father and mother'; and warned us against trying to wriggle out of that responsibility by an over-scrupulous conscience. Yet he also criticized excessive control by the family over the individual: he called his disciples to leave their parents, saying, 'Let the dead bury their dead.' He warned of divisions in the family which could be caused by Christianity. Similarly, the Bible tells us to obey the state: 'Honour the Emperor . . . Render unto Caesar . . . the powers that be are ordained of God.' Yet, at the same time, it warns of the downfall of evil authorities: 'Fallen, fallen, is Babylon the great.'

Love

The apparent contradiction is, however, resolved by the commandment to love. If we love God as our Father, we come to see what a good father should be, and how his children should treat him. We see that good leaders do not arouse resentment, because they understand and sympathize with those they lead, and give them only such orders as are necessary. Good followers will obey gladly, because they have sufficient insight into their leaders' position to know that they only give orders in love, in order to help everyone. All authority comes from God; it should be exercised like his authority and obeyed like his authority.

Leadership

So the Christian insight into the problem of authority is that we need leaders. But they must lead by example, and courteously, from love for the individuals under them. Those who follow must obey gladly, in order that society should work smoothly, from love for their fellows. Unless, that is, the order given is clearly immoral, when love will cause Christians to argue, and, if need be, disobey and face the consequences, acknowledging the leader's right to punish.

Suggested hymns

For the healing of the nations; Judge eternal, throned in splendour; Lord of lords and King eternal; O Lord of earth and altar.

Second Sunday after Trinity (Proper 5)   10 June
Principal Service   **Original Sin**
(*Continuous*): 1 Sam. 8.4–11 [12–15] 16–20 [11.14–15] King Saul anointed, Ps. 138 God's greatness; *or* (*Related*): Gen. 3.8–15 God in the Garden of Eden, Ps. 130 Hope for salvation; 2 Cor. 4.13—5.1 Grace, suffering and resurrection; Mark 3.20–35 Family, obedience

> *'Just as we have the same spirit of faith that is in accordance with scripture – 'I believed, and so I spoke' – we also believe, and so we speak, because we know that the one who raised the Lord Jesus will raise us also with Jesus, and will bring us with you into his presence. Yes, everything is for your sake, so that grace, as it extends to more and more people, may increase thanksgiving, to the glory of God.' 2 Corinthians 4.13–15*

Death

The first few chapters in the Bible tell the story of 'Adam'; the word simply means 'the human race'. We are not accustomed to learning important truths by means of fiction, but that was the normal way of teaching in those days, and unless we accept it we shall miss many of the profound lessons that ancient literature conveys. So God intended human beings to be immortal, but he gave them free will to decide how to behave. Inevitably they disobeyed his command, wanting in their curiosity to explore the depths of evil. So God punished them by taking away their immortality, and they and all their descendants, like you and me, could only live a limited number of years. It is an important lesson to learn, that all our troubles spring from our own self-centredness; but the story is not historically true.

As the fossil record shows, almost every species dies at some time, thus making room for more variants, and enabling the ones most fitted to their environment to replace the less appropriate strains. Miraculously, through this process, God caused human beings to emerge, who were capable of thought, choice, and a relationship with God.

Paul

St Paul was brought up on the Adam and Eve story; he could not talk about evolution because God had not yet revealed that theory. And he had a very clear way of explaining how God gives us good things: we don't earn them. They are God's free gift, arising out of his kindness; Paul calls it God's 'grace'. We all inherit the curse of death, Paul wrote, because we are descended from Adam; we can all become immortal through God's grace if we believe in Jesus and accept God's forgiveness for our own selfishness. This teaching was a colossal leap forward in our understanding of God.

Inherited?

But the Bible itself teaches individual responsibility. This didn't stop Christians down the ages from developing elaborate theories of how we have all inherited the guilt of Adam's sin, which they called the 'original sin'. Original sin is the sinfulness of earlier generations of humans and the effect it has on people today. When Adam was thought of as an historical individual, his disobedience was regarded as the original sin that infected the whole human race. Among those Christians who see the story of Eden as a metaphor for universal sin there is debate on what effects one person's sin has on others and how these are passed on.

- Gnostics believed that the whole material world is evil.
- St Augustine taught that the lust involved in begetting children conveyed sinfulness to them, reducing though not destroying our free will.
- Peter Abelard denied that guilt can be inherited. Because of sin, humans are no longer in the image of God, and it is harder to draw on God's grace.
- St Anselm taught that begetting, not lust, passes on Adam's loss of original righteousness.

- St Thomas Aquinas declared that Adam lost supernatural gifts, but the original 'pure nature' was passed on to his descendants. Our desires can be controlled by the will and by reason. But we all share the corporate guilt of the human race.

Self-centred

Most Christians would argue that human beings are born self-centred in order to survive. This selfishness has to be controlled by education, so that we may live together as a community. The example of others predisposes us to sin; the influence of society constrains but does not remove our free will. We may well feel ashamed for the sins of our ancestors, but guilt cannot be inherited; we have individual responsibility for our actions.

All-age worship

Bring some dolls, and imagine they are old enough to say, 'Mummy, I want this'; 'Daddy, give me that.' If you were their parents, what would you say to them? Does God sometimes have to say that to us?

Suggested hymns

Be thou my guardian and my guide; Dear Lord and Father of mankind; Just as I am, without one plea; O for a closer walk with God.

Second Sunday after Trinity (Proper 5)   10 June
Second Service   Calling Somebody a Jeremiah
Ps. 37.1–11 [12–17] Trust in the Lord; Jer. 6.16–21 Ask for the ancient paths; Rom. 9.1–13 God and Israel; *Gospel at Holy Communion*: Luke 7.11–17

> *Hear, O earth; I am going to bring disaster on this people,*
>   *the fruit of their schemes,*
> *because they have not given heed to my words;*
>   *and as for my teaching, they have rejected it.' Jeremiah 6.19*

Names

What's in a name? Some people's surnames became famous household names, which could be an honour but mostly was a curse:

- Biró gave us the ballpoint pen.
- Blanket was a fourteenth-century weaver.
- Bowdler produced a version of Shakespeare suitable for respectable families.
- The Bowler brothers made hats.
- Mr Boycott was ostracized by his neighbours.
- General Burnside had a hairstyle that turned into sideburns.
- Thomas Crapper was a Victorian inventor of flush-toilets.
- Diesel invented an engine.
- Herr Dobermann bred a fierce guard-dog.
- Léotard invented a gymnastic outfit.
- Lynch formed a mob who took the law into their own hands.
- A McJob is in the dictionary as a low-paid job with few prospects, much to the annoyance of McDonalds Restaurants
- About Messrs Mugger and Hooligan I need say nothing.
- Quisling was a Norwegian who collaborated with the Nazis.
- Alphonse Sax invented the saxophone.

Those were all real people; then there are a lot of fictional characters who are generally remembered as a symbol of a particular characteristic: a Scrooge, a Mrs Mopp, and many others.

Bible

There are many people in the Bible whose names have been famous, from a Judas to a Jeremiah. Poor Jeremiah, he was quite a cheerful person until God sent him to announce the doom of his people in some forthcoming disasters, which he saw as God's punishment for their sins. So now, anyone who is a bit gloomy is told, 'Oh, don't be such a Jeremiah!' He lived through a bad period of history, under some appalling kings of Judah, and he would have been failing in his duty to God if he had not rebuked them. But it was gradually becoming a less monarchic and dictatorial society, yet all the people in high places were as corrupt as the kings, and refused to listen when he spoke to them of God:

> Hear, O earth; I am going to bring disaster on this people,
>   the fruit of their schemes,
> because they have not given heed to my words;
>   and as for my teaching, they have rejected it.

Jeremiah

Jeremiah was a priest from Anathoth, in Judah, from about 630 to 586 BC. He wrote some of the most intimate autobiographical passages in the whole of ancient literature. When Jeremiah was about 21 years old, Jehoahaz, whom Jeremiah called Shallum, reigned for three months. His successor was Jehoiakim; when Jeremiah dictated his somewhat critical poems to the scribe called Baruch, Jehoiakim, in a rage, burnt the scroll in the fire. Soon after this, Jeremiah began to predict that the kingdom of Judah would be taken into Babylon as exiles. First the Babylonian King Nebuchadnezzar deported 3,023 Jews to Babylon. The Jewish King Jehoiachin reigned for only three months in Jerusalem; Jeremiah called him Jeconiah, and/or Coniah; he was exiled to Babylon; Jeremiah wrote to the exiles advising them to work for the prosperity of their new home. In 598, King Zedekiah was enthroned King of the Jews – Jeremiah calls him the 'Righteous Branch'. Zedekiah reneged on a promise to free all the slaves; he sent messengers to Jeremiah; Jeremiah said those Jews left in Jerusalem were 'rotten figs'. When Zedekiah rebelled, the Babylonian King Nebuchadnezzar besieged Jerusalem. Jeremiah was confined in a sort of house-arrest; he bought a field, to show that life would go on after the war; Zedekiah was blinded by the Babylonian soldiers; he and 832 people were deported to Babylon; King Zedekiah died in captivity. The Babylonians appointed Gedaliah Governor of Jerusalem, and Jeremiah was released, taken to Ramah, then set free; an insurrection was raised against Gedaliah. In 587 Jerusalem was totally destroyed, the Temple furnishings were taken to Babylon; many of the priests and other leading citizens were killed. Soon after, another 745 Jews were deported, and Jeremiah was taken to Tahpanhes in Egypt. The so-called 'Lamentations of Jeremiah' are in a very different style and must have been written by somebody else. So no wonder Jeremiah was angry and sad at times; but there are many beautiful passages of hope woven into the texture of his writings. Could you remain hopeful while living a life like his?

Suggested hymns

All my hope on God is founded; Lord of all hopefulness, woe; Through the night of doubt and sorrow.

Third Sunday after Trinity (Proper 6)   17 June
Principal Service   **God's Sense of Humour**

(*Continuous*): 1 Sam. 15.34—16.13 David anointed king, Ps. 20
Give victory to the king; *or* (*Related*): Ezek. 17.22–24 God's call,
Ps. 92.1–4, 12–15 Righteousness; 2 Cor. 5.6–10 [11–13] 14–17 Faith,
life and death; Mark 4.26–34 Parables of the kingdom

> *'With many . . . parables [Jesus] spoke the word to [the crowds],*
> *as they were able to hear it; he did not speak to them except in*
> *parables.' Mark 4.33–34*

Parables

The Sunday school definition of a parable is 'An earthly story with
a heavenly meaning.' St Mark tells us: 'With many . . . parables
[Jesus] spoke the word to [the crowds], as they were able to hear
it.' Earthly stories they understood; high philosophy or advanced
theology would have gone over their heads. This is how God made
us, that we can all get our minds around the things we see every
day. Then we think about them for a bit, and out of the blue, the
heavenly meaning of the story comes to us. Philosophy and theology are useful tools for deep reflection. But for easily absorbed lessons that you can apply to the decisions that you have to make in
your own life, there is nothing to beat a good story.

Jokes

Jesus told stories about the agricultural life of his day, because
that was what the crowds were familiar with. A farmer planted
seed, Jesus said, and the seeds grew into wheat, and he thought
'How clever I am; I did that all by myself!' The crowd laughed,
knowing that God had done it, and the farmer could do nothing without God. Neither could *we* have achieved the things we
boast about without God's help – what fools we are! Jesus also
compared the kingdom of God on earth – approximately what we
call the Church – to a tiny seed of mustard, which people despise
because it is so small and weak. 'Wait and see,' said Jesus, 'it will
grow into a tall plant which birds from all over the world can find
a home in' – in the Holy Land the mustard plants grow as tall as
a man. The crowd probably laughed when Jesus said that too, at

their own lack of faith. For most of the parables were *funny* stories: we could say that Jesus never preached without capping his remarks with a joke!

Laughter

That is why a sense of humour is essential in a Christian. When people were drafted into the armed services in the last war, or National Service afterwards, and they grumbled, they teased each other, saying, 'If you haven't got a sense of humour you shouldn't have joined.' The joke was, of course, that they had had no choice in the matter. Similarly, if God hasn't got a sense of humour, he shouldn't have created the world! He must have plenty of things to grumble about when he sees what we've done to it; but Jesus shows us that God can also see the funny side. Parents love to hear children's laughter; so I hope God smiles when he hears us his children having a good laugh, too. Here are two little poems to make you smile. The first is by a female minister:

Thank God for laughter, and thank God for mirth;
he didn't forget them when he made the earth.
Look at creation. God's nature can joke;
see a goose waddling, or hear a frog croak.

Thank God for laughter, and thank God for wit;
pure, clean and simple, it's always a hit;
just see the bright side, and laugh off the drear,
for laughter is holy and God likes to hear.

Thank God for laughter, and thank God for fun;
thank God for talent in making a pun;
God wants us happy, not deep in the blues,
so he gave us laughter and things to amuse.

And here's a grace by a retired Church of England vicar:

O Lord, your Son was called on earth 'that fellow there who spends
far too much time in dining and in wining with his friends';
be with us when we gather, bless the things we eat and drink,
and help us to enjoy ourselves in all we say and think;
and since we can be certain that among us are some folks

who'll tell us funny stories and crack rather risqué jokes,
we have to ask you in advance and humbly, Lord, that you'll
forgive us if our laughter is unseemly, hard, or cruel;
but you must often laugh at us, so help us heartily
to laugh at jokes that show us, Lord, what fools we mortals be.

All-age worship

*Say and do things to make each other laugh. When does God smile
to hear us laugh, and when does it make him sad?*

Suggested hymns

*Rejoice in the Lord always; Tell me the old, old story; The kingdom
of God is justice and joy; The kingdom is upon you.*

Third Sunday after Trinity (Proper 6)   17 June
Second Service   The Object of the Exercise
Ps. 39 Let me know my end; Jer. 7.1–16 Morality, not nationalism;
Rom. 9.14–26 God and his people; *Gospel at Holy Communion*:
Luke 7.36—8.3 Jesus and women

> 'The scripture says to Pharaoh, 'I have raised you up for the very
> purpose of showing my power in you, so that my name may be
> proclaimed in all the earth.' Romans 9.17

Military manoeuvres

In the British army, they used to organize regular manoeuvres, or
'exercises', when large groups of soldiers move about the countryside, on foot or by lorry. I do not know whether they still do things
like this. One officer used to be charged with drawing up a detailed
plan, listing who was to move where and when, by what transport;
what the chain of command was, and how the units communicate
with one another; and above all, at the head of the paper, was 'The
object of the exercise'. This may be that a particular unit should gain
experience of a type of warfare, or accommodation, or transport; or
that different units may have experience of fighting alongside each
other. But there is no sense in having all those soldiers wandering
aimlessly across the area if they have no idea what the purpose is.

Purpose in life

The same applies to the whole of life. Aimlessness is a waste of time; a waste of the talents that God has given us. Yes, of course, it is all right to drift for a while as you relax, but a whole morning, or even a couple of hours, of purposelessness is disgraceful. If your purpose is to enjoy the scenery and the weather, that is a good thing; remember to thank God for it when you are done. Otherwise, why don't you try to plan your day in advance, and when it goes pear-shaped, form a revised plan, so that no time is wasted? You owe that to God your Maker.

God and the Egyptian Pharaoh

In today's reading from St Paul's letter to the Christians at Rome, he suggests that the Lord God had a purpose for Pharaoh, King of Egypt, even though Pharaoh knew nothing of the Jewish God. God had left the king free will to decide to persecute the Jews, and then to pursue the people of Israel as they fled through the Red Sea. God knew that Pharaoh would behave in that way, and, even though the Israelites complained that God was being cruel to them, God allowed Pharaoh to do this, because God knew that it was serving a wider purpose. God's purpose at the Exodus was to reveal that he is a Saviour God, one who, when we get ourselves into a mess, will save us out of it, eventually, if we will only be patient.

Wider purpose?

Did God have a wider purpose, then, in creating the world? She, or he, is obviously like a great painter and an inspired composer, who gets great pleasure out of creating beautiful things. But has God a plan that involves the human race, or perhaps some even more advanced species that has not yet evolved? Why should he have gone to all the trouble of micro-organizing all the stages of the evolutionary genomes, unless he wanted creatures to emerge who had the power to evolve into beings that were capable of a personal type of relationship with the supreme being?

Heaven

I think the Bible shows us that God had such a purpose. To put it simply, God created earth in order to populate heaven. God wanted creatures whom he could love, and who would respond by loving him in return. Love cannot be created in an instant; it takes a life-time of experience to learn how to love in a community. So God created a universe in which we could learn to love our friends and even our enemies, to prepare us for the next life where all is love. You and I are involved in his plans. As the popular hymn says: 'God is working his purpose out as year succeeds to year.'

Individuals

So that means that God has a purpose for each individual; even for Pharaoh, even for you and even for me! He has given us freedom to choose what we do, but he can use the results of those choices. None of us knows exactly what God's plan for us is; it will certainly involve meeting up again with those who have died. Beyond that we depend on faith and hope; confident that God's plan for us will be far more wonderful than anything we could have imagined.

Suggested hymns

All my hope on God is founded; God is working his purpose out; In heavenly love abiding; O God, our help in ages past.

Fourth Sunday after Trinity (Proper 7) 24 June
(Birth of St John the Baptist)
(For the Birth of St John the Baptist, see page 321.)
Principal Service **How to Be a Christian**
(*Continuous*): 1 Sam. 17.[1a, 4–11, 19–23] 32–49 David and Goliath, Ps. 9.9–20 God lifts me from death, *or* 1 Sam. 17.57—18.5, 10–16 David and Jonathan, Ps. 133 Unity; *or* (*Related*): Job 38.1–11 God's greatness in creation, Ps. 107.1–3, 23–32 Protection from the storm; 2 Cor. 6.1–13 The suffering of the apostles; Mark 4.35–41 Stilling the storm

> *'In our work with God, then, we beg you who have received God's grace not to let it be wasted . . . We do not want anyone to find fault with our work, so we try not to put obstacles in anyone's way. Instead, in everything we do we show that we are God's ser-vants by patiently enduring troubles, hardships, and difficulties.'* 2 Corinthians 6.1, 3–4 (Good News Bible)

168

Representatives

Every Christian is a representative for Jesus, whether we realize it or not. People will look at you and say to themselves or their friends, 'Well, she or he goes to church, they must believe in Jesus. So they must be a bit like Jesus, and Jesus must be a bit like them. Perhaps we ought to find out a bit more about this Jesus they talk about.' Whereas if you are grumpy and bad-tempered they will say, 'Look, you see what religion does to people!'

Causes of decline

Christianity is spreading like wildfire in every part of the world, except Western Europe and the USA. That should make us ask ourselves: what are we doing wrong? Christians in this country seem to be very 'anti': opposed to change, against foreigners, opposed to same-sex marriage that the country at large has accepted, prejudiced against foreigners, and, in some cases, opposed to the discoveries of modern science. People make up their minds about Jesus by what they see in you, yet we are seen as rejecting all the outcasts whom Jesus sought to include.

Attractiveness

St Paul, in today's reading from his second letter to the Corinthians, says every Christian has to be attractive. Other people should look at us and say, 'I wish I was more like her or him. Being a Christian seems to make people better. Perhaps it would even make me into a better person!' So you can bear witness to Jesus Christ without even opening your mouth – except to say something kind to somebody.

Kindness

Kindness involves being loving. That does not mean being all sloppy and sentimental, but putting yourself out to help other people, however much it costs you, like Jesus did. Self-sacrifice is the key-word. It sounds demanding, and it is, but if you develop that sort of personality, you will find you have become much happier than you ever were before. Kindness involves being tolerant and non-judgemental. If the non-Christians hear you criticizing other people, especially your minister and other people in your congregation, they will say, 'I told you so; these Christians are nothing but a load of gossips and scandal-mongers.' And that will give them an excuse to stay away from church for evermore. The criticisms may be true, but you should never speak them aloud.

Suffering

Witnessing to the character of Christ in our lives also means being patient when we are ill or in pain. Nobody wants to be ill, but it comes to most people at some time in their lives. If you grumble, and ask what you have done to deserve it, people will wonder whether you ever read what Jesus said as he hung from the cross. St Paul had suffered a blizzard of troubles in his lifetime, but before listing these, he wrote words that apply to every Christian about every Christian bearing witness to their Saviour.

Readiness

Why don't you thank God, instead, for all the good things that have happened to you, which you have done nothing to deserve? You need to practise hoping for the best and being ready for the worst. In fact everyone needs to learn this, but they can only learn it by watching your example.

Talking

We are all shy to talk about religion. But if you live like that, and look for opportunities, someone will ask you, 'How do you do that?', and will be pleased when you answer how your faith helps you. Leave it there, you do not have to 'ram it down their throats'. That way we shall all be representatives for Jesus, without stirring up any opposition.

All-age worship

Under a picture of Jesus write 'Christ-like behaviour', and list as many characteristics as you can. Then tick those that can be learnt at church.

Suggested hymns

Give thanks with a grateful heart; Oft in danger, oft in woe; One shall tell another; Take up thy cross, the Saviour said.

Fourth Sunday after Trinity (Proper 7)   24 June
Second Service   **Idols**

Ps. 49 Foolishness of the rich; Jer. 10.1–16 Idols; Rom. 11.25–36
Jews and Gentiles; *Gospel at Holy Communion*: Luke 8.26–39
Demons into pigs

> *Their idols are like scarecrows in a cucumber field,*
>   *and they cannot speak;*
> *they have to be carried,*
>   *for they cannot walk.*
> *Do not be afraid of them,*
>   *for they cannot do evil,*
>   *nor is it in them to do good. Jeremiah 10.5*

Forces

One of the most interesting developments in *Homo sapiens* is the understanding that they are under the control of forces stronger than they are. No earlier species understood that, so far as we can tell. They made paintings on cave walls, they gathered around fires, they made life-size models of people and animals. From what happened later it seems they were in some sense 'worshipping' these creatures; asking them for an ample yield from their crops and sufficient meat from their hunts. These images, usually called idols, became an almost universal feature of life, from the hunter-gatherer to the king. Religious people today will say this was a good thing, as it kept them humble, helped them to realize that they were not self-sufficient. It was the beginning of a process that led them to God. Even atheists may admit that it was helpful, as it increased their loyalty to the tribe and obedience to certain mutually acceptable rules of behaviour.

Invisible

But some of the more intelligent humans realized this did not make sense. How could they be talking to a stick of wood in one place and heard by all the clouds, rivers or deer from horizon to horizon? Unless there were some sort of invisible force joining them all together. So the idea arose of invisible gods, with wide power, of whom the idols were only symbols. Of course the less intelligent carried on worshipping the idols because that was what they and their ancestors had always done.

Rivals

The trouble with *this* development was that the different gods or idols became rivals. You could choose to worship the god of war on Mondays and the goddess of peace on Tuesdays, whichever you chose; the reapers prayed for sunshine while those who sowed the seeds prayed for rain. It turned out that none of the idols had any power whatsoever, and they wondered why they worshipped them at all.

Monotheism

So the idea emerged of having one god only. The Bible says that Abraham was the first to whom this was revealed, but probably it emerged shortly beforehand in Mesopotamia. To begin with there was a compromise: yes, there are many gods, but my god is the leader. There are traces of that in the Old Testament: 'God took his place in the council of the gods.' The god of the tribe of Judah was called Yahweh, which we translate as 'the Lord'; the god of the tribe of Ephraim was called Elohim, a plural noun. When the tribes amalgamated they called him 'the Lord God'. The advantage, however, of having only one god is that it leads to a united world. You still hear people saying, 'I will fight your people because they worship a different god from the god my people worship', or, 'We allow female genital mutilation because our god allows it.' Tolerance is essential, but walking to a single moral code is also essential.

Images

Worshipping images still persists, and some religions say that 'it is only a visual aid'. An idol is anything that people worship in place of God in their lives. For many people in the West, their idols are money and fame. We must not condemn a religion, like Jeremiah did, because some of its members kneel down in front of carved images. Nor must we condemn those whose religion tells them to prostrate themselves before icons in their churches, but distinguishes between worshipping and honouring. Where it does get difficult is when our co-religionists say, 'I always pray before the statue in such a place, because they are more likely to be answered if I make them there', which sounds as if we are manipulating our God to do something against his will. Instead we must encourage the three monotheistic religions, Islamic, Judaean and Christian, to march under a single banner of peace; and, without condoning polytheism, encourage all religions to join with us for a single cause. St Paul visited Athens and found an inscription reading, 'To the unknown god'. Instead of rebuking the Greeks for their idolatry, which would have antagonized them, Paul preached: 'What therefore you worship as unknown, this I proclaim to you.' What Christians have to teach is that the one God is a God of love. This should be our approach to all other religions. There is only one God, and we can learn from each other.

Suggested Hymns

Every star shall sing a carol; God is working his purpose out; Hills of the north, rejoice; In Christ there is no east or west.

Fifth Sunday after Trinity (Proper 8) 1 July
Principal Service **Consumerism**
(*Continuous*): 2 Sam. 1.1, 17–27 David's lament over Saul and Jonathan, Ps. 130 Out of the depths; *or* (*Related*): Wisd. 1.13–15; 2.23–24 Made for life not death, *or* Lam. 3.22–33; *Canticle*: Lam. 3.22–33 New every morning, *or* Ps. 30 Healing and life; 2 Cor. 8.7–15 Giving to the needy; Mark 5.21–43 Healing Jairus' daughter, a sick woman's faith

> '*It is a question of a fair balance between your present abundance and their need.*' 2 Corinthians 8.13–14

Consumerism

We live in an age of conspicuous consumerism. Just look at your neighbours. Some of them eat expensive food that they don't really need and that often makes them overweight. Some wear expensive clothes and cosmetics, which make them look ostentatious, not more beautiful. Some of them live in showy houses that are larger than they need. Many of your neighbours buy things just because they see them advertised, using money they haven't got, borrowed at rates they will never be able to afford, which one day they will have to return to the lender. If you doubt what I say about consumerism, look at photographs of homes in your parents' and grandparents' time, and see how many things that you consider as essential now were not even dreamt of then. We should certainly be very thankful to God that we have so many more possessions now than they had then. But ask your parents and grandparents whether they were any less happy then than they are now. Moreover, all this consumerism affects the ability of Christians to give to the Church and to other charities. Which in turn diminishes the churches' ability to advertise and draw in new members and retain those who have recently joined. It is we and our lack of generosity that prevent the churches in this area from growing.

US statistics

I have come across some statistics from the USA. In some ways it is more helpful to look at figures from another country, first because they were in some respects more extreme than we are, and because we can postpone the uncomfortable process of looking at ourselves. In the nineteenth century, most American churches expected every member to look at their pay packet when it first came in, divide it by ten, and give the first tenth, 'the first fruits', to God, through his church and other charities, before they thought about how they would spend the remainder. Nowadays it is mostly only in the African American churches that this continues to be taught, and they are growing fast. Tithing, as it was called, was based on the customs of the Jews. Now only a minority of Americans tithe: a mere 20 per cent are responsible for 80 per cent of the giving. Most giving goes to the benefit of their own church, and very little to Christian work in the rest of the country and overseas. Higher income does not result in higher giving. Very often new members of a church will start to leave as soon as the subject of money is mentioned. Most churches find it difficult to recruit new members under 50, from the generations that grew up after consumerism had taken hold.

Europe

But here in Europe we need regular givers if the Church is to grow and not die. Yet most young people today find giving very difficult. Caught in a net of consumerism, young Christians tend to make giving to other people, to poor people in the developing world, and to their church, an optional extra, when they have already budgeted all they can afford on themselves.

Paul

This is a very different ideal of giving from that which St Paul held up to us. He congratulated his readers on their generosity the year before to the poorer congregations around the Mediterranean shore. But the ideal he held out to them was 'a question of a fair balance between your present abundance and their need'. The apostle envisaged a degree of equality that has seldom been attempted and would be very hard to achieve. But when you contrast the difference in income between the extremely rich and the extremely poor in Paul's day and today, you realize something has gone seriously wrong with our consumer society. Even more so if you look internationally. Compare the extravagant Christmas presents we give and expect, and the people who have only just enough to survive on. There cannot be peace on earth while these difference in income remains. The early Quakers, the Cadburys and the Rowntrees, had the right idea when they gave away most of their wealth. Perhaps only when we rediscover the Christian attitude to giving shall we begin to return to a happy society.

All-age worship

Draw up a budget for your pocket money.

Suggested hymns

Give thanks with a joyful/grateful heart; O Lord of heaven and earth and sea; 'Lift up your hearts!' We lift them Lord to thee; Take my life, and let it be.

Fifth Sunday after Trinity (Proper 8)   1 July
Second Service   **Scientists Prove God Daily**
Ps. [52 Tyrants] 53 Fools; Jer. 11.1–14 Breaking God's covenant;
Rom. 13.1–10 State authority; *Gospel at Holy Communion:*
Luke 9.51–62 Tolerance and sacrifice

> *'The fool has said in his heart, "There is no God."' Psalm 53.1 (Common Worship)*

Science and religion

Why have we Christians allowed ourselves to be portrayed as the enemies of science? If we allowed them to, scientists would do our work of evangelism for us. Looking at it logically, scientists 'prove' the power of God every day. Science depends on our faith that the world works according to logical principles. Most scientists are agreed that the history of our universe began with an event that is popularly known as the 'Big Bang'. This theory is based on observations of the velocity with which all the galaxies are flying apart, calculated by the shift in the frequency of the light they emit; and on the rate of 'decay' of the radioactive elements. Like all scientific theories, we hold to this idea because it gives the best available explanation for our observations – until such time as a better explanation comes along. For example, Newton discovered the law of gravity, but Einstein later produced the theory of relativity, which in certain circumstances provides a more accurate prediction of the speed at which things will travel. Now the law of cause and effect says that everything that happens must have a cause, which was there before the effects that it causes. Matter, and the space it occupies, began at the Big Bang, and so did time, which is a dimension integral to the three dimensions of space. If everything has a cause that precedes it in time, what caused the beginning of space and time at the Big Bang? The only possible answer is a force or beginning that is outside our dimensions of space-time; in other words, something that is eternal. It is unscientific to leave the cause of anything unexplained, so science demands that we should believe in eternity. This does not mean that the first cause is like what Christians call 'God', but you cannot call yourself a scientist unless you believe in something.

Goldilocks

As matter sped out from the Big Bang, within the first few microseconds certain forces came into effect, such as the law of gravity, which caused it to condense into atoms, molecules and eventually into stars. All these scientific constants had to be just right, or the universe would have flown apart into nothing, or collapsed again into itself. Planets had to form, and one of them had to contain water, mostly at a temperature between freezing and evaporation, at the right distance from the sun and of the right size for gravity to stop the atmosphere flying off into space, with the right mix of elements and with a moon to cause tides, before life could emerge and survive. In the fairy tale, Goldilocks tried the porridge that was too hot, and then that which was too cold, before declaring the third bowl 'just right!' So we call the unlikely emergence of at least one planet which could sustain life the 'Goldilocks Effect'. Science demands that we look for a reason for this.

Life

Then life had to be able to diversify and reproduce itself. Mutations happen apparently as random small changes, and some of these were more suited for survival than others. The result of this process, amazingly, was the emergence of humans who could think, choose and love. Darwin tells us *how* this happens, but humans are bound to ask, *why*? The only possible answer is, because something with the power to choose wanted it to, and was involved in the whole process from the beginning until now.

Universes

You could explain the unlikely emergence of a universe like this one by suggesting that there are an infinite number of universes, but that only takes the question back one level: *why* are there so many worlds, and what caused the first one to exist anyway?

Love

This still hasn't told us what the Eternal Being is like, but the best explanation is that its nature is to love. So it wanted creatures to love, which could freely choose to love their Creator in return. And although these creatures might be born in time, the loving relationship thus established should be capable of lasting into a timeless existence. Humans are never going to form this relationship with the Creator when they think of it as an impersonal force; so God had to find a way of showing himself in our world as a person who loves us. And there you have the Christian gospel, established by scientific reasoning. Of course there are still many unanswered questions, but get to know some Christians closely, and you will find they are grappling with all of these.

Eternal ruler of the ceaseless round; Father, Lord of all creation; For the beauty of the earth; Lord of the boundless curves of space.

Sixth Sunday after Trinity (Proper 9)   8 July
Principal Service   **Grace**
(*Continuous*): 2 Sam. 5.1–5, 9–10 David's victory, Ps. 48 God's protection of the city; *or* (*Related*): Ezek. 2.1–5 Speak the word, Ps. 123 Hope for God's grace; 2 Cor. 12.2–10 God's grace is sufficient; Mark 6.1–13 Jesus rejected

> *'"My grace is sufficient for you, for power . . ." is made perfect in weakness.' 2 Corinthians 12.9*

Kindness

Has anyone ever treated you with great kindness, though you had done nothing to deserve it; kindness that was just out of the generosity of their heart? I hope your parents loved you in that way, though most children do not realize until later how great was their parents' love, and how little they did to earn it. Or it may be that somebody promoted you to a place at school or at work, trusting that you would prove yourself a match for the challenges it presented, though you had done nothing so far to prove that you were capable of it.

Grace

We have a special word for this sort of undeserved and overwhelming love. It is called 'grace'. Not the sort of grace shown by a graceful dancer. This is the grace we sing about in the hymn:

> Amazing grace, how sweet the sound
> that saved a wretch like me;
> I once was lost, but now am found;
> was blind, but now I see.

God's love

Mention of John Newton's famous hymn brings us to the most amazing discovery of all. In the time of Jesus, most people thought that God, or the gods, ruled strictly over the human race, judging our actions firmly and harshly. They were quite astonished to hear that God is love; but all their assumptions about life were over-thrown to hear that God's love for us was *this* sort of love, 'grace', the love that pours kindness onto undeserving humans simply because that is God's nature.

Be aware

If that is so, then we should be on the lookout for occasions when he reveals this kind of love to us. For everyone they will be different: for one it will be when God made a glorious sunset for us to look at, which has no physical need to be so beautiful; for another when they met and married a life-partner, who, although not perfect (no-body is), has provided them with a loving environment throughout their lives; or when they fell ill and recovered; when they attended a particularly beautiful concert. Each of you will have your own list; but the important thing is to recognize God's part in this, and thank him for it.

Misfortune

But things don't always go well for us; I don't imagine they could in a particularly complex society. Many people then blame God for their misfortunes. 'How could God do this to me,' they wail, 'at this particular moment? What have I done to deserve it? If that is the God of love they talk about, I don't believe in him any more.' That is a natural, if completely illogical, response to bad times. Yet if so many good things happen to us without us deserving them, what has it got to do with our deserving if occasional bad things happen to us too?

Paul

St Paul had suffered from a particularly painful illness, when he wrote about God's grace. He had prayed three times to be healed from this tormenting pain, yet his prayers were not answered. So he began to realize that a certain amount of pain is essential in every life, to prevent us from feeling conceited. He had been feeling particu-larly pleased with the success of his mission, as if it were something he had achieved on his own, without God's help. So, he said, God had sent him the pain to cut him down to size, and then build up his character by bringing him to realize that God can do wonderful things through quite undeserving people. He imagined God quoting from Isaiah, then Paul completed the sentence in his own words: '"My grace is sufficient for you, for power . . ." is made perfect in weakness.' Isn't it amazing that a man in agony should be able to write so positively about God? But he had learnt that God's love, unlike most human love, is freely given to the undeserving; that is the meaning of 'grace'. Thomas Traherne, the seventeenth-century poet, wrote: 'No man in this world has been loved too much, but many have been loved in the wrong way and all in too short a measure.' That is because we haven't learnt that God's love is totally unconditional. Now we have to make our love for God, and for other people, completely unselfish too.

All-age worship

Write on a badge on your chest, 'I deserve a happy life.' Then change it to 'I don't deserve a happy life, but God gives me one anyway.'

Suggested hymns

Amazing grace; God moves in a mysterious way; God of mercy, God of grace; Rock of ages, cleft for me.

Sixth Sunday after Trinity (Proper 9)   8 July
Second Service   **Gossip**
Ps. [63 My soul clings to you] 64 Protection from enemies; Jer. 20.1–11a Jeremiah's prayer; Rom. 14.1–17 Do not judge others; *Gospel at Holy Communion*: Luke 10.1–11, 16–20 Mission of the seventy

> *'Who are you to pass judgement on servants of another? It is before their own lord that they stand or fall. And they will be upheld, for the Lord is able to make them stand.' Romans 14.4*

Chatter

Chattering with your friends about the world around you is a fascinating and enjoyable occupation, provided everyone promises to distinguish between when they are repeating hearsay and when they have concrete evidence for what they say. This way, we can learn a lot about the world, and possibly about different groups of people. But the big exception to this is that you must never talk about individuals, except to praise them.

Gossip

Those who listen never hear good of themselves, they say. Which just goes to show how much bad-natured criticism of other people goes on in everyday conversation. Some of the criticism may be true. If it is important, it should be shared in confidence with the offender, and nobody else; otherwise, sit on your opinions and tell nobody. You see, the danger with criticizing other people is that your opinion can spread through the community like wildfire through a dry forest. It is no longer 'so and so has this fault', but 'everybody says that so and so is a liability to us all'. And then the trust is destroyed between members of the community. If you are identified as the source of the rumour, your own reputation is ruined because nobody will believe such a notorious scandal-monger. Rabbi Sacks once wrote: 'Gossip kills three people: the one who says it, the person it is directed against, and the person who listens to it.'

Paul

St Paul was obviously having problems with gossip among the congregation of Christians in Rome. He wrote to the Christians there, 'Who are you to pass judgement on servants of another? It is before their own lord that they stand or fall. And they will be upheld, for the Lord is able to make them stand.' That was a clever thrust in what was still a late feudal society. About one in ten of the population was known as a 'freeman'; the remainder belonged to somebody else, as slave, servant, child or wife. If you criticized somebody else in the town, you were in effect criticizing their owner for training them badly; or as if you went out and beat somebody else's dog for being ill-trained. So Paul made a witty aside based on the fact that every Christian belongs to God, so to criticize a fellow believer is an insult to God!

Jesus

Jesus himself said, in the Sermon on the Mount:

'Do not judge, so that you may not be judged. For with the judgement you make you will be judged, and the measure you give will be the measure you get. Why do you see the speck in your neighbour's eye, but do not notice the log in your own eye? Or how can you say to your neighbour, "Let me take the speck out of your eye", while the log is in your own eye? You hypocrite, first take the log out of your own eye, and then you will see clearly to take the speck out of your neighbour's eye.'

Whatever his Roman readers thought, I don't believe Paul was talking in terms of a law court. Jesus judges us every moment of every day, not with any idea of punishing us, but assessing what progress we are making in Christian life and understanding; if our hearts are consumed in criticizing others, he knows we need some good hard shock as a wake-up call to reconnect us with the real priorities in life.

In church

Within the life of a worshipping community, gossip is a disaster and a serious crime. When newcomers arrive in the church, they will decide that this is a very unloving group of people who all dislike each other, and stop coming. Even long-standing members of the congregation will feel the atmosphere has changed, and that there will be no more fun to be had by coming to worship there Sunday by Sunday. The Bible describes the Church as the body of Christ. If your gossiping causes divisions in Christ's body, it is as if you are re-crucifying Christ afresh, and the whole community may die. In the past, churches have ceased to meet because of divisions in the congregation, and it will happen again. But woe to the worshipper whose gossip and criticism brought the unhappy ending about.

Suggested hymns

'Forgive our sins as we forgive'; Just as I am; There's a wideness in God's mercy; When I needed a neighbour.

Seventh Sunday after Trinity (Proper 10)   15 July
Principal Service   **Thanks for Friends**

(*Continuous*): 2 Sam. 6.1–5, 12b–19 The ark comes to the city,
Ps. 24 Lift up your heads; *or (Related*): Amos 7.7–15 The plumb
line: judgement on the city, Ps. 85.8–13 Peace, faith and works;
Eph. 1.3–14 Called to adoption; Mark 6.14–29 Herod beheads
the Baptist

> *'In him you also, when you had heard the word of truth, the gos-*
> *pel of your salvation, and had believed in him, were marked with*
> *the seal of the promised Holy Spirit.' Ephesians 1.13*

Friendship

One of the great medieval Christian writers, Aelred of Rievaulx, said
that 'God is friendship'. I am not quite sure what that means. One half
of that statement is a person, and the other is a relationship, which
does not quite add up. But there is no doubt that the connection between God and friendship is very close. How we come to know God
is not through academic lectures, but by becoming acquainted with
him as our friend. Our relationship with God is like that between two
friends, and in the command to love our neighbour, God is telling us
to treat everybody, even our enemies, as our friends.

Letters

When friends are together they will chatter away together for a while.
Then, because they know each other well enough to tell instinctively
what the other is thinking, they will rejoice in being silent together,
understanding each other absolutely. That also reflects on the
Christian's relationship with God. We set aside a time of prayer each
day, and then we can just chatter to our Maker about anything that is
on our minds; it doesn't always have to be asking for things. But after
a while we shall go quiet, listen to see if God wants to say something
to us, and in the silence simply rejoice in the knowledge of his presence. In the old days, friends who were separated by some distance
would write letters to each other. In the age of emails, Facebook and
tweets, people may only send each other brief messages, and I am
sure the quality of our friendships suffers from this.

Ephesians

Thank God, St Paul wrote many letters to the friends he had made on his missionary journeys around the Middle East. Most of them have not survived, but the ones we have give an intimate picture of the relationship between a new convert to Christianity and the one who first brought them to the knowledge of Jesus. The Letter to the Ephesians begins with a beautiful paragraph of praise to God, which some people know in a fine musical setting, 'Blessed be the God and Father of our Lord Jesus Christ'. Unlike most letters, it does not begin by exchanging the latest gossip, but by acknowledging that God has chosen us to share with others the good news of God's love.

We are chosen

There is a danger in that word 'chosen', that it might lead us to imagine that it was like a job interview, and we got the post because we are the most talented. Quite the opposite! God recognizes that everybody has useful qualities, and where they are lacking, he gives them to us. Paul recognizes that God has given all of us – clever or stupid, practical or clumsy, tactful or blundering – abundant blessings that will enable us to do all he requires of us.

Gifted

Then he turns specifically to the Christians of Ephesus, and thanks God for their wonderful abilities. If he had started the letter like this they would have thought he was flattering them, and ignored what he had to say; doing it this way they can rejoice with the apostle, thanking God for the gifts he had given them.

Thanks to friends

Have you ever written a letter like that to one of your friends, praising them for their good qualities? Admiring them for their acts of kindness? Drawing attention to their compassion for those in difficulties? Thanking them for their hospitality, not only towards you but to anyone who comes to their home? Try it; for a while they will think you are quite mad, but soon it will become the most normal thing in the world.

Thanks to God

But to avoid the charge of mutual flattery, always end by thanking God for each other. Then God may become a natural subject of conversation, whereas you thought it was rather pious to mention religion.

All-age worship

Write a card to three members of the group, ensuring nobody is left out, praising God for their kindness and similar gifts.

Suggested hymns

There is a green hill far away; O Lord of heaven and earth and sea; There's a wideness in God's mercy; To God be the glory, great things he hath done.

Seventh Sunday after Trinity (Proper 10)   15 July
Second Service   Discipline

Ps. 66 What God has done; Job 4.1; 5.6–27 Whom God reproves *or* Ecclus. (Ben Sira) 4.11–31 Wisdom's teaching; Rom. 15.14–29 The apostle to the Gentiles; *Gospel at Holy Communion*: Luke 10.25–37 The good Samaritan

> *'Human beings are born to trouble*
> *just as sparks fly upward.' Job 5.7*

Difficult?

People who read the Bible often shy away from the book of Job, because they think it is gloomy and difficult. Actually it is neither of those things, but you have to remember one important fact: Job is a drama. But first, a warning to those who read it aloud: Job is pronounced with a long 'o', not a short one!

Drama

When I say the book of Job is a drama, I don't necessarily mean that it was acted on a stage, which would have been rather difficult; I mean it was read aloud by several different readers, taking it in turn to recite the different personalities, each presenting a particular point of view. Very often a positive viewpoint is persuasively presented by one speaker, and then completely demolished by the next speaker with an equally convincing outline of the negative point of view. So you should never read one chapter in isolation. Or, at least, if you do, you should have a good idea of the overall pattern of the whole book.

Outline

Wrapped around the central portion, like a plain setting for a beautiful jewel, is an old folk tale about a very rich man called Job, who loses everything, but God challenges Satan – or rather 'the Satan', which means 'the tempter' – to prove that Job is a bad man who didn't deserve his riches anyway. Meanwhile on earth three so-called 'comforters', in the most beautiful verse, try to persuade that good things always happen to good people, so if Job is suffering he must be a bad man. Not very comforting, you may think. Jewish poetry, by the way, does not rhyme, but it has a strict pattern of so many stressed syllables to a line, and uses imagery and beautiful wording. There is a fourth comforter, who dismisses the other three comforters for speaking nonsense.

God

Then God appears. Job lodges a complaint, that God should not have allowed a good man to suffer, and demands that God should explain himself. God does not even try, but instead takes Job on a tour of the natural world, with wonderful descriptions of the earth, the heavens, the rivers and the wild animals. God's question to Job is, 'Could you have created all these on your own, like I did?' There are descriptions of Behemoth, which may not have been the hippopotamus, and Leviathan, who could have been the whale, but is more likely to have been a completely mythical beast.

Humility

So the final message to Job, and to us as well, is to be more humble. Who are we, mere mortals, to think we dare ask God to explain himself? Who are we to imagine that we should be able to understand it if the Almighty, the Incomprehensible, who is above all reason and all human logic, should try to explain to our poor little human minds why he has designed the world as he has? We understand now that God had the brilliant idea of creating organisms which can reproduce and modify themselves, and eliminate those that are not strong enough to survive; but 200 years ago we would have thought anyone who proposed such a laughable idea mad. I wonder what we would say if God explained himself today in the scientific terms of tomorrow. John Milton in *Paradise Lost* tried to 'justify the works of God to man', with only partial success. Every creature has to die sometime to make way for others; in the case of human beings, at least, it is not a tragedy for the one who dies, because they go on to a better life in eternity. So it is right, with Job, to ask the question, 'Why do good people suffer?'; but like Job, we must recognize that we can still believe in a loving God, even though we may never understand the answer. God says to us, as he did to Job, 'Who is this that hides counsel without knowledge?' Therefore we must reply as Job did:

> I have uttered what I did not understand,
>   things too wonderful for me, which I did not know . . .
> I had heard of you by the hearing of the ear,
>   but now my eye sees you;
> therefore I despise myself,
>   and repent in dust and ashes.

Suggested hymns

How shall we sing that majesty?; *Immortal, invisible, God only wise*; *It is a thing most wonderful*; *There's a wideness in God's mercy.*

St Mary Magdalene   22 July
Tears
S. of Sol. 3.1–4 Seeking and finding; Ps. 42.1–10 As deer long for water; 2 Cor. 5.14–17 A new creation; John 20.1–2, 11–18 Go and tell

> *'Jesus said to [Mary Magdalene], "Woman, why are you weeping? For whom are you looking?" Supposing him to be the gardener, she said to him, "Sir, if you have carried him away, tell me where you have laid him, and I will take him away." Jesus said to her, "Mary!"' John 20.15–16*

187

Magdalene

St John's Gospel tells us that Mary Magdalene stood weeping outside the tomb where the dead body of Jesus had been buried. As she wept, she bent over to look into the tomb, and she saw two angels in white, sitting where the body of Jesus had been lying, one at the head and the other at the feet, though she did not actually realize they were angels. They said to her, 'Woman, why are you weeping?' Mary must have thought, 'What a *stupid* question! Why does anybody cry in a cemetery? Have you two never been to visit the grave of somebody you loved, and burst into tears? If so, you're not human.' Fortunately she never spoke those words to the angels. Instead, she sobbed, 'They've taken away my Lord, and I don't know where they've laid him.' A natural complaint – life is so unfair! She came to anoint the body, and some wretch had gone and moved it. Notice that she referred to Jesus as 'my Lord'. Did she just mean 'the boss – the leader of our gang'? Or did she have some inkling that there was a relationship deeper than she could understand between the man she had fallen in love with and the Lord God, creator of heaven and earth?

The gardener

The tears were blurring her eyes, and she could not see clearly. She mopped her eyes, ashamed that anyone should see her crying. When she looked again, the two people in white had gone. But she was aware that there was now a man standing behind her, silhouetted against the rising sun. At once she realized it must be the gardener. He asked her the same stupid question: 'Why are you weeping?' She turned towards him and made her complaint, which sounded more like a wail: 'Sir, if you have carried his . . . body . . . away, just tell me where you have put it, and I'll take him somewhere safe where I can talk to him . . . to it, I mean.' For a moment the gardener said nothing, and she thought, 'What's wrong with all these men? Has nobody got any brains, any compassion?' And then he spoke, just one word, calling her by her name – 'Mary'. There was love and compassion in that voice, with a slight tremble as though her tears had moved him too, and she knew it was Jesus. And then he talked to her tenderly; and now the tears in her eyes were tears of joy. To build up this broken woman's self-respect, he gave her a job to do, telling her she was the only one of his disciples who was up to it. He told her to be the first witness to his resurrection, and to begin by telling the others – she was to be an 'apostle to the apostles'.

Nothing wrong

But first, I expect, Jesus told Mary Magdalene that there is nothing wrong with tears. When we suffer deep emotions, of loss or of joy, it is natural and good to express them. If you try to bottle them up, they will burst out later, at an inappropriate moment. The process of grieving will take much longer, before you learn to accept your loss. When somebody dies whom you love – however strongly you believe in life after death, and that they are happy – still you are sad that you will have to live so long without their visible presence. The shortest verse in the Bible tells us that 'Jesus wept'. That was when his friend Lazarus died. Jesus believed in life after death, though he had a moment of doubt when he cried on the cross, 'Father, why have you gone away from me?' But even though he knew that Lazarus would come to life again one day, he was sad at the thought of the grief his friend's sisters were feeling. So Jesus wept. The strongest people weep sometimes. Sometimes when it rains, people say that God himself weeps, and the raindrops are God's tears, falling in pity on his suffering creation. If anyone tells you to be British and keep a stiff upper lip, tell them that it is Christ-like to cry. But at the last, the Bible promises, 'God will wipe away every tear from [our] eyes' – just as Jesus did for Mary Magdalene on that first Easter morning.

Suggested hymns

Christ is alive! Let Christians sing; Good Joseph had a garden; Mary, weep not, weep no longer; Walking in a garden.

Eighth Sunday after Trinity (Proper 11) 22 July
Second Service **Our High Priest**
Ps. 73 Relief from oppression; Job 13.13—14.6 Job's debate with God, *or* Ecclus. (Ben Sira) 18.1–14 God's majesty; Heb. 2.5–18 Perfected through suffering; *Gospel at Holy Communion*: Luke 10.38–42 Martha and Mary

> *'[Jesus] had to become like his brothers and sisters in every respect, so that he might be a merciful and faithful high priest in the service of God, to make a sacrifice of atonement for the sins of the people.' Hebrews 2.17*

Hebrews

Nobody knows who wrote the Epistle to the Hebrews. But it was clearly written for a Jewish readership, who were soaked in their Scriptures, which we call the Old Testament, and thoroughly familiar with the traditions of Jewish worship. This was based on what they called the Day of Atonement. Only on this day was anybody allowed to enter the Holy of Holies, the central room of the complex of the Jerusalem Temple, where the tablets of stone on which the Ten Commandments were kept, and here God himself was thought to live. Read again Isaiah's vision of the angels singing 'Holy, holy, holy' to remind yourself of how special this room was thought to be.

Background

The one person in the whole world allowed to enter this sacred room, once a year only, was the Jewish High Priest, and he only if he had washed himself thoroughly. There he killed and offered as a sacrifice the Passover lamb, the blood of which was thought to wash the whole Jewish race from the stain of their sins. With that sort of background, you might think that the Letter to the Hebrews would be completely irrelevant to non-Jews like you and me. But wait! Once you have understood the ideas associated with many of the words, Christians can draw a much deeper understanding of what Jesus and his followers thought was happening on what we call Good Friday.

High Priest

The Letter to the Hebrews, or the Letter to Jewish Christians, as it is sometimes called, says that Jesus does for non-Jews what the High Priest did for Jews. First he was baptized, although John the Baptist protested that he had no need of it because he was free from sin, and lived a sinless life to show that he was no less pure than the Jewish High Priest. Then although the High Priest had to deliberately enter God's dwelling-place, Jesus was in heaven, in the bosom of the Father, from the very beginning. Then, as the priests sacrificed the lamb, so Jesus of his own free will submitted to slaughter at the hands of the Roman soldiers, which he could easily have escaped if he had chosen to lie. Then the lamb's body was consumed in the altar fire, and the altar was washed with blood. At the Last Supper, Jesus our great High Priest gave bread and wine to his friends, and by extension therefore to you and me. He said, 'This is my body; this is my blood.' Just as the whole Jewish people were forgiven for every sin they had committed in the whole year, so God chooses to forgive every Christian who receives the bread and wine, for all the sins they have committed since the last time they received Holy Communion.

Covenant

Here an additional metaphor is introduced. The blood of an animal was used as a symbol every time a contract or covenant was, as we would say, 'signed'. The blood was a visible sign of their promises to those who accepted the terms of the contract, just as the signature is to us today. The ancient Jews believed that they had set up a huge overdraft in their account with God because they had done things that were forbidden by one of the hundreds of laws written in the Old Testament. Christians believe that God has given us only two universal laws: to love God with all our heart and mind and soul and strength, and to love our neighbours as much as we love ourselves. So the only sin is lack of love, and God is waiting on tiptoe to forgive that, as soon as we confess it.

Identified

Yet, if we decide to confess, our feeble words seem quite insufficient to express the seriousness of what we have done. So Jesus identifies with us, and absorbs his colossal penitence for the sins of the whole world into your measly, 'Sorry, God, I didn't realize it mattered that much'. So Jesus has to become completely identified with us. As Jeremy Taylor, an eighteenth-century preacher, said, 'When God would save human beings, he did it by way of a human being.'

Suggested hymns

Behold, the great Creator makes; Just as I am without one plea; Love came down at Christmas; Now, my tongue, the mystery telling.

Ninth Sunday after Trinity (Proper 12)   29 July
Principal Service   **Mystery at a Miracle's Heart**
(*Continuous*): 2 Sam. 11.1–15 David and Bathsheba, Ps. 14
Repentance and the needy; *or* (*Related*): 2 Kings 4.42–44 Elisha
feeds a crowd, Ps. 145.10–19 Prayer and providence; Eph. 3.14–21
Prayer and providence; John 6.1–21 Feeding the five thousand

> *'When Jesus realized that they were about to come and take him*
> *by force to make him king, he withdrew again to the mountain by*
> *himself.' John 6.15*

The feeding of the five thousand

The feeding of the five thousand provides an opportunity to pay
attention to Jesus's commentary – though 'commentary' is hardly
an adequate description of this journey into the mystery at the
heart of the miracle. John's interest in the event is quite different
from Mark's, as his careful chronology makes clear. It is near to
Passover and. John casts the whole of Jesus's ministry in a Passover
framework, leading his readers to the denouement in which Jesus
dies as the Passover Lamb of God. Whereas much of the action in
Mark's account centres on Jesus's relationship with the disciples,
John assigns the disciples a more functional role. Their hesitation
over the idea of providing food for such a crowd, Philip's alarming
calculation, and Andrew's despairing mention of the boy who has
'five barley loaves and two fish' emphasize that something is about
to occur that would be impossible on any rational terms. Jesus,
however, 'knew what he was going to do'.

The coming of the kingdom

The people seem to understand the exceptional significance of
what has happened, even if the disciples do not: this is a 'sign', performed by the 'prophet' they have been expecting. That they leap
to the wrong conclusions and want Jesus as their king is only partly
attributable to the limited and opportunistic attention for which
he rebukes them a little later. Though there is no Lord's Prayer
in this Gospel, it has its own way of addressing the coming of the
kingdom – on earth as it is heaven. It is difficult to understand why
anyone would want to demystify the feeding, or Jesus's walking on
the water towards his beleaguered friends some time afterwards.

William Barclay, for instance, reads into the breaking of bread a lesson in generosity and sharing. He goes on to point out that the words translated as walking 'on the lake' in John 6.19 are rendered 'beside the lake' in John 21.1, giving grounds to think that the disciples in fact saw Jesus on the shore.* That doesn't, however, dispose of the fact that Mark, who uses the same words, clearly means 'on the sea'. But more important still is the way in which Jesus identifies himself: 'It is I; do not be afraid.' This instance of divine revelation shows that God has power over the waters, as over the behaviour of the burning bush.

God's generosity

The magnitude of God in generosity and faithfulness is contrasted with the disappointing limitations of the human spirit in the narrative of David and Bathsheba. Here is a king who has conquered in the strength of the Lord in a series of successful battles, forgetting that he is not above the law. Bathsheba's pregnancy is not an unfortunate accident: the useful biological information provided by the writer makes it an extremely likely event. David's desperate attempt at a cover-up, as well as his cowardly arrangements for Uriah's death, show the king in a very poor light against the loyal officer. Yet God will keep the covenant made with David and his house, because God remains God.

A larger hope

Out of that covenant will come a much larger hope, embodied in Jesus, who is born of David's line and in his home town – the 'House of Bread'. It will extend beyond David's house to a spreading community of believers, to whom the Spirit will reveal the 'breadth and length and height and depth' of what the Greek magnificently calls 'the surpassing knowledge love' of Christ. The writer of the letter ends the prayer begun at Ephesians 1.3 on an exalted note, before turning to the details of the new way of life which this knowledge will demand.

All-age worship

Make paper cut-outs of a basket with loaves and fish. Write the names of the children on them, then write on the basket, 'I give you, Lord, all I have and all I am.' Place it on the altar in church.

193

Suggested hymns

Bread of heaven, on thee we feed; Break thou the bread of life; Father, hear the prayer we offer; Let us break bread together.

* William Barclay, *The Gospel of John*, Volume 1, Saint Andrew Press, 1975.

Ninth Sunday after Trinity (Proper 12) 29 July
Second Service **My Redeemer Lives**
Ps. 74 National defeat; Job 19.1–27a My Redeemer lives, *or* Ecclus. (Ben Sira) 38.24–34 Labour; Heb. 8 Mediator of a better covenant; *Gospel at Holy Communion*: Luke 11.1–13 Prayer

> 'For I know that my Redeemer lives, and that at the last he will stand upon the earth; and after my skin has been thus destroyed, then in my flesh I shall see God, whom I shall see on my side, and my eyes shall behold, and not another.' Job 19.25–27

Bail money

Imagine for a moment one of the worst things that could ever happen to you: a case of mistaken identity. Suppose the police arrested you for something you hadn't done, because they thought you were somebody else. It's all right, you think, I can rely on my best friend to come and stand bail for me. He'll pay whatever's necessary to have me set free. But if you're a misanthropist and a recluse, with no friends, there's little hope for you – it's worth making friends, because when the worst happens, you can tell your friends from your enemies, by who sticks by you, and who vanishes into thin air.

Redeemer

The Jews had a special word for this sort of friend; we'll come to that in a moment. The worst-case scenario that haunted them was that they might be captured by an invading army and held to ransom. Or they might be seized by a creditor for non-payment of debt, and held as a slave until the debts were paid off. In either case your hope rested entirely on someone willing to raise the money to pay the ransom or the debt. There were laws which said this was an obligation of your next of kin. But if he failed you, somebody else could turn up trumps. The one who pays off the money to set a slave or captive free was called by a special word, which we normally translate as 'my Redeemer'.

Job

It's a word that will be familiar to you from Handel's *Messiah*, which quotes from the Old Testament book of Job. Poor old Job had lost all his property, and been smitten with a terrible skin disease. It was worse than being a slave; he felt little better than a corpse. For a while, Job lost hope, but then a glimmer of light appeared on the dark horizon. He needed a Redeemer, someone who'd pay the necessary to free him from his suffering. His so-called friends were no use; all they could do was to criticize him. But wait a moment: perhaps God himself would come forward to act as Job's next of kin? Yes, that was it! God would be Job's 'Redeemer'. So with relief and renewed hope he cried out the familiar words:

> For I know that my Redeemer lives, and that at the last he will stand upon the earth; and after my skin has been thus destroyed, then in my flesh I shall see God, whom I shall see on my side, and my eyes shall behold, and not another.

Context

God's on our side! Putting these words in context makes them so poignant, and the modern translation makes more sense than 'though worms destroy this body', which is a complete mistranslation. Job hopes that while he's still alive, God himself will plead for him to be set free. But Handel, or rather Charles Jennens, Handel's librettist, was quite right to give them another slant, which the author of the book of Job couldn't possibly have known. Jesus is the Son of God; Jesus rose from the dead; Jesus pays with his own life to set us free from slavery to sin and death. So Jesus is our Redeemer. Jesus fulfils the role of next of kin for us; Jesus is the friend who pays the bail bond to buy our freedom. After we die, when worms have indeed destroyed our bodies, we shall see, in eternity,

> Jesus, our Redeemer and our God. I know that my redeemer liveth, and that he shall stand at the latter day upon the earth: and though . . . worms destroy this body, yet in my flesh shall I see God: Whom I shall see for myself, and mine eyes shall behold, and not another!

You don't have to be a famous contralto to sing those words with feeling. Any simple Christian, who knows that Jesus died and rose again, and that he has promised that we shall do the same, can say – with heartfelt emotion: After I die, I shall see my God in heaven, because Jesus is my Redeemer, and he's alive for evermore. God's on our side. Halleluiah!

Suggested hymns

I know that my Redeemer lives; Guide me, O thou great Redeemer; My God, how wonderful thou art; You, living Christ, our eyes behold.

Tenth Sunday after Trinity (Proper 13)   5 August
Principal Service   **The Startling Impact of Sudden Recognition**
(*Continuous*): 2 Sam. 11.26—12.13a The parable of the one ewe lamb, Ps. 51.1–13 Forgiveness; or (Related): Ex. 16.2–4, 9–15 The manna, Ps. 78.23–29 The manna; Eph. 4.1–16 Gifts of the Spirit, unity of the Church; John 6.24–35 I am the bread of life

> *'Jesus said to [the crowd,] "I am the bread of life. Whoever comes to me will never be hungry, and whoever believes in me will never be thirsty."' John 6.35*

Seeking and finding

A visitor to Milan happened upon the church of Santa Maria delle Grazie. Mass was just about to start. Joining the elderly priest and congregation of devout women turned out to be a most joyful event. The visitor hoped to see a representation of the institution of the Eucharist with the tourist's mixed motives of reverence, curiosity, self-improvement, and determination not to miss something important. They found they had accidentally stumbled into the real and living continuity of John's extended treatment of the meaning of the feeding of the five thousand as a far more dramatic story of seeking one thing and finding another.

196

The puzzling crowd

The crowd, puzzled that Jesus has disappeared, set off in search of him, boarding the boats that have conveniently arrived from Tiberias. If it seems odd that people who have been 'satisfied' by the food they have been given should feel the need to pursue Jesus across the lake, nevertheless that becomes the narrative's central point. Jesus dispenses with pleasantries and charges the people immediately with seeking him for the wrong reason. They have seen the sign, yet missed its meaning. He is offering them something that will endure; they are thinking of short-term needs that must be regularly replenished. If they had thought about the 12 baskets of food remaining after all had eaten enough, they might have recalled the manna in the wilderness. Only on the sixth day could extra provisions be collected and stored, to be eaten on the Sabbath when no work was done. Jesus has shown them a vision of the great Sabbath that will be the fulfilment of the kingdom of God. That should be the goal of all their efforts.

Work's reward

Work is a recurrent theme in this chapter. It is implied in Philip's estimate of the cost of bread for the crowd—200 denarii translates into 'six months' wages'—and Jesus distinguishes between working for perishable bread and working for 'the food that endures for eternal life'. Like Nicodemus and the woman at the well in Samaria, the people are at a loss to know how to do the 'work of God' that will secure this different food. Fulfilling the law imposed demands, but also offered a discipline. Nicodemus was living by the Mosaic law; the Samaritan woman was living in defiance of the conventions of respectability. Jesus offers each of them something they must work for in a new and challenging way. For the crowd who had crossed the lake, the new working conditions sound too good to be true: 'believe in him whom [God] has sent'. Again, they want a sign.

The greater humanity

This is Jesus's opportunity to reveal his identity. The people have misunderstood him, as an earlier generation had misunderstood Moses. Neither Jesus nor Moses was the giver of bread. Both acted as channels for the gift of God which 'gives life to the world'. With Jesus, it goes further: he is both the channel and the gift itself. Their request, 'Sir, give us this bread always', again misses the meaning. Jesus explains: the bread he is talking about is himself. Sudden recognition in a narrative has startling impact. It is the device that Nathan uses to make David see the wickedness in his greedy appropriation of Bathsheba, when, having told the story of the poor man's ewe lamb, he says to the righteously angry king: 'You are the man!' The Letter to the Ephesians offers its recipients another kind of self-recognition. Now part of the great humanity born in Christ's crucified body, they must recognize what they have accepted.

Back in Milan

The first reading that morning in Milan was Ephesians 4.1–16. 'One Lord, one faith, one baptism, one God and Father of all' is a powerful proclamation in English, and even more so in Italian: 'un solo Signore, una sola fede, un solo battesimo, un solo Dio e Padre di tutti'.

All-age worship

Try your hand at bread-making (because of shortage of time you may have to produce 'one I made earlier').

Suggested hymns

Bread of heaven, on thee we feed; Bread of the world, in mercy broken; Break thou the bread of life; I am the bread of life.

Tenth Sunday after Trinity (Proper 13)   5 August
Second Service   **Heroes**

Ps. 88 The pit of despair; Job 28 Where is wisdom found?, *or* Ecclus. (Ben Sira) 42.15–25 The works of the Lord; Heb. 11.17–31 Heroes of faith; *Gospel at Holy Communion*: Luke 12.13–21 The rich fool

> *'Yet all these, though they were commended for their faith, did not receive what was promised, since God had provided something better so that they would not, without us, be made perfect.'*
> *Hebrews 11.39–40*

Heroes

People are claimed as heroes and heroines when they spend the last few moments of their lives being incredibly brave, and then surrender their lives for their beliefs, or to protect others. Being a hero must surely be the shortest-lived profession, because it usually ends in an early death! Another definition of heroic behaviour is doing not only what nobody else has done, but what nobody else would even think of doing.

We need heroes

There's been a reaction in education against a heroic presentation of national history. In the past, most nations recounted their national story in terms of a series of heroic leaders. Since then, there've been a number of muck-raking biographies of the great men and women of the past, showing up that they were none of them perfect. Well, we could have guessed that; they were human like us, after all. But we don't need to have our attention drawn to their failings; and we are immeasurably poorer because hero-worship has been dropped from the syllabus. We need heroes; even if a misspent youth has been redeemed by one moment of glory, their story is our national story. It's telling the stories of our national heroes that binds us together as a nation; our community's founded on a common respect for the great figures of the past. Please don't take away our heroes; we need them.

Saints

The Christian Church has its heroes too; we call them saints. They weren't all martyrs, but all lived lives of transparent holiness. Yet had you asked any one of them, I'm sure they'd have answered, 'I'm no saint.' A necessary qualification for sainthood is enough humility to be aware of your failings. Yet we need our heroes in Christian history too; with all their faults, they can form role models for us to imitate by their heroism, and their imperfections make them approachable.

Hebrews

In the eleventh chapter of the Letter to the Hebrews, the author, whoever he was, lists great heroes of the faith. This is a list of women and men from the Hebrew Scriptures who are role models for the Christian because of their trust in God. What this wide ranging collection of heroes have in common is their faith.

> Now faith is the assurance of things hoped for, the conviction of things not seen . . . By faith Abel offered to God . . . By faith Enoch was taken . . . By faith Noah . . . built an ark . . . By faith Abraham obeyed . . . By faith Moses . . . refused to be called a son of Pharaoh's daughter . . . By faith the walls of Jericho fell . . . And what more should I say? For time would fail me to tell of Gideon, Barak, Samson, Jephthah, of David and Samuel and the prophets – who through faith conquered kingdoms, administered justice, obtained promises, shut the mouths of lions, quenched raging fire, escaped the edge of the sword, won strength out of weakness, became mighty in war, put foreign armies to flight . . . destitute, persecuted, tormented – of whom the world was not worthy. They wandered in deserts and mountains, and in caves and holes in the ground. Yet all these, though they were commended for their faith, did not receive what was promised, since God had provided something better so that they would not, apart from us, be made perfect.

These are our heroes, and we need our heroes of the faith, so that we can emulate their example of complete and utter trust in God to the very end.

Don't take away our heroes

The sceptic may point out that these heroines and heroes all had their faults – who doesn't? The sceptic may point out that the stories are based on ancient legends, which may have changed many times as they were told around the campfire. So what? They must have been thundering good yarns in the first place to be worth retelling down the years. Someone by the name of Moses must have existed at some time, and of one thing we can be certain: he must have been a man of great faith. We need faith if we're to persevere when things are going badly, and we need the example of the heroes of the faith to strengthen our resolve. Don't take away our heroes: they set up torches in dark streets by the light of which the rest of us can find our way to God.

Christ is the king, O friends rejoice; In our day of thanksgiving one psalm let us offer; One more step along the road I go; Who would true valour see / He who would valiant be.

Eleventh Sunday after Trinity (Proper 14)
12 August
Principal Service   **The Eternal Temptation of Short-term Rewards**
(*Continuous*): 2 Sam. 18.5–9, 15, 31–33 David's grief over Absalom's death, Ps. 130 Grief and forgiveness; *or* (*Related*): 1 Kings 19.4–8 God gives Elijah food, Ps. 34.1–8 Prayer and providence; Eph. 4.25—5.2 Live in love; John 6.35, 41–51 I am the bread of life

> '*Out of the depths I cry to you, O* LORD*! Lord, hear my voice! Let your ears be attentive to the voice of my supplications!' Psalm 130.1–2*

Christian living

There is a tendency to assume that God will listen to our prayers with 'merciful ears' provided we pray for the things he wants us to pray for. But we need to work harder to see God's vulnerability in thinking about what will 'please' God. This is where today's readings can help. Continuing his instructions for Christian living, the writer to the Ephesians begins with the way in which Christians should behave towards one another. This advice is what we might expect, until it turns from human community to humanity's vital relationship with God. Not only are the members of the audience responsible to one another: they must not 'grieve the Holy Spirit of God', whose 'seal' they received in baptism. If Christ gave himself up for them in love, and if God, in Christ, forgives them all their sins, then that is the model they must imitate, continuing to grow into the family resemblance described. Any pattern of behaviour that falls short of this can only wound the God who held back nothing in offering them salvation through Christ.

Our role model

We need look no further than David's grief over Absalom to see a reflection of the infinite grief of God, who offers us the model of Christ, but dignifies us with free will. Nor can there be a more powerful expression of hope that God will forgive – again and again – than Psalm 130. After this exalted picture of Christians living in harmony and obedience to the example of Christ, the Gospel reading brings us down to earth. In practice, it can be difficult to gather people around projects that will not show immediate results, or to persuade them to change their way of life without instant rewards. Jesus makes the most extraordinarily generous offer to the crowd who have followed him to Capernaum: nothing less than the satisfaction of all needs and desires.

Simply believe

All they have to do is to come to him, and believe in him. They respond with rumbling, gargling discontent that is dramatized for us in the Greek word (roughly transliterated), *egonguzon*. 'Complain' gives a rather milder impression of this reaction to the idea that someone whose family is well known locally should be claiming heavenly origins. There are echoes of the hostile reception given to Jesus in Nazareth recorded by Mark, though this is more surprising from people who have just been miraculously fed by the man whose credentials they are questioning. With patience that survives the hurtfulness of rejection and lack of belief, Jesus again explains that he is not claiming the status of the Father, but offering God's people the way to God, and the gift of life.

The eternal life

They are being presented with something better than their ancestors found in the wilderness, the simple choice of life or death. It will take much more of Jesus's patience – to death itself – before they realize that the gift of this living bread to give life to the world demands his own life. It is the same divine patience and self-giving love, always ready to listen to our prayers, ready to run the risk of being hurt by sin and negligence, as works with us, through Scripture and liturgy, to make us ready for eternal life. Charles Wesley caught this exactly:

Author of life divine,
Who hast a table spread,
Furnished with mystic wine
And everlasting bread,
Preserve the life thyself hast given,
And feed and train us up for heaven.

All-age worship

Make pipe-cleaner models of the congregation at Ephesus seated round a rich man's table.

Suggested hymns

Glorious things of thee are spoken; I am the bread of life; Jesus, stand among us at the meeting of our lives; Prayer is the soul's sincere desire.

Eleventh Sunday after Trinity (Proper 14)
12 August
Second Service   **God in Nature**

Ps. 91 Angels guard you; Job 39.1—40.4 God in nature, *or* Ecclus. (Ben Sira) 43.13–33 Nature; Heb. 12.1–17 A cloud of witnesses; *Gospel at Holy Communion*: Luke 12.32–40 Be prepared

> 'The LORD said to Job: "Shall a fault-finder contend with the Almighty?"' Job 40.1–2

Poetry

The book of Job, in the Old Testament, is one of the greatest poems in any language in the world. It deals with the profound question of the problem of suffering, and it's presented as a drama, when God and Satan discuss the faith of an apparently innocent man. Suddenly Job loses his family, his property and his health in one fell swoop. Job and his four friends take it in turns to speak about Job's agony, and finally God himself closes the debate, and recompenses Job for what he's lost. Hardly a line of this long poem passes without some unforgettable image or metaphor. This Hebrew epic was blessed by a translation, in the King James or Authorized Version, which is a paragon of English literature; many of its phrases have entered into everyday speech. If the Almighty wishes to speak to his children, it's through inspiring great poetry that he finds phrases that stir us with the solemnity of what we're hearing.

The problem

The problem that is raised is how God can allow human beings to suffer, when the Bible describes him as great and good. If God is love, surely he wants to take away our pain and grief? If God's all-powerful, surely he's able to do so? We could understand it if a just God sent pain to punish our wrongdoings. Yet wicked people prosper, and men, women and children, all round us, suffer in a way that they've certainly done nothing to deserve. So the poem imagines a completely righteous man; his so-called friends tell him that if he's suffering, then he must be guilty; Job replies that he's lived a blameless life, and wishes God would hear his complaints. Eventually God answers, but not to give an explanation or justification for the problem of innocent suffering. The Lord's unexpected reply is to describe the beauty of nature, and the magnificence of the world he has created. God asks Job: 'Shall a fault-finder contend with the Almighty?' Job at last realizes how self-centred he's been: though he may never understand God, at least he'll trust him.

Nature

So God describes the splendour of the world he created, and teasingly asks Job whether he could have done so well. 'Where were you when I laid the foundation of the earth? . . . when the morning stars sang together, and all the sons of God shouted for joy . . . when I said [to the sea], thus far shall you come and no further, and here shall your proud waves be stopped.'

Descriptions

In the poem, the Lord describes the wonders that make us gasp with awe when we watch nature programmes on television. There is the way the morning light spreads across the valleys when viewed from a hilltop; the depths of the sea and the sources of light. The snow, the wind and the rain; the stars on a dark night; the wild animals and the birds. God asks whether Job knows how the mountain goats give birth. Nowadays we know, but we couldn't have invented such a process if we tried. The wild ass, the wild ox, the ostrich, the war-horse and the eagle are described. Behemoth and Leviathan are mythical animals, but their description owes a lot to the hippopotamus and the crocodile.

Repentance

When God's finished, Job replies, 'I . . . repent in dust and ashes.' Nobody's totally innocent, in the real world. We're meant to love each other, as Jesus loves everybody. All of us have fallen short of that standard; so nobody can say, 'I'm a perfect human being, I completely deserve all the natural blessings that God has showered on me.' You can't measure and compare human sins, and say such a sin deserves this amount of punishment. We must be grateful that God is as merciful as he is.

The answer

Yet this is no answer to the problem of suffering. Nowhere in the book of Job, or anywhere else in the Old Testament, do you find a complete written answer. Only through the experience of life did Job come to an understanding that he couldn't put into words. If we turn to the New Testament, however, we get a completely different sort of answer. In the life and death of Jesus, we find revealed a God who doesn't try to explain our suffering – instead he enters this world of pain and loss, and shares our suffering with us. Perhaps when poor old Job cried, 'I know that my Redeemer lives', he had some dim foresight into how Jesus deals with the problem of suffering.

Suggested hymns

As water to the thirsty; Lord of beauty, thine the splendour; O Lord my God, when I in awesome wonder; The spacious firmament on high.

Twelfth Sunday after Trinity (Proper 15) 19 August
Principal Service **Eat and Live**

(*Continuous*): 1 Kings 2.10–12; 3.3–14 Solomon's dream, Ps. 111
The beginning of wisdom; *or* (*Related*): Prov. 9.1–6 Wisdom's call,
Ps. 34.9–14 Providence and peace; Eph. 5.15–20 Wisdom;
John 6.51–58 Eat and live

> *'[Jesus said,] "I am the living bread that came down from heaven.
> Whoever eats of this bread will live for ever."' John 6.51*

Feed the Minds

Feed the Minds is an ecumenical Christian charity, working with
partners of different denominations and faiths to promote education in Africa, Asia, Latin America and the Middle East. They
believe that education saves lives: if poor people can read, they'll
learn to farm better. But they also speak of the spiritual well-
being of the communities they serve. It's essential that Christians
from richer parts of the world should feed the bodies of the
poor, otherwise they'll die. But feeding bodies only gives people
an animal-like existence, 'nasty, brutish and short'. To make us
more than animals, we must feed our minds and our spirits also.
Acquiring an appreciation of beauty in music and art, and the
ability to love, seems of little practical value, but they're what
make us human.

Cannibalism or Communion?

In the sixth chapter of St John, Jesus recommends us to 'feed on
him'. It seems a strange choice of words, and it led long ago to a
rumour that Christians are cannibals. Of course he didn't mean that;
he meant eating bread and drinking wine in the Holy Communion,
which symbolize his body and blood. The words are chosen, surely,
to remind us that we need more types of nourishment than merely
physical food; we need food for our minds and our souls also.
When we attend a church service, hear the word of God read in the
Scriptures and expounded in the sermon, share with other Christians
in prayer and singing, then we receive spiritual nourishment, leading
to eternal life.

Not only in the sacrament

In St John's Gospel there are many chapters about Jesus as the bread of life and the true vine, about feeding on him and the importance of his blood. Yet curiously, St John gives us no account of the Last Supper itself. He mentions Jesus washing the disciples' feet, teaching and praying; but there's no mention of bread and wine in that chapter. St John meant us to value and honour the sacrament of the Eucharist. But we mustn't stop there. Jesus feeds our minds and spirits in the church services, and we die spiritually if we stop going to church. Yet he can nourish us in other ways too.

Other meals

When you eat together with other Christians, Jesus feeds your souls also. Whether it's a church supper, or an Alpha course, or the refreshments before a church meeting, there's something about eating with one another that binds people together in a particularly loving way. When you arrange your engagements so that your whole family can sit down round a table, Jesus is there too at the family meal. Friends dining together; a cup of tea shared with someone in difficulties; a cheese sandwich at the end of a hard morning's digging, or when you rest during a walk in the countryside, thanking God for his blessings; in all these ways nourishment for the body can also be food for the soul.

A healthy mind

The Roman poet Juvenal wrote about 'a healthy mind in a healthy body'. The two things go together. We can feed on Jesus intellectually, by reading about him, talking with our friends about him, and praying to him. It's sad that so many people let their minds go to sleep when they finish their formal education. You never stop learning, if you're interested in the world around you; you never stop learning about God's love, if you keep your relationship with him alive through daily Bible reading and prayer.

Why?

If you feed on Jesus by worship, table fellowship, reading and prayer, then he'll nourish your souls as surely as bread nourishes your body. The relationship between your soul and God can't be interrupted by the mere death of the physical body, and will grow and blossom in heaven. Jesus said, 'I am the living bread that came down from heaven. Whoever eats of this bread will live for ever.' But the opposite's tragically true, also. If you don't nourish your soul by fellowship with Jesus, even though your body may go on living for a good few years more, you'll be spiritually dead. Why forgo the chance of eternal life by neglecting spiritual nourishment?

All-age worship

Bring coloured card and paper, a hole-puncher and ribbon or raffia. Make small notebooks, decorate them and sell them in aid of Feed the Minds.

Suggested hymns

Alleluia, sing to Jesus; Bread of heaven, on thee we feed; Break thou the bread of life; Let us break bread together.

Twelfth Sunday after Trinity (Proper 15)   19 August
Second Service   **The Burning Bush**
Ps. [92 Giving thanks] 100 All the earth; Ex. 2.23—3.10 The burning bush; Heb. 13.1–15 Outside the gate; *Gospel at Holy Communion*: Luke 12.49–56 Divisions

> *'The angel of the Lord appeared to [Moses] in a flame of fire out of a bush; he looked, and the bush was blazing, yet it was not consumed.' Exodus 3.2*

Myths

Ancient tribal myths are traditional stories, told round the campfire, to do three things. First, they're meant to create a sense of awe and wonder, about the world of nature and about God. Second, they're meant to explain things, origins, words, relationships, that sort of thing. And third, they're meant to unite people – 'We're all one family because we tell the same stories.' The story of Moses and the burning bush does those things superbly. It's supposed to have taken place in a desert, and nomads report seeing mirages and other strange experiences under the desert sun. There's no point in seeking a natural explanation; this is a story about a vision, to remind us that God's close to us at all times, but he doesn't always communicate with us in the ways we expect. Second, the southern tribes called God 'the Lord', and the story goes on to explain this name, which in Hebrew sounds like the verb 'to be'; so God's name is 'I am who I am'. But the tribes who came in with Abraham from the eastern desert called God by a different name, which we translate as just 'God'. So the story unites the north-eastern tribes and the southern tribes, by pointing out that they worship the same God under different names: the God of Abraham is the same as the God they called 'I am'.

What's that to us?

Well, that's all very interesting for archaeologists, anthropologists and social historians, but what's it got to do with us? Actually, it's a very important story, seminal for modern thinking, provided you remember that symbolism is more important than historical accuracy.

Mystery

First, we must remember that God's very mysterious. We don't understand God because God's so much greater than we are. God's everywhere, and wherever we stand we're on holy ground. Sometimes something unexpected happens, and we realize God's trying to tell us something. Unless we're open to the God of surprises, unless we expect the unexpected, we may miss the message when it flashes across our brain. God doesn't only talk to us in church; he can speak through an experience in the desert, or on a mountaintop, on the laboratory bench or in the bosom of our family. Be ready to hear, and to do what he tells you to do.

Not consumed

Second, this story explains something puzzling about the nature of God. The bush was burning, but not burnt up; ablaze, but not consumed. This describes what modern scientists would call a 'steady-state phenomenon'. The sun, around which our planet revolves, seems like that, burning but always remaining the same. But in fact, the scientists tell us, the sun's a huge nuclear reactor, turning nuclear energy into heat and light. There's an awful lot of matter in the heart of a star like the sun, and though it's being used up at a colossal rate, it'll keep burning like that for billions of years yet.

But God is not part of the material world: God's the creator of the material world. God was there before the Big Bang coughed out all that undifferentiated matter, and he'll be there after the universe has run down into undifferentiated matter again in the heat-death. God made time and he isn't affected by it, God's unchanging. Yet, like the burning bush, God's very active; God's a consuming fire, but it's the fire of love. We're made in the image of God, so after we pass from the world of time into the world of eternity, we shall be ablaze with love, too, but not consumed by death.

Inclusive

Third, the story's inclusive. Whatever name you call God by, there's only one God. St Paul, on Mars Hill, told the Greeks, 'the same God, whom you worship without knowing him, is the God we proclaim to you'. Christianity doesn't bring you a new God; but it tells you a lot about God as he's revealed in Jesus, which we would never have guessed at if Jesus hadn't come. Those who use religion to divide people are doing the very opposite of what religion was intended for. It's not meant for judging and condemning other people; religion's meant to be inclusive, welcoming and unifying. The Jews of the northern and southern tribes had plenty to argue about, and, being Jews, argue they did. But the story of the burning bush reminded them that in the end we're all one family; it brings the same message to us Christians, too.

Suggested hymns

Be still, for the Spirit of the Lord; Come, living God, when least expected; Jesus, where'er thy people meet; The God of Abraham praise.

Thirteenth Sunday after Trinity (Proper 16)
26 August
Principal Service   **God is Ready to Hear Us**
(*Continuous*): 1 Kings 8.[1, 6, 10–11] 22–30, 41–43 Solomon prays, Ps. 84 How lovely is your Temple; *or* (*Related*): Joshua 24.1–2a, 14–18 Choose the Lord, Ps. 34.15–22 The Lord's my salvation; Eph. 6.10–20 The armour of God; John 6.56–69 Spirit and life

> *'It is the spirit that gives life; the flesh is useless. The words that I have spoken to you are spirit and life.' John 6.63*

Teaching in the synagogue

Jesus's extended teaching on the bread of life ends on a telling note: 'He said these things while he was teaching in the synagogue in Capernaum.' This suggests, first of all, that the crowd pursuing him from the other side of the lake had found him in the synagogue. More importantly, it suggests that Jesus chose that setting to talk to them about the meaning of the meal they had eaten on the hillside, in order to place his words firmly within orthodox practice. He is illuminating for them the fulfilment of Scripture: 'He gave them bread from heaven to eat', and the synagogue is the place to do this. So there is nothing furtive or unofficial about what he has to tell them, and he will make that point about everything he has ever taught, when he stands before the High Priest after his arrest: 'I have always spoken openly to the world; I have always taught in synagogues and in the temple, where all the Jews come together. I have said nothing in secret.'

Embodiment of God's promises

What the people do not realize, even as the trial takes its course, is that Jesus is not just telling them what the Scripture means, but making God's promises real in his own flesh and blood. That, in the sacraments, God shows us what he does and does what he shows us.

Solomon's journey and wisdom

Solomon's journey from his accession, to the moment when a house where the name of YHWH will be permanently honoured is ready for use, has not demonstrated the unblemished holiness which might be expected of a king who now takes up a priestly role among his people. Having come to the throne by ruthless political scheming, he consolidates his power by systematically annihilating potential opposition. Although commended for his love of the Lord, he sacrifices at shrines which are not all dedicated to YHWH. What allows Solomon to be the king with whom the Lord keeps the covenant made with David is the unusual self-knowledge that moves him to ask for wisdom as a divine gift. Legendary wealth will be added to this, precisely because he has not asked for it. When, at last, he stands before the altar of the new Temple, and prays in the presence of the nation's senior representatives, his prayer comes from what

Robert Wilson describes as a particularly Deuteronomistic point of view. YHWH is the only God, and there is only one legitimate place for worship. The prayer 'asks God to hear the prayers of those who are righteous and truly repent of their sins'. It extends beyond Israel to all who will come to God's house and offer petitions in his name.

Fighting evil through prayer

For the writer to the Ephesians, the movement is outward rather than inward, to communities whose local existence around the eastern Mediterranean takes a larger unity from common trust in the Lord in the face of evil powers in this world, and in the 'heavenly places' beyond. This really is the 'Church militant here in earth', as the vivid metaphors of armour and weaponry indicate. But the most powerful weapon of all is the prayer that runs like a living current from the Spirit, through the 'saints', and overflows in intercession.

Prayer for the people

Making the principle of prayer into something that is genuinely the prayer of the people is a continuing task for those who lead worship and for those who participate. Cranmer's brilliant translation of a collect with its roots in the eighth century uses rhetorical devices native to English to portray a God who is as majestic as, but less austere than, the Latin implies. This God longs for our prayers, even if we are lethargic, and responds beyond what we 'desire or deserve'. We approach in fear, and find forgiveness. Sometimes it is the given, and not the glitteringly extempore, that speaks the needs we did not know we had.

All-age worship

Draw symbols of the seven sacraments: Holy Communion, Baptism, Confirmation, Ordination, Marriage, Forgiveness and Healing. Add other powerful symbols like a kiss.

Suggested hymns

Bread of the world in mercy broken; I am the bread of life; Jesus the Lord says, I am the bread; Seek ye first the kingdom of God.

Thirteenth Sunday after Trinity (Proper 16)
26 August
Second Service　　**Doing Good**

Ps. 116 Recovery from illness; Ex. 4.27—5.1 Aaron speaks for
Moses; Heb. 13.16–21 Do good; *Gospel at Holy Communion*:
Luke 13.10–17 Healing on the Sabbath

> *'Do not neglect to do good and to share what you have, for such
> sacrifices are pleasing to God.' Hebrews 13.16*

Doing good

A Hindu scholar, who was reading the New Testament for the first
time, remarked to his friends, 'I read today about a man who went
about doing good; and I regretted the amount of time I waste just going about.' He had been reading from the Acts of the Apostles, chapter
10, where it says: 'God anointed Jesus of Nazareth with the Holy Spirit
and with power; how he went about doing good and healing all who
were oppressed by the devil, for God was with him.' What a moving summary of Jesus's life is contained in those few words: 'He went
about doing good.' How sad it is that the rest of us fall far short of
Jesus's example, and waste so much of our time just going about, but
seldom doing anything that's going to make the world a better place.

Goodness

Goodness is attractive uprightness in life. Being good to others
involves doing what is in their best interests. Actors say that it's
easy to act a villain, but extremely difficult to act the part of a
really good man. Although most of us have met one or two people
in our lifetime whom we could describe as really good, we've felt
as though we had little in common with them because we ourselves
are so far from being really good.

Goody-goody

Yet really good people have an attractive winsomeness about them.
This is nothing like the false goody-goody goodness of Little Jack
Horner: 'See what a good boy am I!' Really good people are kind
and considerate, imaginative enough to understand your situation
and realize what you really need, before setting about giving it to

you. The goodness of Jesus showed itself in his healing ministry, and his tenderness towards the outcast and poor.

The fruit of the Spirit

So where is true goodness to be found? St Paul tells us that goodness is one of the fruits of the Spirit. 'The fruit of the Spirit is Love, Joy, Peace, Patience, Kindness, Goodness, Faithfulness, Gentleness, and Self-control.' 'For such there is no law,' he adds. Jewish Christians argued that non-Jews couldn't become righteous except by obeying the law of the Hebrew Scriptures. No, wrote Paul, virtues can't be imposed by even the best of laws; they have to grow naturally in the soul. As fruit grows slowly and steadily because nurtured by the life of the tree, so the virtues grow in Christians because of the life God gives through the Holy Spirit.

The goodness of God

Goodness is a description of God's character as revealed in the Bible: when God wanted to reveal his nature, God told Elijah, 'I will make my goodness pass before you.' God is good, God behaves in a reliable and moral way towards us, as well as expecting us to be good to him and to each other. The teaching of Jesus confirms and extends the revelation of the Fatherhood and Love of God in the Old Testament. But Jesus doesn't just tell us to be good: by his death on the cross, he gives us his grace and power to enable us to be good. The Book of Common Prayer describes God as the fountain of all goodness. In the twenty-third psalm, David says that because the Lord is his Shepherd, 'surely goodness and mercy shall follow me all the days of my life'. Though a child is supposed to have misheard this verse, and asked who 'Good Mrs Murphy' was, because they'd been singing 'Good Mrs Murphy shall follow me'.

Our goal

So our goal in life is not to be good, in a smug way, but to go about doing good, as Jesus did. John Wesley made it one of his Rules of Conduct to

Do all the good you can
By all the means you can
In all the ways you can

214

In all the places you can
To all the people you can
As long as ever you can.

It's an attainable goal, because we don't have to do it in our strength, but through the grace of God working in us. Harriet Beecher Stowe, the American author of *Uncle Tom's Cabin*, wrote: 'What makes saintliness in my view, as distinguished from ordinary goodness, is a certain quality of magnanimity and greatness of soul that brings life within the circle of the heroic.' Now there's a target to aim for!

Suggested hymns

God of mercy, God of grace; Let me have my way among you (Do not strive); The Lord's my Shepherd; There is a green hill far away.

Fourteenth Sunday after Trinity (Proper 17)
2 September
Principal Service   **Running after the Scent of God's Garments**

(*Continuous*): S. of Sol. 2.8–13 Love in springtime; Ps. 45.1–2, 6–9 The king's wedding; *or* (*Related*): Deut. 4.1–2, 6–9 Teach your family obedience to law; Ps. 15 The Temple; James 1.17–27 Doers of the word; Mark 7.1–8, 14–15, 21–23 Inner cleanness

> '[Jesus said,] "This people honours me with their lips, but their hearts are far from me; in vain do they worship me, teaching human precepts as doctrines." You abandon the commandment of God and hold to human tradition.' Mark 7.6–8

Faithful living

What is the attractiveness of religious practice? What does faith have to look like, if it is to be a good advertisement for itself? Most people would say that it must be genuine in its enactment of its own principles, practising what it preaches. They might add that it should be sensible and consistent, maintaining a proper relationship between essentials and externals. It should also be practical in a way that allows observers to see what it is about. Less accessible,

215

but nevertheless important, is the requirement for faith to refrain from pre-empting God's action, particularly in the matter of making judgements. Righteous anger, as the Letter of James points out, is not God-given. In fact, the whole letter offers a working guide to being a Christian in the world, and although Luther might have regarded it as unhelpful to a proper understanding of justification, it contains much reassurance for those who want to know how to live their faith, and what a Christian ethic might look like. James advises his readers to 'welcome with meekness the implanted word that has the power to save your souls'. God dwells in us. We need to take our direction from that impulse, being listeners and not just hearers; doers and not just commentators.

Obstructions of ritual and judgement

Jesus's harsh assessment of the Pharisees and scribes is perhaps to be seen in the light of the measured principles that James establishes. They are obeying a law that had evolved with ever greater precision to preserve the distinction between God's holy people and the potential for contamination in their contact with a world outside this distinctive relationship. What Jesus sees in their ritual enforcements is imbalance. They overemphasize external customs, and neglect the real devotion of heart and mind – not necessarily because they are hypocrites, but because they are faulty interpreters. The law that they so zealously defend directs its adherents to the law-giving but also life-giving word of God dwelling in them. Without these secure compass points, it is easy to fall into the trap that James warns against: judging others, and trying officiously to do the work that properly belongs to God.

In love with God

The effect of all of this is to sever people from God rather than to bring them closer; to create in their minds an exacting disciplinarian, and displace the God who always sets obedience side by side with love. It is in response to this latter God that the Church has been happy to allow erotic poetry to erupt into its regime of reading Scripture. Bernard of Clairvaux (1090–1153) saw in the Song of Solomon an allegory of Christ and the Church. We might be even more direct than this, approaching God as if drawn irresistibly and personally by great beauty. The mystics of the Christian tradition have shown through their writings and visions that it is entirely possible to fall in love with God. They have risked the most dangerous of human emotions in seeking the nearest possible apprehension of the God who called them into such close relationship as they prayed and meditated. The most truthful of our human feelings can be our teachers in approaching the God who came close to us in flesh and blood. God is prepared to use all means to draw us closer and to reconcile us to him – and to make us a new creation, capable of proclaiming a kingdom that opens its doors to all who are drawn to its message. Newly baptized Christians in fourth-century Milan heard this more vividly from Ambrose, as he reminded them of their anointing. He mentioned Psalm 133, but went on to say:

> This is the oil of which Solomon said: 'Your name is like fragrant anointing oils poured out; that is why the maidens love you and draw you to them.' How many souls made new today have loved you, O Lord God, saying, 'Draw us after you. We run after the scent of your garments', so that they may drink in the fragrance of the resurrection?

All-age worship

Blow up balloons, and write on them with felt-tips: 'God's Spirit = Life'; 'God's Spirit = Love', etc.

Fourteenth Sunday after Trinity (Proper 17)
2 September
Second Service   **How Can Young People Be Pure?**
Ps. 119.1–16 Happy those who walk in God's law; Ex. 12.21–27; Passover; Matt. 4.23—5.20 Sermon on the Mount

> *'How can young people keep their way pure? By guarding it according to your word.' Psalm 119.9*

Being young

Bliss it was in that dawn to be alive,
But to be young was very heaven.

In that well-known quotation William Wordsworth describes *The French Revolution, as it Appeared to Enthusiasts*. It wasn't long, however, before many people found the new freedom a misery. Then, to be young was not heaven, but more like the other place. What's it like to be young in the twenty-first century, do you think? Young people have many new freedoms today, and enjoy the opportunities for travel, improved education, choice of career, choosing their friends, and making up their own minds. But freedom also brings insecurity. When there are no boundaries, every path is full of peril. When anything goes, nothing's fun any more.

A changed world

We live in a changed world. But of course human nature doesn't change; it's the circumstances in which people grow up that make the difference. Young people in the twenty-first century have much more money than their predecessors. This opens opportunities for enjoyment if they spend it wisely, but only brings misery if they make fools of themselves. And sexual freedom hasn't brought happiness. In the process, we're losing sight of the romantic ideal of love. Falling in love limits your freedom, but it's worth it! The process of choosing a life partner, for young people today, is fraught with difficulties that can hardly be imagined by their predecessors. Long live romance! Long live love! Long live freedom, so long as it doesn't kill romance and love.

Single-mindedness

Psalm 119 asks a very relevant question: 'How can young people keep their way pure?' Now, being pure, in the Bible, doesn't mean what it meant in Victorian times: never thinking about the opposite sex at all. For which Lord Baden-Powell's cure, in the early editions of *Scouting for Boys*, is alleged to have been taking lots of cold showers! Purity in the Bible is more like single-mindedness, concentrating on doing what God wants us to do, to the exclusion of all distractions and temptations. The message of the Bible is that this single-mindedness does indeed bring a happiness deeper than can be known in any other way. 'Blessed are the pure in heart,' says Jesus, 'for they shall see God.' He means those who are single-mindedly trying to live their lives in the best possible way, those who 'hunger and thirst after righteousness'. So it's very important to find an answer to the question, 'How can young people keep their way pure?'

Daily Bible reading

The answer that the psalm gives is simple to say, hard to put into practice: 'How can young people keep their way pure? By guarding it according to your word.' Studying the Bible is the answer to many of young people's problems. Reading a few verses every day, preferably with a set of Bible-reading notes or a book to explain them, and then thinking about what they mean and how they can be applied to your own life, that's the secret. Now, young people often like things to be cut and dried, and to provide simple answers. If you approach the Bible in that way, it'll certainly give you many verses which you can memorize and repeat to yourself when you're tempted. But just because the world has changed so much since Bible times, it's better to take some time thinking about what it meant in the society of those days, and how it needs to be reinterpreted when you apply it today.

Boundaries

Nevertheless, the Bible gives you much-needed boundaries. There are ten commandments which are the rock-bottom foundation of civilized life. If you break them, Jesus reveals a God who'll certainly forgive you, but it cost Jesus his life to win that forgiveness for you, so you won't do it lightly. 'Read your Bible, pray every day, if you'd follow me,' goes the Sunday school chorus. Or as the psalm puts it, 'How can young people keep their way pure? By guarding it according to your word.' Ecclesiastes recommends, 'Remember your creator in the days of your youth.' Then, you may be able to teach a few lessons to those who are older.

Suggested hymns

Blest are the pure in heart; I want to walk with Jesus Christ; Lord, thy word abideth; When we walk with the Lord.

Fifteenth Sunday after Trinity (Proper 18)
9 September
Principal Service   **Zero Tolerance for the Uncleanness of Evil**

(*Continuous*): Prov. 22.1–2, 8–9, 22–23 The needy, Ps. 125 God rewards the righteous; *or* (*Related*): Isa. 35.4–7a Water in the desert, Ps. 146 Healing and salvation; James 2.1–10 [11–13] 14–17 Rich and poor; Mark 7.24–37 Crumbs from the table, healing the deaf

> *'Now the woman was a Gentile, of Syrophoenician origin. She begged him to cast the demon out of her daughter.' Mark 7.26*

Rituals of cleanliness and law

Jesus's confrontation with some Pharisees and scribes over ritual cleanliness in last week's Gospel reading makes an important transition in Mark's narrative. The teaching and ministry that Jesus has exercised among his own people is to be extended to the Gentile regions. Questions of cleanliness, the law, and the special relationships of the Jewish people to God will underpin the next series of encounters.

An unclean spirit

In the first of these, a Syrophoenician woman hears that Jesus is in the district of Tyre, and comes to find him in the house where he is seeking anonymity. The Greek text describes her as 'Greek' rather than 'Gentile', and the lively repartee that follows suggests that she and Jesus may have conversed in Greek. Commentary on the exchange, in which she exhorts Jesus to heal her daughter of an 'unclean spirit', often commends both parties for their wit. It is less direct about the overtones of ethnic discrimination in Jesus's references to 'children' and 'dogs'. On closer inspection, this analogy has some odd features. The word that Jesus uses for 'feeding' the children (the Jews) is normally associated with feeding stalled animals. He goes on to use the diminutive form of 'dogs', suggesting small dogs or puppies. The woman picks this up; for she seems to take Jesus to be referring to household pets, and not outside or feral dogs. Perhaps first-century children were as adept as their modern counterparts at scattering food on the floor in their early attempts at feeding themselves. It was not that the dogs were going to miss out: only that their needs would not receive first consideration. The Gentiles were not Jesus's immediate priority, but their turn would come. Does Jesus respond to the woman's verbal dexterity, or to the deeper intelligence that moves her to address him as *Kyrie*, ambiguously serving as a polite form of address and a greater title? Even the dogs may eventually eat from the table. Even the Gentiles can recognize the Lord. The boundaries of what is externally clean, acceptable and holy are being redefined not only for devout Jews, but also, we may dare to imagine, in the mind of Jesus, as he lives the vocation of God incarnate. What is not ambiguous, however, is his intolerance for the corrosive uncleanness of evil which threatens human wholeness. The demon leaves the child.

Liberation of healing

The return journey describes a further act of healing and liberation. Jesus does not wish for an audience while he deals with the deaf man, but a few of the disciples must have witnessed him touching the man's ears and his tongue with spittle. Unhygienic as this appears, it is a moment of new creation, a sign that the coming kingdom will require a new humanity. That Jesus sighs and looks upwards as he opens the man's senses reminds us that the whole Godhead is involved, and that the doors of heaven are opening, too. The people are properly astonished, and commend Jesus for doing what Isaiah said that the Messiah would do.

The coming of God's kingdom

It is doubtful that the people have drawn the conclusion that the Gospel-writer invites readers to make – that God's kingdom is arriving among them. It will be later, in the light of the resurrection, that Jews and Gentiles who have given their allegiance to this new way of life will be challenged to reassess their own patterns of religious and practical behaviour. To see Christ as 'our glorious Lord' is to see his insistence on loving one's neighbour, not just as the law, but as a 'royal law'. Jesus, who embodies the fulfilment of the law, cannot be followed piecemeal. Only by keeping the whole law – particularly in respect of the poor – can its adherents find the liberty and dignity it offers to them, and to those 'others' whom they embrace as neighbours.

Find out about children with disabilities in your area. What could you do to help?

Suggested hymns

At even, when the sun was set; Give thanks with a grateful heart; Peter and John went to pray; They shall come from the east.

Fifteenth Sunday after Trinity (Proper 18)
9 September
Second Service   **Crossing the Red Sea**
Ps. 119.41–56 Delight in God's commandments; Ex. 14.5–31 Crossing the Red Sea; Matt. 6.1–18 Almsgiving, prayer and fasting

> 'The LORD drove the sea back by a strong east wind all night, and turned the sea into dry land; and the waters were divided.' Exodus 14.21

Biblical epics

When the old, biblical epic films are revived on TV they always find an enthusiastic audience. Small wonder, for the Bible really does contain the greatest stories ever told. It was from these events that God revealed himself as a God who saves. Unfortunately, the special effects stick in the mind until you believe that's how it really happened. In the film *The Ten Commandments*, when Moses led the Israelites through the Red Sea, there's a wall of water as high as a skyscraper on either side of them and they pass through a sort of Grand Canyon. But that isn't quite what the Bible says.

The Red Sea

First of all we have to ask where did this take place? All the English translations of the Bible call it the Red Sea; that great stretch of water, many fathoms deep, which stretches from the southern end of the Gulf of Suez almost to the Indian Ocean. But 'Red Sea' is a mistranslation. The original Hebrew calls it 'the Sea of Reeds'. That could have been anywhere: near the Great Bitter Lakes on the Suez

Canal, or one of the lagoons on the edge of the Mediterranean. But something called the Sea of Reeds can't have been very deep.

A strong wind

So what parted the waters? Some speculate that it was a sort of tsunami, arising from the explosion of the volcanic island of Santorini, causing the waters to recede and then return to drown the Egyptian army. But that's unnecessary if the water was just a shallow marsh. Listen to what the Bible actually says: 'The LORD drove the sea back by a strong east wind all night, and turned the sea into dry land; and the waters were divided. The Israelites went into the sea on dry ground, the waters forming a wall for them on their right and on their left.' Picture the wind pushing the water to the western side of the lake, revealing a sort of causeway, across which the Israelites could pick their way. The shallow water was still there on their right and their left, like a protecting wall, because it prevented the Egyptians making flanking attacks; but when the wind stopped, the water covered the causeway again and stopped the Egyptians following them. Not as dramatic as Cecil B. DeMille's version, perhaps, but easier for the modern scientific mind to accept.

How, why, when, where and who?

The important thing, however, is not how it happened, but why. Whether it was a natural event or a miracle, the hand of God's seen in the fact that these extraordinary events took place exactly when and where they were needed. God's a God who saves, and he provided the Israelites with a way to pass through the water barrier as they escaped from slavery, and to prevent their enemies from following them. Then there was the question of who: Moses was the man of the moment, in the right place at the right time, to recognize that God was behind the events and explain this to the people. They'd never forget; the historical events would be retold in psalm and folklore for ever after, as the foundation story of the nation who believed in a saviour God.

Important to us

That's why the story of the crossing of the Red Sea's important to us, too. The New Testament describes the saving death and resurrection of Jesus as a new exodus. Christians compare our salvation through the waters of baptism to passing through the waters of the Red Sea on our way to the Promised Land of heaven. It's possible, by studying the world of nature, to say there must be a Supreme Being and Creator. But only when God reveals himself through events like the crossing of the Red Sea can we understand that he's a Saviour. God intervened in history by the life of Jesus; and still today he intervenes to save us from slavery. Whether it's slavery to bad habits – to addiction; to greed, envy or anger; to guilt or fear – God will come if we call and lead us through the threatening waters. This is how he proves to us that he loves us. This is how he moves us to love him in gratitude. This is how he saves us from self-centredness, and motivates us to save others from the troubles that entrap them. And we wouldn't have understood all this, if God hadn't first saved the Israelites through the waters of the sea from their Egyptian captors.

Suggested hymns

At the Lamb's high feast we sing; Come ye faithful, raise the strain; The God of Abraham praise; When Israel was in Egypt's land.

Sixteenth Sunday after Trinity (Proper 19)
16 September
Principal Service   **A Dangerous Invitation**
(*Continuous*): Prov. 1.20–33 Wisdom's call, Ps. 19 Law and nature, *or Canticle*: Wisd. 7.26—8.1 Wisdom; *or* (*Related*): Isa. 50.4–9a Suffering, Ps. 116.1–8 Salvation from death; James 3.1–12 Controlling the tongue; Mark 8.27–38 Take up your cross

> '[Jesus said,] "If any want to become my followers, let them deny themselves and take up their cross and follow me."' *Mark 8.34*

Preparing for the end

The feeding of 4,000 people from seven loaves and a few fish, another encounter with the Pharisees, and a blind man's miraculous healing are motifs in Mark's Gospel that are significant in the next stage of his narrative. Jesus now begins to prepare the disciples for the end to which his earthly ministry is heading. To grasp this, they will need to be generous in accepting that he offers salvation to the world, and not just to a small constituency. They will have to distinguish between the values of human powers and the values of a new sort of life. Above all, they will need vision, both to protect themselves in hostile conditions and to see profoundly what the message of Jesus means. All of this is part of Mark's preoccupation with identity, and now Jesus presses the disciples to commit themselves rather than shelter behind the general speculation that he is a returned John the Baptist or Elijah.

The Messiah

It is Peter, the first to answer Jesus's call to follow him, who is the first to acknowledge Jesus as 'Messiah'. That title carries an immense weight of expectation. Matthew and Luke attach it to Jesus from an early stage in their Gospels, establishing him as Saviour and King; this is its first appearance in Mark, and it allows the reader to imagine what it was like for Peter to realize that he knew something he did not know he knew. The perfect moment of epiphany is shattered, however, as Jesus goes alarmingly off-message to introduce his coming death and the extraordinary idea that he will rise again. Peter acts, presumably to save Jesus from himself, knowing the dangers of incautious speech in the volatile climate of their world. By the measure of that world, he acts wisely. But that is not the measure that Jesus is applying. He has in mind a gift of life, bought at great cost, because it is of infinite value. Any life parsimoniously hoarded in a hostile world is mean by comparison; and it is not proof against time. God's life must not be confused with the poor imitation that might tempt someone who feared conflict and pain. Statements such as this are, of course, easier to hear or write down than to live, no matter how sincerely they are believed. The experiences of Christians persecuted and tortured for their faith are evidence enough of that fact. Paul was frank about what following Jesus looked like to the world when he wrote to the Corinthians: 'The message of the cross is folly to those who are perishing, but to those who are being saved, it is the power of God and the wisdom of God.'

Dangerous invitation

Jesus persists in offering his dangerous invitation to the crowd, sparing nothing of what following him will mean. His challenge to them is to consider what they would lose by refusing. Despite the careful distinctions between the foolish and the wise in the proverbs and illustrations provided by the ancient Near Eastern world and kept alive by generations, it must have been hard for the crowd to tell the difference when it came to the lives that Jesus was putting before them. Would it have seemed wayward and complacent to choose a safe and quiet place on earth? Would Jesus's words have seemed like the call of wisdom to a security better than the fickle world could offer, or like the irresponsible mischief-making of the undisciplined tongue? Those questions have confronted followers of Jesus from the earliest times. They have confronted us this past week in two feasts.

Victory of the cross

Holy Cross Day, on 14 September, called us to celebrate the victory of the cross, mindful always that it is a victory scarred by pain and degradation. Then 15 September honoured the third-century bishop and martyr, Cyprian of Carthage, who died in 258, a champion of the unity of the Church. His restoration of those penitents who had denied their faith under persecution recognized compassionately that following Jesus is a hard calling.

All-age worship

Borrow a rucksack, and make a label for it reading 'My burden is light, says Jesus.' Children take turns to put it on, and see how much they can put in it before it is too heavy to carry.

Suggested hymns

I danced in the morning; Take up your cross, the Saviour said; When I survey the wondrous cross; Will you come and follow me?

Sixteenth Sunday after Trinity (Proper 19)
16 September
Second Service   **A Log in Your Eye**
Ps. 119.73–88 Give me understanding; Ex. 18.13–26
Administration of justice; Matt. 7.1–14 Judging others

> '[Jesus said,] "You hypocrite, first take the log out of your own eye, and then you will see clearly to take the speck out of your neighbour's eye."' Matthew 7.5

Broad humour

Broad humour's not a characteristic that most people would associate with Jesus. That's because we've heard his jokes so many times we've forgotten that they *are* jokes. But imagine you're one of the crowd listening to Jesus telling the story for the first time.

A log in your eye

'Once upon a time,' begins Jesus, 'there was this very proud man. He thought he was superior to everybody else, so he was forever telling other people what to do. If the people he met had faults – and who doesn't? – this man took it upon himself to tell them. Even very little failings didn't escape his critical notice. If you got away with only a short telling off for what was wrong about you, you could count yourself lucky. Understandably, he was not popular! One day, he's walking down the street, looking for somebody to criticize, and he can't think why everybody's laughing. Among the laughter, he thinks he hears the words, "Stuck in his eye – stuck in his eye." So he decides it must be one of his neighbours who's got something in his eye, and it's up to him to find out who. The next person he comes to is an inoffensive man, but a harmless old soul. Our proud critic goes up to him and says loudly, "You silly little man, I think you've got something stuck in your eye." There's a gasp from everyone who hears this, and they crowd round to see what'll happen next. The little man stands stock still, flabbergasted, looking up at his critical neighbour. The latter takes out his hankie and begins poking in the other man's left eye. "Yes, here it is," he proclaims. "You've got something stuck in your eye, a little speck of dust, I think. But I can't quite see it clearly, because something's getting in my way." Then there's a great whoop of laughter.' Jesus continued: '"It's you," they're all hooting. "You're the one with something in your eye. You can't see our friend's eye clearly because there's a great log of wood sticking out of your own eye!"' Now that's where the story leaves the real world and becomes totally incredible; you couldn't get a log stuck in your eye, let alone not even notice that it was there. But reality doesn't matter when you're telling a funny story. The joke is that the absurd story reveals something about human nature. The proud man was shown to have been critical of other people's minor failings, but completely blind to his own much more serious faults. The crowd who heard Jesus tell the story screamed with laughter. What a stupid man!

Judging others

Then there was an awkward silence. Why had Jesus told the story? He just looked at them, challenging them to draw their own conclusions. The laughter now became rather embarrassed. One by one they realized they were actually laughing at themselves. *They* were the stupid idiots who were critical of other people, but blind to their own sins. It's true of all of us. The more critical we are of others, the harder it is to see ourselves objectively. 'Well, none of us is perfect, that's obvious,' we think. 'But *my* failings aren't very important. And if you only knew what I have to put up with, you'd understand that it's quite remarkable how patient and basically *nice* a person I really am. Whereas all these other people have got no excuse.' And so we go on, judging other people by totally different standards from those we want them to judge us by. 'That's if anyone has the sheer *nerve* to judge me at all,' we think. And that, my friends, is hypocrisy.

Hypocrisy

Jesus was harder on hypocrisy than on anything else. The quislings who collected tax for the occupying Roman power he could forgive. Those whom respectable people called 'sinners' had simply given up the struggle to keep the nit-picking rules of their religion. Jesus preferred going to dinner parties with people like that, because they were genuine, without a trace of hypocrisy. No, the *real* sinners were the respectable folk: judging other people is the most serious sin of all, because it cuts you off from God. If ever anyone condemns you for wrongdoing, don't try to defend yourself. Just answer, 'Oh, I've done much worse things than that. I've several times criticized other people, and Jesus declared that judging others is the worst sin of all.' Then watch their faces, to see whether they've the grace to laugh at themselves.

Suggested hymns

'Forgive our sins as we forgive'; God forgave my sin in Jesus' name; Our Father, who art in heaven; Thank you for giving me the morning.

Seventeenth Sunday after Trinity (Proper 20)

23 September

Principal Service   **Wisdom from the Ordinary**

(*Continuous*): Prov. 31.10–31 A good wife, Ps. 1 A good person;
or (*Related*): Wisd. 1.16—2.1, 12–22 Conflict, *or* Jer. 11.18–20
Conflict, Ps. 54 Conflict; James 3.13—4.3, 7–8a Wisdom and
works; Mark 9.30–37 Be like children

> *'Who is wise and understanding among you? Show by your good
> life that your works are done with gentleness born of wisdom.'*
> James 3.13

Wisdom as the good wife

Wisdom, personified as a woman or discussed in the practical activity
of working out how to be a Christian in the world, continues to be
a preoccupation this week. The portrait of the good wife at the end
of Proverbs is unlikely to be simply in the interests of presenting a
domestic ideal. If it were only that, then we might admire its emphasis on economic empowerment, but find it somewhat anachronistic
for the modern West. Even in the fourteenth century, Chaucer was
able to parody it in his sketch of that forceful breaker of convention,
the Wife of Bath, with her excellent cloth-making and first place
in the parish offertory, in his General Prologue to *The Canterbury
Tales*. The good wife of Proverbs 31 endures because she is a picture
of Wisdom herself: ordering the world around her, making it functional and profitable; ensuring the nurture of those nearest to her;
remembering the poor; and speaking with kindness as well as with
insight. She offers a radical contrast to the 'loose woman' who is
always ready to lead impressionable subjects astray.

But is it wise?

There remains much in these two figures that will disturb or annoy
anyone committed to opposing female stereotypes. The difficulties
that they pose play an important part in our engagement with texts
that speak out of the cultural milieu of a very different world, even
if there are no immediate answers to the questions. James contin-

ues his discussion of wisdom with another contrast – the distinction between the true wisdom that comes from God, and greedy personal ambition that is not wise at all. In earlier chapters, he has shown great familiarity with a repertoire of proverbs and sayings, but here he sounds much closer to Paul in his presentation of the outward signs by which wisdom marks character. Resolving the internal struggle between two sets of values is the clue, he suggests, to resolving dispute in the community. Asking unwisely delivers only dissatisfaction. The wise person will allow God to shape the pattern of prayer and desire. The doublet in last Sunday's collect, 'perceive and know', is not just a way of padding out a prayer. The two words point to understanding at several levels, and trace a development that begins with correct observation and ends in right action. This is a gift to pray for, but it may not appear instantly in practice.

Misperception of the disciples

The Gospel reading finds the disciples once more unable to perceive what Jesus is trying to teach them, and certainly unwilling to know what it means in any deep way. Since Jesus's last attempt to prepare them for his death, three of them have witnessed the transfiguration; so it seems extraordinary that they should still be resisting his teaching. On the other hand, such a vision of glory arguably makes it inconceivable that the Messiah's exalted status could in any way be attacked. The debate about status which has been in progress on the road to Capernaum may be explained as: if there was to be a messianic kingdom, then there would be important positions to be allocated. Surely some of them would be obvious candidates.

Who will be leader?

Perhaps there is another way of looking at the scene. If, despite their inability to see what Jesus meant about his death, something had sunk in, they would have sensed that, very soon, they would be leaderless. Who, then, should be their leader? Jesus answers with a tableau, embracing a child – the least important person in the social order – in front of them, and instructing them that anyone with ambitions to lead will have to learn a new relationship with status. He began by telling them that the Son of Man would be handed over to the mercy of human beings. He ends by showing how someone else's child could be lovingly held by the Son of God. The kingdom will be learned from the bottom up, not from the top down.

Let older children question the youngest about their earliest memories. What can we learn from small children?

Suggested hymns

A new commandment I give unto you; And now, O Father, mindful of thy love; From heaven you came, helpless babe; Teach me, my God and King.

Seventeenth Sunday after Trinity (Proper 20)
23 September
Second Service   **Consecrating the People**
Ps. 119.137–152 God's righteous judgements; Ex. 19.10–25
Consecrating the people; Matt. 8.23–34 Demons into pigs

> 'The LORD said to Moses: "Go to the people and consecrate them today and tomorrow."' Exodus 19.10

My sainted aunt

In the Greek Orthodox Church, the process of declaring somebody a saint is much more informal than in the West. Men and women who receive popular devotion from their followers have in recent times been addressed as 'Saint' soon after their death. So that there are a number of people in Greece today who, if they spoke English slang, could talk about 'my sainted aunt', and be quite truthful in what they say! Saint simply means holy; in the Roman Catholic Church there's a complicated process of making somebody a saint. Finally, the Pope declares that the dead person is already in heaven, may be called 'Saint (somebody)', and may be prayed to.

Holiness

Yet in the Bible there's a more widespread use of the word 'holy'. St Paul wrote to the Christians in Colossae, 'As God's chosen ones, holy and beloved, clothe yourselves with compassion, kindness, humility, meekness, and patience.' They were holy because God had chosen them. Now he exhorts them to start behaving in a saintly manner. He wrote to all the Christians in Rome, telling them that they were 'called to be saints'. He addressed the Christians in Corinth, some of whom lived lives of dubious morality, as 'the church of God which is at Corinth, with all the saints' in that region. So becoming a saint isn't so much a matter of what standard of morality you've achieved, as the fact that God has chosen you to aim for nothing less than perfect love. No matter how many times you fail and repent, you're a saint because God's chosen you. You've been consecrated by God.

Exodus

In the book of the Exodus, God told Moses to 'consecrate the people'. Having come across the Sinai desert, they were camped at the foot of the Holy Mountain. In three days Moses was going up the mountain to meet God and receive the Ten Commandments. God was going to come near to the people, and although they themselves weren't allowed to climb the mountain, they had to be purified before they could dare to be even in the same vicinity as God. They thought of God's holiness as something like a high-voltage electric current: if you didn't have the correct insulation, coming into contact with the Holy One would give you a fatal shock. The necessary insulation was the personal holiness given to you when you were consecrated. Where we'd disagree with Moses is on what personal holiness consists of. In those days it seemed as though the two things that stood in the way of holiness were dirt and sex. To be consecrated, you had to wash and abstain.

Holy love

Today we'd put the emphasis squarely on love. The more loving you are, the more holy you become. If there's no love in your heart, you're not fit to enter God's presence, no matter how clean or abstemious you may be. So the Christian life's one of progressive sanctification, as you grow in love for God and your neighbours year by year, until you're welcomed into God's holy presence when you die. 'Sanctification' means becoming holy, as does 'consecration'.

Consecration

The word 'consecration' nowadays is mostly used when you dedicate a new church building, setting it aside from secular use for the exclusive worship of the all-holy God; and when a minister or priest consecrates the bread and wine in the Holy Communion service. But perhaps if we had a less narrow view of holiness, and associated it more with progress in love, we could also broaden our concept of consecration. As God told Moses to consecrate the people, maybe we should see the purpose of every church service as to make the people more loving. The people in church, all the congregation, are called to be saints. I'm sure most of us on hearing those words would disclaim them modestly, saying, 'I'm no saint'; and you'd be right, in the sense that none of us is perfect – yet. But if you think of coming to church as your personal weekly consecration, you know you should be heading in that direction. The church service is meant to help you become a more loving sort of person. You, just as much as the consecrated building and the consecrated bread, are being claimed by God as his own: he wants to use you to make the world a more loving place. That's what real holiness means; and that's why you come to church, to help you to build the kingdom of God in love – until you yourself become a sainted aunt, or uncle, or whatever, because you're such a loving person.

Suggested hymns

Holy holy, holy, Lord God almighty; Love divine, all loves excelling; O perfect love, all human thought transcending; Take my life, and let it be.

Eighteenth Sunday after Trinity (Proper 21)
30 September
Principal Service **Doers of Good Works, and Small Steps to Faith**
(*Continuous*): Esther 7.1–6, 9–10; 9.20–22 Esther's victory, Ps. 124 Salvation; *or* (*Related*): Num. 11.4–6, 10–16, 24–29 The Spirit given to leaders, Ps. 19.7–14 Law, guidance, forgiveness; James 5.13–20 Prayer, healing, repentance and conversion; Mark 9.38–50 Causes of offence

> *'So Haman was hanged on the gallows he had prepared for Mordecai. With that the anger of the king abated.' Esther 7.10*

An end to persecution

This week's extract from the book of Esther begins at the story's denouement, when the wicked oppressor of the Jews, who are living in exile under Persian rule, is exposed as a traitor and punished. The book is read in full each year at the start of the Jewish feast of Purim, and its brevity lends itself to that treatment. For Jewish communities, it is a re-creation of an event that ended persecution, and deserved a celebration. But is it history? The story hinges on a staged opposition between Mordecai, the righteous Jew of the tribe of Benjamin, and Haman the Agagite, who is promoted to be the chief state official. This recalls Saul's victory against an Amalekite army led by Agag, in which he disobeyed God's instructions by taking Agag prisoner rather than executing him, and seizing booty instead of destroying it. Saul's family lost the kingdom as a result. Mordecai sets the record right through the mediation of his beautiful cousin Esther, whose position as queen he has partly engineered. Esther herself has her finest moment in revealing Haman as the villain who has plotted against the Jews, and, in so doing, damaging the king's reputation. Her character is given a little more complexity in the Apocryphal Greek version of the book. What she offers, through her persuasion of the king and in the generous dispensation that marks the happy ending of the matter, is an illustration of how good diaspora Jews should live. The Jews of this narrative find a deliverer in the pompous – even gullible – King Ahasuerus. He is not consciously an agent of God's covenant with a particular people, but he is susceptible to influence, good and bad. In Esther, coached by Mordecai, good prevails.

Good works by non-believers

Jesus is not resistant to good works done by those who do not follow him. When John comes to report the activities of the stranger who has been casting out demons, the fact that the man is not 'one of them' interests Jesus far less than his invocation of Jesus's name does. Why should someone who recognizes Jesus as the source of healing power, and uses it for good, be an enemy? A touch of self-consciousness may colour the disciples' anxiety to protect their teacher's ministry. Not so long before, he had rebuked them for their lack of faith in failing to heal a boy afflicted with an evil spirit. They still have much to learn about trusting the intentions and abilities of others – no doubt a formative lesson for the future builders of the Church, who would discover that, for some, commitment is

234

a gradual process. Those who approach Jesus in this more cautious way, trusting his name but not abandoning all to become disciples, are surely the 'little ones' of whom he speaks. Their first moves towards faith are precious to him, precious enough to make him issue a graphic condemnation of anyone who makes it hard for them to come nearer to him.

Avoid becoming a stumbling block

Committed followers are not immune from becoming stumbling blocks to themselves, either. Jesus is probably not actually commending amputation and deoculation as preferable to succumbing to temptation, but he is presenting an unmistakable choice of life or self-destruction – the worm-ridden rubbish heap of Gehenna in Isaiah 66.24. The whole final chapter of Isaiah makes a backdrop to Mark's perplexing words, setting the new Jerusalem and a return for exiles to their rightful place against the destruction of those who choose not to be part of God's promise of salvation. Mark knows the promise, but is not yet ready to show his readers how it is to be fulfilled.

All-age worship

Tie two people back to back, sitting down on the floor. Show how they can only stand up when they learn to co-operate. Let others try, choosing partners who are quite different from them.

Suggested hymns

A new commandment I give unto you; Brother, sister, let me serve you; In Christ there is no East or West; Where cross the crowded ways of life.

Eighteenth Sunday after Trinity (Proper 21)
30 September
Second Service   Forgiveness and Healing
Ps. 120 Lying lips, 121 I lift my eyes; Ex. 24 Blood of the covenant; Matt. 9.1–8 Forgiveness and healing

> 'When Jesus saw their faith, he said to the paralytic, "Take heart, son; your sins are forgiven."' Matthew 9.2

Watership Down

Watership Down is a novel in which all the characters are rabbits. They have a word in their language for what happens to a rabbit when it's caught in the headlights of a car; they call it 'going *tharn*'. It is a paralysis of the mind, leading to a paralysis of the legs, which prevents the rabbit from scampering away to save its life. The word's been adopted by computer programmers, when they have more information than they can cope with, and don't know where to start. There are other situations in which we speak of people being 'paralysed by fear'; it's true that our minds can influence our bodies.

A paralysed man

A paralysed man was carried to Jesus by his friends on a sleeping mat. He couldn't walk, and probably his paralysis was what's called, from the Greek words for mind and body, a psychosomatic illness. Some scribes, the experts in the Old Testament law, taught that all sickness was caused by sin. The sick man had probably committed some misdeed, and was crushed by a burden of guilt, so that he couldn't move. He felt so guilty that he didn't know which way to turn. Believing, as he did, that his paralysis was God's punishment for his sin, he couldn't turn to God, for God was his enemy. So he lay whimpering on his mat, until his friends decided to do something about him, and took him to Jesus the healer.

'Your sins are forgiven'

'Your sins are forgiven,' said Jesus. Today it would be a startling response to a request for healing, but in those days, and with that patient, forgiveness was the only cure that would be effective. Jesus, as a good Jew, wouldn't take the name of God in vain, so he didn't say, 'God has forgiven you', but everyone knew that was what he meant. What shocked the scribes was that Jesus claimed to know what God was thinking, and to speak on God's behalf. Only God can forgive sins. The scribes thought it was blasphemy for Jesus to identify himself with God. Jesus also knew what the Pharisees were thinking, and to justify his claim to speak on behalf of his Father – God – he proved that God had indeed forgiven the guilty man. 'Stand up,' he said to the paralysed man. 'Pick up your mat and walk home.' Then the man believed that God really had forgiven him; his mind was no longer paralysed by fear of God; his legs worked for the first time in weeks; and he walked.

Emotion and illness

Many illnesses have clearly identifiable physical causes in germs and microbes, injury or ageing. But some sickness is entirely psychosomatic. In all cases, the recovery process is speeded up by a clear mind and a firm will. Conversely, if the patient's mind is racked by emotions such as fear or guilt, the body's God-given powers of self-healing may not be able to operate. The most effective cure in most cases is to give, alongside the medical procedures and drugs, a reassurance that the patient is respected and loved. Even those who have no need of a doctor can live their lives more effectively if they believe that God loves and forgives them.

Guilt

Feelings of guilt are a necessary step in taking responsibility for one's own actions, and learning to turn away from sin to a more loving way of life. But they're meant to be dealt with at once; if they drag on they're destructive. Nobody can get on with their life while they still feel guilty.

Forgiveness

So it's our job, on behalf of Jesus, to assure people that God's forgiven them. We can't do that if we bear grudges, or if we always talk of God as a fierce judge. Our sin and guilt cuts us off from God's love, but he wants us to be reconciled. As soon as you feel guilty, it's a sign that you've repented for what you've done. Then God wants you to be sure that he's forgiven you, and he loves you still. 'Your sins *are* forgiven. Stand up and walk.' Walk the way of life, not death; of love, not hatred; of trust in God, not continuing guilt. There may still be work to be done, undoing the harmful effects of your past sins, but you can do it with a light heart, and find new ways of loving, proud in the dignity of being a forgiven sinner.

Suggested hymns

Amazing grace – how sweet the sound; God forgave my sin in Jesus' name; Songs of thankfulness and praise; Thine arm, O Lord, in days of old.

Nineteenth Sunday after Trinity (Proper 22)

7 October

Principal Service   **Precious in God's Kingdom**

(*Continuous*): Job 1.1; 2.1–10 Job tested by suffering, Ps. 26
Righteousness; *or* (*Related*): Gen. 2.18–24 Creation of Eve, Ps. 8
Stewardship of nature; Heb. 1.1–4; 2.5–12 Creation of human-
kind; Mark 10.2–16 Family and children

> '[Jesus said,] "For this reason a man shall leave his father and
> mother and be joined to his wife, and the two shall become one
> flesh."' Mark 10.7–8

Divorce and the law

The Pharisees return in the tenth chapter of Mark's Gospel with
another question that is designed to put Jesus in an awkward
relationship to the law. Jesus is asked to comment on divorce, with
a view to enticing him to pronounce the law wrong, and to offer
something in its place. They, and the scribes, have already tried the
topics of forgiving sins, picking wheat or healing on the sabbath,
and ritual cleanliness; and have evidently failed to learn from these
encounters that Jesus is not to be trapped. Perhaps it goes against
the grain to admit that he is as well versed in the law and the Scriptures as they are. Jesus replies with a question: 'What did Moses
command you?' Their reply allows him to catch them on a techni-
cality; for there is a difference between commanding and allowing,
and if the Mosaic law comprised the whole Pentateuch, then there
was only one command about the duration of marriage—the creation ordinance of Genesis 2.24. Provision is made in Deuteronomy
for ending a marriage under particular circumstances, and this is
the line taken in Matthew's rendition of the same episode: 'Is it
lawful for a man to divorce his wife for any cause?' Mark leaves
matters more open, and although Jesus could have acknowledged
the differing views of conservative interpreters, who thought that
there were very few causes for divorce, and liberals, who were prepared to grant divorce on quite slender grounds, he does not do
this. Instead, he points out that the additional permission came
about because of human failure to live up to the standards set by
God at the very beginning.

Herod's case

There was a particular case in the Pharisees' minds: the marriage of Herod to his former sister-in-law after his own divorce. How satisfying it would have been to persuade Jesus to condemn the king. But that should not distract contemporary readers from the extraordinary difficulties of this discussion in a society where many who hear it read in church will personally have experienced the hurt of divorce, and will know at first hand the many and complex factors that bring marriages to an end.

'Hardness of heart'

The explanation that Jesus gives privately to the disciples seems to offer an inflexible pronouncement. Rather than attempt to find reasons to discount it, we might turn to a less clear-cut matter. It is hard to know exactly what is meant by the 'hardness of heart' that Jesus recognizes in the Pharisees, but a very similar expression is found as he heals the man with the withered hand in the synagogue on the Sabbath. On that occasion, the meaning *is* clear. Jesus is grieved and angry at an attitude that would place rigid rules above the saving transformation of human life. The narrative moves abruptly on to the arrival of parents with their children, presumably seeking blessing and healing. The disciples must share him again, in the midst of this privileged time alone, and only in sharing him will they learn properly what he has to teach them. They have seen him take a child as the picture of a precious citizen of God's kingdom once before.

Salvation and elevation

Now he asks them to be childlike receivers of the gift of the kingdom: people of no social status who are delighted to be given something, not defenders of the rules that exclude others from admission. That salvation and elevation to glory are the destiny of flawed human creatures is the dazzling announcement of the writer of the Letter to the Hebrews. That God finally chooses to speak to us not through angels, but through his Son; who takes on our nature in every respect, and undergoes suffering and death to make us perfect. In Christ we are all offered a better chance and a 'crown of everlasting glory'.

All-age worship

Play at weddings. Read the words of the marriage service.

Suggested hymns

Blest are the pure in heart; Lord Jesus Christ, you have come to us; Love divine, all loves excelling; Will you come and follow me?

Nineteenth Sunday after Trinity (Proper 22)
7 October
Second Service   Francis of Assisi
Ps. 125 Firm as Mount Zion, 126 Like those who dream; Joshua 3.7–17 Crossing the Jordan; Matt. 10.1–22 Mission of the Twelve

> '[Jesus said to his disciples,] "Take no gold, or silver, or copper in your belts."' *Matthew 10.9*

Francis of Assisi

In twelfth-century Italy, the new merchant classes were growing rich and powerful. In the beautiful hill-town of Assisi lived a young man, Francis Bernardone, who belonged to a wealthy family, and lived a dissolute life with his rich friends. During a war between Assisi and the nearby city of Perugia, Francis was taken captive and held for several months. He had a chance to think, and wondered whether the pursuit of pleasure was all there is to life. When he was released, one day he was passing the ruined church of St Damian outside Assisi, and went inside to pray for guidance. He heard the voice of Jesus saying to him, 'Francis, rebuild my church, which is falling down.' He started to reconstruct the ruined edifice, but as he did so, he realized that Jesus had been referring not to the building but to the institutional Church, which was collapsing under the weight of its riches. Like its wealthier members, the Church, too, was beginning to believe that money was all that mattered. Francis decided the only way to overcome this was by personal example. He'd been expected to inherit the cloth business of his father, but he stripped himself of all his fine clothes, put on a peasant's dark coat with a piece of rope around his waist, and 'embraced Lady Poverty'.

Followers

As Francis tramped the dusty roads, people began to walk with him and ask him questions. Soon, one after another, men began to join him. He wrote a simple rule of life to show them how they should live, quoting the Gospels, 'Take no gold, or silver, or copper in your belts, no bag for your journey, or two tunics, or sandals, or a staff; for labourers deserve their food.' They were to be itinerants, wandering from town to town proclaiming the good news of God's love by word and example. 'Preach the gospel at all times,' he said; 'and if you must, use words.' When there were 12 of them, they went to Rome to get the Pope's approval for the rule which formed them into a community. Francis called them the Friars Minor, which means Little Brothers. In 1212, St Clare, a noble woman of Assisi, inspired by Francis, founded an order for women. Due to social customs of the day, they were not able to be itinerant like the friars, but remained in their convent.

Preaching to the birds

Many stories are told of Francis' love of nature. He wrote the famous 'Canticle of the sun', beginning: O most high, almighty, good Lord God: to you belong praise, glory, honour and all blessing. Praise to my Lord God, with all his creatures: and specially our brother the sun, who brings us the day and who brings us the light. Fair is he, and shining with a very great splendour: O Lord, it is you that he signifies to us.' On this is based the hymn 'All creatures of our God and king'. But it would be wrong to sentimentalize Francis; he dictated the Canticle near the end of his life, when he was blind and could no longer see the beauties of nature that he described. He was the first to introduce a Christmas crib into the churches, complete with a live ox and ass. This was an attempt to remind wealthy Christians that Christ was born among the poor. His preaching to the birds was a protest at the unwillingness of the rich to listen to him.

Preaching to Muslims

Francis travelled across southern France and Spain, in the hope of preaching the gospel to the Moors, but he failed to get across the Mediterranean into their homeland, which is now called Mauretania. Then he travelled across Eastern Europe and into Egypt, and arranged a meeting with the Sultan. Francis wanted to make peace between Muslims and Christians. The Sultan listened to Francis with courtesy, but was not convinced. At a time when Muslims and Christians regarded each other as enemies, Francis made a gesture in the right direction; if he'd succeeded, many of the troubles of our own day might have been avoided.

Stigmata

On his return to Assisi, Francis organized his followers into three orders: the itinerant friars; St Clare's sisters who live in an enclosed convent; and the Third Order, or Tertiaries, who carry on their ordinary occupations, but keep a simple rule of life. Then he handed over the supervision of the order to others, and retreated to Mount Alverna to meditate. So intense was his identification with the Crucified that wounds appeared on his hands, feet and side, the 'stigmata'. He died on 3rd October 1226; less than two years later he was canonized as St Francis of Assisi, and 4th October was appointed as his feast day. Even if we can't embrace absolute poverty, we can follow his example in making our lives as simple as possible.

Suggested hymns

All creatures of our God and king; As water to the thirsty; Lord of beauty, thine the splendour; Make me a channel of your peace.

Twentieth Sunday after Trinity (Proper 23)
14 October
Principal Service   **In God's Radical Presence**
(*Continuous*): Job 23.1–9, 16–17 God's greatness and justice, Ps. 22.1–15 Faith and assurance; *or* (*Related*): Amos 5.6–7, 10–15 Justice for the needy, Ps. 90.12–17 Salvation; Heb. 4.12–16 Tempted as we are; Mark 10.17–31 Possessions

> *'Oh, that I knew where I might find him, that I might come even to his dwelling! I would lay my case before him, and fill my mouth with arguments.' Job 23.3–4*

Relationship with God

In our first reading, Job speaks in reply to the first delivery in a third round of speeches by the three people known traditionally as his comforters. Eliphaz has just ascribed Job's misfortunes to his moral failings, and has suggested that Job does not think that God has much to do with human beings. Job's response absolutely denies this allegation. Rather than disregard God, he longs to find him, so that he can plead his cause. He longs for God to listen to him, and yet God cannot be found. Here, as in other places of this book, a skilful piece of parody follows.

Hearing the word of God

The God of Psalm 139, who is always there, no matter how hard his creatures try to distance themselves from him, seems to have vanished. Job is terrified at this state of affairs. He knows that he has kept God's commandments but, at the same time, he knows that this may have nothing to do with God's purpose for him. It would be much less frightening to meet this God face to face in judgement than to live by guesswork. The writer to the Hebrews has considered this matter from a very different angle. In a world perhaps 500 years away, he presents a God who is not radically absent, but radically present. The letter begins by insisting that God has always related to humanity by speaking, once through prophets, but now through his Son. Earlier generations hardened their hearts against this word, but the present audience has a new opportunity to be part of the 'rest', the culmination of all God's saving work in the kingdom, where the Son who suffered is glorified.

God's judgement sees all

There will be no hiding places for anyone with insincere intentions, because the God who speaks also sees and judges. This judgement is not just external, because God works from the inside, dissecting us so that nothing is uninspected. This would be utterly terrifying (and there is certainly no room for complacency) were it not for the key difference, which puts the audience in a position entirely unlike that of their ancestors: 'we have a great high priest who has passed through the heavens, Jesus, the Son of God'. Just as there is nothing that God does not know about us, so there is no part of our weakness that the incarnate Jesus has not inhabited, no test that he has not faced. With such powerful advocacy, the followers of Jesus can be brave in coming to God in the expectation of grace and mercy.

Making the journey

The Gospel reading adds a further element to this gracious gaze of God. The rich young man who wants to share in the good news can assert in good conscience that he has kept the commandments – that his life stands up to inspection. He, however, cannot stand being looked at with a love that wants nothing from him except the growth into a deep relationship with God which appears to entail the loss of all material security. Following a now familiar pattern, Jesus explains the meaning of this encounter privately to the disciples, who wonder whether they have all been duped, and whether there may be nothing at the end of this journey after all. Jesus's answer is comforting, stern and mysterious. What is certain is this: the future embarked on by all who have turned all their priorities upside down in response to the 'good news' will be in the company of the God who is both Jesus's Father and theirs.

All-age worship

Make things which you can sell to raise money for charity.

Suggested hymns

Brother, sister, let me serve you; Good King Wenceslas looked out; Love is his word, love is his way; When I needed a neighbour, were you there?

Twentieth Sunday after Trinity (Proper 23)
14 October
Second Service   **The Walls of Jericho**
Ps. 127 Unless the Lord builds [128 Family life]; Joshua 5.13—6.20 Walls of Jericho; Matt. 11.20–30 Come to me

'The people shouted, and the trumpets were blown. As soon as the people heard the sound of the trumpets, they raised a great shout, and the wall fell down flat; so the people charged straight ahead into the city and captured it.' Joshua 6.20

A spiritual

Joshua fit the battle of Jericho,
Jericho, Jericho,

Joshua fit the battle of Jericho,
and the walls came a-tumbling down.

It's a grand old American spiritual – I suppose 'fit' is a dialect word for fought. It's encouraged generation after generation to fight spiritual battles against seemingly impossible barriers, confident that through the help of God they'll succeed at last.

Spiritual battles

You notice that I said 'spiritual battles'. The Old Testament's a very warlike book, as violent as some of the modern films on TV. If anyone thinks this means that God condones the use of force to overcome evil, they're mistaken. These are old legends; the archaeological evidence is far from clear whether the walls of Jericho, the oldest city in the world, ever collapsed. It's a yarn passed down from generation to generation, and its purpose isn't to encourage physical violence, but spiritual perseverance.

Barriers

There are many spiritual barriers that need to be broken down. There are barriers of mistrust, between individuals and nations. There are barriers of race and class that divide the people within a nation. There are barriers of poverty that prevent the starving people of the third world from sharing in the prosperity that we enjoy. There are trade barriers and sanctions. There are gender barriers, and the famous 'glass ceiling' which prevents women being promoted to a level that their competence deserves. There are barriers of sin and guilt that separate us from God. God wants all these walls to come a-tumbling down, so that we can live together as sisters and brothers to each other, and children of a loving heavenly Father.

Patience and perseverance

But to bring these barriers down requires patience and perseverance. For six days the people of Israel had to walk all the way round the walls of Jericho in silence, with the soldiers in front; behind them the priests with the ark of the covenant and the seven silent trumpets; and after them the rest of the people, without firing a single arrow. Not a sound was to be uttered. The city was besieged, and apparently impregnable, but the Lord told Joshua they were not to give up prematurely. The soldiers of Jericho inside the walls must have become increasingly alarmed at this extraordinary behaviour. Then on the seventh day, the Israelites walked round the city seven times, which must have taken a very long time. At last, when they had done this, they were allowed to shout and blow the trumpets. At this astonishing sound, 'the walls came a-tumbling down', and Jericho was conquered for the Lord. In the case of all the other barriers we've mentioned, also, the process of breaking them down is often a long one, and not for the faint-hearted.

Prayer and praise

We don't know what the Israelites shouted; probably their battle cry will have been the Hebrew equivalent of 'God for Harry! England and St George', and will have involved calling on the name of the Lord. So it was likely to have been a combination of prayer and praise. Both prayer and praise are needed in all our spiritual battles: prayer that God will help us, and praise because we're confident that he'll bring the barriers down.

God will bring them down

For it is only God who can break down walls. In St Paul's time there was a barrier between Jew and non-Jew, of suspicion and mutual hatred – until all races united in one Church as children of the same God. Then, said St Paul:

> In Christ Jesus you who once were far off have been brought near by the blood of Christ. For he is our peace; in his flesh he has made both groups into one and has broken down the dividing wall, that is, the hostility between us. He has abolished the law with its commandments and ordinances, that he might create in himself one new humanity in place of the two, thus making peace, and might reconcile both groups to God in one body through the cross, thus putting to death that hostility through it.

Compared to breaking entrenched barriers of fear and distrust between races and nations, bringing down the walls of Jericho was a cinch. With the patience and perseverance of his people, and their prayer and praise, God in his own time will bring a-tumbling down all the barriers which divide his children. Trust him!

246

Suggested hymns

Be bold, be strong; Disposer supreme, and judge of the earth; Fight the good fight; God is working his purpose out.

Twenty-first Sunday after Trinity (Proper 24)
21 October
Principal Service   **A Ransom for Many**
(*Continuous*): Job 38.1–7 [34–41] Creation, Ps. 104.1–10, 26, 35c Creation; *or* (*Related*): Isa. 53.4–12 The suffering servant, Ps. 91.9–16 Providence, salvation; Heb. 5.1–10 Christ a priest for ever; Mark 10.35–45 Humility and service

> '[Jesus said,] "For the Son of Man came not to be served but to serve, and to give his life a ransom for many."' Mark 10.45

Proud of one's humility

A monk was lying dying, and many people came to his bedside and praised his scholarship, his preaching and his asceticism. When they had all gone he turned to his nurse and said, 'I am very disappointed. None of them mentioned the thing I'm most proud of: my humility.' James and John in the Gospel story were a bit like that. They were very proud of how humbly they'd accepted the hardships of becoming disciples, and thought they should be rewarded by a position of glory. Jesus replied, 'Whoever wishes to become great among you must be your servant. For the Son of Man came not to be served but to serve.' The Son of Man was a title Jesus liked to use of himself, it was a modest way of saying 'me'. The only true glory, said Jesus, is found in humble service of others. I wish our politicians could learn that.

Pride in church life

And I wish church people could learn it, too. In their different ways, the various denominations are tearing themselves apart. The protagonists pretend the arguments are theological, but mostly it's over a desire for power and a wish to control others. 'It's not to be so among you,' says Jesus, sadly; the only true glory is in service.

Biblical interpretation

At the Council of Ephesus, in 461, a hairy Egyptian monk called Shenoudi hurled a brass-bound copy of the Gospels at Nestorius, hitting him in the chest, and cried, 'Thus I refute the heretic with the Scriptures.' Many people use the Bible in a hardly more subtle way today, claiming that the Bible proves that they are right and everybody else is wrong. People talk about 'biblical morality' who haven't actually read what the Scriptures say, but are imposing their own prejudices on the Bible. Jesus said that the greatest sin of all is judging and condemning other people. But then people always rip verses of the Bible out of context to reinforce their prejudices. A text without a context is a pretext. We should always be humble in interpreting the Bible, and never twist it to our own advantage: remember Jesus, the Son of Man, 'who came not to be served but to serve, and to give his life a ransom for many'.

Sacrificial life and death

That verse is the clearest evidence from the Gospels that Jesus regarded his death as a sacrifice. Jesus took the idea of the lamb led to the slaughter in Isaiah as a metaphor for his own death. In fact, he uses an interesting word: 'ransom'. Today, this is what we pay for a hostage who's been kidnapped to be set free. In Jesus's day it was commonly used for redeeming a slave. To give anyone their freedom always comes at a price; Jesus is saying that by his death he's already paid the price to set us all free. Free from what?

- bad habits
- fear
- prejudice
- oppression
- dependence on material possessions.

Anything you want to be set free from, the death of Jesus will do it.

Payment to whom?

We can never take our freedom from sin and death lightly, because the price of our freedom was the death of Jesus. What we must never ask is, to whom was that price paid? That's pushing the metaphor too far. If it was paid to God, that means God is cruel and mercenary. If it was paid to the devil, that puts God in the devil's power. No, sacrifice is only a metaphor for something too deep for words. Somehow, the Creator of the cosmos came down to live among us, and died so as to win our love. The humility we see in Jesus is the character of the Creator. All we can do in response is to put away our pride in our own goodness, our own achievements; then love God, in gratitude for what God's done for us, and humbly become the servant of all our neighbours. Down, peacock's feathers; we are servants of the servant King, and proudest when we can be of service to others!

All-age worship

Older children can spend some time helping younger children to read. Discuss whether the pleasure you gain from their success is worth the effort.

Suggested hymns

A man there lived in Galilee; Brother, sister, let me serve you; From heaven you came; Praise to the Holiest in the height.

Twenty-first Sunday after Trinity (Proper 24)
21 October
Second Service   **Sunday Observance**
Ps. 141 Prayer like incense; Joshua 14.6–14 Caleb; Matt. 12.1–21 God's servant

'It is lawful to do good on the sabbath.' Matthew 12.12

Chariots of Fire

The film *Chariots of Fire* concerns the great Scottish runner, Eric Liddell, known as 'the Flying Scotsman', and his rivalry with the Jewish athlete Harold Abrahams. Both were victims of prejudice in different ways, and both triumphed in the end. When Liddell went to compete in the 1924 Olympic Games, the 100-metre race was fixed for a Sunday. But Liddell, a devout Christian, refused to break the law of the Sabbath as he understood it, and wouldn't take part. He gave up his chance of winning a medal, but his religion was more important to him than his sporting achievements. The gold medal was won by Abrahams, whose Sabbath, of course, was on the Saturday. To everyone's surprise, however, on a later day Eric Liddell went on to win bronze in the 200 metres, then gold in the 400 metres, at which he was comparatively inexperienced, in the, then, record time of 47.6 seconds. The next year, he completed a degree in science and a degree in divinity, and, sacrificing his chances of a brilliant career in the UK, he went to China to work as a missionary.

Sabbath

But was the law of the Sabbath worth sacrificing a gold medal for? Liddell would have said yes. The Ten Commandments tell us that the seventh day of the week is holy to God; on it we must do no work. Jesus rose from the dead on a Sunday, so Christians transferred the Sabbath observance on to the first day of the week, called the Lord's Day. The Old Testament ruling that anyone who works on the Sabbath day should be put to death hasn't been applied for centuries. Yet in those countries where people still don't work on Sundays, there's an air of relaxation and calm on that day which is quite unknown among the rush and bustle of the seven-days-a-week nations. Workers who have no regular day off produce less in seven days than others do in six, and are less healthy.

Jesus

But Jesus came into conflict with the Pharisees over the Sabbath. Five times he healed people on the Sabbath, which was considered to be work. The Pharisees were willing to bend the rules to save an animal, said Jesus but objected when he saved a human life. Once, Jesus gleaned ears of corn on the Sabbath. He quoted King David, who ate sacrificial bread in a temple, showing that human need overrides the letter of the law. 'The sabbath was made for human beings,' he said, 'not human beings for the sabbath.' Yet Jesus didn't abolish the Sabbath law for Jews, he only called for a common-sense approach.

Gentiles

A different situation arose when non-Jews became Christians. In the Roman Empire everybody worked on Sundays: employees would be fired and slaves whipped if they refused. So the Church decided that the whole Jewish law doesn't apply to Gentiles, only the laws against pagan sacrifices, murder and adultery. Yet the Sabbath law wasn't really about working hours, but about setting time aside to worship God. Without worship, life can turn 100 per cent materialistic. As a sign outside a church put it, 'Seven prayer-less days make one weak'.

Sabbath observance

So where do we strike the balance? Jesus wouldn't want us to be like strict sabbatarians who object to all forms of pleasure. Provided we devote at least an hour a week to worshipping the Almighty, our day of rest can be spent in recreation, or re-creation of our mind and body. 'The family that prays together stays together', so we should make time when the whole family can relax together at least once a week. But worship's a voluntary choice, and we can't insist that others should worship unless they want to. Yet by devoting Sundays to shopping and professional sport, we risk making worship impossible for some faithful Christians, whom we compel to work for us in catering, travel, retail and entertainment.

Sacrifice

So all praise to those like Eric Liddell, who are prepared to sacrifice their careers and their wealth for their principles. An old book quotes the singers Jenny Lind and Harry Lauder, both famous in their day, as examples of people who were willing to do just that. We should give everyone freedom to spend an hour with God if they want to. Would you be willing to risk opposition and mockery by your insistence on coming to church on Sundays, from your employer or your family? And how do you feel about the number of people who are made to go in to work and prevented from worshipping on Sundays by your insistence on shopping and watching professionals performing on the Lord's Day?

Suggested hymns

Dear Lord and Saviour of mankind; I danced in the morning; Prayer is the soul's sincere desire; This is the day, this is the day which the Lord has made.

SS Simon and Jude, Apostles   28 October
Two Low-profile Apostles

Isa. 28.14–16 A foundation stone; Ps. 119.89–96 I am yours, save me; Eph. 2.19–22 The foundation of the apostles; John 15.17–27 You have been with me

> *'So then you are no longer strangers and aliens, but you are citizens with the saints and also members of the household of God.'*
> *Ephesians 2.19*

Who they are not

Today, the Church remembers two disciples defined by who they are not: not Simon Peter or Judas Iscariot. Anyone living in the shadow of someone else with his or her name has these patron saints. Perhaps unsurprisingly, we know little about them. Simon was known as 'Simon the Cananaean' or 'Simon the Zealot' – possibly because he was a member of the Zealots, Jewish freedom-fighters not averse to seeing off the odd Roman in a dark alley; or possibly because he was zealous for the Jewish law, but without any connotation of extremism. To avoid any confusion, John describes Jude as 'Judas, not Iscariot', while Matthew and Mark use another name altogether, Thaddaeus. If he wrote the letter of Jude, then, influenced by Jewish eschatological thought, he yearned for the day of the Lord to right all wrongs. His religious zeal would be strong, perhaps verging on the fanatical, making the Zealot Simon a kindred spirit.

With Jesus from the beginning

Somewhere in history, Jude became the patron saint of lost causes. It has been suggested that, to avoid any possible confusion with Judas Iscariot, people avoided invoking the aid of anyone called Judas until they were completely desperate, or because his epistle emphasizes that the Christians should persevere in difficult circumstances. History tells us that people with lost causes can be violent in their desperation, but, in contrast, Jude discouraged persecuted Christians from violence, exhorting faithfulness to God. What we do know is that Simon and Jude were with Jesus from the beginning, and stuck with him faithfully, without shining in the limelight for good or ill.

Passionate action

When Jesus was being somewhat obscure, the night before he died, Jude asked: 'Lord, how is it that you will manifest yourself to us and not to the world?' Since both the question and questioner are remembered, it seems that the others were glad that he had asked it. If you or I were to go down in history for asking one important question, what would we want that to be? The answer that Jesus gave to Jude centred on loving him and keeping his word. After Jesus's death, what did these keen disciples do with their devotion? Unlike Judas Iscariot, they both made the leap from religious fanaticism to zeal for the way of Jesus who suffered and died. They are associated with the proclamation of the gospel in several countries, from Libya to Armenia, including Persia, where both were martyred around AD 65, Simon (gruesomely) by being sawn in two. Their passion for the kingdom of God led to passionate action, and any latent Jewish nationalism was recast as zeal for all nations to hear the gospel.

Role models of discipleship

The question how we direct our enthusiasm is a topical issue in the world today, most obviously in the decisions that some people make to use violence to pursue their ends. But what of the violence of words that can be used destructively everywhere, from politics to domestic disputes, including (to our shame) in the Church? Simon and Jude's conversion to being passionate disciples rather than violent religious fanatics was testimony to the power of the gospel to transform not their passion – that was never quenched – but their pattern of living. They give us an example to emulate of zeal directed to godly ends. Most of us are fairly ordinary people who want to be faithful to God day by day, and who have ideals and causes about which we are passionate.

Rediscovering our passions

Our faith should be among them. In the midst of daily discipleship, what is God calling us to do with our zeal? This affects decisions about our whole lives: careers, money, time. Perhaps we need to rediscover our passions, if they have been lost in the routine plod of daily life. If we experience the desolation that Jesus described in the Gospel, or if despair or loneliness tempt us to give up as a lost cause, then the reading from Ephesians reminds us that we are members of the household of God, built together spiritually into a dwelling place for God on the foundation of people such as Simon and Jude, with Christ Jesus as the cornerstone. Simon and Jude would never have expected that future when they first followed Jesus in the shadow of their better-known namesakes.

Suggested hymns

Captains of the saintly band; Come, O thou traveller unknown; Like the murmur of the dove's song; Ye watchers and ye holy ones.

Last Sunday after Trinity (Proper 25)   28 October
Second Service   The Bible is Better than Gold

Ps. 119.121–136 Better than gold; Eccles. 11; 12 Youth and age; 2 Tim. 2.1–7 Soldiers of Christ; *Gospel at Holy Communion*: Luke 18.9–14 Pharisee and tax-collector

> *'Therefore I love your commandments above gold, even much fine gold.' Psalm 119.127 (Common Worship)*

Gold

Gold is one of the group of elements known as the Noble Metals. This is because they don't dissolve in acids or oxidize in the atmosphere, so unlike other types of treasure they never rust or perish. It's been known since ancient times. Gold is found in veins of quartz, or in river sands which have been formed out of a lode. It's extracted with cyanide, and purified in a furnace, when the impurities are skimmed off the molten metal as dross. It's found in the gold mines of South Africa, Russia, Canada and the USA, where it was panned out of the rivers during the gold rush. For millennia, gold's been used to make gold coins, which never rust. It's also used in decoration, usually as rolled gold or gold leaf, in gold rings and other jewellery, in electronic circuits and electrical contacts. Pure gold's too soft to use, so it's mixed with other metals in an alloy, up to 24 carat, which is pure gold.

Value

The value of gold comes from its scarcity, its imperishability and its beauty. So we use gold as a metaphor for something of great worth, like the gold medals at the Olympic Games; the bullseye at the centre of an archery target; a golden jubilee or golden wedding; a golden handshake; the golden mean and the Golden Rule; golden oldies and golden opportunities; as scarce as gold-dust; or a child who's as good as gold. Until 1914 the currencies of Great Britain and several other countries were linked to the Gold Standard, meaning that the value of a pound note corresponded to that of a certain weight of gold. But those who use gold as a measure of value are often criticized as knowing the cost of everything but the value of nothing.

The Bible

Psalm 119, the longest of the psalms, is a hymn of praise to the value of the Scriptures. So we read in verse 127 the words, 'Therefore I love your commandments above gold, even much fine gold.' The Holy Bible's worth its weight in gold. That's because those who've studied it and try to live by it find it the most precious thing in life. But how many people who call themselves Christians actually regard knowing the Bible as of more value to them than becoming rich? The Last Sunday after Trinity is celebrated in some churches as Bible Sunday, when we thank God for the gift of the holy Scriptures, and pray for those who translate the Bible into other languages; who distribute it to places where it's hard to come by; who study the languages in which the Bible is written, and the society of the time, which forms the context in which the Bible's to be understood. Please pray also for those who explain the meaning of the Scriptures for today and expound it to the Christians in the pews.

The value of the Bible

The Holy Bible's worth its weight in gold. That's because the Bible contains the word of God. God himself inspired the writers, and when you read the Bible, the Creator of the universe is speaking directly to you. The Bible advises us how to live, how to pray and how to inherit eternal life. Through the words of the Bible we learn how to know the love of our heavenly Father, have Jesus as our friend, and receive the Holy Spirit. The Bible tells us how to live life triumphantly and joyfully, following the example of Jesus, resisting temptation and walking in the way that God has planned for us. The teaching of Jesus shows us the importance of love in our treatment of others, and the danger of surrounding ourselves with a hard, unforgiving attitude, cutting ourselves off from our neighbours and from God. The Bible's teaching on prayer, and the examples of prayer in the Psalms and the Gospels, builds a habit of daily intimate communication with our loving heavenly Father. Reading the Bible each day helps us to open our hearts to the Holy Spirit, so that the love of God may fill us and work through us to spread God's caring compassion to our neighbour. There's an old saying that before using any gadget, you should always read the maker's instructions. God is the maker of our body and soul, our life and the world we inhabit. To know how to use those things effectively, we should unfailingly read the Maker's instructions. Truly we should love God's commandments above gold, even much fine gold.

Suggested hymns

Break thou the bread of life; God has spoken by his prophets; Lord, thy word abideth; Tell me the old, old story.

All Saints' Day   1 November
(see pages 347 and 352.)

Fourth Sunday before Advent   4 November
(or All Saints' Sunday; see page 352)
Principal Service   **Love God, Love Your Neighbour**
Deut. 6.1–9 Love God, teach the law to your children; Ps. 119.1–8 Joy in the commandments; Heb. 9.11–14 Salvation through the sacrifice of Christ; Mark 12.28–34 Love God, love your neighbour

> *'"You shall love the Lord your God with all your heart, and with all your soul, and with all your mind, and with all your strength." The second [commandment] is this, "You shall love your neighbour as yourself." There is no other commandment greater than these.'*
> *Mark 12.30–31*

Laws

A London barrister was showing some visitors around his chambers. They commented on the number of law books on his bookshelves. 'Yes,' he replied, 'they contain every law a British Parliament's ever passed. The first volume contains those passed in the twelfth, thirteenth and fourteenth centuries. The next three centuries are in seven volumes. There are over 50 volumes in all, with a new volume issued every year. Most of the laws that the present Parliament's passed have never been tested in court!' The visitors soon realized that the more laws you have, the less effective they become.

Old Testament

The Bible contains hundreds of laws, beginning with the Ten Commandments. They were followed by many more telling the Israelites what to do when every imaginable misdemeanour was brought to trial. These were the written law; but there was also a long tradition of spoken law, explaining how to interpret these texts in more and more detailed circumstances. The scribes were those who made it their profession to record all these rules and regulations, discussing how to apply them to particular cases. It became more and more unwieldy, until some Jews gave up and decided to ignore God's law altogether, it was too complicated. They weren't bad people, just too busy, but the scribes lumped them together as 'the sinners'. Jesus said the 'sinners' would enter the kingdom of God ahead of the scribes and Pharisees, because they instinctively went to the heart of what the law was about, and were kinder and more loving people.

Simplifying

Some at least of the rabbis realized that a simplification of the law was necessary. Some believed there were lighter and weightier requirements of the law; the lighter ones could be broken occasionally, but the heavier ones never. The prophets pointed people away from ritual towards the moral heart of the law: Hosea speaks for God when he says, 'I desire steadfast love and not sacrifice, the knowledge of God rather than burnt offerings.' Rabbi Hillel was challenged to recite the whole law while standing on one leg. He replied, 'What you hate when it's done to you, don't do it to your neighbour. This is the whole law, the rest is commentary.'

Jesus

A scribe, who'd obviously been puzzling about all this, came to Jesus and asked him, 'Which commandment is the first of all?' Jesus answered, 'The first is, "Hear, O Israel: the Lord our God, the Lord is one; you shall love the Lord your God with all your heart, and with all your soul, and with all your mind, and with all your strength." The second is this, "You shall love your neighbour as yourself." There is no other commandment greater than these.' The commandment to love God is quoted from Deuteronomy; it begins every synagogue service, and is contained in those little *mezuzah* cylinders which Jews nail to their doorposts. The commandment to love your neighbour is from Leviticus. Originally it only applied to people who live near your home, or perhaps to all your fellow Jews. But Jesus tells us to love everybody, of every race, without exception.

God and neighbour

Jesus was the first to put the commandments to love God and your neighbour together. A life full of love is more pleasing to God than a struggle to observe every detail of the written law. But the two commandments of Jesus have to go together. You can't claim to love God, and then ignore your neighbour, whom God loves at least as much as he loves you. You'll fail to love your neighbour if you do it in your own strength; you must love God first, then let him pour his love into your heart, so that it's really God who loves your neighbour, using you as his instrument. The scribe who challenged Jesus could see the connection between loving God and loving your neighbour, and Jesus said he was 'not far from the kingdom of God'. There are too many laws, of state and religion. Do you try to cut through the undergrowth to follow the two loves, of God and neighbour? Of course we fail over and again. But if the intention to love is there, Jesus smiles at us, saying, 'You, too, are close to God's kingdom.'

Suggested hymns

Brother, sister, let me serve you; Gracious Spirit, Holy Ghost; My God, I love thee – not because; When I needed a neighbour.

Fourth Sunday before Advent   4 November
Second Service   **Living on Earth as if in Heaven**
Psalm 145 (*or* 145.1–9) Praise the Lord; Daniel 2.1–48 (*or* 1–11, 25–48) To dream; Revelation 7.9–17 Salvation; *Gospel for Holy Communion*: Matthew 5.1–12 Rejoice and be glad

'[Jesus said,] "Blessed are the peacemakers, for they will be called children of God."' Matthew 5.9

The vision of John

The vision of John in the book of Revelation takes us into the world of holy mystery. John, who lived at a time of persecution of the early Church, had a vision of the unending worship in heaven that we join every time we gather for worship. Our worship never begins at 10.00 a.m. on Sundays and lasts for an hour. Instead, at 10.00 a.m. on Sundays we join in for an hour with the ongoing worship of heaven, and occasionally we are lifted out of ourselves and have the numinous sense that we are caught up in something bigger than ourselves, greater than our corporate effort.

Live fully on earth

In apparent contrast, we hear difficult words from Jesus speaking to his disciples – including John who, decades later, was to have this extraordinary vision which set his years of faithful discipleship in a heavenly perspective. The beatitudes are not directives but statements of fact, inviting us to a new way of seeing which incorporates the outlook and way of life of people who live fully on earth, wading into life with both feet and with their sleeves rolled up. They are merciful and meek, they mourn, they are peacemakers, they hunger and thirst for righteousness, they are reviled and persecuted. Their perspective is that of heaven – they know that this life is not all there is, but that grief will be comforted, righteousness will come in fullness, the pure in heart will see God, the peacemakers will be called children of God, and that they have a reward in heaven. This perspective frees them from the necessity to seek reward in this life, and thus enables them to be more fully involved because they have no ulterior motive except to live as those who know they are blessed by God.

Faith unlimited

The beatitudes describe a way of life that is not unworldly, but immensely worldly and in the thick of things. Daniel lived such an engaged life despite being an exile employed in the royal court of the enemy nation that had conquered his own. He could have found all sorts of reasons, indeed justification, for not living faithfully, but instead had risked his life to negotiate an alternative to the royal court's diet so he and his companions could fulfil their religious duties while also serving the king. They proved themselves utterly reliable and wise despite their precarious existence. Daniel lived in a fraught situation on earth with his eyes fixed on heaven, winning first respect (as recounted in this reading), but later potentially deadly opposition.

We cannot live the beatitudes without getting messy, because they involve living amid the grief and mourning for a world that is not as it should be, in the midst of unjust and unrighteous situations, in the places where mercy is missing, where there is no peace, where purity of heart is undermined at every turn, where power-hungry people scorn and manipulate meekness for their own ends. People who live this way – Daniel, Jesus's disciples, the saints – we remember in this kingdom season. They live risky lives as fully and as passionately as they can. For some, this is done in the face of 'the great ordeal', once endured by the people John saw now robed in white in heaven. In a sense they gamble with their lives for the sake of Jesus Christ.

Between heaven and earth

People who live in the way of the beatitudes also have a sense of balance between heaven and earth. They know that the present moment counts in God's purposes. Some religious people are so heavenly minded they are no earthly good, and some non-Christian people are very earthly minded, driven by an admirable desire to right the injustice they see, but with no knowledge of the ultimate redemption of all creation in Christ. As Christians, we are called to move between the heavenly and earthly worlds, totally immersed in each, letting each inform the other as the light of heaven shines through our lives.

All-age worship

Copy stained-glass pictures of a saint, with crayons or appliqué. In a 'scroll' design underneath, write one of the beatitudes that you think applies to that saint.

Suggested hymns

Blest are the pure in heart; For all the saints who from their labours rest; Seek ye first the kingdom of God; Take my life, and let it be.

Third Sunday before Advent   11 November
Principal Service   **Parishes**

(*For a service that is not a Service of Remembrance.*)
Jonah 3.1–5, 10 God's forgiveness of Nineveh; Ps. 62.5–12 God's
greatness and love; Heb. 9.24–28 Salvation through Christ; Mark
1.14–20 Fish for people

> *'Jesus said to them, "Follow me and I will make you fish for people."'*
> *Mark 1.17*

St Martin

Today's not only Armistice Day, it's also Martinmas, the feast day
of St Martin of Tours. St Martin was a soldier and was born around
AD 316, in a non-Christian family. He joined the Roman army, but
was fascinated by the story of Jesus of Nazareth. But in those days,
you couldn't be a soldier if you were a Christian. One cold day, as
Martin was riding his horse, he saw a half-naked beggar shivering
by the roadside. On a sudden impulse, he drew his sword and cut
his warm military cloak in two, giving half to the beggar. The beggar revealed himself as Jesus Christ, calling Martin to resign from
the army and be baptized.

Monks

Martin became a monk, living in a cave in the banks of the River
Loire. Other monks settled nearby, his cell grew into a monastery,
and Martin was appointed Bishop of Tours. Christianity spread
along the Roman roads in those days, and the only Christians were
in the larger towns. Monks were free to travel out from their monasteries, or Minsters, to preach and minister to the people in the
country villages. Many villagers were converted and baptized, but
when the monks moved on, there was nobody to teach the new
converts the faith. Martin had a brilliant idea, which changed the
social history of Europe throughout the Middle Ages, and is still a
powerful influence today.

Parishes

The Roman Empire had been divided into areas by the government,
each administered by a governor. These areas were called dioceses,

and when Christianity became the religion of the Empire, it was natural that bishops should be appointed to each diocese to administer the Church there. Martin's idea was to divide the ecclesiastical dioceses into parishes. Everyone in the diocese lived in one parish or another; and parish priests were appointed to be responsible for each parish, care for the people and evangelize the pagans there. At first there were no church buildings, but soon the local landowners gave land and resources to build a parish church, often very beautiful but very cold and plain. Later, more land was given to the Church as glebe, which was often farmed by the priest, who could now afford to live in the parish, and who received a tenth of the income of all the other farmers to maintain the church building, and care for the poor and sick.

Today

So St Martin's brainwave meant that the church was responsible for every person living in the parish, whatever their faith. Of course, if a group of Nonconformists wanted a church and a minister, they had to raise the costs among themselves, but Anglicans in the British Isles, like Roman Catholics and Lutherans in other parts of Europe, grew up thinking that someone else would always pay the bills for them. These days the tithes have been abolished; health and welfare workers are paid by the government, and landowners don't feel responsible for the physical and spiritual needs of those who live on their lands. Many other forms of meeting place and entertainment are available, and fewer people see any need to go to church, or to support the parish where they live. The old sense of local community has been lost. Higher expectations in the upkeep and heating of buildings, support of the minister's family and provision of pensions, with costly administration in the diocese, all mean that the parish system, Martin's brainwave, is breaking down all over the country.

The future

Nonconformists, independent churches and Roman Catholics each have their own problems, but all are asking what the future holds for the Church. Everybody here loves *their* church, and would do anything in their power to keep it open, but nationally many people say we may have to go back to the minster system. That means small numbers of paid clergy going out from a central base. Local churches would be cared for by ministers who earn their living in other ways, and each congregation would care for and evangelize the residents in their area. Some buildings may have to be handed to the local authority for social centres, and let out to different groups at different times. I don't know the answer to all this, but it's something we should all be thinking and praying about, especially at Martinmas.

All-age worship

Find out about the finances of your church, and draw up a rough budget. What could you do to increase church income?

Suggested hymns

An army of ordinary people; Soldiers of Christ arise; Through the night of doubt and sorrow; Will you come and follow me?

Remembrance Sunday   11 November
A Just War?

(The readings of the day, or those 'In Time of Trouble', can be used. These readings are for 'The Peace of the World'.)
Isa. 57.15–19 Peace too far and near; Ps. 72.1–7 May peace abound; 1 Tim. 2.1–6 Prayers for peace; John 14.23–29 My peace I give you

> *'[Jesus said,] "Peace I leave with you; my peace I give to you. I do not give to you as the world gives. Do not let your hearts be troubled, and do not let them be afraid."' John 14.27*

Pacifists

Christians can start with the Bible, and reach sincerely held but opposite conclusions on war and peace. If you mention the phrase 'a just war', at once you'll have two sorts of people gunning for you. Pacifists say that war's always evil; there can never be a just war. War involves killing, and killing's always wrong. Even with television we seldom grasp the horror of looking on the mangled bodies of people we love. We need the pacifists to remind us that we must strive, as hard as we can, to avoid war.

National defence

The second group of people who get angry at talk about a just war are those who've decided that some particular battle is necessary for the defence of their country, and don't want to be held back by quibbling Christians mouthing moral scruples.

How to lose friends

So if I begin to talk about just-war doctrine today, I know that many in this congregation will get very angry with me, and I might have no friends at all by the time I'm done! I'd just ask you to hear me out to the end; I may turn out to be saying something different from what you expect. I'm not going to tell you what to decide; I'll succeed in my purpose if I set you arguing among yourselves, passionately but rationally.

Just war?

St Thomas Aquinas is credited with inventing the doctrine of the 'just war', but it isn't a specifically Christian idea. Every nation feels that some behaviour on the battlefield's honourable and other behaviour's not. Aquinas only summarized what earlier writers had said. First he considered the pacifist position.

Non-retaliation

Jesus told us to 'turn the other cheek'. That's fine for individuals; but does it apply to whole nations? The commandments say, 'Thou shalt not kill.' But love overrides all commandments. For instance, a robber enters your house and starts beating your granny to death. To kill the robber's a wicked thing to do. But not to kill him, and allow him to kill your grandmother without trying to defend her, is also evil. So we're forced to choose 'the lesser of two evils'. Or are you going to turn your granny over, and say, 'You've hit her on one cheek, now hit her on the other'?

Should we fight?

But if you decide that you must use force to defend the innocent when they're attacked, then you've got to think about the doctrine of the just war. It's in two parts: should we go to war, and how should we fight if we do? Aquinas said we should never go to war unless we can meet *all* of the following five conditions. There must be:

1 a just cause – self-defence is a just cause for fighting; seizing other people's land is not;
2 proper authority – a self-appointed dictator does not have proper authority to start a war; a democratic government may have;
3 right intention – to get justice for everybody is a right intention; to seize power is not;
4 the probability of success – sometimes you win a battle, but lose the struggle for peace;
5 *and* proportionate means – there's a limit to the number of innocent civilians you can justifiably kill.

So the Church says to those who are not pacifists: you still need to meet strict conditions before you can declare war with a clear conscience.

How?

But we haven't finished yet. Aquinas said if you decide to fight, you must meet three more conditions:

1 Discrimination means attacking the right targets.
2 Proportionality means using only as much force as you have to.
3 Responsibility means helping people get their lives back to normal afterwards.

Peace

Jesus promised in the Gospel to give us his peace, in heaven if not on earth. God promises eternity to everyone, not just those who believe the same as we do: think about the parable of the sheep and the goats. One very good reason for loving your enemy is that you will one day come face to face with him or her in eternity.

How to make friends

A Chinese emperor vowed to destroy all his enemies within a year. Twelve months later his advisors complained that the enemies were all still alive. 'But I have no enemies left now,' replied the emperor, 'because I've made them all my friends.' Wouldn't it be wonderful if we could all do that?

Make a list of what the children would like to be when they grow
up. Make up a prayer asking God to help them achieve their ambitions, and remembering those who died before they could do so.

Suggested hymns

God is our strength and refuge; Peace is flowing like a river; Peace,
perfect peace?; Saviour, again to thy dear name.

Second Sunday before Advent   18 November
Principal Service   **Paroxysms of Goodness**
Dan. 12.1–3 Conflict and resurrection; Ps. 16 Resurrection, life and
death; Heb. 10.11–14 [15–18] 19–25 Assurance and faith; Mark
13.1–8 Conflict

> '*Let us consider how to provoke one another to love and good
> deeds, not neglecting to meet together, as is the habit of some,
> but encouraging one another.*' Hebrews 10.24–25

Punishment vs promise of salvation

Jesus's answer to the disciples' question about the end of all things
is a gift to those of an apocalyptic turn of mind. Their interest in
cataclysmic events, which can usually be conveniently attached to
current items in world news, is not blunted by the cautionary opening: 'Beware that no one leads you astray.' Nor is it modified by
what follows. Jesus will go on to speak of the personal cost of being a disciple, disowned by family, punished by civic authorities,
and hated for speaking in his name. There is a difference between
apocalypse and eschatology, between a vision of our relationship
to God cast in terms of violent punishment of sin in a series of
cosmic disasters, and one framed in the light of a promise of salvation already given in Christ. Knowing that difference may not make
circumstances easier for the victims of war, persecution, famine,
drought and earthquakes. It is certainly not a quick and easy answer to perplexity about the action (or not) of a loving God in all
these things.

Living with purpose

But, knowing the difference between apocalypse and eschatology does make it possible to be purposeful about living in the good time that is given to us. It is this time that interests the writer of the Letter to the Hebrews, who continues to explore Jesus's high priestly ministry in contrast to the kind of priesthood familiar to the audience. The distinction is itself best defined in terms of time. Conventional priests repeat the offering of sacrifices, 'day after day', because human sin is repetitive. As sinful human beings themselves, they can never get beyond the daily need for atonement. Jesus, perfectly human and perfectly divine, has offered a sacrifice not confined by time, but 'for all time', needing no repetition. And, having done that, he has reset the clock according to the time of salvation, sitting down at God's right hand to wait until those for whom he died catch up. This is not passivity or disengagement. Waiting is dependent on relationship, imagined as a covenant, and kept alive by the presence of the Holy Spirit. The writer, recalls Jeremiah, who wrote of the covenant that God would establish with Israel after the exile – not as a theoretical agreement, but as a living and embodied promise, written on the hearts and minds of the people. In this new covenant, there is an answering embodied element in the blood of Jesus that washes sin away, and the flesh that becomes the way for our imperfect flesh to find its way to God.

Provoking one another

How should this time of active waiting be used? The writer offers urgent practical advice to those who have received the hope and assurance of sin forgiven. They are to goad one another 'to love and good deeds'. English translations have not retained the energizing picture of a sudden outburst of love, suggested by the Greek *paroxusmon* and still used to convey extremes of behaviour – from paroxysms of weeping to paroxysms of overspending. They focus on the root word (*oxus* – sharp), and choose the more prosaic 'provoke one another' to describe the almost competitive encouragement demanded of the Christian community with its eye on the end of 'the race that is set before us'. Such incitement is best achieved by meeting regularly for worship, study and hospitality – all part of a training for life in God's eternal kingdom.

Model lives

Last week we commemorated vernacular saints whose stories are models of these good principles made real in dedicated lives. Margaret (16 November), the English princess who grew up in exile in Hungary while the Danes ruled England, returned to marry the King of Scotland after the Conquest, and devoted herself to the feeding of the poor and the good governance of the Church. Hugh, Bishop of Lincoln (17 November), reorganized his vast diocese, cared for the poor, the lepers and the oppressed, and opposed the persecution of Jews. This week we remember Hilda, Abbess of Whitby (19 November), who presided over the reconciliation of the Roman and Celtic traditions in Britain at the Synod of 664, and brought greater peace and unity to the Church. Edmund, King of the East Angles (20 November), died under a hail of Danish arrows, refusing to renounce his Christian faith. They are among the great 'cloud of witnesses' who show us that, however harsh its conditions, there is much to be done with the time we have.

All-age worship

Cut out from newspapers and magazines advertisements for science fiction or action adventure films. Are these characters examples or warnings about how we should live?

Suggested hymns

All my hope on God is founded; And can it be?; Glorious things of thee are spoken; What are these like stars appearing?

Second Sunday before Advent   18 November
Second Service   **The Fiery Furnace**
Ps. 95 Let us sing; Dan. 3 (*or* 3.13–30) The fiery furnace;
Matt. 13.24–30, 36–43 Betrayal and denial

'Then King Nebuchadnezzar . . . said to his counsellors, "Was it not three men that we threw bound into the fire?" They answered the king, "True, O king." He replied, "But I see four men unbound, walking in the middle of the fire, and they are not hurt; and the fourth has the appearance of a god."' Daniel 3.24–25

Shadrach, Meshach and Abednego

The book of Daniel starts in the reign of King Nebuchadnezzar, who exiled the people of Judah to Babylon. He then chose some of the promising young men to be trained up in the literature and language of Babylon, so that they could serve as advisors in the royal court. Among these was Daniel, whom he renamed Belteshazzar, and Hananiah, Mishael and Azariah, who were given the names Shadrach, Meshach and Abednego. Soon, they were all four promoted to high positions. In chapter 3, Daniel isn't mentioned. King Nebuchadnezzar makes a golden idol, and says that anyone who doesn't worship it will be thrown into a fiery furnace. Shadrach, Meshach and Abednego refuse to worship the idol, and the furnace is made so hot that it kills the men who threw the three young men into the fire. The king was astonished to see not three but four men walking around unharmed in the midst of the flames. 'And the fourth', exclaimed the king, 'has the appearance of a god.' The three are taken out of the furnace, not even scorched, and the king is so impressed he passes a new law threatening dire punishment to anyone who speaks blasphemously about the God of Shadrach, Meshach and Abednego. According to the Apocrypha, the three young men then sang the song we know as the Benedicite.

Repetitions

The story's beautifully told, and the storyteller obviously enjoyed repetitions. The list of those who served under the king comes twice: the 'satraps, the prefects, the governors, and the king's counsellors'. The new law says that everybody's to worship the golden idol when they hear the sound of the musical instruments, and this list is repeated in full four times: 'When you hear the sound of the horn, pipe, lyre, trigon, harp, drum, and entire musical ensemble, you are to fall down and worship the golden statue that King Nebuchadnezzar has set up.' Nobody's quite sure what instruments the Hebrew words are referring to. Somebody was once asked to read this lesson from the Authorized Version. He came across these strange words, and guessed at a pronunciation for 'the cornet, flute, harp, sackbut, psaltery, dulcimer, and all kinds of musick...' Then he turned the page and saw that the same words came up again, and he couldn't remember how he'd pronounced them the first time. So he stammered out: 'At what time ye hear the, er, the orchestra ...' and hoped nobody would notice!

Keep the faith

The story's told to encourage Jews to remain faithful under persecution. They were persecuted by the Persians in Babylon, then by
the Greeks, and then by the Romans. They must have often been
tempted to compromise, and worship the idols of the foreign gods.
But if they did, the message about the one God who cares how we
treat each other would be lost, and the Jewish nation, God's messengers, might disintegrate. After centuries of anti-Semitism, Jews
still have to tread a narrow line between assimilation to the customs
of the nation where they live, and faithfulness to the traditions that
have kept them together down the ages.

The fourth man

Then who was the fourth man, who was walking in the fiery furnace along with Shadrach, Meshach and Abednego? The one who
had 'the appearance of a god'? Nebuchadnezzar obviously thought
it was the Jewish God come to encourage and rescue his followers.
But the Jews have always been reluctant to talk of God appearing in
human form. For Christians there's no problem. God appeared in
human form when Jesus came to earth, so, for us, the fourth person
in the furnace represents Jesus, the Son of God.

Furnace of affliction

So, for the Christian, the story of the burning fiery furnace reminds
us that Jesus is always with us. Even in the furnace of affliction,
whether it's pain, persecution, depression or mockery, we must
keep the faith, make no compromise with evil, and trust in the
invisible presence of our Saviour. Nothing, nothing can separate us
from the love of God, ever.

Suggested hymns

*All creation, bless the Lord; Do not be afraid, for I have redeemed
you; Let us, with a gladsome mind; Onward, Christian soldiers.*

Christ the King   25 November
Principal Service   **Mysteries of the Kingdom**

Dan. 7.9–10, 13–14 The kingship of Christ; Ps. 93 The Lord is
King; Rev. 1.4b–8 The greatness of Christ; John 18.33–37 Are you
the King?

> *'Pilate . . . summoned Jesus, and asked him, "Are you the King of
> the Jews?"' John 18.33*

Kingdom

There is an edge to Pilate's address to Jesus, as he returns to the
Praetorium to hear the Jews' complaint, which goes beyond the
routine identification of the defendant. 'Are you the King of
the Jews?', or even 'So you are the King of the Jews', assumes either
a false and dangerous claim, or a case of severe delusion. Jesus
refuses to play this game. He has already made seven statements
that begin 'I am', but 'I am the King of the Jews' is not one of them.
In his reply to Pilate, he shifts the noun from 'king' to 'kingdom',
something he has referred to only once, in John's narrative, in his
nocturnal conversation with Nicodemus. There, the kingdom is
explicitly God's, and it is reached through new vision and new
birth.

Reborn son of man

Nicodemus struggles to comprehend this new birth. It will be
through the resurrection, when the 'Son of Man' is 'lifted up', and
that lies some way ahead, although clues to salvation are already
to be found in the prophets' writings. Jesus's possible allusion
to Daniel's prospect of a world justly ruled by 'one like a son of
man' after disorder and oppression, is available in most translations except the NRSV, which opts for 'like a human being'. The
explanation of the kingdom which Jesus gives to Pilate is no less
complex. This is not a question of territory. There is something
about Jesus, recognized very early in his public ministry as an
astonishing authority. John associates it firmly with the Father,
who is the source of all authority exercised by the Son. The Son
can do nothing on his own.

271

Paradox

It is out of this vital relationship that Jesus speaks to Pilate, reminding him again that it is he who has named Jesus as a king. The paradox of Jesus's power becomes more and more compelling through his trial: it derives its strength not from claims of importance, but from a complete putting aside of self and status. Its mission is to 'testify to the truth', a simple statement in its own right, but world-changing in its implications. Pilate, through cynicism, nervousness, or plain indifference, chooses not to probe the implications.

Mystery

The Feast of Christ the King, which we keep today, invites us to approach the mystery of the kingship that is celebrated. Here, we are challenged by the ordering of the Church's year, which ends with this feast and begins again officially on Advent Sunday. At one level, it is logical that 'the year that begins with the hope of the coming Messiah ends with the proclamation of his universal sovereignty' (*Common Worship: Times and Seasons*). Yet, at another level, this ignores the longer development running through the readings from the Sunday after All Saints' Day to the final week of Advent. These readings reveal the 'full manifestation of the reign of the Lord', an insight taken from the Advent Project, which promotes the recovery of a seven-week Advent that concentrates on the rich development of this theme (http://the adventproject.org/rationale.htm).

Judgement

Judgement is certainly part of the final and eternal reign of Christ over the world, but it is rooted in love for the world – love that gives its own life, and leads those for whom it dies into new life. Christ gains his title to kingship by doing what no earthly king could do: dealing with sin, the ultimate enemy, by offering at great cost liberation from sin. The kingdom he establishes is a structure of worship, not of power, and the judgement that it brings comes in the hardest and gentlest form. One way to imagine it is to sing Charles Wesley's great Advent hymn as a meditation, not a war cry, in the weeks to come:

> Every eye shall now behold him
> Robed in dreadful majesty;
> Those who set at nought and sold him,

Pierced and nailed him to the tree,
Deeply wailing,
Shall the true Messiah see.

All-age worship

Make paper crowns. Write on them, 'A True King'. Wear them during the service, then cast them down before the altar.

Suggested hymns

Lo! He comes with clouds descending; Christ triumphant ever reigning; Crown him with many crowns; For the beauty of the earth; Let all the world in every corner sing.

Christ the King 25 November
Second Service **The Moving Finger Writes**
Morning Ps. 29 Enthroned, 110 The king at your right hand;
Evening Ps. 72 An ideal king; Dan. 5 Belshazzar's feast;
John 6.1–15 Feeding the crowd

> *'This is the interpretation of the matter: MENE, God has numbered the days of your kingdom and brought it to an end; TEKEL, you have been weighed on the scales and found wanting; PERES, your kingdom is divided and given to the Medes and Persians.'*
> *Daniel 5.26–28*

The moving finger

Edward Fitzgerald's translation of *The Rubaiyat of Omar Khayyam* contains the famous lines:

> The Moving Finger writes, and having writ Moves on;
> nor all thy piety nor Wit Shall lure it back to cancel half a Line,
> Nor all thy Tears wash out a Word of it.

This reference to our deeds being written in an indelible record is probably a reminiscence, conscious or unconscious, of the story of the banquet given by King Belshazzar in Babylon, where the finger of God writes on the wall behind the feasting king the judgement on his crimes. It's a memorable image, and the story's made even more memorable in Sir William Walton's oratorio, to words arranged from the Bible by Osbert Sitwell, called *Belshazzar's Feast*.

The divine message

Belshazzar and his guests, his wives and concubines, were drinking from the sacred vessels which had been looted from the Temple in Jerusalem, an appalling blasphemy. As they drank, instead of recognizing the one true God to whom the goblets belonged, they praised their idols of gold and silver, bronze, iron, wood and stone. The fingers of a human hand wrote on the plaster of the wall the words which Daniel read as 'Mene, mene, tekel upharsin'. These are the names of Babylonian coins, and the story is told ironically to suggest that they could have been written by the treasurer working out the cost of the refreshments, and not until Daniel interpreted them was it realized that this was a divine message.

Double meanings

The literal meanings of the words are 'number', 'weight' and 'division'. The coin known as a 'mina' was named after the counters used for calculations. The coin now known in Israel as the 'shekel' was originally a fixed weight of silver, just over 11 grammes. A half-shekel was named from the word 'peres', meaning 'divided'. The plural of peres was parsin, and the letter 'u' in front of it in the old translations simply means 'and'. So Daniel interpreted the message about the coins according to the literal meanings of their names: numbered are your days; weighed is your wickedness; and divided shall your kingdom be. These historical details make the fabulous story even more significant.

Judgement

Turning to British history, it was the achievement of Magna Carta to show that even the king is not above the law. Belshazzar's crime was to consider that he was even above God's law. But no, God keeps a record of all our wickedness: 'The moving finger writes, and having writ moves on.' Revelation depicts 'the dead, great and small, standing before the throne, and books were opened . . . And the dead were judged according to their works, as recorded in the books.' It's good to be reminded that God cares about the way his children treat each other, and what we do to our own bodies through misuse of alcohol, food and so on.

Forgiveness

It was Belshazzar's misfortune that he died that very night, before he had had a chance to repent. King Nebuchadnezzar before him had been judged, punished, but when he repented and praised God, he was forgiven and restored to his kingdom. Jesus implies that judgement is something we do to ourselves: 'And this is the judgement, that the light has come into the world, and people loved darkness rather than light because their deeds were evil.' It's undoubtedly true that much of our suffering in this life is caused by our own self-indulgence. If we thank God for the good things that happen to us, it seems logical that our sufferings are sent by him as punishment. But the God whom Jesus describes doesn't sound like one who'd willingly cause his children to suffer. He might give us a short, sharp shock to bring us to our senses, but God always holds open the possibility that we can repent and be forgiven.

The moral

So the story of Belshazzar's feast is a stern warning that God is aware of, and judges, everything we do, and we must repent before it's too late. Numbered are your days; weighed is your wickedness; and divided shall your possessions be. But the Christian cannot agree with Omar Khayyam that:

> The Moving Finger writes, and having writ
> Moves on; nor all thy piety nor Wit
> Shall lure it back to cancel half a Line,
> Nor all thy Tears wash out a Word of it.

It is the tears of the penitent, joined to those of God himself, that can wash the slate clean.

Suggested hymns

God of grace and God of glory; Judge eternal, throned in splendour; O God of earth and altar; Rejoice, the Lord is King.

Sermons for Saints' Days
and Special Occasions

SAINTS' DAYS

When his friends described the martyrdom of St Polycarp in about AD 156, they declared their intention of 'celebrating the birthday of his martyrdom' every year in the future. When churches could be built to enshrine the bodies or relics of the martyrs, they were often dedicated on the anniversary of their death, and an annual dedication festival was held on that date. Other churches dedicated to the name of a saint soon celebrated the saint's day as their 'patronal festival'. The Bible describes the heroes of the Old Testament as a 'cloud of witnesses' around us, and all believers as being united in the body of Christ, as 'fellow citizens of the saints, and of the household of God'. Since the time of the Maccabees it had been held that those who had died heroically are praying for those who are alive, the Church Triumphant interceding for the Church Militant. It seemed natural to ask the departed for their prayers, and to talk to our dead friends just as we did when they were alive. But superstition grew up around devotion to the saints in the Middle Ages, and it was rejected by most Protestants. Yet many congregations wished to continue honouring the saints, especially on their own patronal festival. When the Book of Common Prayer was printed in two colours, the more important saints' days were listed in the calendar as 'Red Letter Days'. This book provides sermons for all the 'Festivals' in the modern calendars, including the patron saints of England, Scotland, Wales and Ireland, and Corpus Christi; as well the 'Principal Feasts' commemorating the Epiphany, the Annunciation and All Saints' Day; Harvest Festival, and sermons for Baptisms, Weddings and Funerals. *Common Worship: Services and Prayers for the Church of England* gives rules for transferring the observation of Festivals when they coincide with Principal Feasts, as well as suggesting colours for the hangings and vestments in church; in general, feasts of martyrs are red, all others are white, with an option to use gold on Principal Feasts.

St Stephen, Deacon, First Martyr   26 December 2017
Keeping the Law

2 Chron. 24.20–22 The stoning of Zechariah, *or* Acts 7.51–60 The
death of Stephen; Ps. 119.161–168 Persecuted without a cause;
(*if the Acts reading is used instead of the Old Testament reading,
the New Testament reading is* Gal. 2.16b–20 Crucified with Christ);
Matt. 10.17–22 Persecution

> '[St Stephen said to the Jewish leaders,] "You are the ones that
> received the law as ordained by angels, and yet you have not kept
> it."' Acts 7.53

Anti-Semitism

The Jewish people have suffered as a persecuted minority throughout history. But especially because of the Second World War, where
they endured the horrific torture of the Holocaust, they deserve the
sympathy and respect of people of all religions. So any criticism
of Jewish people runs the risk of being regarded as anti-Semitism.
Unless, that is, the criticism is made by other Jews. St Stephen,
whom we commemorate today, made a long speech when he was
accused of criticizing the Law of Moses, which in a non-Jew would
have been disgraceful. In his defence, he described the history of the
Jewish people, and God's goodness and mercy to them throughout
their history. One of God's greatest gifts was when he gave the Jews
the Law, which helped them to think carefully and logically about
how God expects us to behave. But, said Stephen to the priests and
Pharisees, '*you have never kept it!*'

Shocking

Shock, horror! They thought *they* were the only people to observe
the complex regulations found in their Scriptures, and here was a
fellow Jew lecturing them on their disobedience. But his criticism
was firmly based on two facts. First, their law included a command
to love their neighbours as much as they loved themselves, and Jesus
had explained that all the other laws depended on this. If you dress
as the Scripture tells you, avoid the foods that it forbids, wash before
you pray, and do no work on the Sabbath – but if you don't observe
these laws with love in your heart, you are breaking them. Secondly,
Stephen's name is the Greek word for a crown, so he probably came

from one of the many Jewish families who had settled abroad, and spoke better Greek than they did Hebrew. So he understood that God had revealed to the Jews that there is only one God for all the world, who cares about the way we treat each other, so that they could spread this good news to all the other nations on the earth. But instead of teaching foreigners to be loving and tolerant, as God wishes, they had told them that all nations must observe the ancient customs and pernickety regulations that the Jews had developed for themselves. For saying this, Stephen was stoned to death. In Acts 15 we read that the first Christians decided that most of the ritual laws of the Old Testament don't apply to non-Jews. We all owe to the Jews almost all we know about God and his will for us. But we cannot share their concentration on the complexities of the Law.

Islam

Maybe this teaches us something about how we should treat people of other religions, as well as the Jews? They all have something to teach us about God, which we should accept gratefully. But when they tell us we should follow their customs, we should politely disagree, because the Law of Love overrides all other laws. For instance, we can admire the spiritual insights of the Holy Qur'an, with its emphasis on Allah the merciful and compassionate; we should copy their submission to the will of God – 'Islam' means submission, and 'Muslim' means one who has submitted – but we cannot accept the entire Shariah law. We can learn much from our Muslim friends, and we must live together in peace and tolerance. But, just as with the Jews, we must ask them to adapt their laws to modern circumstances, and base their behaviour on love.

Christians

Judaism, Islam and Christianity all worship one God. Yet although we have so much in common, we are not good at living together in peace, as God wishes us to. We Christians are not guiltless in this, either. From the Crusades, to setting up the State of Israel on Arab lands, to arbitrarily redrawing their boundaries after the First World War, we have disobeyed God's commandment to live together in mutual love. We, too, judge people on whether they observe our traditional morality, ignoring whether or not they are more loving than we are. Christians can sometimes be as hyper-legalistic as the people who martyred St Stephen.

Law

Ours, like Judaism and Islam, is a religion with high standards of behaviour. There is a place for the guidance of traditional morality. But we must never let our laws triumph over the Law of Love that Jesus taught to us.

Suggested hymns

Come down, O love divine; Let there be love shared among us; Love came down at Christmas; Love divine, all loves excelling.

St John, Apostle and Evangelist   27 December
St John's First Letter

Ex. 33.7–11a The tent of meeting; Ps. 117 Praise God, all nations; 1 John 1 The word of life; John 21.19b–25 The Beloved Disciple

> 'We declare to you what was from the beginning, what we have heard, what we have seen with our eyes, what we have looked at and touched with our hands, concerning the word of life.' 1 John 1.1

Readers

You can never understand a letter unless you know to whom it was written, and why. Otherwise you may fail to understand it, or worse, you may gain a totally mistaken idea of what the writer was trying to say. Often that does not matter; but in the case of the letters included in the Bible, it could be extremely dangerous.

John

There are three Letters of John in the New Testament, and none of them make any mention of who they are addressed to. Perhaps they were meant to be copied to a number of churches, dealing with a common problem that all of them shared. John was a common name, but we can be sure that the letters, headed '1 John', '2 John' and '3 John', were written by the same man who wrote the book headed 'The Gospel of John', because the style of language is so similar, and they deal with similar problems. Today we celebrate

'St John, Apostle and Evangelist'; we might add, 'also letter-writer'. So how should we understand his letters?

First Letter

Today, let's look at the First Letter of John. Like the Gospel, it lays great stress on love, and light. But in the letter, John describes some people that he deeply disagrees with. John believed that Jesus was 'the Word made flesh'. By that he meant that Jesus was God's way of communicating with us, so he was completely divine; yet at the same time he was only able to save us because he had become as completely human as we are. John's opponents did not believe that. Some said that Jesus was not at all human, he was God, temporarily occupying a human being when Jesus was baptized, and leaving him again when the human Jesus cried out, 'My God, my God, why have you forsaken me?' They asserted that the world was made up of an uneasy mixture of two things: spirit and flesh. The spirit was entirely good, and would have nothing to do with our fleshly part, which was completely evil.

Dangerous

Why did St John think this was so dangerous? If the flesh is bad, Christians should have nothing to do with caring for their op-pressed neighbours, and the joys of sex. Some even went so far as to say that God himself is a mixture of light and darkness, and we should have as much dirty sex as we can because it takes us deeper into the dark side of God. Others said, if the spiritual side of life is all that counts, then the only Christians are those who have re-nounced material concerns; and we should despise those filthy sub-humans who are concerned with how to earn their living and meet the material needs of others. These attitudes are still found in some Christians, even today; in fact we sometimes slip into saying things like that ourselves.

Answer

John's answer is to stress the twofold nature of Jesus, wholly human and wholly divine. As one of the early Christians wrote, 'He became what we are to make us what he is.' If you believe that, you will be repelled by sin and attracted by love. Listen to what a difference this understanding of the context makes to our understanding of what John meant when he wrote:

- 'Every spirit that confesses that Jesus Christ has come in the flesh is from God, and every spirit that does not confess Jesus is not from God.'
- 'This is the one who came by water and blood, Jesus Christ, not with the water [of baptism] only but with the water and the blood [of crucifixion].'
- 'If we say that we have fellowship with him while we are walking in darkness, we lie and do not do what is true; but if we walk in the light as he himself is in the light, we have fellowship with one another, and the blood of Jesus his Son cleanses us from all sin.'
- 'If we walk in the light as [God] himself is in the light, we have fellowship with one another, and the blood of Jesus his Son cleanses us from all sin.'
- 'We know that we have passed from death to life because we love one another . . . How does God's love abide in anyone who has the world's goods and sees a brother or sister in need and yet refuses help?'

When you get home, read the First Letter of John, and see how it challenges your own selfish assumptions.

Suggested hymns

From heaven you came; Lead, kindly light; Let there be love; The Spirit lives to set us free.

Holy Innocents   28 December
Innocent Children
Jer. 31.15–17 Rachel weeping for her children; Ps. 124 When our enemies attacked us; 1 Cor. 1.26–29 God chose what is weak; Matt. 2.13–18 The massacre

> *'When Herod saw that he had been tricked by the wise men, he was infuriated, and he sent and killed all the children in and around Bethlehem who were two years old or under, according to the time that he had learned from the wise men.' Matthew 2.16*

281

Innocents

The grief of parents when one of their children dies is indescribable. They think of the empty void in their lives, how they will miss the one they love, and the destructions of all the dreams and hopes in which they had invested so much love. Nobody *deserves* a long and happy life, and if we are given one, we have to thank God for his mercy. But when a child dies young, we begin to question why something so unjust should happen, for they have done no evil deeds that they need to be punished for. When we look in the eyes of a sleeping child, there is an incredible innocence in their expression. They may have been what we call 'a little bit naughty' at times, but that is only the survival instinct we find in the young of any species; they have not deliberately chosen to do evil.

Bethlehem

So, if that is what we feel about the death of one child, just imagine what the parents of Bethlehem must have felt when the soldiers of King Herod slaughtered every one of their children who was two years old or less. This was because Herod had learnt that this village was where a future king would be born, who would drive out Herod's dynasty. The wise men told him that the birth had already taken place, within the past two years, because that was the length of time they had been following his star. The only way Herod could defend his throne against a usurper was to decapitate all the babes under two years old, before the eyes of their parents. But he was unsuccessful, because baby Jesus and his parents had already fled to Egypt. Yet dying because of Jesus, condemned of crimes you have not committed, is what the saints down the ages have done. So we count the children of Bethlehem within 'the noble army of martyrs'. They are known as the 'Holy Innocents', for whether you spell the word H.O.L.Y. or W.H.O.L.L.Y., they were totally without blame.

Virgin

There is an aroma of innocence in the way we use the word 'virgin'. But that word, in the Bible, has two meanings. The words of Isaiah that we know as 'a virgin shall conceive' are correctly translated in modern Bibles as: 'The young woman is with child and shall bear a son, and shall name him Immanuel.' Sex was not considered sinful in those days, and any young mother could be described as a virgin. It was St Matthew who first saw in these words a prediction of the miraculous birth of Jesus. St John, in the book of Revelation, uses the word in both senses, when he writes:

> And I heard a voice from heaven . . . like the sound of harpists playing on their harps, and they sing a new song before the throne . . . No one could learn that song except the one hundred and forty-four thousand who have been redeemed from the earth. It is these who have not defiled themselves with women, for they are virgins; these follow the Lamb wherever he goes. They have been redeemed from humankind as first fruits for God and the Lamb, and in their mouth no lie was found; they are blameless.

Redeemed

This is symbolic. There will be far more than 144,000 people in heaven. They will include men as well as women, and many of them will be parents. Yet because they have repented of their sins, God has forgiven them and restored them to the sort of innocence they had as children; that is why they are called 'virgins'. So when we get to heaven, we can be sure that we shall see again those 'holy innocents' who died as children. But you and I will also be welcomed before the throne of God, provided we have repented of our many sins. Then God will restore our childlike innocence. We shall skip together through the streets of the New Jerusalem, where, said the prophet Zechariah, 'Old men and old women shall again sit in the streets of Jerusalem, each with staff in hand because of their great age. And the streets of the city shall be full of boys and girls playing in its streets.'

Suggested hymns

Lully, lullay, thou little tiny child; There's a song for all the children; Unto us a boy is born; When Christ was born in Bethlehem.

Naming and Circumcision of Jesus   1 January 2018
The Past and the Future

Num. 6.22–27 Aaron's blessing; Ps. 8 From the mouths of babes;
Gal. 4.4–7 Born under the law; Luke 2.15–21 Naming and
circumcision

> *'But when the fullness of time had come, God sent his Son,*
> *born of a woman, born under the law, in order to redeem those*
> *who were under the law, so that we might receive adoption as*
> *children.' Galatians 4.4–5*

New Year

New Year's Eve, or New Year's Day, is a point of transition. We
say farewell to the year that has passed, and we look forward to the
year that stretches in front of us. There are many things in the past
that need to be repented for, forgiven and then forgotten. Yet there
are also lessons to be learnt from our mistakes, and we must fix
these firmly in our memories, so that we can build on the foundations we laid at that time. We may have made resolutions, some of
which were unrealistic and unrealizable, but others that are worth
labouring over in the year to come, to make our lives more useful
and the world a better place.

Turning points

Our lives are full of these turning points: every midnight when we
lay one day to rest and embark on another; every month when the
seasons change; every new school and every new job we enter upon;
every new friendship or new relationship we form, every death and
every birth, closes the door on one section of our lives, and opens
up a new phase of our existence. So perhaps the way we handle
New Year will give us some guidelines about how we should deal
with other moments of transition.

Past

The past is past. We admired Edith Piaf when she sang, 'Non, je
ne regrette rien.' But it could easily be misunderstood. 'No, I don't
regret anything,' it means. Neither the good things that people have
done to me, nor the bad things, it's all the same to me . . . The lovers

are all swept away . . . I start again from zero . . . Because my life, my joys, begin with you . . . today! That's what the words mean. They don't deny the importance of repentance for the bad things we have done. Only when we have done that and received God's forgiveness can we shut the door on them; only then will they cease to trouble us with feelings of guilt.

Future

Another sentiment from an old film is the final line of *Gone with the Wind*: 'Tomorrow is another day.' Just because today was terrible doesn't mean that tomorrow cannot be the best day of your life. You just have to seize the day with hope, and ask God to turn it into a blessing. Every today is yesterday's tomorrow, and tomorrow's yesterday. So we should always approach it in hope, and try to make it a day we shall look back on with pride and gratitude. Sometimes facing the challenges of a difficult day and overcoming them can do us more good than coasting idly through a day that presents us with no problems. Challenges are character-forming, and give us a new beginning.

Progress

Even God can't do everything at once. He has to advance step by step, taking us with him at the fastest pace we can comfortably manage, and teaching us as much as we can take in, one day at a time. Jesus didn't say, 'you will learn all the truth at once'; he promised that the Holy Spirit will 'lead you into all truth'. I wonder what new truths the Spirit will reveal to us this year?

Children

St Paul wrote, to the Christians in Galatia, 'But when the fullness of time had come, God sent his Son, born of a woman, born under the law, in order to redeem those who were under the law, so that we might receive adoption as children . . . So you are no longer a slave but a child, and if a child then also an heir, through God.' Paul recognized that salvation is a long, slow process. *Homo sapiens* learnt quite quickly that there is a spiritual dimension to this material world. But it took God thousands of years to drum into their thick heads that there is not a different god for every tribe and district, who would fight for 'his' tribe against all the other tribes; but, rather, one God for everybody. Then God sent his Son into the world, to free us from slavery to codes of law, and slavery to greed, when we enter into a father–son (or father–daughter) relationship with God. Jesus taught us to pray that God's kingdom of Love might come on earth, as it is in heaven. Let us all make it our New Year's resolution to work as hard as we can to bring that to pass this year.

Suggested hymns

God is working his purpose out; Lord, for the years; One more step along the world I go; Thy hand, O God, has guided.

Epiphany   6 January
(or may be transferred to Sunday 7 January)
Wise Men from Wherever
Isa. 60.1–6 Bringing gold and incense; Ps. 72.[1–9] 10–15 Kings will bow before him; Eph. 3.1–12 Preaching to Gentiles; Matt. 2.1–12 Visit of the Magi

> *'In the time of King Herod, after Jesus was born in Bethlehem of Judea, wise men from the East came to Jerusalem, asking, "Where is the child who has been born king of the Jews? For we observed his star at its rising, and have come to pay him homage."' Matthew 2.1–2*

Magi

Wise men came from the East to worship Jesus, the King of the Jews. You may not realize how shocking those words were to the Jews who first read them. 'The East' probably means Persia, or modern-day Iran. The 'Medes and Persians' took over the Babylonian Empire. The wise men were Magi, a sect of astrologer-priests, who thought you could tell the future by studying the stars. From the Magi we get our word 'magic'. So to the Jews, they represented everything that was bad. The point of the story is that even people from a different country, a different race and a different religion may have things to teach us about our God, and we should welcome them to lay their spiritual gifts at the feet of Jesus.

Wherever

But that was all long ago and far away. How are we going to get this message across to people of today? I am now going to quote from the script of a nativity play called 'The Secret Name'. It has not yet been published, but I have seen parts of the script. Here they are not 'wise men from the East', but 'wise people' – to be politically correct and make casting easier – from Africa, from the Far East, and from the West. But if you are writing your own nativity play, you could make them 'Wise People from Wherever'. Let 'the star' tell you about them:

> From far-off, three wise persons, not certain what they seek,
> have followed me; with stardom they're possessed;
> the first one is a digital technology-type geek,
> who hails from prosp'rous countries in the West.
> From Asian lands there follows next a mystic type of seer,
> a truly clever person from the East.
> The third one comes from Africa, informing people here,
> black races are the greatest, not the least.

First we hear from 'The wise person from the West':

> We have linked all our computers in a universal net,
> we can access all the data that we want,
> on a laptop we can process all the words that we can get,
> and print them out in any fancy font.
> Yet I've searched the World Wide Web to find the purpose of
>   the whole,
> and always get this message from above:
> Information has no meaning till it finds its hidden soul
> in a Babe whose secret name is Love.

You remember that the play was called 'The Secret Name'? Next comes 'The wise person from Asia':

> I have studied world philosophies, done all that God requires;
> spent days in meditation and in prayer;
> I have mortified my flesh, I have denied all my desires,
> and felt I wasn't getting anywhere.
> So I battered heaven's portals with my loud petitioning,
> and always got this message from above:

The meaning of existence lies in one quite simple thing:
in a Babe whose secret name is Love.

Finally comes 'The wise person from Africa':

I have joined with other black folk as we talked into the night
of the suffering of our people and its worth.
Where can we find the freedom then for which we seek to fight?
How's justice to be built upon the earth?
Yet ever as we argued on, we felt the slipp'ry slope;
we always got this message from above:
all our struggle's self-destructive till we place our final hope
in a Babe whose secret name is Love.

Then they **all** speak in turn to the audience:

So all you many people here, who think that you are wise,
or who dream of understanding human life;
who think that your discoveries will take you to the skies,
or who simply hope to understand your wife!
Take heed from our example as you travel on your way;
you'll always get this message from above:
you will find the wisdom sought for when you see its shape one
    day
in a Babe whose secret name is Love.
© Michael Counsell

Message

Although you may find that rather strange, I think it brings home to
people of today the same message as the old story taught to the people
of their time. That is, that what is unique about Christianity is its teaching about a God of love, which we would like to share with everybody.
But we also have things to learn from what God has taught them.

Suggested hymns

Brightest and best of the sons of the morning; From the eastern
mountains; Hills of the north, rejoice; In Christ there is no east or
west.

Week of Prayer for Christian Unity   18–25 January
To Gather into One the Dispersed

Ezek. 36.23–28 Back to your own land; Col. 3.9–17 No longer
Jew and Greek; Ps. 122 A city at unity; John 11.45–52 Gather the
dispersed

> *'He did not say this on his own, but being high priest that year he
> prophesied that Jesus was about to die for the nation, and not for
> the nation only, but to gather into one the dispersed children of
> God.' John 11.51–52*

Pharisees

The leaders of the Jewish nation were in two groups. The Pharisees
were those who were devoted to observing the Jewish law, in every
minute detail. Not only that, but they had developed a complete
corpus of traditions as to how that law should be applied. It was
a whole culture of tradition. Then Jesus came and attacked their
traditions: 'In vain do they worship me, teaching human precepts
as doctrines. You abandon the commandment of God and hold
to human tradition.' No wonder they wanted him destroyed, for
he was destroying the lovely fabrication of tradition which they
worshipped – *instead of worshipping God!*

Sadducees

The other group was the Sadducees. They were the priestly party,
the rich aristocracy. They were prepared to collaborate with the
occupying power, the Romans, so long as the Romans supported
their wealth, privilege and power. The Jewish historian Josephus
wrote that 'The behaviour of the Sadducees to one another is
rather rude. And their dealings with their equals are rough, as
they are with strangers.' They were afraid that Jesus, having just
raised Lazarus from the dead, might win a following among the
people, who would raise a riot. Then, they feared, the Romans
would clamp down on the Jews, and the Sadducees would lose
their ruling position. No wonder they were afraid of Jesus, because
he might take away the power that they clung to – *instead of clinging to God!*

Unconscious irony

So, with unconscious irony, the High Priest Caiaphas warned them that it was better that one man should die for the people, than that the whole nation should be destroyed. His rejection of Jesus led to continuing stubbornness in the Jewish nation, and 40 years later the Romans destroyed Jerusalem and the nation did perish. Who can imagine what an age of peace would have dawned if the Jews had instead accepted Jesus? So by clinging to their tradition and their power, *instead of God*, the Pharisees and Sadducees lost their nation, lost their traditions, and lost their power.

The Dispersion

St John says that Jesus died to gather into one the dispersed children of God. What does he mean by that? The Jews who lived outside the Holy Land, scattered and doing business throughout the Roman Empire, were known as the Dispersion. But John was thinking beyond them to the non-Jews, the Gentiles, who in his eyes were also children of God. Jesus died to gather all the peoples of the world into one family. Jesus died to overcome the divisions and suspicions between nations and races and gather everyone together into a worldwide unity of love and harmony. The way Jesus would do this, John hoped, was by a united Church demonstrating to the world how Jew and Gentile could break down the dividing wall of partition between them. A Church which showed how people could accept, tolerate and love each other, in spite of major differences, could overcome, in time, all the divisions of humankind. *So why hasn't it happened?*

Disunity

I'll tell you why, in my opinion. It's because of you and me, and all the other church members who've allowed the one Church of God to shatter into fragments. The division of the one Church into denominations has happened because, just like the Pharisees and Sadducees, we're not willing to surrender our traditions and our power. We've broken the Body of Christ into pieces, as they did, because we've worshipped our traditions and clung to our power – *instead of worshipping and clinging to God!*

290

The *Didache*

One of the oldest Christian prayers outside the Bible comes from a book called the *Didache*, written about AD 100. At the breaking of bread, as we remember the body of Christ broken on the cross, these words are to be said: 'As this bread was once grain scattered upon the mountains, as was brought together into one loaf, so may your Church be brought together from the ends of the earth into your kingdom.' If we pray that prayer ardently in our hearts at every service, then the Church will begin to do what we were chosen for, and what Jesus died for: *to gather into one the dispersed children of God.*

Suggested hymns

Broken for me, broken for you; In Christ there is no east or west; Jesus stand among us at the meeting of our lives; O thou who at thy Eucharist didst pray.

Conversion of St Paul   25 January
A Changed Man

Jer. 1.4–10 The call of a prophet; Ps. 67 Let all the peoples praise you; Acts 9.1–22 Saul's conversion (*if the Acts reading is used instead of the Old Testament reading, the New Testament reading is* Gal. 1.11–16a Called me through his grace); Matt. 19.27–30 The reward of eternal life

> 'And immediately something like scales fell from [Saul's] eyes, and his sight was restored. Then he got up and was baptized.'
> Acts 9.18

Change

None of us, if the truth be told, really likes change. We have got used to the old familiar ways; though we wouldn't admit it, we are in a bit of a rut. If someone suggests a change, 'You can't expect me to throw away all the things I've learnt,' we grumble, 'and embark on a whole new way of life at my age.' You probably know the story of the bishop who said to a churchwarden, 'You've been the warden here for forty years, they tell me. You must have seen a lot of changes in that time.' 'Yes bishop,' replied the warden. 'And I've resisted every one of them!' And yet without change we cannot have progress, and without progress our society will gradually decay into a moribund and ineffective talking-shop, with very little in common, and no concern with helping others to improve.

Paul

I think St Paul must have been rather like that, before his conversion on the road to Damascus. He was brought up a Pharisee, one of the narrowest sects in Judaism. He describes himself as 'a Jew . . . brought up in [Jerusalem] at the feet of Gamaliel, educated strictly according to our ancestral law, being zealous for God'. You see, Paul believed passionately that God had made a covenant or contract with the Jewish people, to protect them and guide them, provided that they obeyed the Old Testament laws scrupulously without exception. So when Christians began preaching that Jesus said that love is at the heart of the law, Paul thought that was the end of the contract. Jesus reportedly said that if you have love in your heart, it doesn't matter how many laws you break; but if you obey all the laws and have no love, you are as bad as the worst of sinners. To Paul such an idea was an abomination. So, as he himself said, 'I persecuted [the Christians] up to the point of death by binding both men and women and putting them in prison, as the high priest and the whole council of elders can testify about me. From them I also received letters to the brothers in Damascus, and I went there in order to bind [the Christians] who were there and to bring them back to Jerusalem for punishment.' He just couldn't cope with any changes in the beliefs on which he had built his entire life.

Changed

Then he saw the light, and became a changed man. He heard Jesus saying to him, 'Why do you persecute me?' Then Paul realized that Jesus is God incarnate. So all the prejudices on which Paul had built his career collapsed into a pile of dust, and he had to start all over afresh. God gave him a job to do: to retranslate the whole of the teaching of Jesus, into an entirely different language and culture that would attract the non-Jews throughout the Roman Empire. So Paul began to preach in favour of the ideas that up until then he had condemned. And he was very successful. Through the power of Jesus, the most dyed-in-the-wool conservative, with a small 'c', can change radically and gain a new character altogether.

Us

If Paul could do it, so can anyone of us. You may have read of famous people who suddenly changed. You may have friends who have come through a similar 'light-bulb moment', and whose life has taken an entirely new direction as a result. But of course it could never happen to you – or could it? Is there any aspect of your attitudes that has remained rigid and unchangeable for as long as you can remember? Is God maybe calling you to make a radical change in your views? You may think change is beyond you; but if you think it through you may realize that God is calling you to do something special for him. Then step out in faith, and God will give you the grace to cope with the collapse of your hitherto universe and the rebuilding of a new one on fresh foundations. Then you, like Paul, will become a changed man or woman. You will learn how much God loves you, and increase in self-respect, and in the respect of others, for your ability to shake off the past and begin a bright new future. God may be saying to all of us what the railway porters used to say: 'All change!'

Suggested hymns

Lead me, O thou great Redeemer; Sometimes a light surprises; We sing the glorious conquest; Will you come and follow me?

Presentation of Christ in the Temple   (Candlemas)
2 February (*or may be observed on Sunday 28 January*)
Malachi

Mal. 3.1–5 The Lord shall come to his Temple; Ps. 24.[1–6] 7–10 Open the gates for the Lord; Heb. 2.14–18 Jesus became like the descendants of Abraham; Luke 2.22–40 The presentation of Christ in the Temple

> 'See, I am sending my messenger to prepare the way before me, and the Lord whom you seek will suddenly come to his temple. The messenger of the covenant in whom you delight – indeed, he is coming, says the LORD of hosts.' Malachi 3.1

Festival

On this day we remember how Mary and Joseph brought the new-born baby to the Temple in Jerusalem, and 'presented' him as a thanksgiving gift to God. This was a Jewish custom based on the story of the Exodus, when all the firstborn sons of the Egyptians died, and the first son born to an Israelite couple was given to God to thank him for sparing them. Then the parents bought their son back again by making a gift to God! This was the first time Jesus had been inside the Temple. But, because we believe Jesus is the Son of God, Christians have regarded this as a fulfilment of the prophecy of Malachi, in the Old Testament, that God himself would come to the Temple: 'The Lord whom ye seek will suddenly come to his temple.' Got it?

Malachi

Malachi is the last book in the Old Testament; the final chapter predicts the return of Elijah, who will prepare the people for the coming of the Lord, as John the Baptist prepared them for the coming of Jesus. Nobody knows who wrote it – 'Malachi' means 'My Messenger', and was probably a pen-name – nor do we know when it was written, though with its concentration on the failings of the priests and Levites, it may come from soon after the Jews returned from Babylon and re-established the worship in the Temple of Jerusalem. Some believe that the author was himself a Levite, the lower of the two grades of priests in Jerusalem, originating in the northern kingdom of Israel and its capital, Samaria. The passage from Malachi that we read today was set by Handel in his great oratorio *Messiah*, where the soloist sings, 'The Lord whom ye seek shall suddenly come to his Temple, but who may abide the day of his coming . . .' and the chorus sing, 'And he shall purify the sons of Levi.' Malachi was disgusted at the slackness of both grades of priests in carrying out their duties.

Priesthood

Baby Jesus, when he grew up, was frequently in conflict with the priests and Levites. He criticized them for their overemphasis on strict ritual, as against the social justice that the prophets had called for. Malachi's protest was 'against those who swear falsely, against

294

those who oppress the hired workers in their wages, the widow and the orphan, against those who thrust aside the alien, and do not fear me, says the LORD of hosts.' Similarly, Jesus, in his so-called Nazareth Manifesto, proclaimed: 'The Spirit of the Lord is upon me, because he has anointed me to bring good news to the poor. He has sent me to proclaim release to the captives and recovery of sight to the blind, to let the oppressed go free, to proclaim the year of the Lord's favour.'

Jesus

The Letter to the Hebrews in the New Testament sees no further use for the Jerusalem priesthood. Instead, Jesus is our sinless Great High Priest: 'For it was fitting that we should have such a high priest, holy, blameless, undefiled, separated from sinners, and exalted above the heavens. Unlike the other high priests, he has no need to offer sacrifices day after day, first for his own sins, and then for those of the people; this he did once for all when he offered himself.'

All believers

If we remember these warnings, there is no harm in calling our Christian ministers priests, as they offer the sacrifice of prayer daily for the people whom they serve. But the New Testament speaks not of individual priests, but of the priesthood of all believers: 'like living stones, let yourselves be built into a spiritual house, to be a holy priesthood, to offer spiritual sacrifices acceptable to God through Jesus Christ'. When Jesus came first to the Temple as a baby, the old priest named Simeon called him 'a light to give light to all the nations of the world', which is why today is also called Candlemas. But if all Christians are called to be priests like Jesus, that means we have to sacrifice our time, our convenience, our comfort, even our lives if necessary, in the service of the whole world, and especially the poor and needy. The sacrifice called for is great, but the promised reward is greater.

All-age worship

www.liturgies.net/Epiphany/Candlemas/candlemas.htm
https://www.churchofengland.org/media/1264590/gs1549.pdf
(page 316)

Suggested hymns

Faithful vigil ended; Hail to the Lord who comes; Of the Father's love begotten; When candles are lighted on Candlemas Day.

St David, Bishop of Menevia, Patron of Wales
c. 601   1 March
Windows

Ecclus. (Ben Sira) 15.1–6 Whoever holds to the law will obtain wisdom; Ps. 16.1–7 I have a goodly heritage; 1 Thess. 2.2–12 Entrusted with the gospel; Matt. 16.24–27 Take up your cross

> *'So deeply do we care for you that we are determined to share with you not only the gospel of God but also our own selves . . . As you know, we dealt with each one of you like a father with his children.' 1 Thessalonians 2.8, 11*

Evangelist

St David was called to share the good news of Jesus and his love with the people of Wales. He was famous for his rousing open-air preaching. But I am sure that he also had many private conversations with individuals, listening to their life-stories, and quietly sharing how Jesus was the answer to all their problems. For St David, like St Paul, had been called to Christ 'to share . . . the Gospel of God', and, like St Paul, St David will have done it by preaching and also when he 'dealt with each one . . . like a father with his children'. I want to tell you a true story that illustrates one way in which this softer form of evangelism can be carried out.

Visitors' Chaplain

Many cathedrals today have a team of 'Visitors' Chaplains': volunteers who spend, perhaps, one day a month, near the door, saying a few words to each person who enters, to make them feel welcome. They may be serving or retired clergy, lay readers, or others who feel a calling to this wonderful experience. This is a fascinating and enjoyable task, because the chaplains meet all sorts of people, from the ones who say, 'I've lived in this city all my life and passed this building every day, but this is the first time I've come inside', to those who say in broken English, 'I have just arrived in this country, and I wish to hear what Christianity teaches.' Each of these presents an opening for sharing the good news in a fatherly – or motherly – way.

Windows

Two women came into a cathedral, and the chaplain advised them to look at the colourful windows, and come back to him if they had any questions. In a few minutes they were back and asked him, 'What is that one about? I've seen the other which shows Jesus going up into heaven, surrounded by angels, with 12 men watching him. This one also has Jesus on a cloud, but the people seem very different, a real mixture, and one of the angels is carrying a chain.' 'Ah, that will be the Last Judgement,' replied the Visitors' Chaplain. 'What does that mean?' they asked. The chaplain gulped, and told them that after we die, we shall get a chance to tell God we are really, really sorry for all the naughty and selfish things we have done. Then, if we really mean it, God will forgive us, and welcome us into heaven. There are all the dirty buildings of this city falling to the ground because we shall have no need of them in heaven.' 'Good,' the visitors exclaimed. 'And what is the chain for?' The chaplain explained that they had been taken from the people, who had been prisoners of death in the grave and were now set free. Then he added as an afterthought: 'Well, their bodies were in the tombs, but they believed then that the souls went to wait in a place called purgatory.' 'Do you believe that?' asked the visitors.

Time

'Actually, no, I don't,' answered the chaplain. 'You see, since then, Albert Einstein has taught us a whole new way of looking at time, which is a property of space. Where there is no space there is no time. So when you have your chance to get into heaven, it will feel as though you have just died.' One of them grumbled, 'There's not much chance for someone like me, then.' 'On the contrary,' said the chaplain, 'God has promised that those who admit that they don't deserve it are the very ones who will have a place with Jesus throughout eternity.' The visitors went home to think about this. Whether they came to a decision, then or later, I do not know. But the stained glass had formed a window of opportunity for sharing the gospel, for sure.

David

This applies to all of us, including St David. We are all called to be evangelists – not in the sense of those who wrote the four Gospels, but meaning those who share the good news with others. Before we can do this, we have to learn to speak their language – in St David's case that was Welsh and the Celtic appreciation of nature; in our case today, it is the language of modern science.

Suggested hymns

Author of life divine (Rhosymedre); Guide me, O thou great Redeemer (Cwm Rhondda); Hail the day that sees him rise (Llanfair); Judge eternal, throned in splendour (Rhuddlan).

St Patrick, Bishop, Missionary, Patron of Ireland
c. 460 17 March **The Steadfast Man**

Deut. 32.1–9 Let my teaching drop like rain, *or* Tob. 13.1b–7 In the land of my exile; Ps. 145.1–13 Make known to all peoples; 2 Cor. 4.1–12 This ministry; Matt. 10.16–23 Warnings for missionaries, *or* John 4.31–38 Ripe for harvest

> *'The Lord is loving to everyone*
> *and his mercy is over all his creatures.'*
> Psalm 145.9 (Common Worship)

Biography

The Bible tells us that God is a god of love. As the psalm puts it, 'The Lord is loving to everyone'. This love is revealed in the humility and suffering of Jesus for our sake. There are many echoes of this in the life of St Patrick, the patron saint of Ireland, whom we commemorate today. Paul Gallico, an American novelist, author of *The Snow Goose* and *The Poseidon Adventure,* also wrote a biography of St Patrick. He called it *The Steadfast Man.* In an appendix to Gallico's epic are the only extant primary sources (in translation, of course) of the life of Patrick, in two volumes that were translated into Latin from the words the saint himself dictated. The first is called the *Confessio.* St Patrick wrote this book to defend himself against slanderous charges. He

298

recounts the story of his conversion and missionary labours. The second is much shorter, and is called *A Letter to the Soldiers of Coroticus*. Coroticus was a Welsh chieftain, who, with a group of soldiers, attacked some Christians who had just been baptized, killing some and taking the rest into slavery. Patrick's letter demands repentance from the chieftain and his soldiers for this wicked act of terrorism.

Paraphrase

Here are a couple of paraphrases of the translations of Patrick's writings given in Gallico's book:

> When I was about sixteen years old, and knew nothing of the one true God, I was taken to Ireland with thousands of other British people, as a slave. I fully deserved my sufferings because I turned away from God and disobeyed his commandments. But God opened my eyes, and my heart was turned to him. I have long wanted to write about this, but I was afraid, because I have not studied like others, nor do I know the Latin tongue in which the Scriptures came to us, and what I write here had to be translated for me. God inspired me, an outcast, to serve the people whom Christ gave me, for as long as my life endures, humbly and sincerely. Then one night in a dream I heard a voice telling me to return to my native land, and I walked two hundred miles to the port, where I took a passage on a ship to my own home and my own people. There I was ordained, but when I was appointed a bishop some of the senior people made a case that I was not good enough. Yet God called me to return to Ireland and become a 'fisher of men'. I baptized thousands, but would not accept a penny from them when they offered me gifts. Some opposed me, and there were times when I longed to return to Britain, but I endured it patiently because God has chosen me to remain here until I die . . .

And from the Letter to Coroticus:

> The day after some of the newly baptized, anointed with oil, had been slain, I sent a presbyter, asking that their captors should send to us the others whom they had taken prisoner. But they only jeered at him. So I have sent this second letter, to be read in the hearing of all the people and of Coroticus himself. May God

inspire them to come to their senses, to repent of their wicked deeds – murderers of the brothers and sisters of Jesus – and release the baptized women whom they had enslaved . . .

Gallico

Paul Gallico commented in his biography that St Patrick did not have an easy life. Yet he persevered in spite of everything, sacrificing the comforts and certainties of everyday life to bring the good news of God and his love to the people of Ireland. Yet his humility is revealed in his writings, first in his self-criticism and his repeated assertion that he is unworthy to hold this position, but more especially in the way he 'skips over', in a few words, the description of the hardships and opposition he had to endure, from when he was 16 years old until the day he died, because he thought they were unimportant, and he did not wish to bore his readers! Patrick truly was 'a steadfast man.'

Suggested hymns

I bind unto myself today (St Patrick); I cannot tell why he whom angels worship (Londonderry); Lord, while for all mankind we pray; Inspired by love and anger (Salley Gardens).

St Joseph of Nazareth   19 March
Brother of Cleophas?

2 Sam. 7.4–16 Descendants of David; Ps. 89.26–36 David's line; Rom. 4.13–18 Abraham's descendants; Matt. 1.18–25 Joseph's dream

> *'Hoping against hope, [Abraham] believed that he would become "the father of many nations", according to what was said, "So numerous shall your descendants be."' Romans 4.18*

Joseph

St Joseph, whom we commemorate today, was not the father, but the stepfather of Jesus. Because of the virgin birth, Jesus had no earthly father; but the Bible tells us that 'Joseph . . . took [Mary] as his wife, but had no marital relations with her until she had borne a son'. The people of Nazareth referred to the brothers and sisters of Jesus – James and Joses and Judas and Simon, and some unnamed girls. Roman Catholics believe that Mary was a perpetual virgin, and they were actually Joseph's children from a previous marriage, and only half-brothers and -sisters to Jesus. Protestants believe they and Jesus were true siblings.

Marys

However, I read something the other day which made me think again about the way different families were related to each other. The item referred to Joseph as the brother of Cleopas – more about him later. I don't think that was true, but it set me thinking about what we would call the extended family tree of Jesus, through his mother and his stepfather. I start by looking at the number of people called Mary in the New Testament. There were Mary Magdalene, Mary and Martha the sisters of Lazarus, and Mary the mother of John Mark, who were friends of Jesus but not related to him. But there is also a mysterious woman called 'the other Mary' in the accounts of the death and burial of Jesus. I am not going to give you all the references, but these quotations all come from the four Gospels in the New Testament:

- At the crucifixion, 'there were also women looking on from a distance; among them were Mary Magdalene, and Mary the mother of James the younger and of Joses . . .'.
- But in St John's Gospel, it says, 'standing near the cross of Jesus were his mother, and his mother's sister, Mary the wife of Clopas, and Mary Magdalene'. Matthew calls her 'the other Mary'.
- At the burial, 'Mary Magdalene and Mary the mother of Joses saw where the body was laid.'
- 'When the Sabbath was over, Mary Magdalene, and Mary the mother of James, and Salome bought spices, so that they might go and anoint him. And very early on the first day of the week, when the sun had risen, they went to the tomb . . . As they entered the tomb, they saw a young man, dressed in a white robe, sitting on the right side; and . . . he said to them, ". . . Jesus of Nazareth . . . has been raised."'

Relationships

So we are building up a family tree. Jesus, his brothers and sisters, were the children of Mary and Joseph. The Virgin Mary's sister appears to have been called Mary also, but it would be very unusual for siblings to be given the same name; so perhaps it means 'sister-in-law'. In which case this Mary was Joseph's sister; the wife of Clopas; and the mother of James and Joses. Joses was also called Joseph, after his mother's brother, perhaps. Got it? But, confusingly, the father of James the apostle is also called Alphaeus, as well as Clopas. They are both Greek names, and many people from 'Galilee of the Gentiles' spoke Greek. It makes you wonder whether the little Jewish boy couldn't pronounce the name he had been given, so 'Clopas' was the nearest he could get, and the name stuck.

Cleophas

So Clopas could have been Joseph's brother-in-law. What he couldn't have been was the same as Cleophas, who met the risen Christ on the road to Emmaus. For that couple said that 'some women of our group . . . were at the tomb early this morning', which seems a very off-hand way to speak of your own wife. For what it's worth, Cleopas is considered to be a shortened version of 'Cleopatros'.

Families

Of course, none of this matters a jot, though it is fun doing a Sherlock Holmes on the New Testament; 'Elementary, my dear Watson!' But what it does is provide a very different idea of the childhood of Christ. Instead of a lonely little boy standing in his stepfather's carpentry shop alone with his parents, the place must have been chock-a-block with relations and in-laws, the children running in and out and getting under the feet of the grown-ups. What fun! And that reminds us that, although there is much we can learn in solitary silence, the natural home of Christianity is in families and communities; and its purpose is to spread love through extended families, building us all into supportive communities.

Suggested carols

As Joseph was a-walking, he heard an angel sing; Joseph dearest, Joseph mine; Once in royal David's city; The great God of heaven is come down to earth.

Annunciation of Our Lord to the Blessed Virgin Mary   9 April (transferred)

Be Not Afraid

Isa. 7.10–14 The sign of Immanuel; Ps. 40.5–11 I love to do your will; Heb. 10.4–10 I have come to do your will; Luke 1.26–38 The angel's message

'The angel said to her, "Do not be afraid, Mary, for you have found favour with God."' Luke 1.30

The angel's words

If an angel suddenly appeared in your kitchen and gave you a message, would you remember what the message was? Or would you be so shocked at what happened that you'd forget what was said? That would be a pity, because when an angel brings a message it's bound to be important. Let's look at the words which Gabriel said to Mary when he visited her in Nazareth: 'Greetings, favoured one! The Lord is with you . . . Do not be afraid, Mary, for you have found favour with God. And now, you will conceive in your womb and bear a son, and you will name him Jesus. He will be great, and will be called the Son of the Most High, and the Lord God will give to him the throne of his ancestor David. He will reign over the house of Jacob for ever, and of his kingdom there will be no end . . . The Holy Spirit will come upon you, and the power of the Most High will overshadow you; therefore the child to be born will be holy; he will be called Son of God. And now, your relative Elizabeth in her old age has also conceived a son; and this is the sixth month for her who was said to be barren. For nothing will be impossible with God.'

Grace

Gabriel's first words were 'Greetings, favoured one! The Lord is with you.' A second later he said, 'for you have found favour with God'. 'Highly favoured' means that God, in his mercy, has been very gracious to Mary, and given her a privilege that nobody could have deserved. The Latin Bible mistranslated these words as 'full of grace'. This led some people to think that Mary had an inexhaustible supply of a magic substance called 'grace', which she would give to those who pray to her. We should obviously honour her very highly because she was chosen by God. But it's wrong to suggest that God

303

won't answer our prayers until Mary persuades him to. God's love is unconditional, and he's 'more eager to hear than we to pray'.

Be not afraid

'Do not be afraid', or 'Be not afraid', said the archangel. These words occur more than 50 times in the Bible. That's a promise from God for every week of the year: God wants us to know that there's nothing to be afraid of.

- We mustn't be afraid of God – we must trust him.
- We needn't be afraid of our enemies – for God will look after us.
- We needn't be afraid that we shan't be able to cope with the challenges that confront us – for God will give his grace to us, as he did to Mary. Grace gives us the strength to overcome all our problems.
- There's no need to be afraid of the future – for God in his providence will see us through to the end.
- And if we trust in God, we needn't fear death – because it's the gateway to everlasting life.

Saviour and king

Gabriel continued, 'And now, you will conceive in your womb and bear a son, and you will name him Jesus.' 'Jesus' means 'God saves'. Gabriel promises that Mary's son will save us from the guilt of sin and the fear of death. 'The Lord God will give to him the throne of his ancestor David,' said the archangel, 'and of his kingdom there will be no end.' Jesus is to be a king.

Son of God

'The Holy Spirit will come upon you . . . therefore the child to be born will be . . . called Son of God.' God himself has come to earth.

Nothing's impossible

'And now, your relative Elizabeth in her old age has also conceived a son . . . For nothing will be impossible with God.' Nothing's impossible! A virgin birth's not impossible for God. And if Jesus is our Saviour, our king, and the Son of God come to earth, nothing's impossible for us, either. Find your dictionary, and cross out that word 'impossible'! There's no such thing as impossible for the Christian. In that case, what have we got to be afraid of?

Response

Mary remembered exactly what the angel said to her. And Mary's response was: 'Here am I, the servant of the Lord; let it be with me according to your word.' That should be our response too, whatever life throws at us. We know that all things are possible, so we shall not be afraid.

Suggested hymns

Do not be afraid; Fear not, rejoice and be glad; The angel Gabriel from heaven came; Through all the changing scenes of life.

St George, Martyr, Patron of England c. 304
23 April
Britishness

1 Macc. 2.59–64 Be courageous, *or* Rev. 12.7–12 Michael fights the dragon; Ps. 126 Restore our fortunes; 2 Tim. 2.3–13 A soldier of Christ; John 15.18–21 They will persecute you

> *'My children, be courageous and grow strong in the law, for by it you will gain honour.'* 1 Maccabees 2.64

Englishness

St George is the patron saint of England. Yet he was not an Englishman and never visited England. He was chosen by the Crusaders because he was a soldier saint. Several other nations, and some Arab groupings, also chose him for the same reason, and the English Crusaders brought home with them his 'bloody cross' over their armour to encourage others to fight for their country. It is good that nations should have a patron saint, as it encourages them to feel proud of the nation where they were born, or where they have settled, with all its faults, simply because it is theirs. Today, all that most people know of St George is that football supporters fly his flag, or drape themselves in it, to demonstrate their belief, despite what the scoreboard says, that the English team is better than any other. Rivalry is quintessential to sport, but it is not a good thing when learning to live peacefully with your neighbours in the world outside the football stadium.

Britishness

The patron saint of Scotland is St Andrew; St David is the patron saint of Wales; and Ireland proudly claims St Patrick as theirs. It is a pity there is no patron of Britain, to encourage unity and cooperation between the nations still known as the 'United Kingdom'. Schools have been criticized for not teaching 'British values' to their pupils, to prevent them becoming terrorists, and it is suggested that immigrants should demonstrate that they accept the tradition of their host country before they settle here. But we cannot do that until we have agreed on what 'Britishness' consists of. A liking for warm beer and a cuppa every hour of the day is insufficient. Before the Reformation it was adherence to the teaching of the Roman Catholic religion; afterwards it would have been a question of following Puritanism. By the beginning of this century a high proportion of the population adhered to non-Christian religions, or had no religion at all. An attempt to include Christian values in the European constitution proved divisive and had to be abandoned.

Contract

Canon Alan Billings suggested in the *Church Times* some years ago that what is needed is a set of contractual arrangements for people to agree to live together tolerantly in a liberal modern state. He proposed:

- respect for the rule of law;
- equality of all citizens before the law;
- democratically elected government;
- freedom of speech;
- freedom of assembly;
- freedom of worship;
- freedom of the individual to live his or her life as he or she wishes, subject only to not interfering with the rights of others;
- and finally, tolerance and respect for those who differ from us.

There is nothing specifically Christian in this; on the other hand few sincere believers in any religion would disagree with it. Christians would say that it is a true exposition of what Jesus meant by a community based on love.

Change

Society is changing, and most religions are slowly changing, too. The reason so many immigrants want to come to this country is because they would rather live somewhere where these ideals of mutual tolerance and respect are sought after than in the dictatorships they have fled from. St George was killed by those who wished to make him change his religion by force. Sadly, that attitude continued for centuries, even among Christians. We used to say that anyone who did not proclaim their belief in some ancient creedal statement, which we ourselves could not fully understand, was a heretic or, worse, an infidel, and deserved to die. But Jesus was talking about recognizing the good in people of other faiths when he said of the Roman centurion: 'I tell you, not even in Israel have I found such faith.' Nowadays we are prepared to see the good in other religions, and we would be more likely to speak about the teaching of Jesus concerning love and mutual self-sacrifice, and try to demonstrate it in our lives as individuals and as a community. If people are attracted by this, we will welcome them with open arms. But even with a soldier-saint as our patron, we will never use force as a means of evangelism.

Suggested hymns

Judge eternal, throned in splendour; In Christ there is no east or west; Lord, while for all mankind we pray; O God of earth and altar.

St Mark the Evangelist   25 April
A Letter from St Mark to St Paul

Prov. 15.28–33 Good news, *or* Acts 15.35–41 Paul rejects Mark; Ps. 119.9–16 How can young people keep their way pure?; Eph. 4.7–16 The gift of an evangelist; Mark 13.5–13 Staying power

> *'Barnabas wanted to take with them John called Mark. But Paul decided not to take with them one who had deserted them in Pamphylia and had not accompanied them in the work.'* Acts 15.37–38

Dear Uncle Saul,

I hope you don't mind me calling you by the name I used to use, when we were friends. Of course it's Uncle Barnabas who's my blood relation. But you were his best friend, so I looked up to you and loved you as my honorary uncle. But because I was so unsure of myself, I probably came across as a very arrogant young man. You'll be surprised to hear from me again after such a long time.

The only thing I had to boast about was that the Lord Jesus chose my mother's house in Jerusalem for his last Passover supper. The story of the supper was one that I passed on to you.

But after supper I slipped out of the house with just a linen tunic on, and followed them down into the Kidron Valley. And then . . . I came home without my tunic. That's the story of my life: whenever things get difficult I run away.

And I ran away again in Perga, and you were so angry with me, Uncle Saul. You see, I thought we'd be doing a nice tour of the synagogues in Cyprus, preaching to fellow Jews, and then come back home.

I first realized things were going wrong when we were summoned to the house of the Governor, Sergius Paulus, in Paphos. We'd never thought of talking to the hated Gentiles about Jesus. And there you were, trying to convert the Roman Governor!

Then, you told Uncle Barnabas you were taking over as leader of the expedition. We were taking the next ship to Pamphylia, you said. Pamphylia, which means 'all races'! Well, you preached in the synagogue in Perga, but also in the marketplace.

Then you went down with the marsh fever. I felt very sorry for you, trembling in your bed and sweating. But at the same time I was secretly glad, because I thought it would bring the expedition to an end.

And then you dropped your bombshell. We were going up into the dangerous mountains. I didn't know Sergius Paulus came from those parts, and had family in Pisidian Antioch. I went to Uncle Barnabas. 'Uncle Barnabas,' I sobbed, 'what are we going to do? I thought we were coming to preach to Jews, and now Saul's heading deep into Gentile country.'

Dear old Uncle B, he was so sympathetic. 'Never mind, my boy,' he said, 'if you can't face it, go back home to Jerusalem, and I'll explain it to Saul.' You and I never spoke again after that. My uncle told me you were quite incandescent with rage. Called me 'a deserter from the army of Jesus Christ'.

Eventually I made my way back to Jerusalem and my mother's house. All the Christians used to break bread there in those days, and that's where I met up again with dear Rhoda, our servant girl. We fell in love and got married.

Simon whom Jesus called Peter had grown very fond of Rhoda, too, in a fatherly way, after that dreadful muddle when she didn't recognize him when he came to our door from the prison! He began to speak of me as his son.

Then to my utter grief dear Rhoda died in childbirth. I think I grew up from a child to a man in that year.

So after Rhoda died, Peter asked me if I'd come with him to Antioch as his translator. It was also a wonderful opportunity to write down the good news of Jesus the Christ in Greek, based on what Peter told me. But still we were apostles to Jews. Although Peter had baptized Gentiles, he said he was leaving that ministry to his friend Saul of Tarsus.

Peter can manage without me now. He suggested my place is with the mission to the Gentiles. He says I'm free to go to Rome, which I have always longed to visit. He may come to Rome himself, one day, he says, but not this year. I'm sending this letter with a fast courier. I am really looking forward to seeing you there.

So this letter is to ask, will you take me back? I've said I'm sorry for letting you down in Perga. Please, Uncle Saul, will you forgive me? I would so like to help you.

John Mark

Suggested hymns

'The kingdom is upon you'; The kingdom of God is justice and joy; The saint who first found grace to pen; We have a gospel to proclaim.

SS Philip and James, Apostles   1 May
Blessings of Adversity

Isa. 30.15–21 This is the way; Ps. 119.1–8 The way of the Lord; Eph. 1.3–10 The mystery of forgiveness; John 14.1–14 Show us the Father

> '[Jesus said to the Twelve] "Do not let your hearts be troubled. Believe in God, believe also in me. In my Father's house there are many dwelling-places. If it were not so, would I have told you that I go to prepare a place for you?"' John 14.1–2

Philip

The passage from St John's Gospel is chosen for St Philip and St James' Day because it reports Philip making a debating point at the Last Supper: 'Lord, show us the Father, and we will be satisfied.' Yet he seems to be a spokesman for all the 12 disciples, and Jesus addressed his reply to them all. At what was supposed to be a happy occasion, Jesus told his friends that he was about to die, and they would all desert him. This was disastrous news, and they were all shattered. But Jesus said, 'Do not let your hearts be troubled.' It sounds unsympathetic at first. Yet Jesus was not denying that it was an almost unbearable disaster for them. Their attitude would make all the difference. They would still feel it was unfair. But if they trusted in God, then the disaster could yet become, in a strange way, a sort of blessing.

Disasters

Almost every year we read of shattering natural disasters. It may be an earthquake, or a tsunami caused by an underwater earthquake. Or it may be a hurricane, or some other atmospheric condition, which causes so much loss of life. We read in the paper, or see on the television, that so many thousands of people have been killed, or buried alive, or bereaved or left homeless. And we shout, 'How appalling! Why did God allow it? Couldn't he somehow have prevented it?' A natural reaction. But Jesus would have said, 'Do not let your hearts be troubled. Believe in God, believe also in me.' That is a lot to ask of us. But then we knew that God is infinitely greater than we are, and we shall never fully understand the workings of his mind. Yet he did promise us that God is love, and this does not seem to fit in with that. So look at it this way: God created a planet where life could evolve, with continents and mountains caused by moving and colliding tectonic plates – the very things that cause earthquakes. These things were there long before human beings arrived. Once they realized this, all our ancestors should have accepted, as the Japanese did, that you must build your houses away from the fault zones, and from materials that will not fall on people in an earthquake. It is hard to blame God for the fact that we still have not learnt that lesson. Atmospheric turbulence produces the rain that waters the crops, too.

Relief

Secondly, natural disasters evoke a wonderful reaction of human sympathy and compassion, with millions raised around the globe for the relief efforts. This creates, in the donors, a new awareness of the problems of their fellow human beings, of whatever race, which could not have come any other way. It may only last a short while, but over a lifetime, there may grow an awareness that God created a wide variety of humans, and he loves them all, not just the 'people like us'. Once that lesson sinks in, we are on the way to making this world a more peaceful, compassionate place. For the victims, too, there will be a change in attitude; they now know from personal experience that the human race is not all bad, and there are some who have put themselves out to help people in need like me.

Afterlife

Finally, we are all forced to look again at the question of life after death. Christians talk about it, but it doesn't seem to change their basic fear of death. Probably because of that, many others have given up belief in an afterlife altogether, regarding it as a primitive superstition. But if there is no proof there is an afterlife, there is no proof that there isn't, either. The evidence gives a very strong probability that there is, and if so, we would be stupid not to prepare ourselves. We should feel compassion for the survivors, but not for the dead, because they have gone to a new life where all is happiness and joy, and where we shall meet again eventually. Jesus said, 'In my Father's house there are many dwelling-places.' So in three ways, we can change our attitudes if we trust Jesus, and those new attitudes will be useful to us in the rest of our lives. It is not unsympathetic to say that faith can bring blessings out of adversity. I am sure the 12 disciples realized that, after Jesus rose again.

Suggested hymns

Alleluia, sing to Jesus; Christ triumphant, ever reigning; Father, hear the prayer we offer; Thou art the Way – by thee alone.

St Matthias the Apostle   14 May
Villains

Isa. 22.15–25 Eliakim replaces Shebna; Ps. 15 Who shall dwell
in your house?; Acts 1.15–26 Mathias replaces Judas (*if the Acts
reading is used instead of the Old Testament reading, the New
Testament reading is* 1 Cor. 4.1–7 Stewards of God's mysteries);
John 15.9–17 I have appointed you

> *'Peter stood up . . . and said, "Friends, the scripture had to be
> fulfilled, which the Holy Spirit through David foretold concerning
> Judas, who became a guide for those who arrested Jesus . . ."'*
> Acts 1.15–16

Matthias

St Matthias is remembered for one thing and one thing only; he
was appointed to be a member of the Twelve who followed Jesus,
after Judas Iscariot had villainously betrayed Jesus, and then committed suicide.

Villain

I call Judas a villain because what he did was wicked, and had the
awful result of the crucifixion of the Son of God. People can make
excuses for him – I have done it myself. He may have been so disappointed in the policy of non-violence that Jesus was following, that
he wanted him out of the way so that a more belligerent Messiah
would take over. He may have thought that he would start a war
between the Jews and the Romans which Jesus, having broken free,
would win. But the fact remains that to betray your best friend to
what would almost certainly mean an unjust trial, and death by
crucifixion, is an act of unimaginable awfulness. Judas definitely
deserves the title of villain.

Today

There are plenty of villains around these days – the newspapers are
full of reports of villainy. For some types of crime – illegal actions
that have some justification – we feel a degree of sympathy with the
criminal. Some audacious burglaries are rather amusing – except to

the victims. We can almost imagine ourselves into the criminal's shoes, and sympathize with him or her. But with truly wicked deeds, like paedophilia, I find it quite impossible to identify or sympathize. 'I could never be tempted to do such a revolting thing,' I say.

Needed

Perhaps for that very reason we actually need villains, to show us our own vulnerability to temptation. First, try to imagine the awful things that have been done or said to the villain when they were children. Consider the conditions in which they were brought up. Then think about the things that may have happened to them recently, to drive them to the very brink of breakdown. Their attitudes and priorities may have become irretrievably twisted. To be tempted into villainy may have become all too easy. This does not justify what they have done. We should still describe it as totally unforgivable – though the generous heart of God may yet find ways to forgive them if they repent. But we need to ask ourselves, if we had had to undergo the horrors they endured, in our own lives, might we not have been a little tempted to get our revenge on the society that had treated us so badly by doing something truly horrific? Perhaps not. But if you follow that train of thought, you may be able to recognize that the villain was born as a human being like you, however they may have been damaged and distorted by what happened to them subsequently.

Humility

This does not answer the question of how we treat the villain; for some, nothing less than imprisonment for life is the most loving sentence we can apply – at least it gives the criminal time to repent and seek God's forgiveness. The biggest error Judas made was to kill himself, before he had had time to demonstrate his true remorse and ask God to pardon him. But what I am thinking of today is the question we often ask: why did God allow Judas to do it? The main answer to that question is that God will never take away our freedom to make our own decisions, in all circumstances. But there is a secondary answer to the question, which is this: God allowed Judas to betray Jesus to teach us all that none of us is immune to temptation. Our friends trust us, and we hope they are right. But, if we are humble, each of us has to admit that, at times, we have been tempted to do things we know to be wrong. There is nothing wrong with this; even Jesus was tempted. But we need to make up our minds well in advance, that when we are tempted, even to do things that are slightly wrong, we shall say a firm 'No'. One thing follows after another, and to cover up the little lie you have told, you may have to tell a bigger lie, and so on. Admit it; none of us is immune to temptation; we must be ready for it and fight it. Don't be complacent. Judas can teach us that.

Suggested hymns

Be thou my guardian and my guide; Forty days and forty nights; The highest and the holiest place; There's a wideness in God's mercy.

Day of Thanksgiving for the Institution of Holy Communion (Corpus Christi)   31 May
Feeling the Kiss of God

Gen. 14.18–20 Melchizedek brought bread and wine; Ps. 116.10–17 The cup of salvation; 1 Cor. 11.23–26 The Last Supper; John 6.51–58 Living bread

> *'The Lord Jesus on the night when he was betrayed took a loaf of bread, and when he had given thanks, he broke it and said, "This is my body that is for you."' 1 Corinthians 11.23–24*

Automata

The Holy Communion can easily become something of an automatic routine. We have spoken the words, 'The Lord Jesus on the night when he was betrayed took a loaf of bread, and when he had given thanks, he broke it and said, "This is my body that is for you"', and gone through the motions so many times that they no longer make any impression on us. We become almost like robots or automata, going through the rituals as if we were machines, having no feelings about it at all. Part of the trouble is that we have heard so many theological discussions about what precisely is happening to the bread and wine, that we forget to attend to what is happening to us and to our emotions. Has the bread suffered transubstantiation, where its accidents remain the hardness and flavour of bread, but its inner substance changes

314

from the nature of bread into the inner nature of the body of Christ? Or is it 'consubstantiation', where it has both natures at the same time? Or is it merely symbolic? Does it matter? So we leave the church full of puzzlement in our brains, but quite dead in our hearts.

Imagination

So I want you instead to make full use of your emotions for a moment, and forget what your brain tells you. In St John's Gospel there is a very full account of the Last Supper, much longer than that in the other three Gospels and St Paul's Letter to the Corinthians. One of the sections is about the love that Jesus has for us, and how he wants us to be his friends:

> 'They who have my commandments and keep them are those who love me; and those who love me will be loved by my Father, and I will love them and reveal myself to them.' Judas (not Iscariot) said to him, 'Lord, how is it that you will reveal yourself to us, and not to the world?' Jesus answered him, 'Those who love me will keep my word, and my Father will love them, and we will come to them and make our home with them.'

This is quite shocking to everybody who has been brought up to think of God as distant and judgemental. God is in love with me! God wants me to think of him as my housemate! And Jesus loves me in the same way. They are my friends.

Emotional

British people are not very good at expressing their emotions; we are too keen in keeping the stiff upper lip. Other nations are much more open. Members of the same family will hug and kiss each other, no matter which gender they are. They will even kiss people who are unrelated, but whom they count as their friends. You may not approve of this or enjoy it. But imagine that you come from such a background, which Jesus almost certainly did. Then Jesus loves you, and wants to kiss you to demonstrate his love. Next think that Jesus wants you to regard the bread as though it was his body. You are shortly going to receive a piece of that bread onto your lips, or onto your hands which will then place them into your mouth.

Kissing Jesus

So, if you will let your imagination run freely, you can tell yourself that you are about to kiss Jesus. Of course we all know that it is not factually true – that doesn't matter. If you can tell yourself that you are about to kiss Jesus, and Jesus is kissing you, and in this way you are both able to show your love for each other. This turns a dull routine into an exciting emotional experience, which may make a profound change in your behaviour. I am not suggesting that you go round kissing all your friends. But you may learn to love them more, and be kinder to them, because you think of what happened to you in church on Sunday as a deep emotional experience: when the bread touched my lips, I was able to give Jesus a kiss.

Suggested hymns

And now, O Father, mindful of the love; Be still, for the presence of the Lord; Hands that have been handling; Lord Jesus Christ, you have come to us.

Visit of the Blessed Virgin Mary to Elizabeth
1 June (transferred)   Mutual Support
Zeph. 3.14–18 Sing, daughter Zion; Ps. 113 Making her a joyous mother; Rom. 12.9–16 Hospitality; Luke 1.39–49 [50–56] Magnificat

> *'. . . love one another with mutual affection . . .' Romans 12.10*

Support

One of the signs by which you can, or ought to be able to, recognize a group of Christians is by the mutual help and support they offer to one another. They may be too modest to admit that they need help, but each of them is probably sensitive enough to recognize when another Christian is in difficulties. Then one may cook a meal for the other, or offer to clean their house. Best of all, they may give up time just to listen to the other recounting what the problem is; offering advice if it is asked for, or helping the one who is in trouble to work out the solution for themselves. In his list of the characteristics of the Christian life, St Paul wrote to the Christians in Rome, 'love one another with mutual affection'.

Mutual

In the case of the Blessed Virgin Mary and her cousin Elizabeth, both were in deep trouble. So Mary made the excellent decision to visit the older woman. No one is quite certain where Elizabeth and her husband, Zechariah the priest, lived, though it was probably not far from Jerusalem, where Zechariah ministered in the Temple, and therefore a long distance from Nazareth, where Mary had received the message of her forthcoming pregnancy from the archangel Gabriel. The Bible does not tell us how Mary travelled, but whether she was on the back of a bumpy and obstinate donkey or on foot, the journey would have left Mary feeling absolutely exhausted. She may even have travelled alone. But making a sacrifice for somebody else is one of the best ways of showing that they are important to you.

Elizabeth

Elizabeth was an old woman, past the menopause, or what we call nowadays 'the change of life'. She had been expecting a quiet retirement with few demands on her strength. Then her husband went to Jerusalem to perform a tour of duty in the sanctuary, and came home dumb, but by some means conveying the message that his elderly wife was likely to become pregnant. So she had to face it all over again: the 'morning sickness', carrying round a heavy child in her tummy, then the labour pains, the agony of childbirth, and the sleepless nights of caring for a young baby. You can imagine her saying, 'Oh no, not again, at my age. I had thought all that was behind me.' And then there were the neighbours. Admittedly, some famous Israelites had been born when their mother was old and apparently barren: Isaac, the son of Abraham and Sarah when they were both well advanced in years, and Samuel, son of the barren Hannah and her equally elderly husband Elkanah. In each case their children were prophesied to be significant figures in history, so Elizabeth could not have been surprised to hear that her son, called John the Baptist, was predicted to be a prophet; but it would only increase the burden of responsibility she felt in bringing him up. That is what Elizabeth knew; but there were bound to be one or two neighbours who made fun of her behind her back for involvement in intercourse at her age.

Mary

The Virgin Mary probably suffered from mockery too. Few women in that society remained virgins for long after puberty, so she was probably in her early teens, and for many girls, a first pregnancy at a young age was not an easy experience. But worse still, she was engaged to Joseph but not yet married. The neighbours will therefore naturally have assumed that she had been a young flibbertigibbet who had conceived a child while not married. And they let her know that they disapproved.

Encouragement

So these two women, coming from widely different age groups, yet suffering from basically similar problems, were able to support and encourage each other because Mary had arranged that they should meet. Both Mary and Elizabeth belonged to the same family, and so, as St Paul had recommended, they supported each other with family love. But all Christians, whether or not they are physically related, belong to the same Christian family, and even to the same family of the human race. So we should support each other through our difficulties. There is no need to pry into somebody else's circumstances; you can probably detect when somebody else looks worried, and befriend them to offer your help. If they want to, they will tell you what their problem is; if not, no matter, just offer them your friendship and support. Thus we shall be built together into the same Christian family, and never lack for supportive friends.

Suggested hymns

Lord of the home, your only Son; Shall we not love thee, Mother dear?; Tell out, my soul, the greatness of the Lord; Ye watchers and ye holy ones.

St Barnabas the Apostle   11 June
The Life of Barnabas

Job 29.11–16 Like one who comforts; Ps. 112 Generous; Acts 11.19–30 Barnabas encourages Saul (*if the Acts reading is used instead of the Old Testament reading, the New Testament reading is* Gal. 2.1–10 Barnabas and me); John 15.12–17 Love one another

> *'They sent Barnabas to Antioch. When he came and saw the grace of God, he rejoiced, and he exhorted them all to remain faithful to the Lord with steadfast devotion; for he was a good man, full of the Holy Spirit and of faith. And a great many people were brought to the Lord.'* Acts 11.22–24

A good man

St Stephen was stoned to death for proclaiming that non-Jews could just as easily become members of God's kingdom as Jews. Furious nationalist Jews then persecuted non-Jews and Greek-speaking Jews who claimed to be Christians all over the Middle East. Mostly the apostles preached only to Jews, but in Antioch Greek-speaking people heard the gospel message and many of them were converted to Christianity. Then the need arose for Jewish Christians who could also speak Greek to minister to the new converts who spoke no Hebrew. One of these, a Jew from the Greek island of Cyprus, was named Barnabas. He seems an insignificant figure in the New Testament, but his influence on relations between different language groups in the Church lasts until today. To help with the multilingual mission in Syrian Antioch was Barnabas, who is described as 'a good man, full of the Holy Spirit and of faith'. Barnabas called for St Paul, who was brought up in Greek-speaking Tarsus. His partnership with Paul may have lasted only a short time, but its effect on Paul was enduring. We had already heard of Barnabas because he sold a field he owned and gave the proceeds to the apostles to use for feeding hungry Christians, and he had introduced Paul to the 12 apostles.

Antioch

The focus of the Christian story now shifts to Antioch. It was in Antioch that the believers were first called by the Greek name

'Christians'. After a successful year's mission in Antioch, Barnabas and Paul were sent to Jerusalem with the money that had been collected in Antioch to feed the hungry Christians in the region around Jerusalem; a gesture of compassion, but also of reconciliation between the language groups.

Cyprus

Then Barnabas had the brainwave, inspired as he said by the Holy Spirit, of showing Paul round his home country of Cyprus. They took with them John Mark, the nephew of Barnabas and later the author of the first ever Gospel, the Gospel of Mark, and they travelled along the south coast, visiting all the synagogues where Barnabas was well known. Eventually they reached Paphos at the western end of the island. There a Jewish magician named Elymas or Bar-Jesus had insinuated himself into the court of the Roman proconsul Sergius Paulus. He seems to have had long conversations with St Paul. It was at this point that Saul of Tarsus changed his name to Paul, presumably in honour of the proconsul; and the proconsul may have given him the idea of uniting the Roman Empire by spreading the idea of a single religion for everybody, with only one God. If he started at the chief city of each province, it might be taken up by the government. So Paul went to the remote border town of Pisidian Antioch where the consuls were related to Sergius Paulus.

Persecution

They crossed over to the north Mediterranean mainland, where John Mark was so scared by this change of plan that he deserted them and returned to Jerusalem Wherever they went, Paul and Barnabas made converts, but were fiercely persecuted. In Lystra the people thought Barnabas, the leader, was an incarnation of the Roman god Zeus, and Paul the spokesman was Hermes, the chief speaker. They returned at last to Jerusalem, strengthening and encouraging their new converts on the way.

The Council of Jerusalem

It was in Jerusalem that the first world gathering of Christians, the Synod of Jerusalem, was held, and it was agreed that non-Jewish

Christians should not have to obey any of the Old Testament laws except those about murder, fornication, meat offered to idols and meat that had been strangled.

Separation

After this, Paul and Barnabas separated; Barnabas in family loyalty wanted to take John Mark with them, but Paul refused to take a coward who had deserted them when things got dangerous. That is all we know from the Bible about Barnabas, but legend says he was martyred in the stadium and buried in a church near Salamis, now called Famagusta, which is where Shakespeare set the story of Othello. What a thrilling story! What an inspiring man!

Suggested hymns

Brother, sister, let me serve you; How bright these glorious spirits shine; Make me a channel of your peace; The 'Son of Consolation'.

The Birth of St John the Baptist   24 June
John the Baptist's Birthday

Isa. 40.1–11 A voice in the wilderness; Ps. 85.7–13 Salvation is at hand; Acts 13.14b–26 A baptism of repentance, *or* Gal. 3.23–29 The law our schoolmaster; Luke 1.57–66, 80 Birth of the Baptist

> *'[Zechariah] called for a writing-tablet and wrote, "His name is John."' Luke 1.63*

Birthdays

For everyone, birthdays are a time of celebration. For the parents and relations, it is joy that a new member had joined the family. For the individual whose birthday it is, though they could not put their joy into words on the day they were born, later on there were birthday parties, to express their joy that they had come into this wonderful world. Finally, God must rejoice that another of his children has survived the 'Call the Midwife' process and entered into the world of joys and pleasures that he has prepared for us to enjoy.

Tribal

When human society evolved from the fragile family, where the death of one means the death of all, into the extended family we call a 'tribe', attitudes changed somewhat. Selfishness became the ultimate sin, and altruism the principal good; everyone lived for the good of the tribe. So men's main duty was to father as many children as possible, and a woman's place was in the home, bringing up as many children as possible. Those who failed in this duty were scorned and despised: barren women, gay men, for instance.

Elizabeth

Elizabeth, the mother of John the Baptist, whose birthday we celebrate today, was despised and mocked because she had reached the menopause, the age after which women are usually considered not to be able to bear children any more, without bearing one single child. She had failed, thought the neighbours, in the principal purpose of her existence. You can imagine the scorn of her neighbours. Her husband Zechariah was also childless of course, but it is less easy to tell when a man ceases to be fertile; and anyway, he was a highly respected priest at the Temple in Jerusalem. So imagine the joy of both of them when an angel appeared to Zechariah who told him they were to have a son and call him John. He was to be a total abstainer from alcohol, was to be great in God's eyes, spread the Holy Spirit, and bring reconciliation between the generations. Zechariah laughed at this ridiculous message, and was punished by being struck dumb until the baby was born. You should never laugh at God's promises, or that he has chosen you, of all people, to carry them out.

Birth

The birth was a perfectly normal one, despite Elizabeth's age and the scorn of her neighbours. Added to the usual pride of a mother was the realization that she had proved her worth as a human being after all. Children were normally named after a relative, or some feature of their appearance, or a circumstance of their birth. They asked Elizabeth what her child should be called, and she replied, 'John', which means 'God has shown favour'. The name turned out to be particularly apposite.

The Baptist

Then, as St Luke tells us, the story continues in the way with which we are all familiar:

> [Zechariah] asked for a writing-tablet, and wrote, 'his name is John'. And all of them were amazed. Immediately his mouth was opened and his tongue freed, and he began to speak, praising God. Fear came over all their neighbours, and all those things were talked about throughout the entire hill country of Judea. All who heard them pondered them and said, 'What then will this child become?' For indeed the hand of the Lord was with him.

John's life and death

When John grew up he became a prophet. He wore the clothing characteristic of a prophet, and lived in the wilderness. He preached that everybody, not just the non-Jews, needed to repent and tell God they were sorry for the wrong things they had done if they wanted a place in the kingdom of God, But the Pharisees and Sadducees he called a brood of vipers fleeing from a fire. He said he was preparing the way for Jesus, saying: 'I baptize with the water of forgiveness, but he will baptize with the fire of judgement.' John was reluctant to baptize his cousin, but Jesus insisted it should be so, and everyone saw the Holy Spirit descending on him like a dove. The cousins exchanged messages, John one of doubt, Jesus one of praise. John criticized King Herod for marrying his dead brother's wife, so Herod beheaded him. What a man! What a life!

Suggested hymns

Hark, a herald voice is calling; Lo, from the desert homes; On Jordan's bank the Baptist's cry.

SS Peter and Paul, Apostles   29 June
A Letter from Peter in Rome

Zech. 4.1–6a, 10b–14 Two anointed ones; Ps. 125 Stand fast for ever; Acts 12.1–11 Peter released from prison (*if the Acts reading is used instead of the Old Testament reading, the New Testament reading is* 2 Tim. 4.6–8, 17–18 Poured out); Matt. 16.13–19 Peter recognizes the Messiah; *or for Peter alone*: Ezek. 3.22–27 Preaching to his own; Ps. 125; Acts 12.1–11; (*if the Acts reading is used instead of the Old Testament reading, the New Testament reading is* 1 Peter 2.19–25 Suffering for God); Matt. 16.13–19

> '*Jesus answered him, "Blessed are you, Simon son of Jonah! For flesh and blood has not revealed this to you, but my Father in heaven. And I tell you, you are Peter, and on this rock I will build my church."' Matthew 16.17–18*

Dear brother apostle,

I hope this reaches you in time to warn you not to come to Rome. The situation here's very dangerous. You'll have heard about the great fire? By a convenient coincidence it broke out where the Emperor has been trying to clear some slums so that he can build himself a new palace. So naturally you can guess whom the people blame for starting it. Then Nero has to shift the blame onto someone else, and we hear he is already blaming us Christians. Before long the *vigiles* will come knocking on our doors at midnight, and then the arrests will start. You must not, I repeat not, be in Rome when that happens.

Today, I tried to escape myself. I had only got a few miles down the Appian Way when I met the Lord. Well of course I recognized him, because unlike me he hasn't grown any older since he was crucified, and I could still see the marks of the nails. Although I was among the first to see him after he rose again, you, Paul, were the only one who has actually seen him since the 40 days he spent with us then. Until today.

You know me. Impetuous Peter, who always has to blurt out something when I'd do better to keep my mouth shut. 'Where are you going, Lord?' I demanded. 'Into Rome to be crucified again,' I heard him say. 'The Christians there are my body; when they

St Peter in the Forum at Rome

suffer, I suffer. The good shepherd does not abandon his sheep. And where are you going, Peter?'

So here I am back in Rome, waiting for the knock on my door, expecting a spell in the Mamertine prison if nothing worse. The church here was strong and growing when you first came, under arrest four years ago. After you were acquitted and set off on your travels among the Gentiles again, I came here to minister to the Jewish Christians, and found the church leaderless. So I took charge, preached the sermon at Passover and sent your colleague Silas to carry copies of it to the churches in the most dangerous areas, warning them of the possibility of persecution. But if I'm executed by you-know-who, times will be hard for the church here. There's nobody who could take over from me, so it's essential that you remain free, so that when the fuss dies down you could come here to take charge of the whole church.

I know we've had our disagreements in the past, but I've learnt my lesson. The Twelve were appointed by the Lord to be leaders of the twelve tribes of the Jewish church – you were appointed apostle to the Gentiles, and we're all equal. I supported you over accepting Gentiles into the covenant community. Well I had to, after I'd seen the Gentile Cornelius receive the Holy Spirit.

I'm staying at present in the house of our friend Clement, and John Mark is with me. Clement, being an imperial freedman of the house of Titus Flavius Clemens, has a fine house on the Lateran Hill. When he heard that the church here needs leaders, he came back from Philippi where you met him, and now he's a highly respected elder. He's a promising lad, and could do well in politics if he chooses. He could act as spokesman for the church here, but I don't think he could take charge on his own.

So, dear Paul, please keep yourself safe. It would be a disaster if you were arrested again. Don't worry what happens to me, though;

I believe firmly that I shall meet my Master again when I die, and I'm looking forward to the day when he releases me from earthly service. I'm not so sure as I used to be that the Lord will return to earth in our lifetime. See you in heaven, where there are no rivals.

Simeon Cephas, also known as Peter

Suggested hymns

Forsaken once, and twice denied; Lord, the light of your life is shining; The church of God a kingdom is; 'Thou art the Christ, O Lord'.

St Thomas the Apostle   3 July
History and Meaning

Hab. 2.1–4 The righteous live by faith; Ps. 31.1–6 I trust in the Lord; Eph. 2.19–22 The foundation of the apostles; John 20.24–29 Doubting Thomas is convinced

> *'Jesus said to [Thomas], "Have you believed because you have seen me? Blessed are those that have not seen and yet have come to believe."' John 20.29*

Fortunate

St Matthew, in his Gospel, lists nine types of people who are especially privileged: blessed are the poor, those who mourn, the meek, the hungry, the merciful, the pure, the peacemakers, the persecuted and reviled. We call these sayings the 'Beatitudes', from the Latin word for 'blessed'. But St John's Gospel has only one beatitude, which Jesus addresses to the so-called 'Doubting Thomas'. Jesus said to Thomas, 'Have you believed because you have seen me? Blessed are those that have not seen and yet have come to believe.' It comes at a climax of the Fourth Gospel, and, to be frank, it comes as rather a surprise. We would have thought that the lucky ones were those who had seen Jesus in the flesh. But not so; the contemporaries of Jesus suffered from the handicap of having visible and tangible proof of the presence of God on earth. They were necessary as the means of spreading this message throughout the world and down the ages. But the purpose of the whole operation, beginning with the incarnation, is that ordinary people like you and me should come to have faith and trust in God's love, without having any proof. We must learn not to rely on proof, and trust only in what we have heard of God's reliability and love.

Doubters

John's Gospel begins, after stating that 'The Word became flesh', with the down-to-earth story of Nathanael, who would not believe because, he objects, no good thing could possibly come from a God-forsaken place like Nazareth. Soon after that, Jesus had an interview with a Pharisee called Nicodemus, who objects to being told he must be born again, a phrase that he takes literally, protesting that a man cannot be born when he has already grown old. Then, at the end of John's Gospel, comes the story of Thomas, who will not believe until he can touch the wounds in Christ's body. It is almost as though John has an obsession with doubt, which he has, rightly, because true faith can only be born out of profound doubt. Those who want proof, or evidence, are missing the point: we must learn to stand on our own feet, without any props or crutches. Those who ask for 'proofs' of the existence of God are heading up a blind alley. There are no proofs of God, only arguments that make it probable that God exists, which you then have to test in your own experience. St Thomas, then, is a hero for all true believers, because he started where we all have to start: in doubt. There is nothing irrational in the good news of God's love; but only when we realize that there is no irrefutable logical course to the truth can we learn faith. If you want to persuade another human to love you, you do not use force, but gentle persuasion, leaving the other freedom to choose. So it is with God.

Dark times

We used to call those terrible times that most Christians go through when they realize that reason has abandoned them in their search for God 'the dark night of the soul'. It is fatal if you then give up, moaning that there is no such thing as a loving God. Instead, we should make firm vows of faithfulness, promising to obey all the commands of God, even though our hearts are devoid of feelings. It may last a month, or several years, but these times of darkness are essential for the growth of true faith, which depends on trusting obedience more than on indulgent emotionalism.

The way to faith

Don't, for God's sake, despair when these dark times come. But, like St Thomas, use them as a stepping stone to true faith, which knows that God in Jesus is very close to you all the time, whether you feel it or not, and whether or not you have any rational proof. St John, writing of his Gospel, said, 'These things are written so that you may come to believe that Jesus is the Messiah, the Son of God, and that through believing, you may come to have life in his name.' Blessed is Doubting Thomas, because he has shown us how this is possible even for those who are in the depths of doubt.

Suggested hymns

Firmly I believe and truly; If you believe and I believe; Lead kindly light, amid th'encircling gloom; The spacious firmament on high.

St Mary Magdalene   22 July
(see page 187)

St James the Apostle   25 July
Modern Pilgrims

Jer. 45.1–5 Seeking greatness; Ps. 126 Sow in tears, harvest in joy; Acts 11.27—12.2 Herod kills James (*if the Acts reading is used instead of the Old Testament reading, the New Testament reading is* 2 Cor. 4.7–15 Treasure in clay pots); Matt. 20.20–28 Seeking greatness

> *'About that time King Herod laid violent hands upon some who belonged to the church. He had James, the brother of John, killed with the sword.' Acts 12.1–2*

Which James?

At least three people named James are mentioned in the New Testament.

1 James 'the Just' was the brother of Jesus, and principal leader of the church in Jerusalem after the resurrection. The Jewish historian Josephus says he was stoned to death. He was not one of the Twelve, called apostles. He is celebrated together with Philip on 1 May.

2 James 'the Less' was one of the Twelve, however, and the son of Alphaeus. He is celebrated on 3 May.

3 James 'the Great' was also one of the Twelve, son of Zebedee and brother of John; they were called 'Sons of Thunder'. Today's reading reports that he was killed by King Herod, and today is his feast day. According to Spanish legends, he came to Spain and evangelized here, and the Virgin Mary appeared to him on a pillar. He returned to Israel, was killed by Herod as described in today's reading, and his remains were taken back to Spain and buried at Compostela.

You may not be convinced that any of these went to Spain, but Compostela is a popular destination for pilgrims, and up to a million people each year go on pilgrimage to the supposed site of his burial. So perhaps historical accuracy is not important when someone makes a journey with a spiritual purpose. It is the fact that many others have taken the same journey that makes a place holy; as T. S. Eliot wrote, 'To kneel where prayer has been valid'.

Journeys

Christian visitors to Jerusalem have described their journeys as pilgrimages from at least the fourth century. When the Holy Land was inaccessible because of the Crusades, most pilgrimages stopped at Rome. Since then other sites have grown up, including Canterbury, Lindisfarne, Iona, Assisi, Lourdes, Guadalupe and many others. If you are planning to visit any of these, it is worth reading the history first, so that you can turn your journey into a pilgrimage. If you are free of other demands you could go with a specialist pilgrimage company when everything is planned for a group in advance. If you are not able to travel, it is very helpful to regard your whole life as a pilgrimage.

Purpose

The first difference between a pilgrimage and any other journey, or any other life, is that you live with a purpose, expecting to change in yourself, and to feel nearer to God. This requires an effort, either to make the physical journey, or to discipline your life with certain times for prayer each day. Sometimes you will forget; that does not matter, so long as you learn to say sorry to God and accept his forgiveness. At other times you will be strongly tempted to give up. This is much more serious. The Christian life is never easy, and sometimes it can be described as 'the way of the cross'. You may not feel that God is present, or that he cares what happens to you. This is in fact one of our heavenly Father's greatest gifts, because, if you can grit your teeth and keep going, you can build up strength of character, and cease to be so dependent on fickle feelings.

Companions

You are not the only person who has these dry spells. On your pilgrimage, physical or spiritual, be open to those who travel with you, and make time to encourage your fellow pilgrims. Some people find that out of the blue, as it were, after a long period of dryness, there comes a sudden moment of joy, and sweet awareness of God's presence. If this happens to you, thank God for it, and reserve a special space for it in your memory, so that when things are not going well later, you can remember it, and say to yourself, 'Well, at least when I was in such and such a place, I knew that God is with me, and that he can use me to do his will.' And if your fellow pilgrim has a memorable moment, congratulate them, reminding them that you, like God, feel that they are a heroic soldier with a place in God's plans and a purpose to their life.

Suggested hymns

Guide me, O thou great Redeemer; He who would valiant be; O happy band of pilgrims; Through the night of doubt and sorrow.

The Transfiguration of Our Lord   6 August
We Saw

Dan. 7.9–10, 13–14 The Son of Man; Ps. 97 Clouds are around him; 2 Peter 1.16–19 We saw; Luke 9.28–36 The transfiguration

> *'We did not follow cleverly devised myths when we made known to you the power and coming of our Lord Jesus Christ, but we had been eyewitnesses of his majesty. For he received honour and glory from God the Father when that voice was conveyed to him by the Majestic Glory, saying, "This is my Son, my Beloved, with whom I am well pleased." We ourselves heard this voice come from heaven, while we were with him on the holy mountain.'*
> *2 Peter 1.16–18*

Eyewitness

The reason that war correspondents run such colossal risks in dangerous situations is because an eyewitness report is worth more than any number of second-hand accounts. 'I was there, I saw it with my own eyes, it was going on all around me.' The television viewer's attention is gripped by that sort of reporting. It's sad that so many worthy interviewers and cameramen have been injured, even killed, in consequence, but that's human nature. We don't pay much attention to a report, unless it's given by an eyewitness.

Second Peter

In that case, you'd think the Second Letter of Peter in the New Testament would be one of the most respected books in the whole canon of Scripture. 'We had been eyewitnesses,' it says; 'we ourselves heard this voice.' It claims to be a first-hand account; 'we heard', 'we saw'. But in fact many readers ignore this letter, because it's such an odd one. It makes big claims for its own truthfulness:

> So we have the prophetic message more fully confirmed. You will do well to be attentive to this as to a lamp shining in a dark place, until the day dawns and the morning star rises in your hearts. First of all you must understand this, that no prophecy of scripture is a matter of one's own interpretation, because no

prophecy ever came by human will, but men and women moved by the Holy Spirit spoke from God.

But none of the other writers whose letters are contained in the holy Scriptures actually describe their own writings as Scripture; it sounds a bit conceited; most other writers leave it to others to praise their work. 'Methinks [he] doth protest too much.' Therefore some scholars conclude that Second Peter is not by St Peter at all. Maybe they're right; though whenever you have two scholars together discussing the Bible you're sure to have at least three opinions! But the church leaders who drew up the list of what books are to be included in the canon of Scripture during the Council of Carthage at the end of the fourth century AD were satisfied that this letter was worthy to be included, and it's their authority, speaking for the whole worldwide Church, that we rely on when we say that the transfiguration really happened. Whoever wrote this letter, he was resisting 'false teachers' who claimed that the apostles had made it all up. Consequently, the false teachers continued, there's no need to follow the moral teachings of the apostles: everyone can do what they like.

Who Jesus was

The transfiguration was a vision, when the disciples saw who Jesus really was. They saw him shining with bright glory; they heard the voice of God saying, 'This is my Son.' So they were right to say that we should believe what Jesus taught. For if Jesus really is the Son of God, then what Jesus taught his disciples is what God himself wants us to believe. When Jesus taught in the Sermon on the Mount that God wants us to treat each other in a profoundly moral way, Jesus was right. When Jesus summed up God's commandments to us as loving God and loving our neighbours, Jesus was right. When Jesus compared God to the astonishingly forgiving father of the Prodigal Son, Jesus was right. When Jesus promised that those who believe will live with him in eternity, he was right again. These are the central beliefs of the Christian faith, and they're true, not just because they're in the Bible, but because they were spoken by God's Son. Whether or not the writer of Second Peter really was an eyewitness, the real St Peter, and all the other early disciples, actually were. They saw Jesus, a humble man, but with incredible authority, healing the sick, forgiving sinners and rebuking the proud, and the disciples became convinced they were watching God himself at work. We listen to the news reports of the war correspondents, and believe them because they're eyewitnesses. How much more should we listen to the apostolic account of the teaching of Jesus, believe it and act on it, because God himself was speaking to us through his Son.

Suggested hymns

Christ, whose glory fills the skies; Lord, the light of your love is shining; Mine eyes have seen the glory of the coming of the Lord; 'Tis good, Lord, to be here.

The Blessed Virgin Mary   15 August
Exalted but Human

Isa. 61.10–11 As a bride, *or* Rev. 11.19—12.6, 10 A woman in heaven; Ps. 45.10–17 You shall have sons; Gal. 4.4–7 Born of a woman; Luke 1.46–55 Magnificat

> *'A great portent appeared in heaven: a woman clothed with the sun, with the moon under her feet, and on her head a crown of twelve stars.' Revelation 12.1*

The exaltation of the Virgin

What a pity that Christians should argue among themselves about the Blessed Virgin Mary. It's not what she herself would have wanted; in fact, it may be part of that sword that the old priest Simeon said would pierce her own heart: it must break her heart to see people arguing about her. Yet there are two views about Mary held with equal sincerity by different Christians. One group sees her as the perfect mother, the greatest woman who ever lived. Mary was sinless, they say, from before she was born, for she was immaculately conceived in the womb of St Anne, her mother, and was the perfect saint for the rest of her life. She was an example of purity, ever-virgin, and when she died, or 'fell asleep' as we say, she was the only human being worthy to be taken straight into heaven, without having to wait in any intermediate state like the rest of us. There she hears our prayers, and prays on our behalf to God almighty. She is full of grace, which she can give us from her treasury, to help us to live better, and to ensure our place in heaven. The Blessed Virgin Mary, the Mother of God.

The humility of the peasant girl

But there's another view of Mary, which doesn't completely contradict that one, but places the emphasis very differently. This is Mary the humble peasant girl, chosen by God's grace, not because she was better, but because she was willing to do what no woman before had ever been asked to undertake. She bore the baby Jesus, and bore also the shame and scorn of not being married at the time he was conceived. She was the author of one of the most revolutionary songs in the history of political literature, which we call the Magnificat. She bore other children, Jesus's brothers and sisters, and because Joseph seems to have died when Jesus was little more than 12 years old, she brought up this large family on her own. Mary didn't understand the direction her son's ministry was taking, and tried to warn him off going to Jerusalem. Then she stood broken-hearted at the foot of the cross, and John, the Beloved Disciple, was asked to look after her.

Two ideas in tension

These two views of Mary aren't completely incompatible, though certain points in each description are impossible to believe if we take the other description seriously. Both stories contain truths that we ignore at our peril, and somehow we have to find a way to hold these two concepts together in our minds in creative tension.

Purity and temptation

Mary was certainly the greatest of saints. The difficulty in reconciling the two views arises from different ideas of what saintliness means. It includes purity, the absence of any corrupt or vicious behaviour. But this purity's always hard-won, by a very real struggle against temptation. Even Jesus, the Bible says, 'was tempted in all things the same as we are, only he didn't yield to sin'. If Jesus was tempted, then surely the Virgin Mary was, and she didn't sail through life surrounded by an aura of sanctity. Which gives hope to us who struggle with temptation, too. Virginity, and celibacy also, doesn't consist in having no sexual feelings at all; it means having the same temptations as everybody else, but sublimating one's desires in such a way that we can care for others in a positive way.

Our example

If Mary was human like us, then we can and must pray to her, and think of her as the loving Mother of Us All. But that mustn't distract us from prayers to Jesus, who was also tempted, who knows what it's like to be human, and who's the sole mediator between us and the Father. For Jesus's sake we love Mary his mother; it was from her that he learnt what human love means. But we won't fall into the trap of exalting her to a superhuman level in our prayers, which would take away our sense of the very real feminine aspects of God our Father and Mother. Mary's one of us, on our side of the dividing line between human and divine. But she is the best, the kindest, the most loving human being who's ever lived; for that, we honour her as highly as it's possible to honour another human being, and try to copy her example of pure and selfless love.

Suggested hymns

Blest are the pure in heart; Her Virgin eyes; Shall we not love thee, Mother dear?; Tell out, my soul, the greatness of the Lord.

St Bartholomew the Apostle 24 August
Witnesses on Oath

Isa. 43.8–13 My witnesses; Ps. 145.1–7 Speak of your wondrous acts; Acts 5.12–16 The apostles heal (*if the Acts reading is used instead of the Old Testament reading, the New Testament reading is* 1 Cor. 4.9–15 The shame of the apostles); Luke 22.24–30 Judging the twelve tribes

'*You are my witnesses, says the Lord.*' Isaiah 43.10

Who was Bartholomew?

St Bartholomew, whom we commemorate today, is listed among the Twelve, that group of disciples who were closest to Jesus.

Jesus committed the leadership of his church after he died to the Twelve. But apart from his mention among the Twelve on each of the four occasions that they're listed in the New Testament, nothing else is known of Bartholomew at all. St John's Gospel doesn't mention Bartholomew, but there's quite a lot about somebody called Nathanael in St John, who's not mentioned in the other Gospels, so some have suggested that Nathanael was his first name and Bartholomew was his surname. There's another theory, too. Because they were close to Jesus, either Bartholomew or Nathanael, or Nathanael-Bartholomew if they were one and the same, must have been present at the Last Supper. Nathanael is named among the seven disciples who saw Jesus making breakfast beside Lake Galilee after his resurrection, but none of them is reported as saying anything; whereas somebody called 'the disciple whom Jesus loved' is mentioned repeatedly. It's usually assumed that the Beloved Disciple was John the son of Zebedee. But he could possibly have been Nathanael-Bartholomew. In which case he was the one

- who reclined next to Jesus at the Last Supper
- who asked Jesus who was going to betray him
- whom Jesus asked to care for his mother
- who was the first to enter the empty tomb
- who, some people believed, would never die until Jesus came again
- and whose witness is the basis of the Fourth Gospel.

Nobody will ever know whether Bartholomew was the Beloved Disciple; but it's worth a mention, so that we can honour 'the disciple whom Jesus loved' on this day.

Witness

The last-but-one verse of the Fourth Gospel refers to the Beloved Disciple, and reads, 'This is the disciple who is testifying to these things and has written them, and we know that his testimony is true.' The important question's not who wrote the words of the Gospel, but whose evidence is being reported. The qualification to be an apostle is to be a witness. When they had to choose a replacement for Judas, Peter said they must select 'a witness with us to [Jesus's] resurrection'. So even if we know nothing else for sure about poor old Bartholomew, at least we know he was a witness.

Police witnesses

A large policeman with a magnificent bass voice was asked for the first time to read from the Bible in church. The set passage was Isaiah chapter 43, so he stood at the lectern and boomed out, 'YOU ARE MY WITNESSES, SAYS THE LORD.' Some of the more nervous choirboys were observed to be all-of-a-tremble and looking for a door to scuttle through! Now, when a policeman tells you to be a witness in court it needn't be frightening; but it's an awesomely solemn responsibility. You have to swear an oath to tell the truth, the whole truth and nothing but the truth. If you don't do that to the best of your ability, some poor innocent person may go to prison, or a guilty person may be set free to harm somebody else.

Apostles

So when the apostles were called to be witnesses for Jesus, they had no less a responsibility than to tell the truth about Jesus, the whole truth about Jesus, and nothing but the truth of Jesus. You don't find the people who wrote the Bible telling casual lies, or partial truths; they were on oath to be truthful witnesses, and you can trust what they wrote: 'we know that his testimony is true', said their friends. The apostles were prepared to die for the truthfulness of their evidence; according to legend, Bartholomew was flayed alive and then beheaded. He could have avoided that fate if he'd withdrawn his evidence, but he couldn't do that because he knew it was true.

Our witness

We honour Bartholomew for his witness; and you and I are called to be witnesses, too. You've prayed to Jesus, and your prayers have been answered; that proves that Jesus is alive, so get out there and tell people. You don't need to be brilliantly clever or expensively educated to be a witness: just tell the truth as you know it. Don't forget, though, that you're under oath to tell the truth, the whole truth, and nothing but the truth about Jesus. Bartholomew did it, and so can you.

Suggested hymns

God forgave my sin; Jesus is Lord! Creation's voice proclaims it; O for a thousand tongues to sing; Tell out, my soul.

Holy Cross Day   14 September
Obedient unto Death

Num. 21.4–9 The bronze serpent; Ps. 22.23–38 All the earth shall turn to the Lord; Phil. 2.6–11 Obedient to death on the cross; John 3.13–17 God so loved the world

> 'He humbled himself and became obedient to the point of death – even death on a cross.' Philippians 2.8

The Dutch boy

We all know the story of the little Dutch boy and the dam. The land had been drained and the sea was held back by the earthen dyke. The land which the people farmed, and on which they lived, was, as in so many other parts of Holland, lower than the level of the sea outside the dam. One bitterly cold night a little boy was walking home alone alongside the earthwork, and he noticed a tiny hole in the soil, through which a trickle of water was beginning to flow. If he left it like that, the trickle of water would wash away more earth, until it became a steady flow and then a flood, which would breach the wall and drown everyone in the village. The boy looked around for something to fill the hole with while he went for help, but he could find nothing. So he stuck his finger in the hole, and waited for somebody to come by. But nobody came, and soon the cold made him unconscious. When they found him in the morning he was dead, but his finger was still blocking up the hole in the dam. The water hadn't been able to get through, and the lives of the villagers had been saved, but at the cost of the boy's life. Yet he'd done what he knew he had to do, and sacrificed his life that others might live.

Obedience

There are many similar stories of heroic sacrifice. Many a member of the armed forces or emergency services has been given his or her orders and carried them out to the letter, even at the cost of their own life. Maybe they were instructed to defend a position, and were told that if that point was defeated the whole front might collapse. So they were obedient unto death. I'm sure there must be stories, though I can't remember any, of a child being told by his or her father to look after the smaller brothers and sisters, and surrendering their own life while protecting the others, obeying their father to the point of dying for the sake of those they loved. If there is such a case, it would form a perfect comparison for the words of St Paul in his letter to his friends in Philippi. The 'colony' of Philippi, by the way, was mostly made up of ex-soldiers and their families.

Jesus was obedient

To the Philippians, Paul wrote:

> Let the same mind be in you that was in Christ Jesus, who, though he was in the form of God, did not regard equality with God as something to be exploited, but emptied himself, taking the form of a slave, being born in human likeness. And being found in human form, he humbled himself and became obedient to the point of death – even death on a cross.

Jesus, believe it or not, left the glories of heaven behind him, renounced his power of command, and came to earth as a poor, hungry Galilean preacher. He did this in obedience to orders he received from God his heavenly Father; and then, even more incredibly, he was obedient even unto death: death by hanging on a gibbet. He sacrificed his life that others might live. That's why we sometimes call the sacrificial deaths of brave heroes 'lesser Calvaries'. The same principle of sacrificial love and obedience is at work, only Jesus had so much more to sacrifice.

Like Father, like Son

But here we're grasping for truths beyond where human language will take us. If you can imagine a supremely loving human father and son, where the father asks his son, in love, to do something which he knows might lead to his death for the sake of others, and the son obeys because his love for his father's so great that he'll even sacrifice his life, you're coming somewhere near it. But then you have to go on to say that the father loved the son so much that he was actually beside him, suffering with him, when the son laid down his life. Like father, like son. Perhaps there never has been human love as close as that. But that's the sort of image we have to hold in our mind when we think of God the Father and the cross of Jesus. The story of the little Dutch boy is the beginning of a long trail; follow it to its logical conclusion, and it will lead you to the cross in the heart of God.

And can it be that I should gain?; In the cross of Christ I glory; Were you there when they crucified my Lord?; When I survey the wondrous cross.

St Matthew, Apostle and Evangelist   21 September
The Call of Matthew

Proverbs 3.13–18 Wisdom more precious than jewels; Ps. 119.65–72 Better than gold; 2 Cor. 4.1–6 The open statement of the truth; Matt. 9.9–13 The call of Matthew

> *'As Jesus was walking along, he saw a man called Matthew sitting at the tax booth; and he said to him, "Follow me." And he got up and followed him.' Matthew 9.9*

The call of Matthew

The account in the Gospel of the call of Matthew to follow Jesus is very brief; all it really tells us is that Matthew was a tax-collector, and that he followed Jesus immediately. That evening, Jesus was having supper with many tax-collectors and sinners. When the New English Bible was published, that verse was translated as 'tax-collectors and other sinners', and the Inland Revenue Staff Association contemplated taking the translators to court for libel! Collectors and inspectors of taxes these days may be unpopular with their clients, but they're no more sinful than any other profession. But the tax-collectors in Jesus's day bought from the hated occupying Roman government the right to collect customs dues from everybody who crossed the provincial boundary in a particular place, and to charge as much as they liked. So Matthew was not only a cheat and a swindler, but he robbed his own people on behalf of their enemies – he was a quisling and a traitor. No wonder he was hated.

What Jesus saw in Matthew

But Jesus saw the potential in the despised tax-collector. It goes without saying that this can't have been the first time they met, though no previous encounters are recorded. Perhaps Jesus had chatted with Matthew at the boundary post where you crossed the River Jordan between Bethsaida and Capernaum, from the tetrarchy of King Herod Philip into the territory of Herod Antipas. Maybe Matthew had stayed on the edge of the crowd when Jesus spoke in the open air, or slipped quietly in at the back when he preached in a synagogue. Possibly Matthew had been a guest at a previous dinner party when Jesus had astonished everybody by enjoying the company of all those terrible taxmen. Anyway, Jesus recognized that Matthew had gifts of fellowship, administration, loyalty to his friends, and possibly the literary gifts needed of anybody who was going to write a gospel.

What Matthew saw in Jesus

What did Matthew see in Jesus? The first thing must have been his open, tolerant friendship. Jesus took people as he found them, not rushing in to judge them, not approaching them with ready-formed prejudices, but willing to see the best in people, and forgive them their faults. If only Christians were a bit more like Jesus in that respect, we might not put off so many people who want to come to Jesus at their time of need, but are frightened away because they find his followers so judgemental. Second, not only was Jesus open and tolerant; he spoke about a God who's the same. The God Jesus spoke of wasn't like the god the nationalists described, who fought for the Jews against anyone who opposed them. Neither was he the god of the Pharisees, who rejected anyone who failed to keep every jot and tittle of the Jewish law and tradition. The God whom Jesus described as his Father was more like the father of the prodigal son, ready to meet people halfway, to forgive them as soon as they repented, and to throw a celebration party at the drop of a hat. A God you could talk to; a God who'd be your friend, loyal to you if you were loyal to him. A God like an ideal tax-collector, who kept fair accounts, but was willing to wipe out any debt if you genuinely couldn't pay. A God who accepted the outcasts whom others despised.

He got up and followed him

Matthew the tax-collector had never dreamt that Rabbi Jesus would be interested in him. Matthew needed someone like Jesus to make sense of his life. But what possible need could Jesus have for Matthew? Then Jesus called him, saying, 'Come, follow me!' Jesus wanted him; that astonished poor outcast Matthew. He'd no idea what use Jesus had for him, or what task he'd be put to. Enough for Matthew that Jesus called him; he left his post, his prospects and his fortune, and fell in, marching in step behind Jesus, to follow him wherever he led, to let the future hold whatever tasks, trials and tribulations it might. That's what it means to be a Christian; not clinging to our past, our status and our security, but setting out joyfully on the wonderful game of follow-my-leader, confident that wherever Jesus leads us to, he'll be there with us, and will give us the strength to fulfil the tasks he sets us.

Suggested hymns

He sat to watch o'er customs paid; Jesus calls us – o'er the tumult; The kingdom of God is justice and joy; There's a wideness in God's mercy.

St Michael and All Angels   29 September
Heavenly Choirs

Gen. 28.10–17 Jacob's ladder; Ps. 103.19–22 Bless the Lord, you angels; Rev. 12.7–12 Michael fought the dragon (*if the Revelation reading is used instead of the Old Testament reading, the New Testament reading is* Heb. 1.5–14 Higher than the angels); John 1.47–51 Angels descending on the Son of Man

> 'Bless the Lord, you angels of his, you mighty ones who do his bidding, and hearken to the voice of his word.' Psalm 103.20 (Common Worship)

A Welsh bass

A Welsh singer had a powerful bass voice. He died and went to heaven, and a few days later his best friend also died. 'Tell me, Jonesie,' he asked, 'what's the singing like up here?' 'Well, boyo,' the other replied, 'the first morning the archangel Gabriel led us in a choir practice, and he said the balance wasn't quite right. He asked a couple of million basses to be quiet, and then a few million more. Finally he said, "That's better, it's nearly balanced now. But we still need a little less in the bass, Mr Jones."'

Heavenly choirs

We often picture angels as singing the praises of God, based on the heavenly choirs who sang to the shepherds at Bethlehem, and the book of Revelation. To those people who are tone-deaf, that provides a depressing image of heaven. But perhaps when God makes us all perfect in the afterlife, he'll give even the unmusical the gift of song. Choir members here below have an ambitious task in trying to echo the tones of the heavenly choirs, and must remember that God doesn't expect perfection, only that we should do the best for him that we can.

Imagery

But then, all our talk about heaven is metaphor and imagery. Heaven's the state of being with God, outside space and outside time, or perhaps we should say in another dimension, where space and time aren't measured as they are on earth. The angelic choirs are another element in the symbolism, through which we grasp that the indescribable afterlife is like the best joys and pleasures we've experienced on earth, improved and enlarged to the nth degree. For many people, some of the most pleasurable experiences they've enjoyed in this life have been in connection with making music or listening to music. The tone-deaf will have to forgive the musical for imagining heaven as the sum of all these musical experiences multiplied to infinity.

Angels

So on Michaelmas Day, what can we learn by thinking of the angels as singers? Surely that praising God's the most important activity in the universe, and that it doesn't only take place in the visible world, but is going on around us in the spiritual world all the time. When we praise God, together with others in church or on our own, we're not starting something fresh. We're simply joining our voices to a great tide of worship which flows day and night towards the throne of God. In this flood of praise already participate the angels and archangels; cherubim and seraphim; thrones, principalities, dominions, virtues and powers; day and night eternally worshipping the eternal Trinity.

Church music

This justifies us in using music in the worship of the Church. Both Jesus and St Paul sang hymns. Music was used for the Psalms of

David in the worship of the Jerusalem Temple, and some think that this was a direct ancestor of the Byzantine chant of the Eastern Orthodox Churches, and the medieval plainsong of the Roman Catholic Church. Polyphony brought new harmonies to the church music of the thirteenth to sixteenth centuries, and enriches cathedral services today where the congregation worship by offering to God the music they can only listen to. Much of the music of the great composers of the classical, baroque, romantic and modern periods was not only commissioned by the Church but expressed the personal faith of the composers. The Reformation was marked by the Genevan Psalms and the Lutheran Chorales. Hymns and hymn-singing emerged in the Nonconformist churches, became central to Methodism, and have become a normal part of Anglican and Roman Catholic parish worship. It's been said that Christians learn more theology from the hymns they sing than from the sermons they hear. General William Booth, the founder of the Salvation Army, used the styles of Victorian popular music for his brass bands to play in the street. The folk music of many races and cultures has been used in worship. Ira D. Sankey and Dwight L. Moody popularized sentimental and rousing hymns in revival meetings, and the charismatic movement has encouraged modern worship songs, which have enriched the hymnbooks of even traditional churches. Such is the Church's 'catholic' and diverse taste in music, offering every type of melody to God in inspired and inspiring worship. In this we follow the example of the heavenly choirs of angels.

Suggested hymns

Angel-voices, ever singing; Come, let us join our cheerful songs; How shall I sing that majesty?; Ye watchers and ye holy ones.

St Luke the Evangelist   18 October
Blind, Deaf, Lame and Dumb
Isa. 35.3–6 Healing in the new age, *or* Acts 16.6–12a The Macedonian call; Ps. 147.1–7 God heals the broken hearted; 2 Tim. 4.5–17 Only Luke is with me; Luke 10.1–9 Sending out the seventy

'Then the eyes of the blind shall be opened, and the ears of the deaf unstopped; then the lame shall leap like a deer, and the tongue of the speechless sing for joy.' Isaiah 35.5–6

344

Political correctness

We laugh at 'political correctness gone mad'. Taken to extremes it can certainly be comical. But the reason for it is deadly serious. We speak in a PC way because many folk, who struggle with problems in their lives, feel marginalized and robbed of their dignity when treated as a category, rather than as individuals. So we've learnt to speak of handicapped people as 'people with disabilities', so that each one should be treated as unique, not just be defined by their disabilities.

Isaiah

St Luke, whom we commemorate today, and whom St Paul describes as 'the beloved physician', usually describes ill people as those 'who were sick with various kinds of diseases'. As a doctor, he knew that not even Jesus could heal sufferers by pigeon-holing them. The prophet Isaiah would have got into hot water if he'd written today that 'the eyes of the blind shall be opened, and the ears of the deaf unstopped; then the lame shall leap like a deer, and the tongue of the dumb sing for joy'. Yet Isaiah was writing poetry, and poets must be allowed to take liberties with the language in order to make a point. Christians have interpreted this passage as a prediction of the coming of the Messiah. When Jesus healed people who were blind, and so forth, this was seen to fulfil that prophecy. But as well as their surface, literal meaning, those words also have a deeper, symbolic significance. St Luke knew that any doctor who heals a physical illness has to consider the patient's emotional and spiritual needs as well. Jesus pointed out that, as a result of his ministry, 'the blind receive their sight, the lame walk, the lepers are cleansed, the deaf hear, the dead are raised, and the poor have good news brought to them'. Yet he wasn't only talking about the physically disadvantaged – he was helping us to see that we're all spiritually blind to the love of God and the needs of others, and we all need Christ's healing.

Blind

So let's draw out the spiritual symbolism of each of the disabilities Isaiah mentions. He wrote, 'Then the eyes of the blind shall be opened.' People who have what we should really call visual impairment used to be put in a corner as a nuisance. Now, if they're partially sighted, they can read large-print books and enlarged text on the computer screens. Those with little or no sight can use a guide-dog, and even become members of the cabinet. But when it comes to spiritual blindness, as the proverb says, 'There's none so blind as those that will not see.' We're so wrapped up in our own desires, we don't even notice what God's doing for us, and what he wants us to do for others.

Deaf

Isaiah wrote, 'the ears of the deaf [shall be] unstopped'. Those with a hearing impediment can now be helped with hearing aids and sign-language. It's harder to help the spiritually deaf. Don't you wish that God would speak to you? Have you considered that maybe he's talking to you all the time, through nature, the Bible and the sermons, and you don't hear him because you're too busy with your own affairs?

Lame

Next, said Isaiah, when Messiah comes, 'the lame shall leap like a deer'. Saints Peter and John healed a lame man in the Temple, who went 'walking, and leaping, and praising God'. If you feel insignificant and ineffectual, perhaps you need Jesus to heal your spiritual lameness?

Dumb

Finally, Isaiah mentions the dumb, though in the USA that word means 'stupid'. So the NRSV translates it as 'the tongue of the speechless [shall] sing for joy'. Maybe you don't have an impediment in your speech, can speak persuasively or chatter for hours on most subjects. But when it comes to talking to your friends about Jesus and what he means to you, you're completely tongue-tied. Then you need Jesus to remove the impediment of shyness and heal you.

Healing

You hadn't realized how spiritually sick you are, had you? Luke the physician knew that physical and spiritual healing go together. Jesus heals you, so that you may enjoy life more, but also to make you more useful to God. God wants you to see his love for everybody, hear his guidance, then walk the walk and talk the talk for Jesus.

Suggested hymns

Give thanks with a grateful heart; Lord, I was blind, I could not see; Make way, make way; O for a thousand tongues to sing.

SS Simon and Jude, Apostles   28 October
(see page 252)

All Saints' Day   1 November
Embracing Poverty
(*If 4 November is not kept as All Saints' Sunday, the readings on page 351 are used on 1 November. If those are used on the Sunday, the following are the readings on 1 November.*) Isa. 56.3–8 My house for all people, or 2 Esd. 2.42–48 Crowned by the Son of God; Ps. 33.1–5 Rejoice, you righteous; Heb. 12.18–24 Come to Zion; Matt. 5.1–12 The Beatitudes

> '[Jesus said], "Blessed are the poor in spirit, for theirs is the king-dom of heaven."' Matthew 5.3

Egypt

Most people haven't time to celebrate a different saint every day, so on All Saints' Day we think of the ones we have ignored. One important but little-known saint was St Antony, who lived in Egypt, in the third century AD. Many people in the Roman Empire at that time had become immensely rich through trade and commerce. Most of the rest were thoroughly materialistic, eager to become rich also. The poor were very poor, and the rich were corrupt. Most people were nominally Christian, but there was little interest in spiritual things. Yet many good Christians agonized over the state of the world, then as now. A few, of whom Antony was one, decided that the only way to avoid the temptations of materialism was to give up everything and escape. In the desert they could meditate alone in silence. These hermits were known as the Desert Fathers, though there were some women among them also.

347

Embracing poverty

One day, Antony heard the Gospel read in church, and was struck by the words of Jesus to the rich young man, 'If you wish to be perfect, go, sell your possessions, and give the money to the poor, and you will have treasure in heaven; then come, follow me.' So Antony gave away all his possessions and went to live alone in the desert. In the stunning silence of the desert, Antony found he could pray as never before. He was free from the distractions of having money and wondering how to spend it. He found that poverty, when it's not imposed on you but is willingly chosen, is a great blessing, and he embraced poverty gladly. Jesus said, 'Blessed are the poor in spirit, for theirs is the kingdom of heaven.'

Attracting followers

The discipline of Antony's life of self-denial was in contrast to the luxury of the world around. The news of what he had done began to spread, and other Christians travelled out into the desert to ask him questions and learn from him. Some of them stayed and built their hermit cells nearby so that they could pray and discuss with him daily. Soon, so many followers flocked out to learn from them that it was said 'the desert was made a city'. It seemed as though the whole purpose of his flight into the desert had been destroyed, but Antony knew where his duty lay. He came out of his self-imposed isolation for a while, to form them into a loose-knit community with a common rule of life. This was something never seen before. Before that there had been hermits living alone; now there were communities of monks living together.

Work and prayer

Once Antony was filled with despair. His loneliness brought many sinful thoughts. He said to God, 'Lord, I want to be saved, but these thoughts won't leave me alone. How can I be saved?' Soon afterwards, he noticed a man sitting at his work, plaiting a rope, then getting up from his work to pray. He went on like this all day long. Antony realized God was telling him that prayer needs to be combined with physical exercise and work. In this way, Antony lived to over 100. Once he asked God, 'Lord, why do some people die young, while others drag on to extreme old age? Why are some people poor and others rich? Why do wicked people prosper while good people are needy?' He heard a voice saying to him, 'Antony, concentrate on yourself; God decides these things; it won't do you any good to know the reasons.'

Today

So what about us today? What must we do to be saved? Antony clearly saw that poverty is not a good thing when people are forced to be poor. But it does have its advantages when it's willingly chosen. So we should work and pray to lift other people out of their poverty. That will mainly consist in creating fairer patterns of trade. It will cost us, by removing the protection enjoyed by our own industries and agriculture. But after making adequate provision for our families, we should give away our surplus wealth, and enjoy the blessings that come with a simpler lifestyle. We can 'live simply, so that others may simply live'. As Antony discovered, it's much easier to pray when your life isn't cluttered with a lot of possessions.

Suggested hymns

All for Jesus, all for Jesus; Blest are the poor in heart; Take my life, and let it be; Teach me, my God and king.

Commemoration of the Faithful Departed

(All Souls' Day)   2 November

Souls of the Righteous

Lam. 3.17–26, 31–33 New every morning, *or* Wisd. 3.1–9 Souls of the righteous; Ps. 23 The Lord my shepherd, *or* Ps. 27.1–6, 16–17 He shall hide me; Rom. 5.5–11 Christ died for us, *or* 1 Peter 1.3–9 Salvation ready to be revealed; John 5.19–25 The dead will hear his voice, *or* John 6.37–40 I will raise them up

> *'The souls of the righteous are in the hand of God, and no torment will ever touch them.' Wisdom of Solomon 3.1*

The book of Wisdom

One of the Scriptures' most moving meditations on death is in the book of Wisdom, also known as the Wisdom of Solomon. This is written as if it were penned by King Solomon, but it's written in Greek, and is familiar with Greek philosophy. It was obviously written by a Jew, around the time of Jesus, probably intending to honour the great king of the past by writing in Solomon's name, which was not an uncommon practice in those days. This wasn't considered dishonest, and the book of Wisdom was included in the Christian Bible up until the Reformation, when Martin Luther included it in the Apocrypha. The beginning of the third chapter of the Wisdom of Solomon will be familiar to many people, probably in the Authorized or King James Version, because of its use at funerals. It is very appropriate to read it today, All Souls' Day, or the Commemoration of the Faithful Departed.

The souls of the righteous are in the hand of God, it begins.
It was a Greek idea that human beings have souls which survive after their bodies perish at their death, but the Jewish author seizes upon it gladly. He is writing about 'the righteous', those who may not have been famous or successful in worldly affairs, but tried to live their lives in the most upright way they knew. God doesn't prevent the death of the body, but he does care for our souls.

And there shall no torment touch them.
Jews believed that wicked people were destroyed in the fire of Gehenna; Greeks thought that evildoers were punished in a part of the underworld called Tartarus. Not the righteous, says Wisdom. Christians would add that this includes penitent sinners to whom has been imputed the righteousness of Christ.

In the sight of the unwise they seem to die:
their departure is taken for a misfortune,
and their going from us to be a disaster.
Those who don't have the gift of God's wisdom regard death as a disaster. For those who are left behind to mourn the departed, it's often a misfortune. But for those who've died, whose souls are in the hand of God, it may rather be a blessing, because,

They are in peace.
As Shakespeare puts it in *Cymbeline*,

> Fear no more the heat o'th'sun,
> Nor the furious winter's rages.
> Thou thy worldly task hast done,

Home art gone and ta'en thy wages.
Golden lads and girls all must
As chimney-sweepers, come to dust.

Yet when the dead souls no longer have a body, they are untroubled by the pains and fears of bodily life, and we may well envy them that.

For though they appear to be punished,
yet they were full of hope for immortality.
Wisdom sums up its teaching in one word: immortality. The Greeks taught that the soul is naturally imperishable, and they regretted that they were forced to survive for ever. The immortality that Wisdom speaks of is the gift of God to those whom he regards as righteous, and, for us, that includes those who have faith in Jesus. When Jesus rose from the dead, Christians changed their talk about death. Obviously God's gift to us, after our death, is that, like Jesus, we shall have a means of praising God, recognizing each other and speaking to each other. St Paul called this 'clothing the soul with a spiritual body'. What a glorious life that will be!

Their sufferings were light compared with the glory they will receive.
For God tested them, and found them worthy to be with him.
Like gold in the furnace he tested them, and accepted their sacrifice.
When God comes to reward the righteous their goodness will shine out; and the Lord will be their king for ever.
The conclusion of this passage from the book of Wisdom is to bring us hope in our sufferings, through belief in a glorious future beyond death. All Souls' Day is an occasion for commemorating those who've died, and giving thanks for their lives, in which they at least aimed at righteousness. It's also a time for looking forward with hope to the eternity which will be ours when we too die, when we shall rejoice in the glorious kingdom of heaven.

Suggested hymns

Immortal, invisible, God only wise; Jesus lives! Thy terrors now; The Lord's my Shepherd; Thine be the glory.

351

All Saints' Sunday   4 November
Who Is Good Enough?

(These readings are used on the Sunday, or if this is not kept as All Saints' Sunday, on 1 November itself; see page 347.) Wisd. 3.1–9. The righteous in God's hand, *or* Isa. 25.6–9 A refuge for the needy; Ps. 24.1–6 Open the Temple gates for the Lord; Rev. 21.1–6a The new Jerusalem; John 11.32–44 The resurrection of Lazarus

> *'Who shall ascend the hill of the Lord? And who shall stand in his holy place? Those who have clean hands and pure hearts.'* Psalm 24.3–4

Churchgoing

St Paul wrote a letter 'To the church of God that is in Corinth, including all the saints in [that area]'. Then he gave them a right telling-off for some very un-saintly behaviour! In the language of the Bible, 'all saints' doesn't mean people who are perfect, but all Christians, everyone who goes to church. For some people, going to church is a duty, a grudging obligation. All praise to them if they keep on attending – particularly if you don't like the style of worship or the choice of music, but you keep coming because your family want to, or to support your local community. In that case, what the Bible calls 'the sacrifice of praise' may be a real sacrifice for you, but one that God accepts because it's a way of showing that he is important. We're in church to worship God, not just to enjoy ourselves. But if you *are* enjoying yourself it helps a lot! For many people, coming to church is the high point of the week. Many people like meeting their friends, or enjoy the beauty of the building and music, or like singing, or mental stimulation, or being told that God loves them, or even in some cases all of the above. If circumstances prevent them being in church one Sunday, the week seems to get off on the wrong foot, and they feel something important is missing from their lives. If you haven't reached that point yet, examine your attitude when you come to church, make up your mind to enjoy the service and the socializing and to ignore the minor irritations, and the pleasure of churchgoing will grow on you.

Pottering

It's not only during Sunday services that this pleasure is to be found. Many people go into church at other times, arranging the flowers, dusting the pews, practising the organ, or visiting old churches while they are on holiday, and find an atmosphere of indescribable peace. There's a real satisfaction to be found in pottering about in church. Logic tells us that if God exists, he must be everywhere. But it's easy to forget that. In church, the beauty and the calm, and the inspiring worship, remind you of the presence of God. It's above all in church that you can feel the presence of God close to you. When you step through the church door, say, silently or aloud, 'Hello, Jesus!'

God's presence

Then, when you have been in church, you can take God with you when you leave. Something jogs your memory later in the week, reminding you that, even if we forget God, he never forgets us and never leaves us. Gradually you become increasingly aware that every moment of every day you are living in the presence of God. This isn't anything solemn; God likes to watch you enjoying yourself in many different ways. Knowing that God is with you and loves you increases the enjoyment. Going to church once a week or more can transform your whole life.

Saints

Also, the saints are with us in church. When somebody dies we say they have gone to be with Jesus. Where's Jesus? In heaven, certainly, but he's everywhere. He's very specially present in God's house, the church. So when you feel the presence of Jesus in church, you are also especially close to those you love who've died. That's why church-going is such a comfort to the bereaved. The long list of famous Christians that you've read about are also with Jesus; so they, too, are close to us when we're in church. We call this 'the communion of saints'. Eastern Orthodox Christians fill their churches with icons because they are not only visual aids, but 'win-dows to eternity', reminding us of the great crowd of saints always present with us.

Family

For the Church is God's family. The communion of all the saints, in heaven and on earth, is our family life. Yet any family needs to meet regularly. I hope God never has cause to say to you, 'I love you, my child, and nothing will stop me loving you, because I'm your Father; but it's not much of a relationship, because you're hardly ever in my house with the rest of my family.'

All-age worship

Make a cardboard model of the screen in an Orthodox church, with pictures of famous Christians – www.kosovo.net/news/ archive/2005/November_10/1.html

Suggested hymns

O what their joy and their glory must be; Give us the wings of faith to rise; Let saints on earth in concert sing; Who are these like stars appearing?

Saints and Martyrs of (our own nation)
8 November   Eulogies and Epitaphs

Isa. 61.4–9 Build up the ancient ruins, *or* Ecclus. (Ben Sira) 44.1–15 Let us now praise famous men; Ps. 15 Who may dwell in your tabernacle?; Rev. 19.5–10 A great multitude invited; John 17.18–23 To be with me to see my glory

> *'Let us now sing the praises of famous men, our ancestors in their generations.' Ecclesiasticus 44.1*

Ecclesiasticus

In between the Old Testament and the New Testament, some Bibles print a selection of other books. Mostly they were written by Jews, but in Greek, during the time between the Old and New Testaments. St Jerome included them in his Latin translation of the Bible; Martin Luther separated them out in his German version, calling them 'The Apocrypha'. One of these is headed 'The Wisdom of Jesus son of Sirach'. It became known as 'The Church Book', or in Latin, Ecclesiasticus. Don't confuse it with another book, which *is* in the Old Testament, called Ecclesiastes. Sirach, or Ecclesiasticus, is all poetry, most of it very beautiful, and many people believe that it's truly inspired.

Vaughan Williams

One of the most moving passages, often used at funerals and memorial services, has been set by the composer Ralph Vaughan Williams as an anthem, once heard, never forgotten. So I'll quote it in the King James Version, as Vaughan Williams did. It's appropriate today, the commemoration of the saints and martyrs of our own nation:

> Let us now praise famous men, and our fathers that begat us.
> The Lord hath wrought great glory by them
> through his great power from the beginning.
> Such as did bear rule in their kingdoms,
> men renowned for their power,
> giving counsel by their understanding, and declaring prophecies:
> Leaders of the people by their counsels,
> and by their knowledge of learning meet for the people,
> wise and eloquent are their instructions:
> Such as found out musical tunes, and recited verses in writing:
> Rich men furnished with ability,
> living peaceably in their habitations:
> All these were honoured in their generations,
> and were the glory of their times.
> There be of them, that have left a name behind them,
> that their praises might be reported.
> And some there be, which have no memorial;
> who are perished, as though they had never been;
> and are become as though they had never been born;
> and their children after them.
> But these were merciful men,
> whose righteousness hath not been forgotten.
> With their seed shall continually remain a good inheritance,
> and their children are within the covenant.
> Their seed standeth fast, and their children for their sakes.
> Their seed shall remain for ever,
> and their glory shall not be blotted out.
> Their bodies are buried in peace;
> but their name liveth for evermore.
> The people will tell of their wisdom,
> and the congregation will shew forth their praise.

Eulogies

The author of that poem was thinking of famous men among his ancestors, the Jews. But every race can boast some heroes and heroines of the past. We shouldn't idolize them – nobody's perfect, and they wouldn't thank us for pretending that they were. But to describe their virtues encourages us to follow their example, in serving God and our neighbours. Concentrating on our fellow countrymen and -women doesn't imply that we're better than anyone else; but we naturally want to serve our own nation, in gratitude for all that earlier generations have left for us. Such a speech, in praise of somebody who's died, is called a 'eulogy'. Sometimes eulogies are carved into a tombstone, when they're called 'epitaphs'.

Funerals

Some day you may be called to deliver a eulogy at a funeral. A newspaper once gave guidance on how to do this, suggesting you ask yourself the following questions:

To whom am I speaking?

How would the person like to be remembered?

What made the person special? What were their favourite pastimes and interests, likes and dislikes?

When was the person happiest?

Who was really close to him or her?

What did I like about the person? What did other people like about him or her?

What are the highlights of the person's life story?

If I could only say three things about him or her, what would they be?

Do I want someone else to give the eulogy on my behalf on the day?

Is anyone else speaking about the person at the funeral? Should we avoid saying the same things?

Olden days

Whether you have to speak at a funeral, or write an obituary, ask yourself those questions. Yet while there are still people living who loved them, you shouldn't speak ill of the dead. However, when you're considering people from the olden days, famous or obscure, you can balance the lessons to be learnt from their good points with warnings to avoid their mistakes.

Suggested hymns

God, whose city's sure foundation; Let saints on earth in concert sing; Rejoice in God's saints, today and all days; We sing for all the unsung saints.

St Andrew the Apostle   30 November
News from the Front Line

Isa. 52.7–10 The messenger who announces peace; Ps. 19.1–6 The heavens declare God's glory; Rom. 10.12–18 God's messengers reconcile Jew and Greek; Matt. 4.18–22 The call of the fishermen

> *'How beautiful upon the mountains are the feet of the messenger.' Isaiah 52.7*

Combatants and civilians

The civilians left at home are always hungry for news from the battle zone – especially those who have loved ones serving among the combatants. They devour the newspapers; they are glued to the television; they await the next post with a mixture of hope and dread. The news hounds are expected to put themselves in positions of real danger, so that they can send back first-hand news right from the front line. 'Is the battle going our way?' they ask. 'Are we winning? Is the end of the long struggle in sight? Is there any news of a peace accord?'

Isaiah

This very real and poignant human situation lies behind the imagery used in Isaiah. 'How beautiful upon the mountains are the feet of the messenger who announces peace, who brings good news.' This passage was written when the majority of the Jewish people were in exile in Babylon. Those who had been left behind in Jerusalem for 50 years had little news of how their brothers and sisters were faring in their captivity. If only somebody could bring a message as to how things were going! And then, as they stared hopelessly out from the walls of Jerusalem, in the distance, where the path from Babylon in the east came over the summit of the Mount of Olives, one of the watchers spied a small cloud of dust. What was it?

The dust had been kicked up by the feet of a runner . . . a messenger perhaps! Yes, yes, that's what it is, there's somebody running along the mountain road towards us. What will he have to report? Is the exile nearing an end? Will our friends and relations be coming home soon? Yes, it's good news at last – an outbreak of peace. Our God is in charge of history, and he's saved us.

How beautiful upon the mountains are the feet of the messenger who announces peace, who brings good news, who announces salvation, who says to Zion, 'Your God reigns.'

The New Testament

And from this simple but powerful image comes much of the language used in the New Testament. The word 'gospel' means 'good news'; preaching means proclaiming good news; those who do so are 'good-news-ers' or evangelists; evangelism is spreading the good news. An apostle means somebody who's been sent: a messenger. And what's the good news that they have to proclaim? The good news of the kingdom, or kingship, of God – our God reigns! In the struggle between good and evil, our side's won. Peace at last!

St Andrew

When St Andrew met Jesus, the first thing Andrew did was to share the good news with his brother Peter, saying excitedly, 'We've found the Messiah!' The long-awaited leader, who would usher in the kingdom of God, and bring them peace. Andrew and Peter were fishermen; Jesus called them to fish for people. 'Jesus came to Galilee, proclaiming the good news of God, and saying, "The time is fulfilled, and the kingdom of God has come near; repent, and believe in the good news."' Andrew realized he was in the front line of the battle, where goodness was overcoming evil, and he had to tell people about it. Jesus sent his apostles or messengers out as evangelists, with the words: 'Go nowhere among the Gentiles . . . but go rather to the lost sheep of the house of Israel. As you go, proclaim the good news, "The kingdom of heaven has come near."'

World mission

Jesus began training his disciples close to home, among their own people. Then their vision widened out. Andrew was a Jew, but he spoke Greek also. So when some Gentiles, non-Jews who spoke Greek, wanted to meet Jesus, it was bilingual Andrew who brought the Greeks to Jesus. Jesus realized that with Andrew's multi-racial tolerance, the mission was entering into a new phase. 'The hour has come,' said Jesus. Christianity was not to be a narrow sect of Judaism, it was to evolve into a world mission, to bring the good news of peace to every nation.

Sharing

The message was this: all your sins can be forgiven; you can be reconciled with God; and God wants you to live with him in eternity. How can you keep a message like that to yourself? No, you have to share it with your nearest and dearest, then you have to set out on your journey across the mountains to the farthest corners of the earth, proclaiming the good news of victory, of our redemption, and of the promise of eternal life.

Suggested hymns

Jesus calls us – o'er the tumult; How lovely on the mountains are the feet of him; I danced in the morning when the world was begun; Will you come and follow me?

Sermon for Harvest Festival
Lilies of the Field

Joel 2.21–27 Eat and be satisfied; Ps. 126 Sow in tears, reap in joy; 1 Tim. 2.1–7 Thanksgiving for everyone, *or* 1 Tim. 6.6–10 Money the root of all evil; Matt. 6.25–33 Lilies of the field

> '[Jesus said,] "Consider the lilies of the field, how they grow; they neither toil nor spin, yet I tell you, even Solomon in all his glory was not clothed like one of these."' Matthew 6.28–29

Lilies

In the area around Lake Galilee in the springtime, the hillsides are covered with wildflowers, especially crimson anemones. Jesus is described in Matthew's Gospel standing on a hill near Galilee, delivering what's called the Sermon on the Mount. He would only have to look around him to see 'the lilies of the field'. The word simply means the wildflowers.

Don't worry

'Don't worry about what you'll eat, or drink or wear,' Jesus said. 'Isn't life more than food, and your body more important than clothing? The wildflowers don't work like you do, yet even glorious King Solomon wasn't dressed as splendidly as they are. God gives glorious clothing to the short-lived grass in the fields; isn't he even more likely to clothe you? How little faith you have! . . . Work, as your first priority, for the kingdom of God; and food, drink and clothing will be given to you as well. If you're going to worry, today's quite enough to worry about today – you just haven't time to worry about tomorrow!'

Comfort

You can read this as comfort or challenge. 'If you're fearful about the future,' Jesus says, 'don't be. How can you doubt God's love? Of course God will look after you. Trust him.' That's great comfort, for many people are more fearful about the future than they'd care to admit.

Challenge

But the other way of reading it is as a challenge. What do you spend most time on? Material things and money, making sure you've enough, planning how you're going to get more, and what you'll spend it on. So money's obviously the most important thing in life to us; it's become an idol. Money has taken the place in our lives that God ought to occupy. Seek first the kingdom of God, says Jesus. Make God your king, obey him as king, and help others to, then live in a kind and unselfish, righteous way. If you do that, you may not be quite as stinking rich as if you spent all your time money-grubbing, but you'll have enough, and you'll be a lot happier. People who visit poor countries are always struck when they return home by how many possessions people in the rich countries have, and how miserable they all seem compared with the people in poor countries.

Harvest Festival

So the parable of the lilies in the field is a great comfort, but it's also extremely challenging. Harvest Festival has the same two sides to it. First it's a chance to rejoice that we've enough to eat, and to remember that we're entirely dependent on God and the weather as to whether we get anything to eat at all. But Harvest also challenges us: not only do we have enough to eat in spite of the fact that others are hungry; very often we have enough to eat *because* others are hungry. Because of our food subsidies, our home-produced food items are cheap in the shops, and the producers in the poor countries can't sell theirs here. Moreover, we can export our produce to the poor countries, and sell it for less than it costs the farmers there to produce their own. Yes, I know it's more complicated than that, but whenever I eat a cheap meal, or wear cheap clothes, a poor man, woman or child somewhere may be dying of malnutrition because of the subsidies my elected representatives are paying.

Politics

Politicians want to be re-elected. If we tell them what we think, they'll do something about world hunger. A bishop from Mozambique was invited to a hearty lunch in the UK. When he described the starvation in his country, his hosts felt ashamed at the amount of food on their table. He replied, 'Don't be. There's no way you can get that food to Mozambique. Enjoy your prosperity and thank God for it. But pray for the decision-makers, who cause us to go hungry so that you can be well fed.' That's a good message for any Harvest Festival.

All-age worship

Draw two tables; on one the food an average person in your country eats in a week, and on the other the amount eaten by an average African. Send it to your MP.

All things bright and beautiful; Come, ye thankful people, come; For the fruits of his creation; We plough the fields and scatter.

Sermon for a Wedding
The Saturday Big Tent Wedding Party
John 15.9–13

> 'Jesus said, "This is my commandment, that you love one another, as I have loved you."' John 15.12

Books

I wonder whether any of you have read one of the comical books by Alexander McCall Smith about life in the African nation of Botswana. The first book was called *The No. 1 Ladies' Detective Agency*, and tells of two women, proud to be local, who set up a private detective agency. Among the gentle humour there is a lot of simple wisdom in what they say and think. One of the recent titles was *The Saturday Big Tent Wedding Party*, and it ends with an account of how one of the female detectives at last gets married, and it has some things to say that are very relevant to us at this wedding service today.

Welcome

The book never specifies the denomination of the Church in which Mma Makutsi is married, so the welcome that the minister gives to the couple and the congregation at the beginning of the service does not have to adhere to any known service book. He begins by saying that the couple are here because they love each other, and they are declaring that love before the congregation and the whole of Botswana. There is no attempt to define the purpose of marriage, but the minister immediately asks anyone who knows any reason why they should not be legally married to say so. That is a legal requirement, like reading the banns in church, to ensure that neither of them is already married and committing bigamy. Then they move on to make their promises to each other. I think that defines in a few words what is important in Christian marriage.

Love

At the very centre of married life, of course, is love. The magic of falling head over heels in love is one of the most beautiful things that God ever invented. It is one of the deepest emotions that many people ever experience; and emotions are designed to motivate us and set us in motion. But that is only the beginning; it requires a great deal of dedication to go on caring for somebody from the depth of your heart for the whole of your life. That sort of perseverance can only come from a deep gratitude that your partner is in love with you and a determination never to let them down. The ebullience of first love fades, but it must grow into a much deeper and longer-lasting devotion. One of the reasons for making your love for each other public in a church wedding, is that you can remind yourself in later years of how you felt on this day, and give each other a treat of some sort to bring back the strength of your feelings for each other.

Legal

That brings us to the importance of legal marriage. When you sign a marriage licence in the presence of others, you are making your commitment to care for each other for the rest of your lives. Your relationship is no hole-and-corner thing; it is a legal commitment made in public. It will be difficult at times, but you won't give up easily when you remember what you said today.

Promises

But to many people the vows, the promises that you make to each other, looking the other in the eyes, in the marriage service, are even more important than the legal documents. 'How could I let him or her down,' you think, 'after making those promises face to face?'

Jesus

Jesus said, 'This is my commandment, that you love one another, as I have loved you.' There are many types of love, from soppy romantic love to the love of the soldiers who surrender their lives for their country because they love her. Jesus says our love for each other must always include an element of self-sacrifice. There is no demanding to have everything our own way in a truly loving marriage. But you can never force anyone to love by telling them to. So Jesus promised that his loving presence will always be around us, supporting us, encouraging us, and inspiring us to love each other. That is why people get married in church: because it sets our love for each other in the context of the unending love of Jesus for each one of us.

Sermon for a Baptism or Christening
God Provides the Cleansing
Mark 7.1–8, 14–15, 21–23

> 'For the Pharisees, as well as the rest of the Jews, follow the teaching they received from their ancestors: they do not eat unless they wash their hands in the proper way.' Mark 7.3–4 (Good News Bible)

Have you washed your hands?

When young people come to eat their meals, what do good parents ask them before they sit down? Yes, 'Have you washed your hands?' Why is that important? Because dirt and germs on your hands might easily get into your mouth, and then make you sick. You don't want a week in bed with an upset tummy, so it's worth spending a minute washing your hands clean. Also, it's polite to all the other people; they don't want to watch a dirty child eating next to them. Always wash your hands. Now these ideas help us to think about baptism or christening.

Jewish tradition

But first a question: which nation did Jesus belong to? Was he British, Spanish, Nigerian? No, he was a Jew. The Jewish people in his day were very strict about washing their hands. We read in the Bible that 'The Jews follow the teaching they received from their ancestors: they don't eat unless they wash their hands in the proper way.' I'm sure these traditions started off as useful rules for healthy living. But it sounds as though some Jews had made of them what we call a 'fetish': a sort of magic that they must do to make sure God's on their side. They thought God wouldn't love them unless they washed thoroughly; God wouldn't listen to their prayers unless they gave themselves a scrub before starting to talk to him.

What is God interested in?

Now, God doesn't want you to get sick, so he's pleased when you wash your hands before meals. But I don't believe that God's more interested in cleanness than anything else; it's important, but not very high up on the list of God's priorities; as American people say, it's 'no big deal'. Yet the Jews in Jesus's time had become obsessed with cleanliness, as if it mattered more to God than anything else.

John the Baptist

What's all this got to do with pouring water on a baby's head? Well, who can tell me the name of Jesus's cousin? Yes, John the Baptist. The Jews were so obsessed with washing that if anybody who wasn't a Jew wanted to pray to God as they did, the 'filthy foreigners', as they called them, had to wash themselves clean of their nasty habits and become Jews. They called this ceremony 'baptism', which is simply another word for washing. John the Baptist told them not to be so high and mighty; it's not just the foreigners, everybody needs to be pure before they can talk to God, so everybody needs to wash. But it's not clean hands that God's interested in, so much as a clean heart. Hating other people and criticizing them makes our hearts dirty; it's only when our hearts are full of love that we're pure enough to talk to God. But how can we possibly become pure enough to talk to God; how can we fill our hearts with love? Not by washing our hands, said John. So God himself provides the means: God gives us a once-and-for-all washing, which means we'll be able to talk to God for the rest of our lives. Then John took the people down into the River Jordan and baptized them.

Christening

So when we baptize baby N. today, we're doing what John the Baptist, and all the followers of Jesus did. We call it 'christening', which means 'Christian-ing': making someone a Christian, a member of God's family the Church. From now on, the new Christian won't have to struggle to become clean enough to talk to God. You and I, who were christened a few years ago, we're already pure, because God himself has washed our hearts. Mind you, once you realize how much God loves you, how much he wants you to talk to him, then you'll try to avoid all the naughty deeds that upset God, and you'll want him to make your heart a loving heart, and kind to all the people round you. But that's an offer, not a condition. Loving other people isn't something we have to do before God will listen; it's something we can't help doing because we've been talking to God.

Today

So thank God that baptized Christians don't have to struggle to make themselves good enough to talk to God, because God's already provided us with a once-and-for-all washing at our baptism. Help young children to grow up as good Christians, by loving them and setting them a good example. And by the way, it's also quite a good idea to wash your hands before every meal.

Suggested hymns

Guide me, O thou great Redeemer; O Jesus, I have promised; On Jordan's bank the Baptist's cry; When Jesus came to Jordan.

Sermon for a Funeral or Memorial Service
A Spiritual Body
1 Cor. 15.20–25, 35–38, 42–44a, 54–58 in a new paraphrase

A reading from St Paul's first letter to the Christians in Corinth, chapter 15:

> Jesus Christ has been raised out of death. He is the beginning of the harvest, the first to wake up of those who by dying have fallen asleep. The Scripture says it was because one man, Adam, disobeyed God, that death came into the world. So it is fitting that through one man, Jesus, the resurrection of the dead should begin. For as we all die because of our common humanity as descendants of Adam, we shall all come alive again because of our common Christianity, as believers in Jesus. But it will all happen in the proper order: first Jesus rose again, and when he comes to us, those who belong to him will come back to life. Then, at last, he will put God the Father back in charge of everything, after he has destroyed

366

all rival authorities. For Scripture says, 'He must rule until he has crushed all his enemies beneath him.' The last enemy to be destroyed will be death itself. But perhaps you are asking, 'How can dead people come alive again? What sort of body will they have?' Now that is, in fact, a silly question! Think of this example: when you sow a seed in the ground, new life can only come out of it if it stops being a seed. When you bury the seed under the earth, what you put there is not the plant that is going to come up; it is just a seed, a grain of wheat, for instance. But God will bring out of it a beautiful new plant. The type of plant that comes up depends on what sort of seed you sow. Now the resurrection of people who have died is like that. When you bury a dead body it decays; when we come alive again we shall never decay. The body you bury is weak and feeble; when we come alive again we shall be strong and beautiful. You bury a mere physical body; God raises up what we could call a 'spiritual body'. It is as though we shall strip off our mortal body, and then put on an immortal body like new clothes. Then the words of Scripture will come true, which say, 'Death itself has died, victory is won!' The prophet Hosea asks, 'Death, where is your victory? Grave, what harm can you do us?' Death harms us because we are guilty, and sin gets its power from the Old Testament law. But thank you, God, you have given us victory over death, because of the powerful forgiveness of our Lord Jesus Christ! So, my friends, stand firm and steady! Keep on doing your work for the Lord, because you know that everything you do has eternal results, if it is done for him.

(© 2005 Michael Counsell)

Longing for immortality

I think most people have a sort of yearning to believe in life after death. To some it's obvious and simple; they know deep down that the one they loved isn't really dead, but lives on somewhere where we can talk to them and they know what we're doing. But for others it's not so easy; they half believe, but the other half of their mind tells them it's old-fashioned and unreasonable. That's probably because they don't know what the Bible says about the afterlife. The Bible doesn't talk about harps and haloes and wings. St Paul had to invent a new word to describe what we're like in heaven: he called it a 'spiritual body'. But to make it easier he started by talking about sowing seeds.

Sowing seeds

Most people in St Paul's day had personal experience of sowing wheat seeds in the fields. And most people when they died were buried directly into a hole in the ground – there was no cremation then. So the comparison was obvious. Burying a body is like sowing a seed, said the Apostle. The plant which comes up is beautiful, whether it's an ear of wheat or an exotic flower. The seed you plant is rather plain. It appears to rot away, though it's actually being used by the germ at the centre to make a plant out of. It stops being a seed, that's for sure. But we shouldn't be sorry for the seed we plant, because we know soon it will have turned into something much more wonderful. In fact, we know more science these days than St Paul did. We know that at the heart of every cell there's a string of DNA that determines what sort of plant comes up.

Rising to new life

So it is when we go to heaven, says St Paul. We shan't be the same as we are now; we'll be much better. But the pattern of personality which we've built up in this life continues into the next. We may not have a physical body in heaven; it's not that sort of place. But the personality we form on earth will be the same personality we have in heaven. Well, thank God, that's not quite true: all the bad parts of our personality, the character traits we're ashamed of, will be put away with the old physical body when we've finished with it. We lay aside our worn-out physical body when we die. It's rather like taking off an old set of clothes, and putting on new ones. But the new clothes aren't made of material substances; for the spiritual world of heaven, we need a 'spiritual body'.

Our hope

Of course we can't fully understand heaven. Our words were coined for talking about time; they can't cope with eternity. It's like trying to explain grown-up life to children. But we can use picture language, like St Paul does. What matters is that when we get to heaven, we can recognize each other, talk to each other, and praise God together. And that's a great comfort.

Suggested hymns

Alleluia, alleluia! Hearts to heaven and voices raise; Now the green blade riseth from the buried grain; The Lord's my Shepherd, I'll not want; Thine be the glory, risen, conquering Son.

Scripture Index to Sermon Texts

Subject Index

378

Author Index

Notes

Notes

Notes

Notes

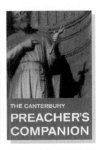

Advance order for the 2019 editions *(available May 2018)*

quantity

Prices are subject to confirmation and may be changed without notice

CANTERBURY CHURCH BOOK & DESK DIARY 2019 *Hardback*   £19.99 + p&p* ....

CANTERBURY CHURCH BOOK & DESK DIARY 2019 *Personal Organiser (loose-leaf)*   £19.99 + p&p* ....

CANTERBURY CHURCH BOOK & DESK DIARY 2019 *Personal Organiser (A5)*   £19.99 + p&p* ....

CANTERBURY PREACHER'S COMPANION 2019 *Paperback*   £19.99 + p&p* ....

For details of special discounted prices for purchasing the above in any combinations
or in bulk, please contact the publisher's Norwich office as shown below.

Order additional copies of the 2018 editions
Subject to stock availability

Hardback Diary **£19.99*** ....   Organiser **£19.99*** ....

Preacher's Companion **£19.99*** ....   A5 Personal Organiser **£19.99*** ....

Ask for details of discounted prices for bulk orders of 6+ copies of any individual title when ordered direct from the Publisher.

Sub-total £................

*Plus **£2.50** per order to cover post and packing (UK only): £................

All orders over £50 are sent POST FREE to any UK address.
Contact the Publishers office for details of overseas carriage.

TOTAL AMOUNT TO PAY: £................

I wish to pay by ...

... **CHEQUE** for £ .... made payable to **Hymns Ancient and Modern Ltd**

... **CREDIT CARD**   All leading credit and debit cards accepted *(not American Express or Diners Club)*
Your credit card will not be debited until the books are despatched.

Card number: ....   Expiry: ____ /____

Issue No: ____ Valid from: ____ /____

Switch or Maestro only

Signature of
cardholder: ....   Security code:_____

Last three digits on signature panel

Please PRINT all details below.

Title: ....   Name: ....

Delivery address: ....

....

....

.... Post Code: ....

Telephone or e-mail: .... Date: ....

Please ensure you have ordered the edition you require for the correct year. No liability will be accepted for incorrect orders

Return this order form or a photocopy – with details of payment – to

Norwich Books and Music, 13A Hellesdon Park Road, Norwich NR6 5DR
Telephone: 01603 785900   Fax: 01603 785915   Website: www.canterburypress.co.uk